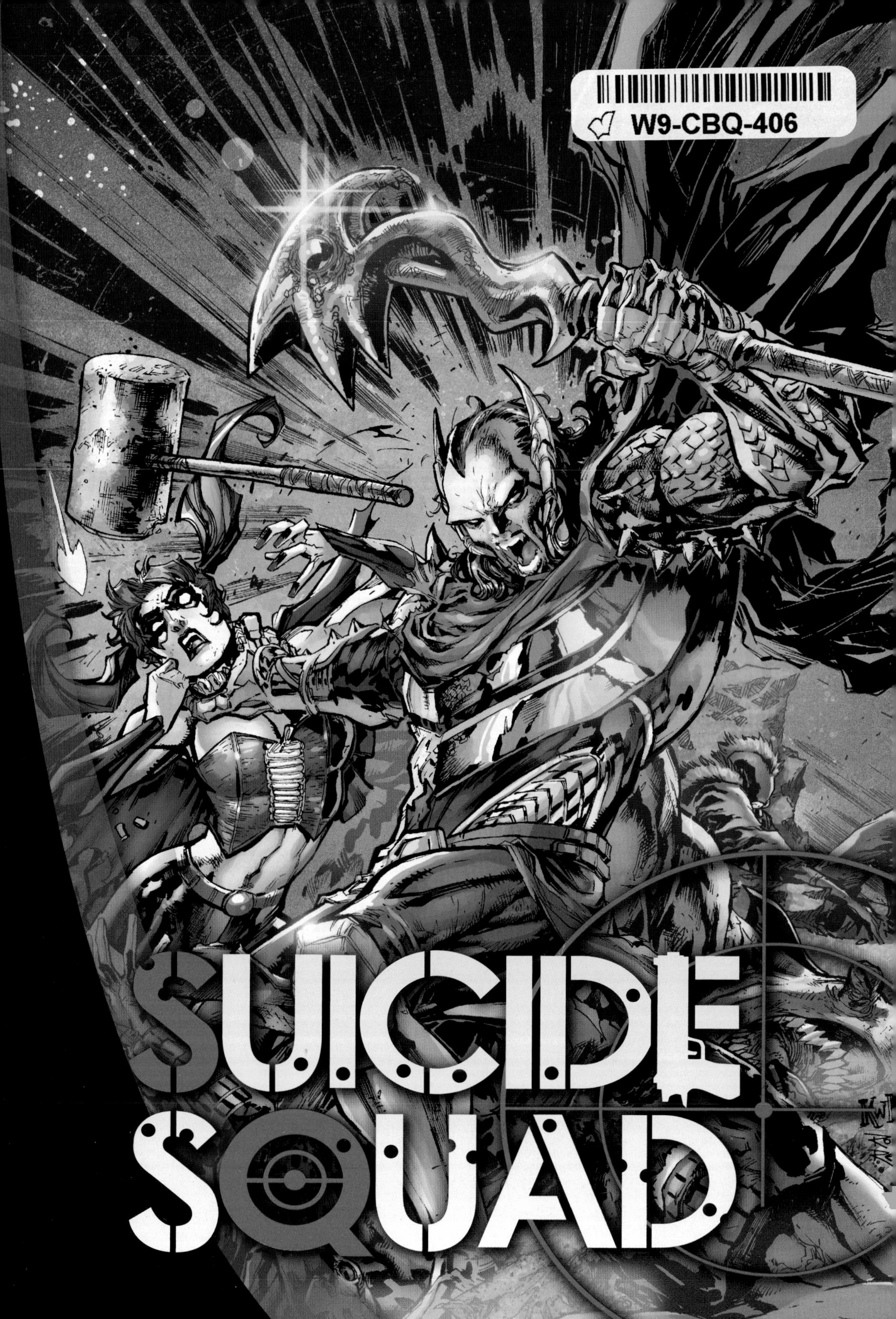

SUICIDE SQUAD

VOLUME 2 BASILISK RISING

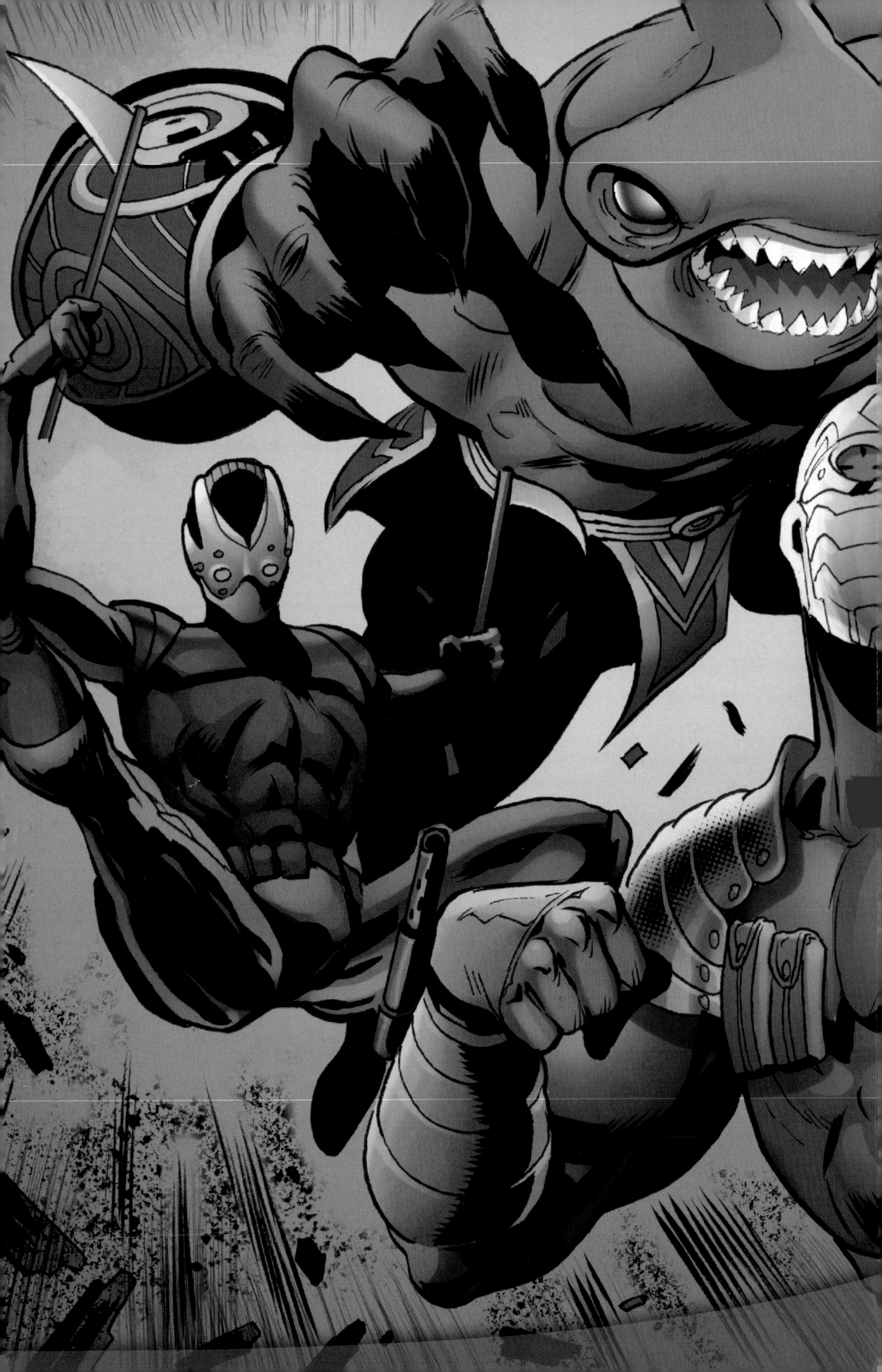

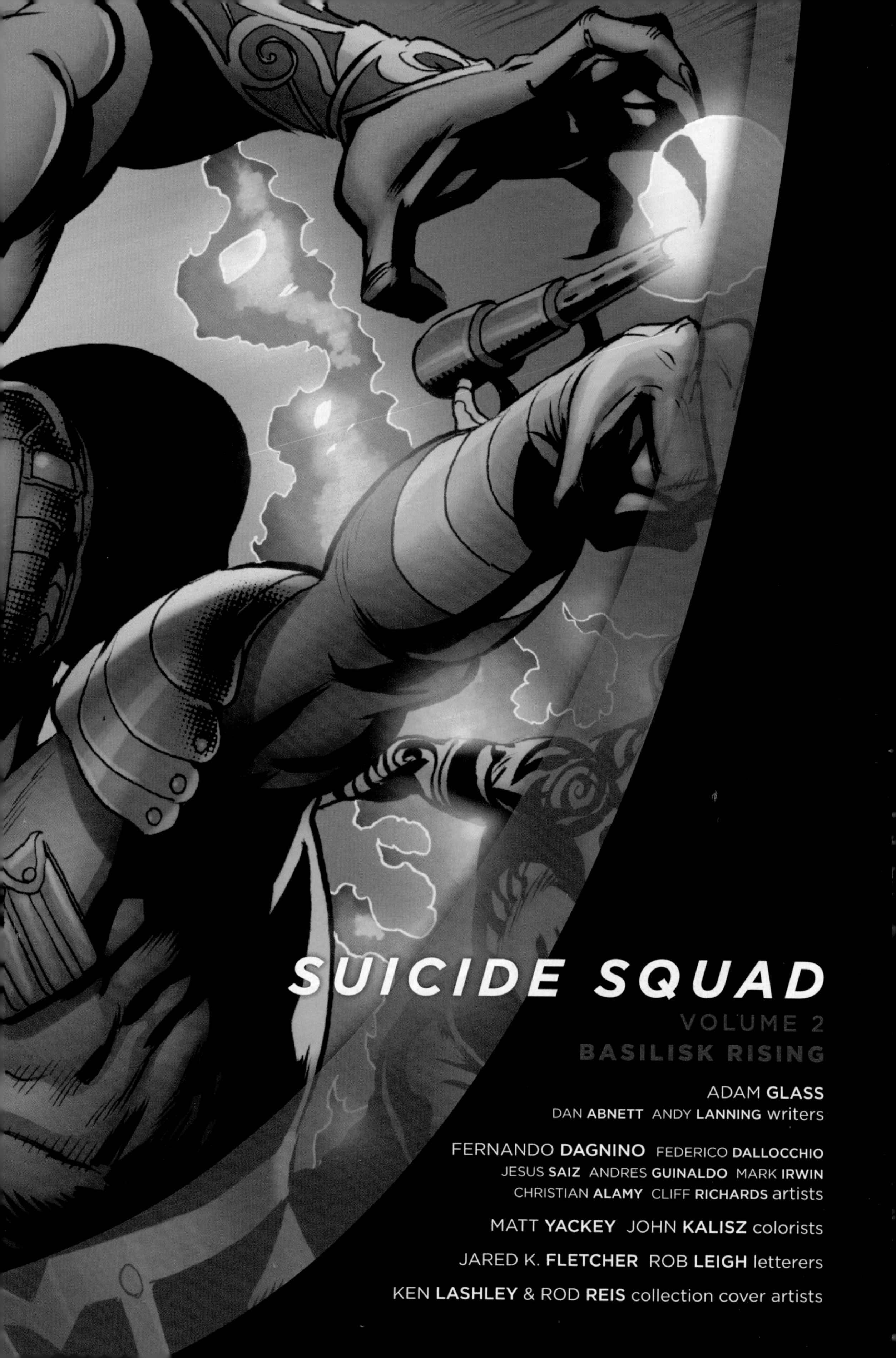

SUICIDE SQUAD

VOLUME 2
BASILISK RISING

ADAM **GLASS**
DAN **ABNETT** ANDY **LANNING** writers

FERNANDO **DAGNINO** FEDERICO **DALLOCCHIO**
JESUS **SAIZ** ANDRES **GUINALDO** MARK **IRWIN**
CHRISTIAN **ALAMY** CLIFF **RICHARDS** artists

MATT **YACKEY** JOHN **KALISZ** colorists

JARED K. **FLETCHER** ROB **LEIGH** letterers

KEN **LASHLEY** & ROD **REIS** collection cover artists

BOBBIE CHASE BRIAN CUNNINGHAM Editors – Original Series KATIE KUBERT Assistant Editor – Original Series
JEB WOODARD Group Editor – Collected Editions ROWENA YOW Editor – Collected Edition ROBBIE BIEDERMAN Publication Design

BOB HARRAS Senior VP – Editor-in-Chief, DC Comics

DIANE NELSON President DAN DIDIO and JIM LEE Co-Publishers
GEOFF JOHNS Chief Creative Officer AMIT DESAI Senior VP – Marketing & Global Franchise Management
NAIRI GARDINER Senior VP – Finance SAM ADES VP – Digital Marketing BOBBIE CHASE VP – Talent Development
MARK CHIARELLO Senior VP – Art, Design & Collected Editions JOHN CUNNINGHAM VP – Content Strategy
ANNE DEPIES VP – Strategy Planning & Reporting DON FALLETTI VP – Manufacturing Operations
LAWRENCE GANEM VP – Editorial Administration & Talent Relations ALISON GILL Senior VP – Manufacturing & Operations
HANK KANALZ Senior VP – Editorial Strategy & Administration JAY KOGAN VP – Legal Affairs
DEREK MADDALENA Senior VP – Sales & Business Development JACK MAHAN VP – Business Affairs
DAN MIRON VP – Sales Planning & Trade Development NICK NAPOLITANO VP – Manufacturing Administration
CAROL ROEDER VP – Marketing EDDIE SCANNELL VP – Mass Account & Digital Sales
COURTNEY SIMMONS Senior VP – Publicity & Communications JIM (SKI) SOKOLOWSKI VP – Comic Book Specialty & Newsstand Sales
SANDY YI Senior VP – Global Franchise Management

SUICIDE SQUAD VOLUME 2: BASILISK RISING

DC Comics, 4000 Warner Blvd., Burbank, CA 91522
A Warner Bros. Entertainment Company
Printed by RR Donnelley, Salem, VA, USA. 9/8/15. Sixth Printing.

ISBN: 978-1-4012-3844-5

Library of Congress Cataloging-in-Publication Data

Glass, Adam, 1968-
Suicide squad. Volume 2, Basilisk rising / Adam Glass, Fernando Dagnino.
p. cm.
"Originally published in single magazine form in Suicide Squad 8-13, 0, Resurrection Man 9."
ISBN 978-1-4012-3844-5
1. Graphic novels. I. Dagnino, Fernando, 1973- II. Title. III. Title: Basilisk rising.
PN6728.S825G58 2012
741.5'973–dc23
2012040575

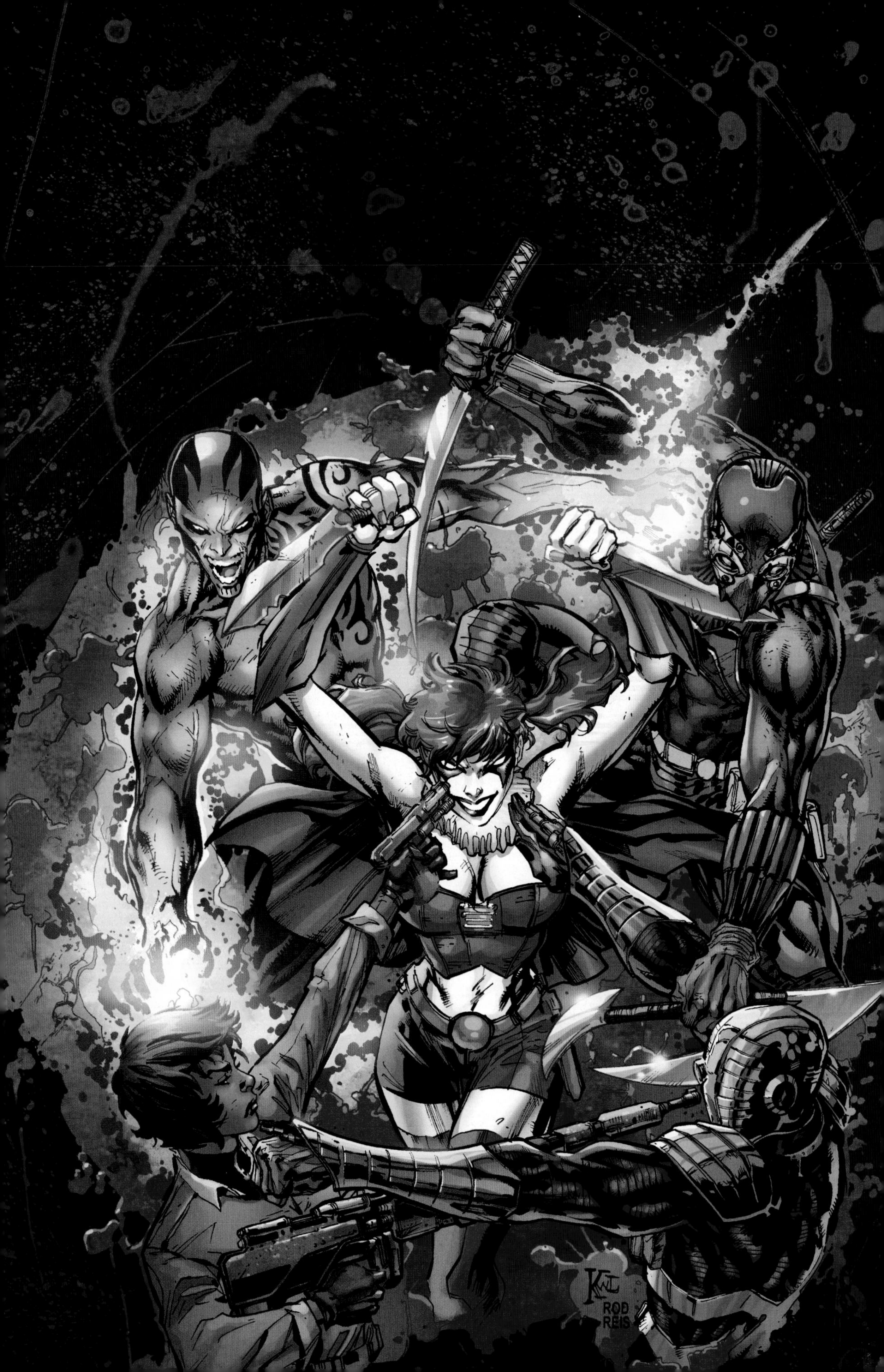
ROD
REIS

AFTERMATH

ADAM GLASS
writer

FEDERICO DALLOCCHIO
artist

cover art by KEN LASHLEY & ROD REIS

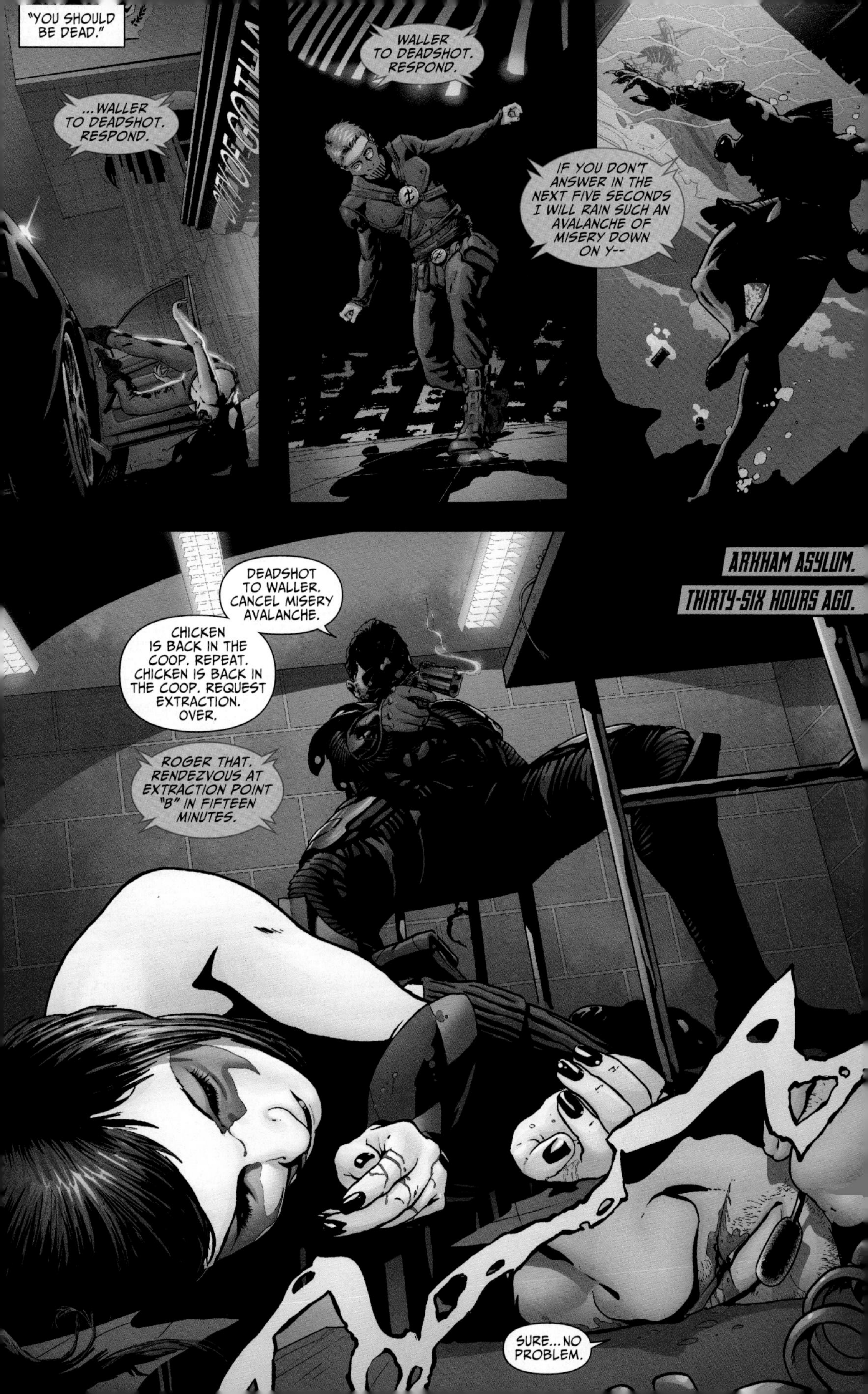
"YOU SHOULD BE DEAD."
...WALLER TO DEADSHOT. RESPOND.
WALLER TO DEADSHOT. RESPOND.
IF YOU DON'T ANSWER IN THE NEXT FIVE SECONDS I WILL RAIN SUCH AN AVALANCHE OF MISERY DOWN ON Y--
ARKHAM ASYLUM.
THIRTY-SIX HOURS AGO.
DEADSHOT TO WALLER. CANCEL MISERY AVALANCHE.
CHICKEN IS BACK IN THE COOP. REPEAT. CHICKEN IS BACK IN THE COOP. REQUEST EXTRACTION. OVER.
ROGER THAT. RENDEZVOUS AT EXTRACTION POINT "B" IN FIFTEEN MINUTES.
SURE... NO PROBLEM.

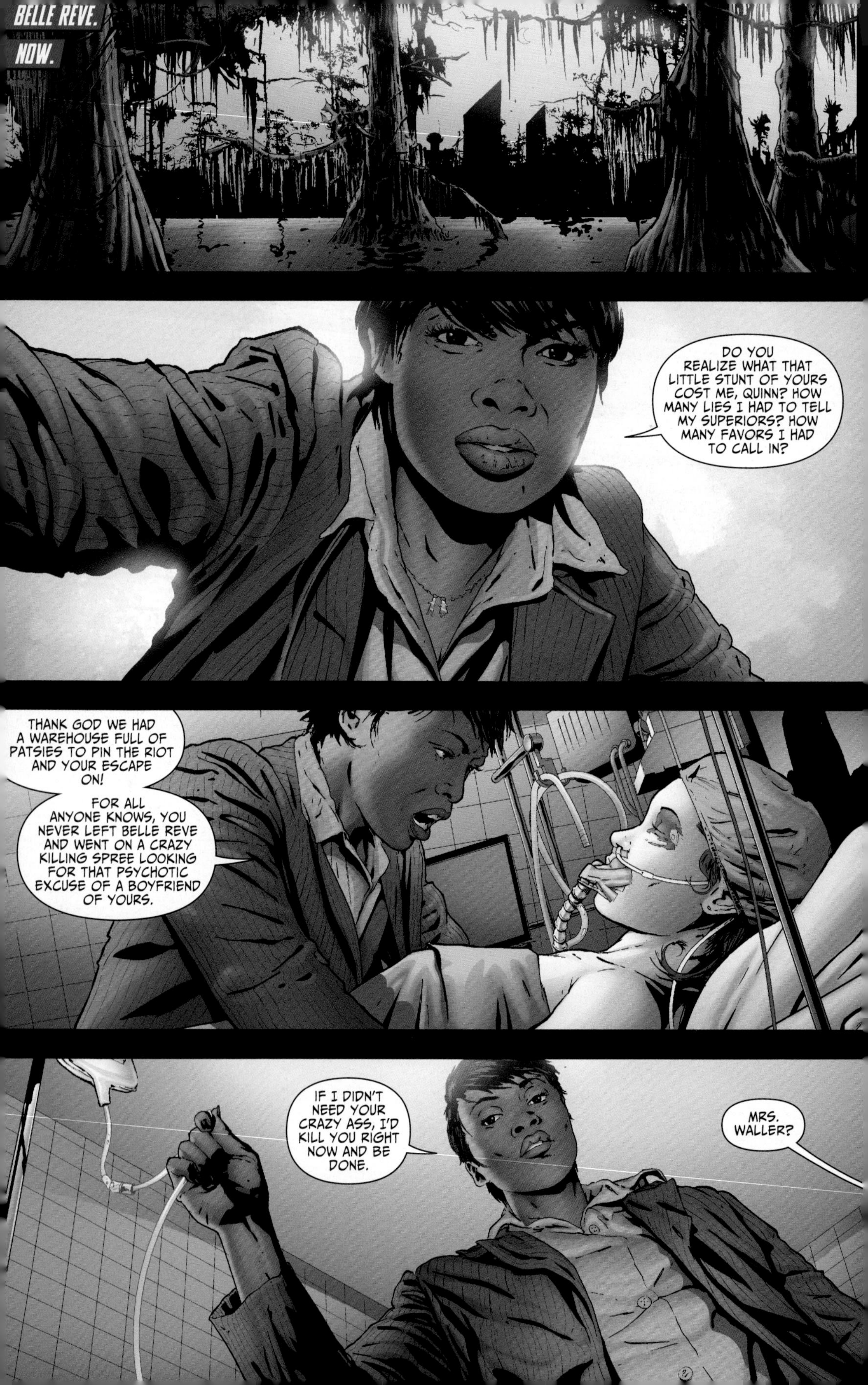
BELLE REVE.
NOW.
DO YOU REALIZE WHAT THAT LITTLE STUNT OF YOURS COST ME, QUINN? HOW MANY LIES I HAD TO TELL MY SUPERIORS? HOW MANY FAVORS I HAD TO CALL IN?
THANK GOD WE HAD A WAREHOUSE FULL OF PATSIES TO PIN THE RIOT AND YOUR ESCAPE ON!
FOR ALL ANYONE KNOWS, YOU NEVER LEFT BELLE REVE AND WENT ON A CRAZY KILLING SPREE LOOKING FOR THAT PSYCHOTIC EXCUSE OF A BOYFRIEND OF YOURS.
IF I DIDN'T NEED YOUR CRAZY ASS, I'D KILL YOU RIGHT NOW AND BE DONE.
MRS. WALLER?

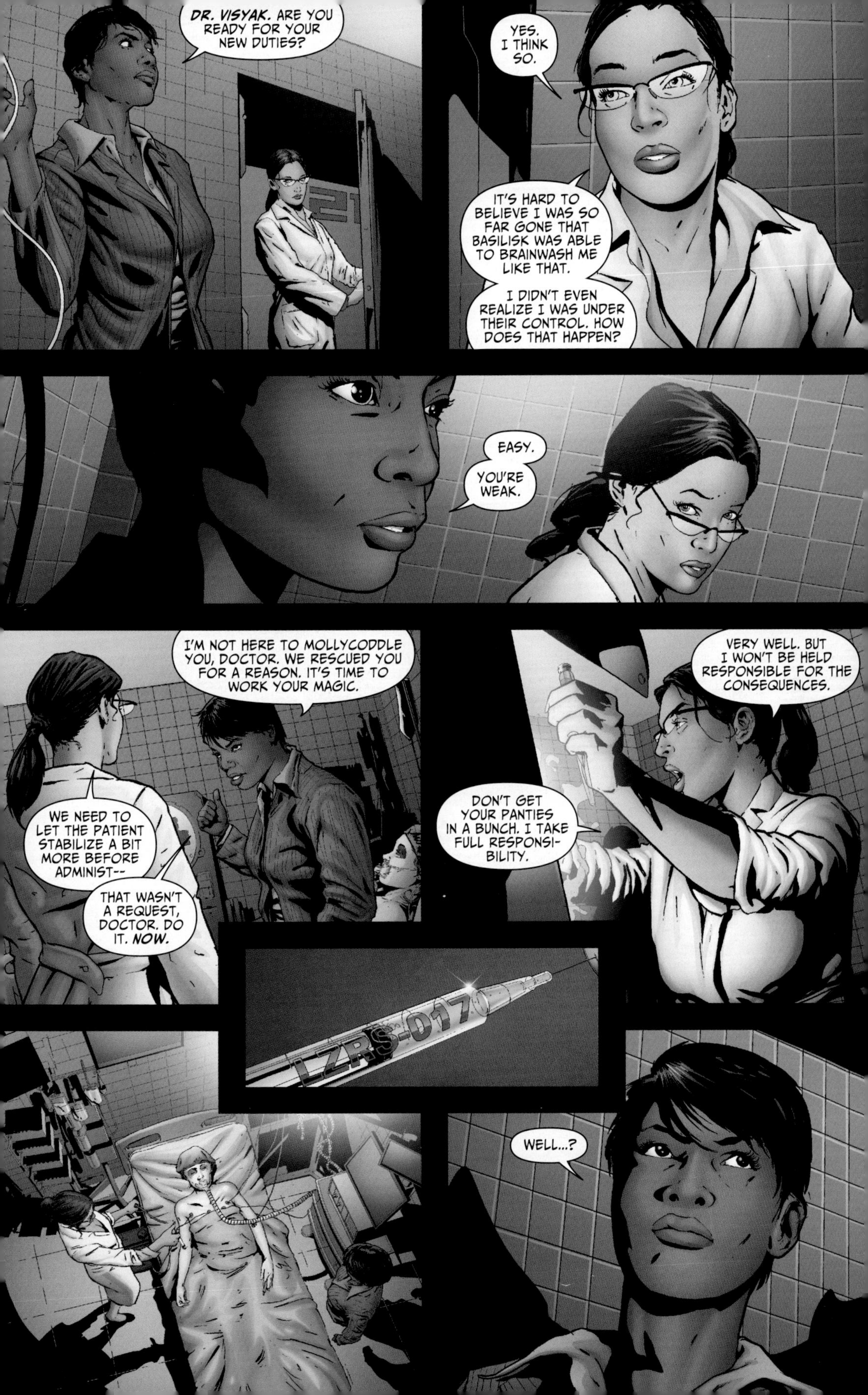
DR. VISYAK. ARE YOU READY FOR YOUR NEW DUTIES?
YES. I THINK SO.
IT'S HARD TO BELIEVE I WAS SO FAR GONE THAT BASILISK WAS ABLE TO BRAINWASH ME LIKE THAT.
I DIDN'T EVEN REALIZE I WAS UNDER THEIR CONTROL. HOW DOES THAT HAPPEN?
EASY.
YOU'RE WEAK.
I'M NOT HERE TO MOLLYCODDLE YOU, DOCTOR. WE RESCUED YOU FOR A REASON. IT'S TIME TO WORK YOUR MAGIC.
WE NEED TO LET THE PATIENT STABILIZE A BIT MORE BEFORE ADMINIST--
THAT WASN'T A REQUEST, DOCTOR. DO IT. NOW.
VERY WELL. BUT I WON'T BE HELD RESPONSIBLE FOR THE CONSEQUENCES.
DON'T GET YOUR PANTIES IN A BUNCH. I TAKE FULL RESPONSIBILITY.
LZRS-017
WELL...?

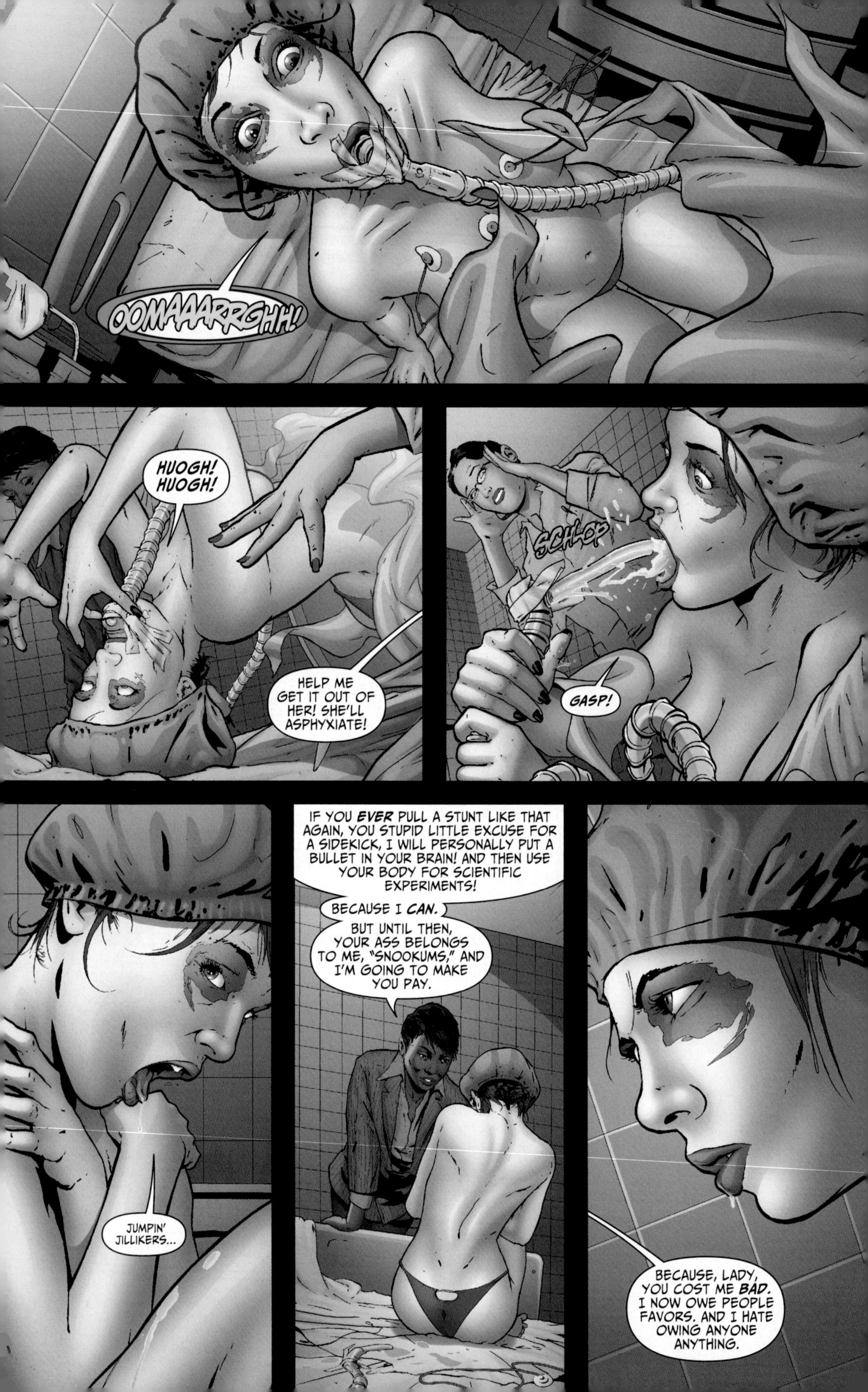
OOMAAARRGHH!
HUOGH! HUOGH!
HELP ME GET IT OUT OF HER! SHE'LL ASPHYXIATE!
SCHLOP
GASP!
JUMPIN' JILLIKERS...
IF YOU EVER PULL A STUNT LIKE THAT AGAIN, YOU STUPID LITTLE EXCUSE FOR A SIDEKICK, I WILL PERSONALLY PUT A BULLET IN YOUR BRAIN! AND THEN USE YOUR BODY FOR SCIENTIFIC EXPERIMENTS!
BECAUSE I CAN.
BUT UNTIL THEN, YOUR ASS BELONGS TO ME, "SNOOKUMS," AND I'M GOING TO MAKE YOU PAY.
BECAUSE, LADY, YOU COST ME BAD. I NOW OWE PEOPLE FAVORS. AND I HATE OWING ANYONE ANYTHING.

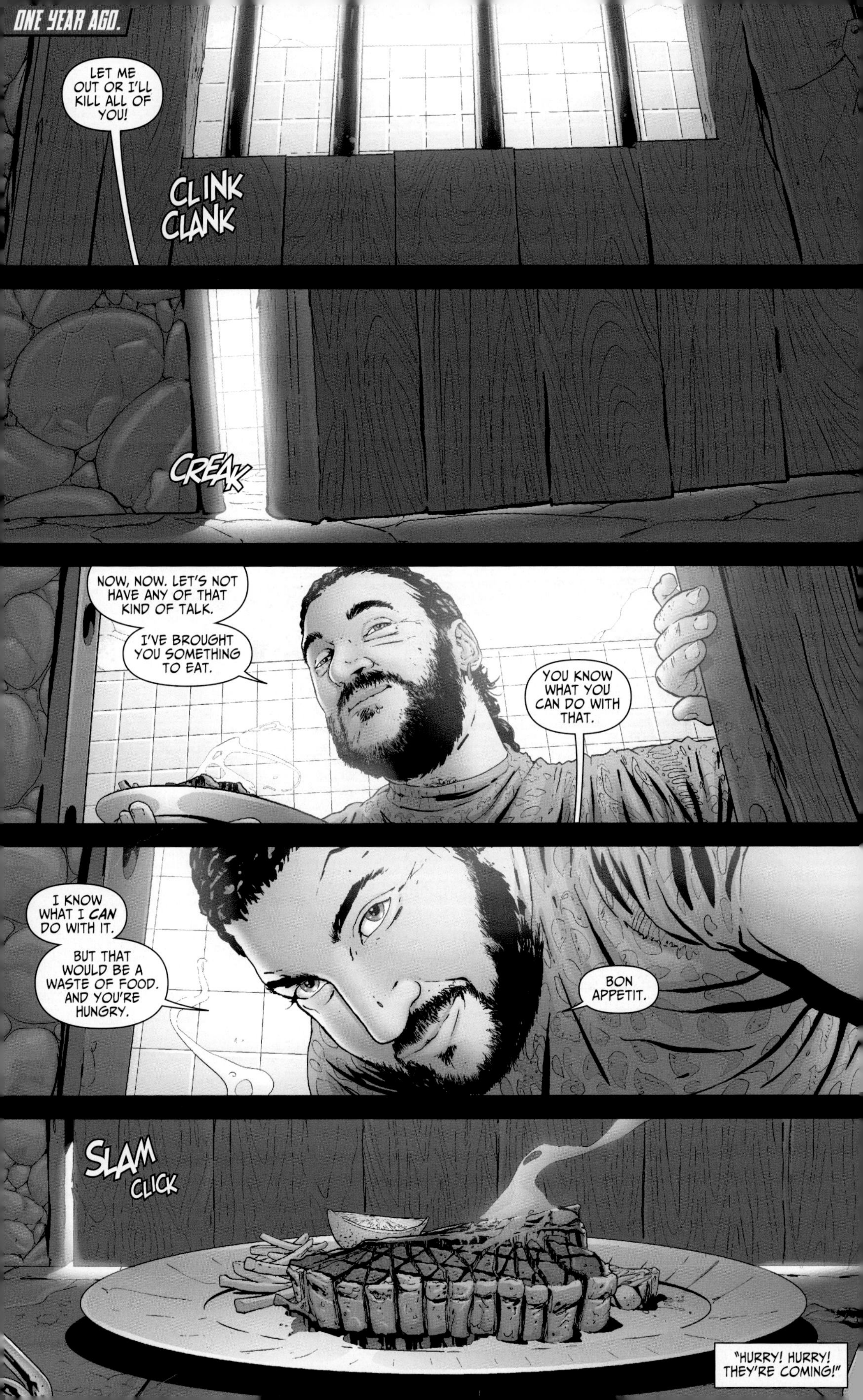
ONE YEAR AGO.
LET ME OUT OR I'LL KILL ALL OF YOU!
CLINK CLANK
CREAK
NOW, NOW. LET'S NOT HAVE ANY OF THAT KIND OF TALK.
I'VE BROUGHT YOU SOMETHING TO EAT.
YOU KNOW WHAT YOU CAN DO WITH THAT.
I KNOW WHAT I *CAN* DO WITH IT.
BUT THAT WOULD BE A WASTE OF FOOD. AND YOU'RE HUNGRY.
BON APPETIT.
SLAM
CLICK
"HURRY! HURRY! THEY'RE COMING!"

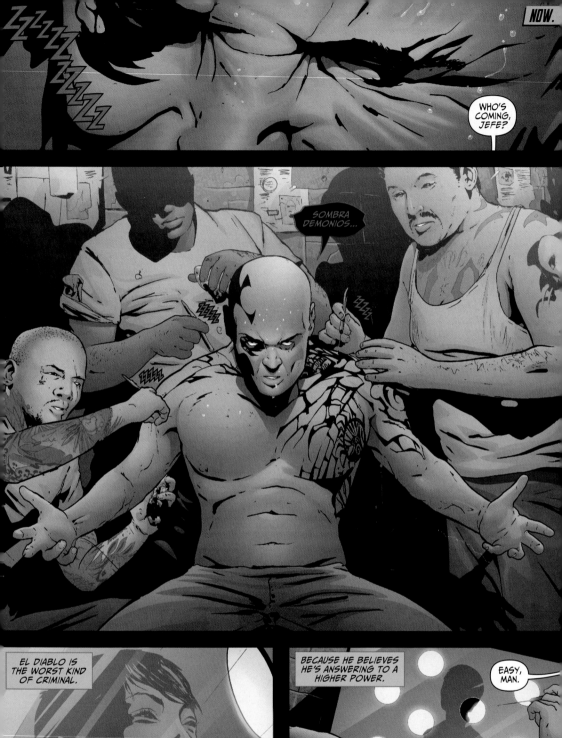

ZZZZZ
ZZZZ
ZZZ

WHO'S COMING, JEFE?

SOMBRA DEMONIOS...

EL DIABLO IS THE WORST KIND OF CRIMINAL.

BECAUSE HE BELIEVES HE'S ANSWERING TO A HIGHER POWER.

EASY, MAN.

SHADOW DEMONS!

THERE! RIGHT THERE IN THE CORNER!

CAN'T YOU SEE THEM?!

IN THE SHADOWS.

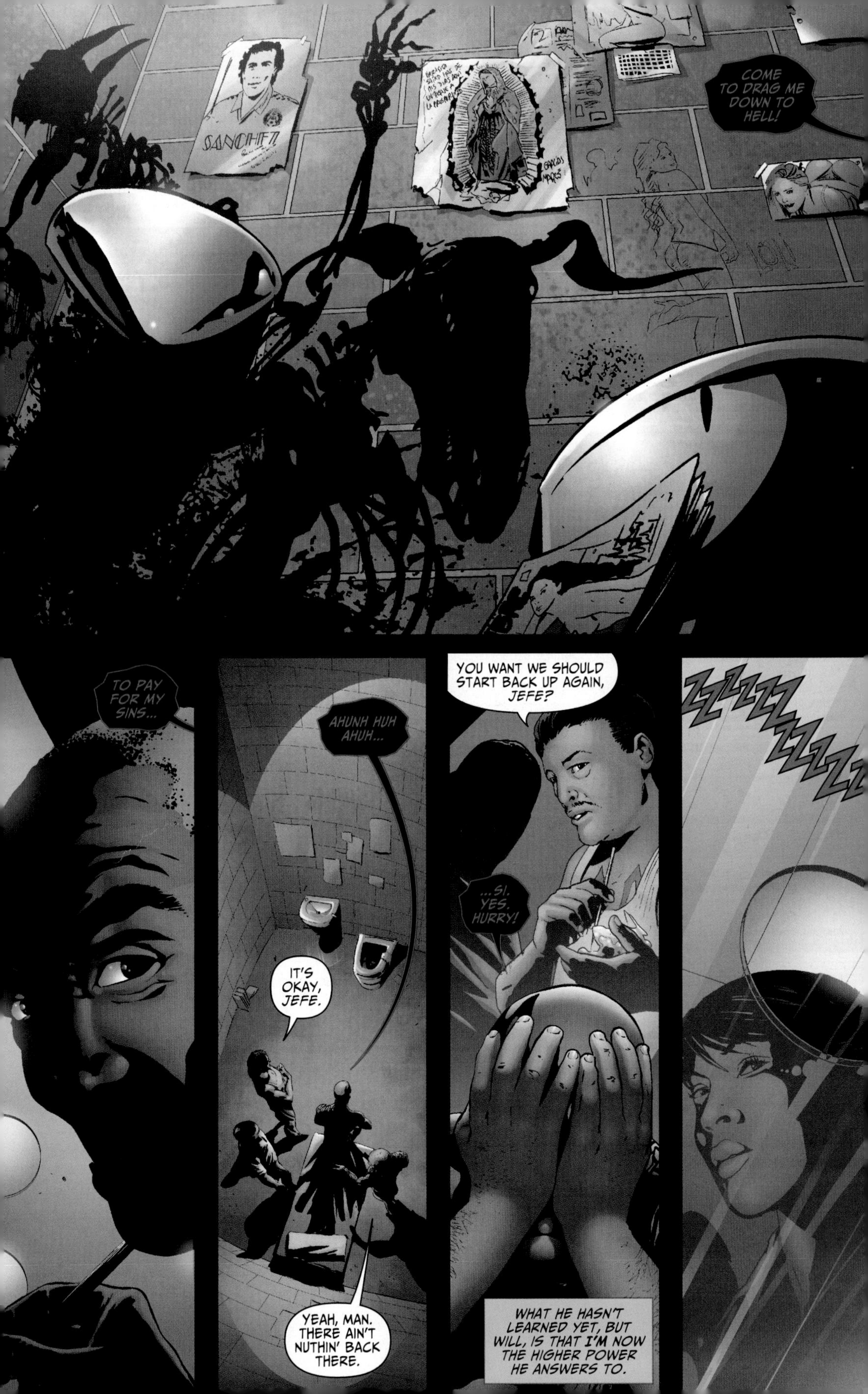
COME TO DRAG ME DOWN TO HELL!
TO PAY FOR MY SINS...
AHUNH HUH AHUH...
IT'S OKAY, JEFE.
YEAH, MAN. THERE AIN'T NUTHIN' BACK THERE.
YOU WANT WE SHOULD START BACK UP AGAIN, JEFE?
...SI. YES. HURRY!
WHAT HE HASN'T LEARNED YET, BUT WILL, IS THAT I'M NOW THE HIGHER POWER HE ANSWERS TO.
ZZZZZZ

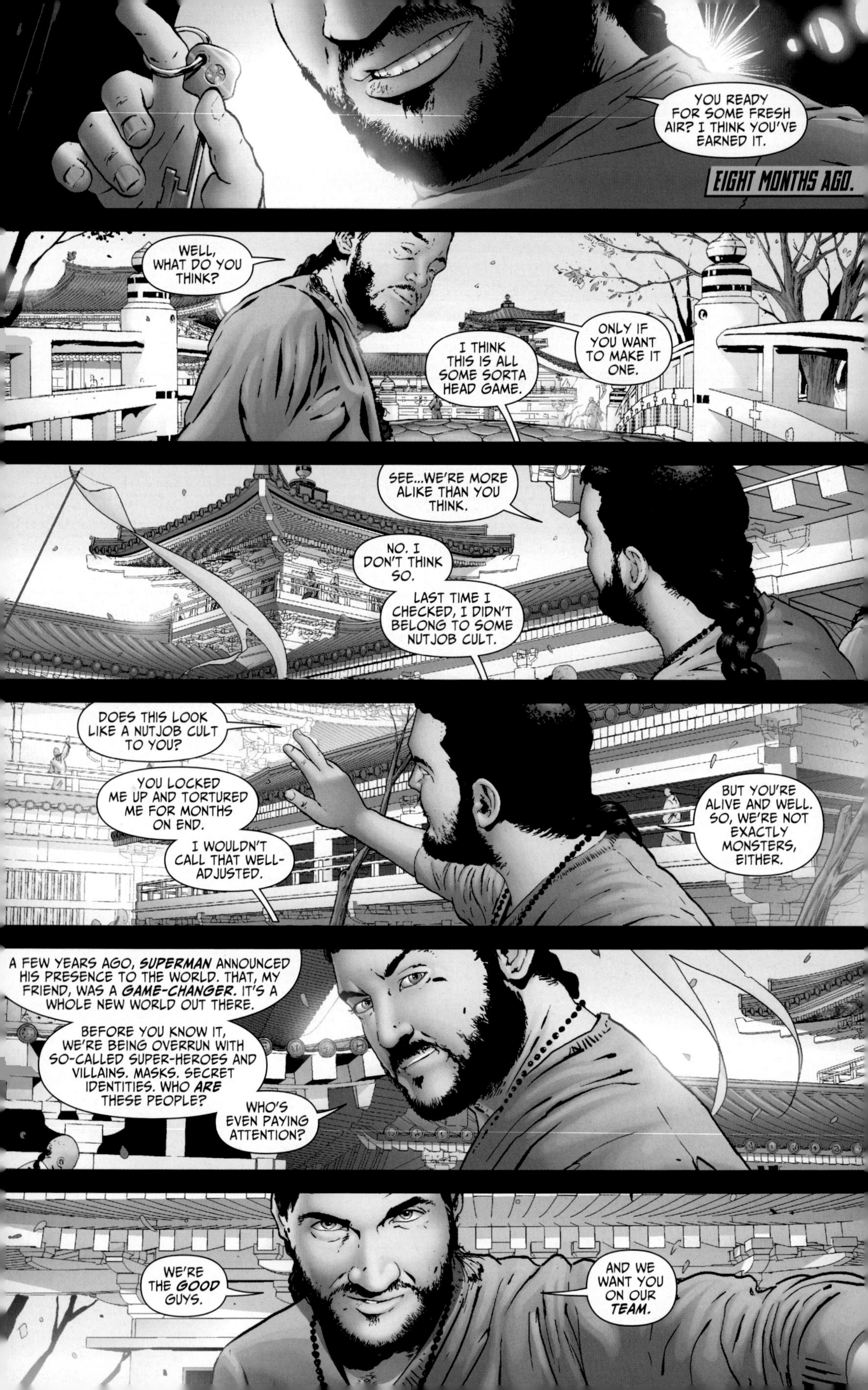
YOU READY FOR SOME FRESH AIR? I THINK YOU'VE EARNED IT.
EIGHT MONTHS AGO.
WELL, WHAT DO YOU THINK?
I THINK THIS IS ALL SOME SORTA HEAD GAME.
ONLY IF YOU WANT TO MAKE IT ONE.
SEE...WE'RE MORE ALIKE THAN YOU THINK.
NO. I DON'T THINK SO.
LAST TIME I CHECKED, I DIDN'T BELONG TO SOME NUTJOB CULT.
DOES THIS LOOK LIKE A NUTJOB CULT TO YOU?
YOU LOCKED ME UP AND TORTURED ME FOR MONTHS ON END.
I WOULDN'T CALL THAT WELL-ADJUSTED.
BUT YOU'RE ALIVE AND WELL. SO, WE'RE NOT EXACTLY MONSTERS, EITHER.
A FEW YEARS AGO, SUPERMAN ANNOUNCED HIS PRESENCE TO THE WORLD. THAT, MY FRIEND, WAS A GAME-CHANGER. IT'S A WHOLE NEW WORLD OUT THERE.
BEFORE YOU KNOW IT, WE'RE BEING OVERRUN WITH SO-CALLED SUPER-HEROES AND VILLAINS. MASKS. SECRET IDENTITIES. WHO ARE THESE PEOPLE?
WHO'S EVEN PAYING ATTENTION?
WE'RE THE GOOD GUYS.
AND WE WANT YOU ON OUR TEAM.

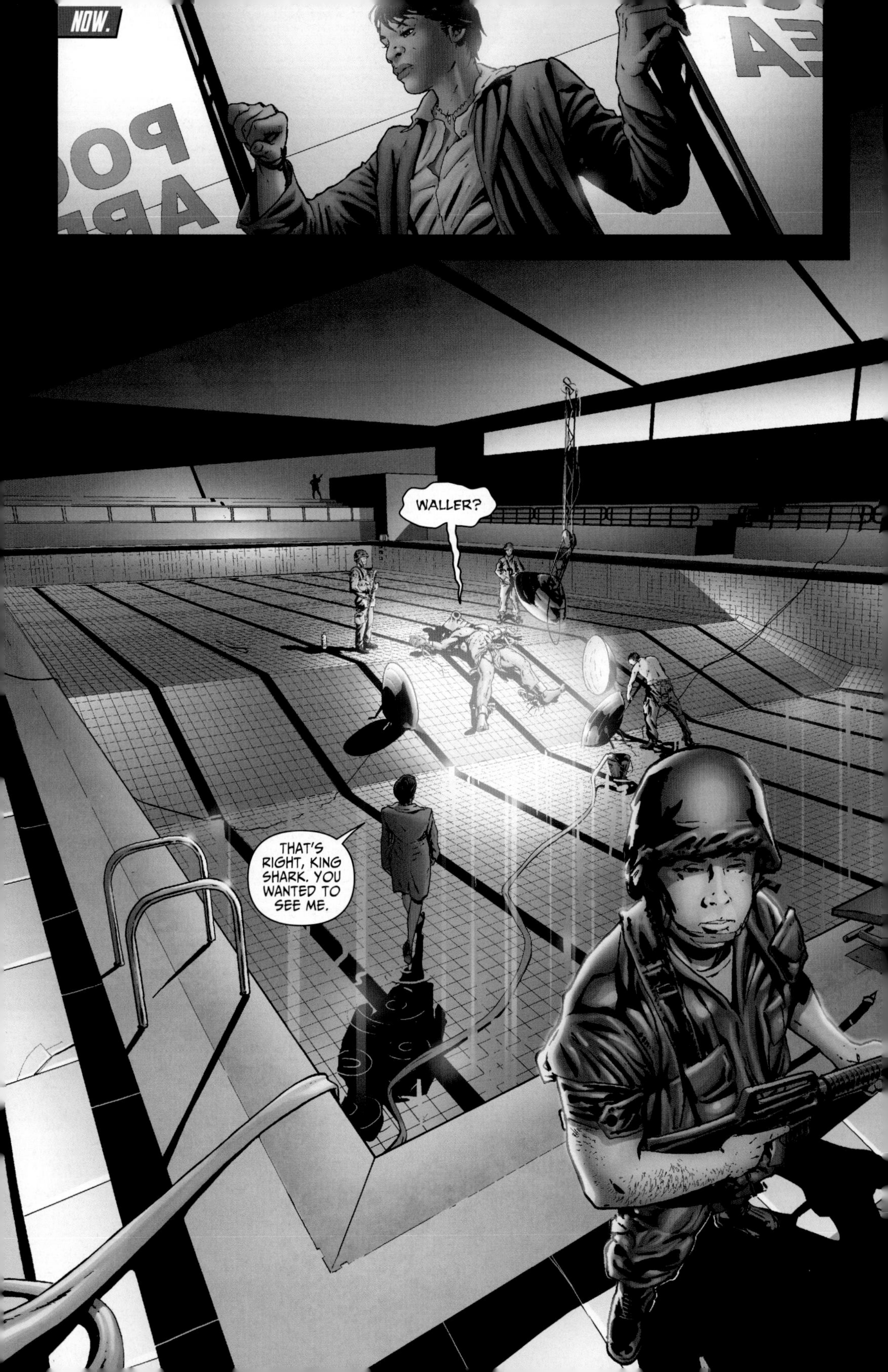
NOW.
WALLER?
THAT'S RIGHT, KING SHARK. YOU WANTED TO SEE ME.

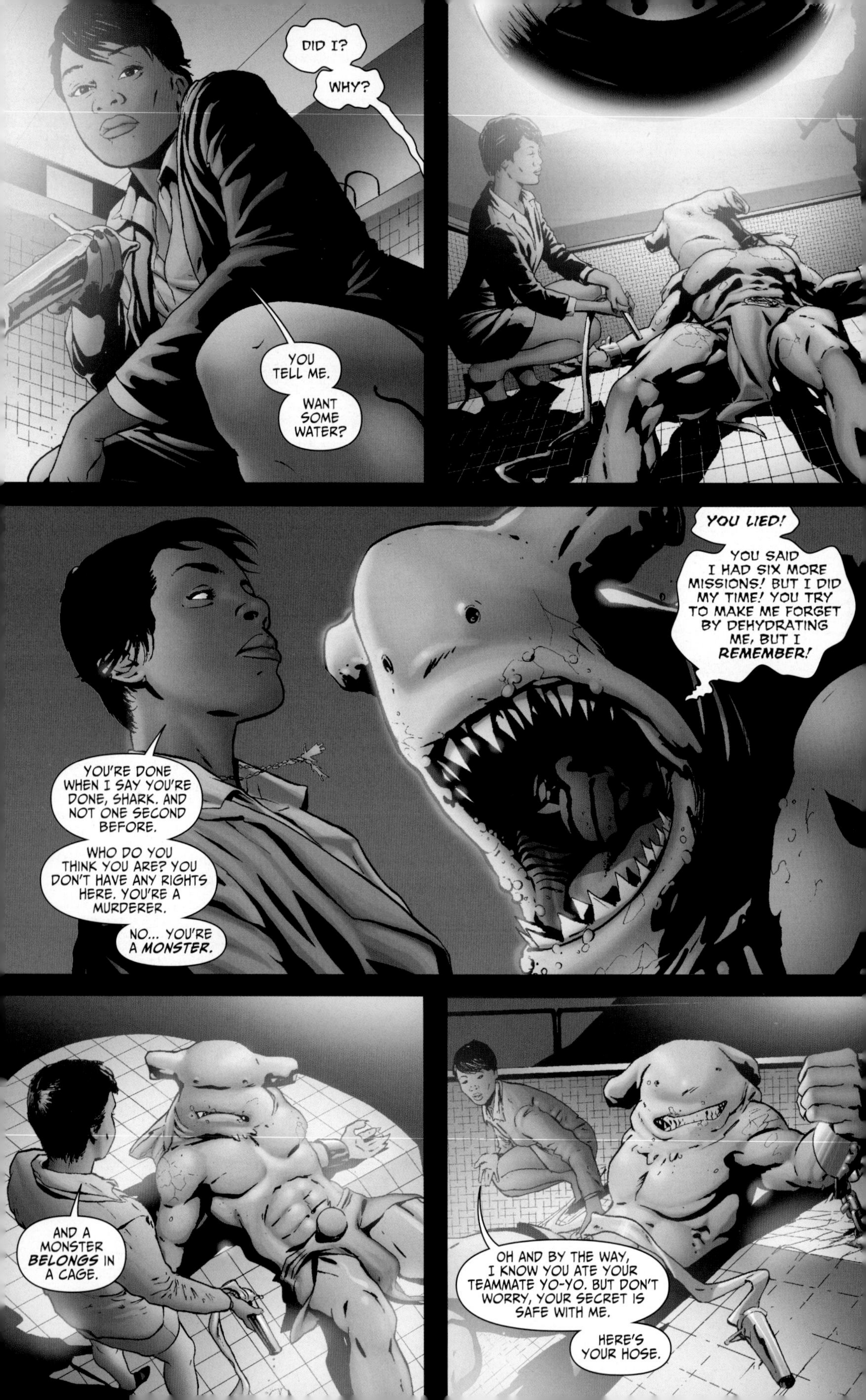
DID I?
WHY?
YOU TELL ME.
WANT SOME WATER?
YOU LIED!
YOU SAID I HAD SIX MORE MISSIONS! BUT I DID MY TIME! YOU TRY TO MAKE ME FORGET BY DEHYDRATING ME, BUT I REMEMBER!
YOU'RE DONE WHEN I SAY YOU'RE DONE, SHARK. AND NOT ONE SECOND BEFORE.
WHO DO YOU THINK YOU ARE? YOU DON'T HAVE ANY RIGHTS HERE. YOU'RE A MURDERER.
NO... YOU'RE A MONSTER.
AND A MONSTER BELONGS IN A CAGE.
OH AND BY THE WAY, I KNOW YOU ATE YOUR TEAMMATE YO-YO. BUT DON'T WORRY, YOUR SECRET IS SAFE WITH ME.
HERE'S YOUR HOSE.

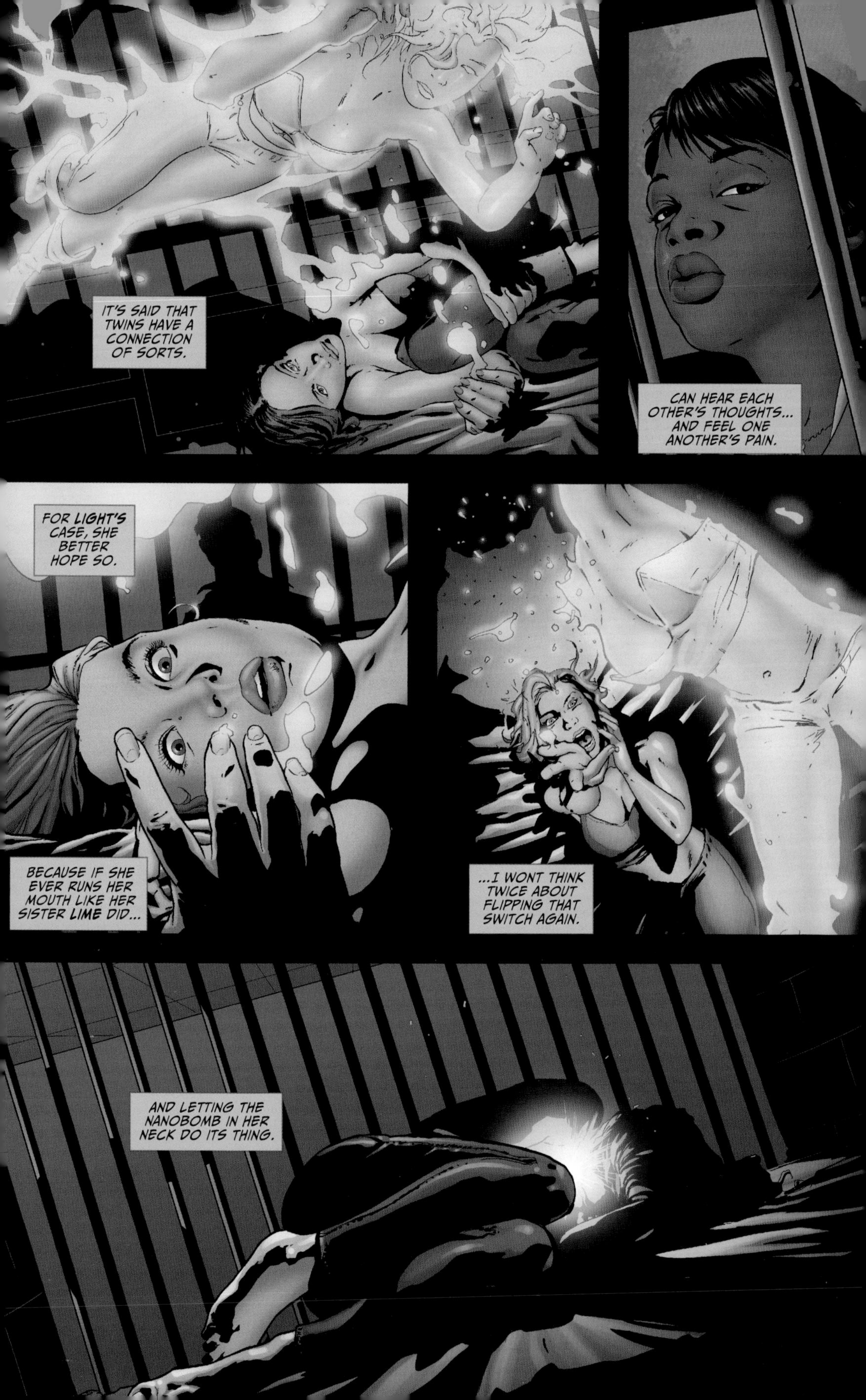
IT'S SAID THAT TWINS HAVE A CONNECTION OF SORTS.
CAN HEAR EACH OTHER'S THOUGHTS... AND FEEL ONE ANOTHER'S PAIN.
FOR **LIGHT'S** CASE, SHE BETTER HOPE SO.
BECAUSE IF SHE EVER RUNS HER MOUTH LIKE HER SISTER **LIME** DID...
...I WONT THINK TWICE ABOUT FLIPPING THAT SWITCH AGAIN.
AND LETTING THE NANOBOMB IN HER NECK DO ITS THING.

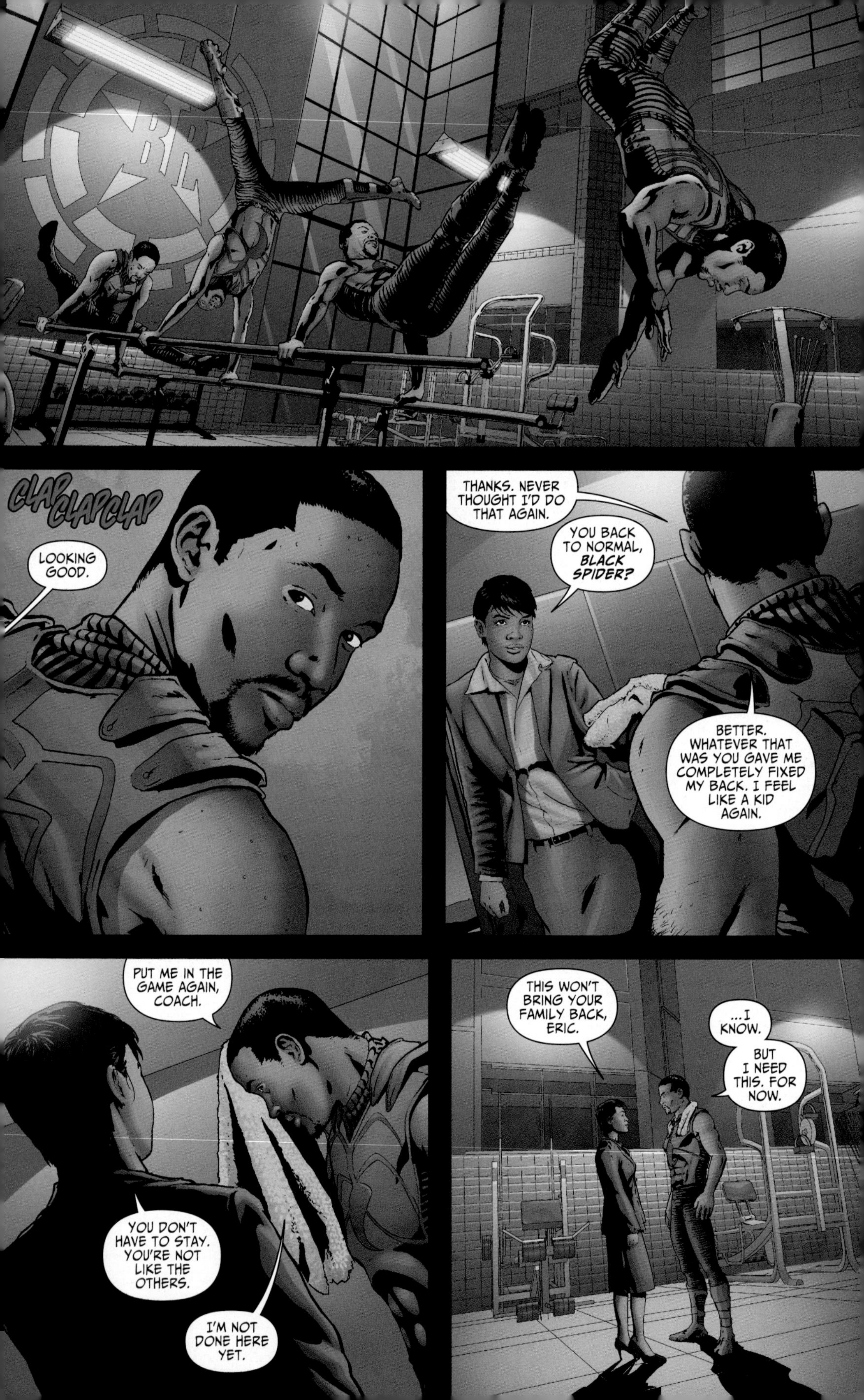
CLAP CLAPCLAP
LOOKING GOOD.
THANKS. NEVER THOUGHT I'D DO THAT AGAIN.
YOU BACK TO NORMAL, BLACK SPIDER?
BETTER. WHATEVER THAT WAS YOU GAVE ME COMPLETELY FIXED MY BACK. I FEEL LIKE A KID AGAIN.
PUT ME IN THE GAME AGAIN, COACH.
YOU DON'T HAVE TO STAY. YOU'RE NOT LIKE THE OTHERS.
I'M NOT DONE HERE YET.
THIS WON'T BRING YOUR FAMILY BACK, ERIC.
...I KNOW.
BUT I NEED THIS. FOR NOW.

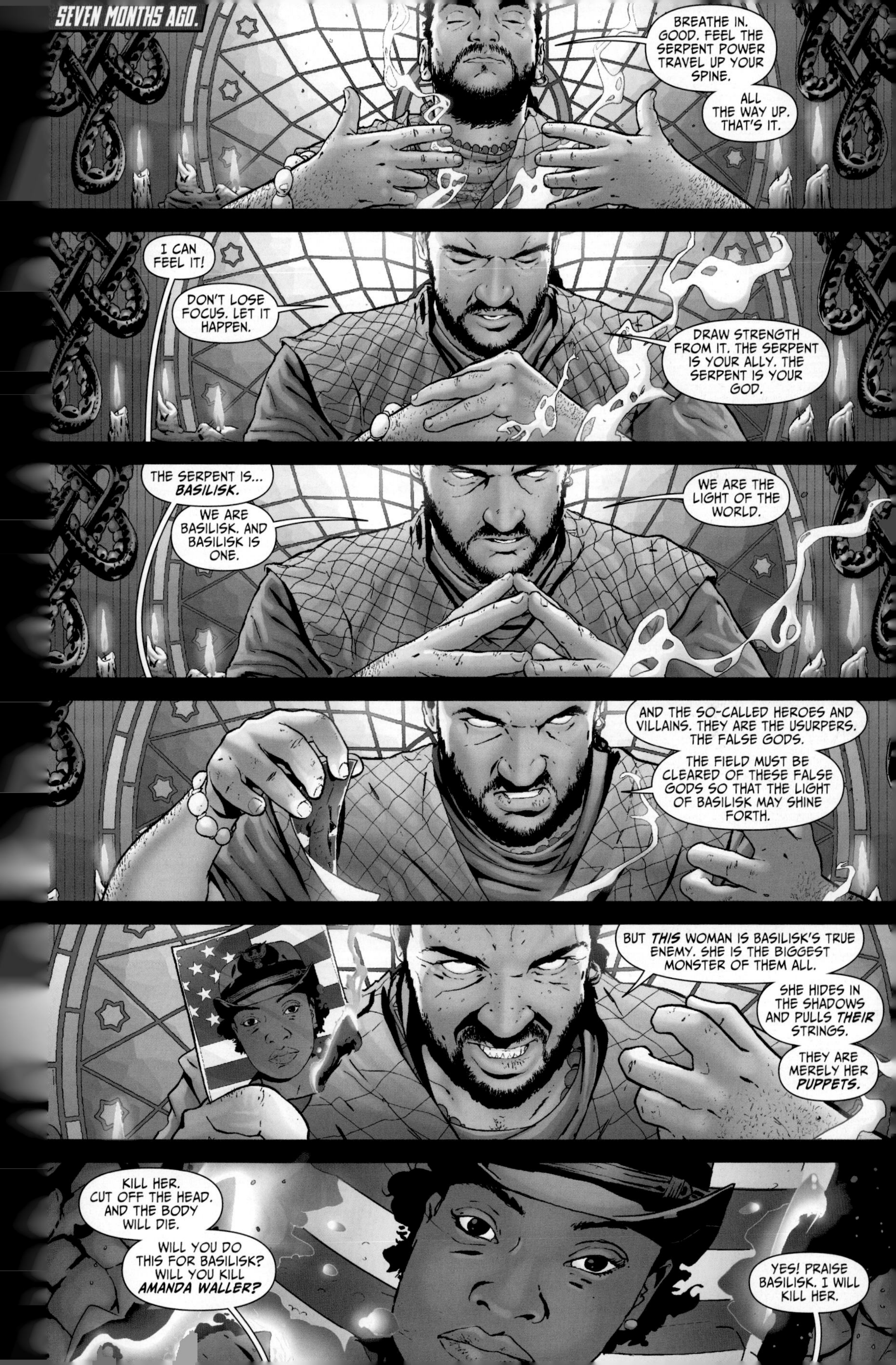
SEVEN MONTHS AGO.
BREATHE IN. GOOD. FEEL THE SERPENT POWER TRAVEL UP YOUR SPINE.
ALL THE WAY UP. THAT'S IT.
I CAN FEEL IT!
DON'T LOSE FOCUS. LET IT HAPPEN.
DRAW STRENGTH FROM IT. THE SERPENT IS YOUR ALLY. THE SERPENT IS YOUR GOD.
THE SERPENT IS... BASILISK.
WE ARE BASILISK. AND BASILISK IS ONE.
WE ARE THE LIGHT OF THE WORLD.
AND THE SO-CALLED HEROES AND VILLAINS. THEY ARE THE USURPERS. THE FALSE GODS.
THE FIELD MUST BE CLEARED OF THESE FALSE GODS SO THAT THE LIGHT OF BASILISK MAY SHINE FORTH.
BUT THIS WOMAN IS BASILISK'S TRUE ENEMY. SHE IS THE BIGGEST MONSTER OF THEM ALL.
SHE HIDES IN THE SHADOWS AND PULLS THEIR STRINGS.
THEY ARE MERELY HER PUPPETS.
KILL HER. CUT OFF THE HEAD. AND THE BODY WILL DIE.
WILL YOU DO THIS FOR BASILISK? WILL YOU KILL AMANDA WALLER?
YES! PRAISE BASILISK. I WILL KILL HER.

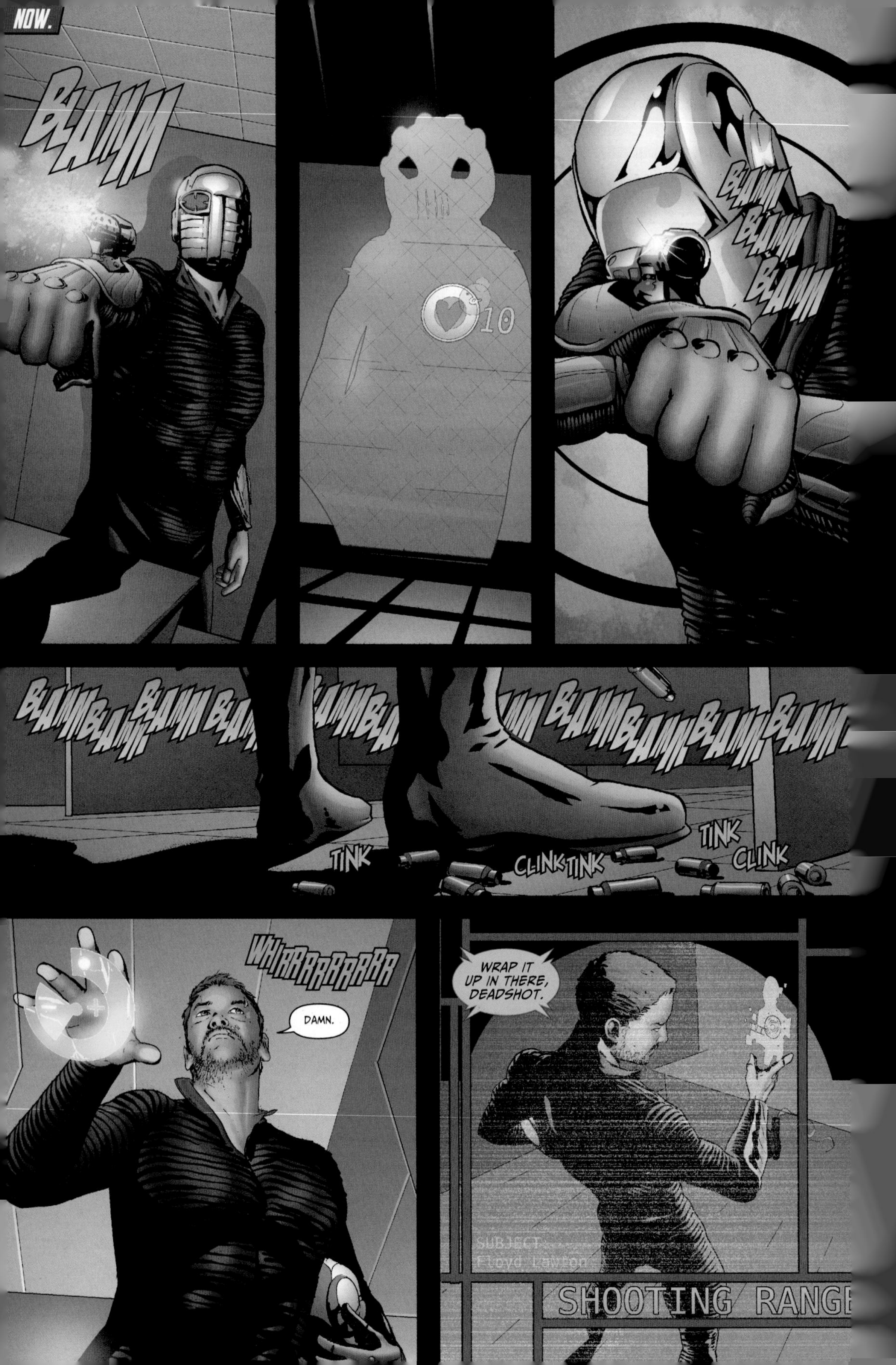
NOW.
BLAMM
10
BLAMM
BLAMM
BLAMM
BLAMMBLAMMBLAMM BLAMM
BLAMMBLAMM
BLAMM BLAMMBLAMMBLAMMBLAMM
TINK
CLINKTINK
TINK
CLINK
WHIRRRRRRRRRR
DAMN.
WRAP IT UP IN THERE, DEADSHOT.
SUBJECT
Floyd Lawton
SHOOTING RANGE

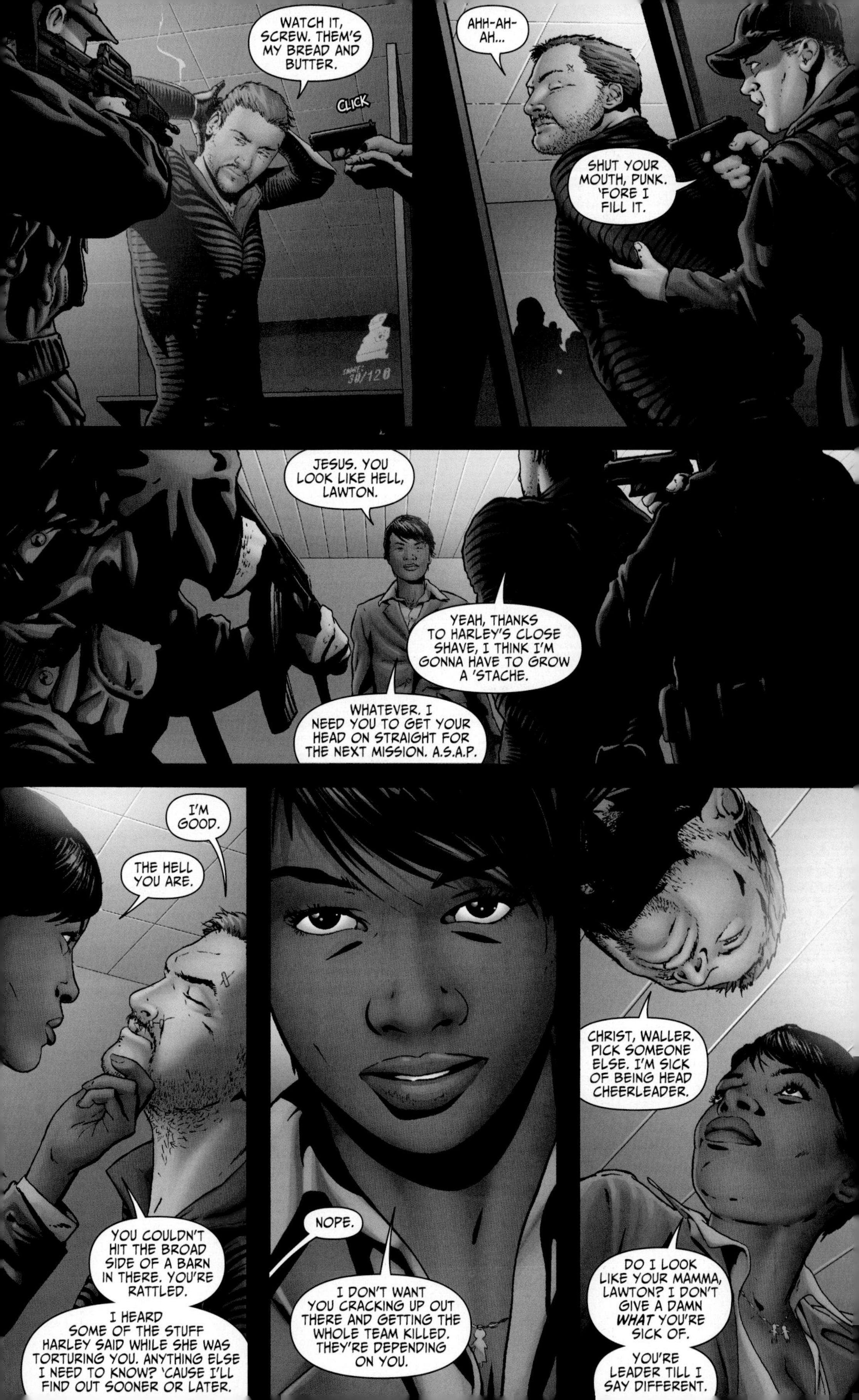
WATCH IT, SCREW. THEM'S MY BREAD AND BUTTER.
CLICK
AHH-AH-AH...
SHUT YOUR MOUTH, PUNK. 'FORE I FILL IT.
JESUS. YOU LOOK LIKE HELL, LAWTON.
YEAH, THANKS TO HARLEY'S CLOSE SHAVE, I THINK I'M GONNA HAVE TO GROW A 'STACHE.
WHATEVER. I NEED YOU TO GET YOUR HEAD ON STRAIGHT FOR THE NEXT MISSION. A.S.A.P.
I'M GOOD.
THE HELL YOU ARE.
YOU COULDN'T HIT THE BROAD SIDE OF A BARN IN THERE. YOU'RE RATTLED.
I HEARD SOME OF THE STUFF HARLEY SAID WHILE SHE WAS TORTURING YOU. ANYTHING ELSE I NEED TO KNOW? 'CAUSE I'LL FIND OUT SOONER OR LATER.
NOPE.
I DON'T WANT YOU CRACKING UP OUT THERE AND GETTING THE WHOLE TEAM KILLED. THEY'RE DEPENDING ON YOU.
CHRIST, WALLER. PICK SOMEONE ELSE. I'M SICK OF BEING HEAD CHEERLEADER.
DO I LOOK LIKE YOUR MAMMA, LAWTON? I DON'T GIVE A DAMN *WHAT* YOU'RE SICK OF.
YOU'RE LEADER TILL I SAY DIFFERENT.

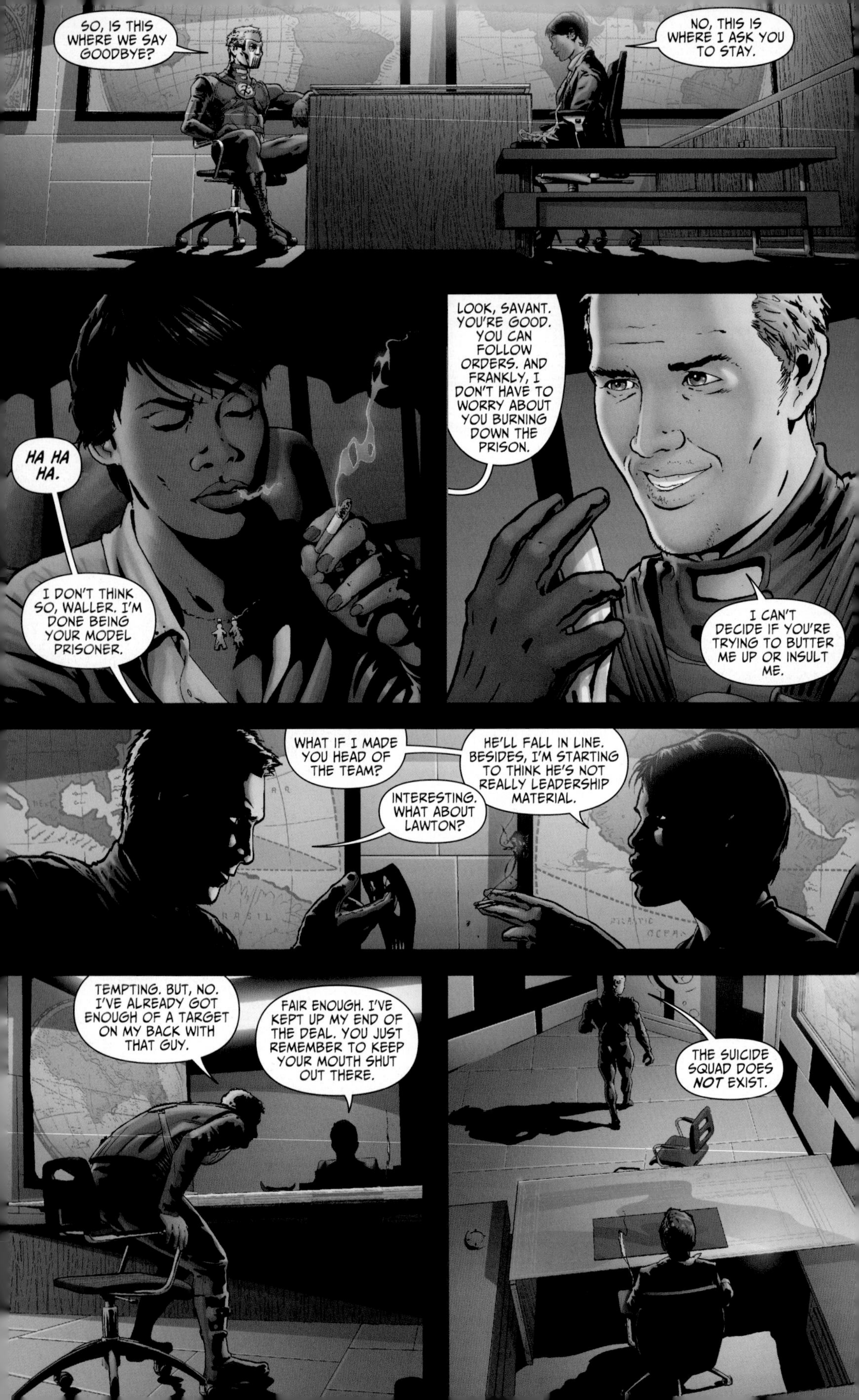
SO, IS THIS WHERE WE SAY GOODBYE?
NO, THIS IS WHERE I ASK YOU TO STAY.
LOOK, SAVANT. YOU'RE GOOD. YOU CAN FOLLOW ORDERS. AND FRANKLY, I DON'T HAVE TO WORRY ABOUT YOU BURNING DOWN THE PRISON.
HA HA HA.
I DON'T THINK SO, WALLER. I'M DONE BEING YOUR MODEL PRISONER.
I CAN'T DECIDE IF YOU'RE TRYING TO BUTTER ME UP OR INSULT ME.
WHAT IF I MADE YOU HEAD OF THE TEAM?
INTERESTING. WHAT ABOUT LAWTON?
HE'LL FALL IN LINE. BESIDES, I'M STARTING TO THINK HE'S NOT REALLY LEADERSHIP MATERIAL.
TEMPTING. BUT, NO. I'VE ALREADY GOT ENOUGH OF A TARGET ON MY BACK WITH THAT GUY.
FAIR ENOUGH. I'VE KEPT UP MY END OF THE DEAL. YOU JUST REMEMBER TO KEEP YOUR MOUTH SHUT OUT THERE.
THE SUICIDE SQUAD DOES *NOT* EXIST.

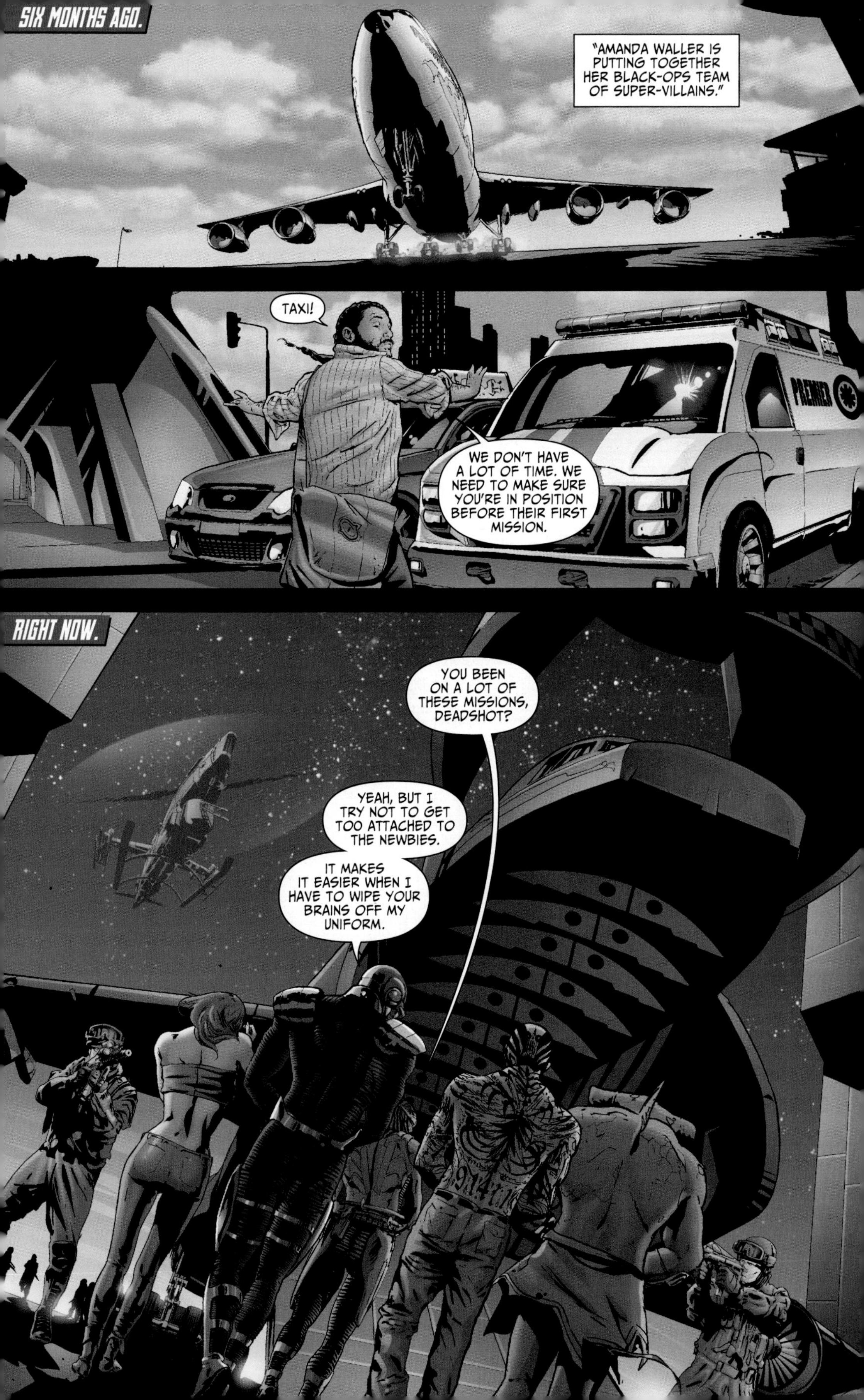
SIX MONTHS AGO.
"AMANDA WALLER IS PUTTING TOGETHER HER BLACK-OPS TEAM OF SUPER-VILLAINS."
TAXI!
WE DON'T HAVE A LOT OF TIME. WE NEED TO MAKE SURE YOU'RE IN POSITION BEFORE THEIR FIRST MISSION.
PREMIER
RIGHT NOW.
YOU BEEN ON A LOT OF THESE MISSIONS, DEADSHOT?
YEAH, BUT I TRY NOT TO GET TOO ATTACHED TO THE NEWBIES.
IT MAKES IT EASIER WHEN I HAVE TO WIPE YOUR BRAINS OFF MY UNIFORM.

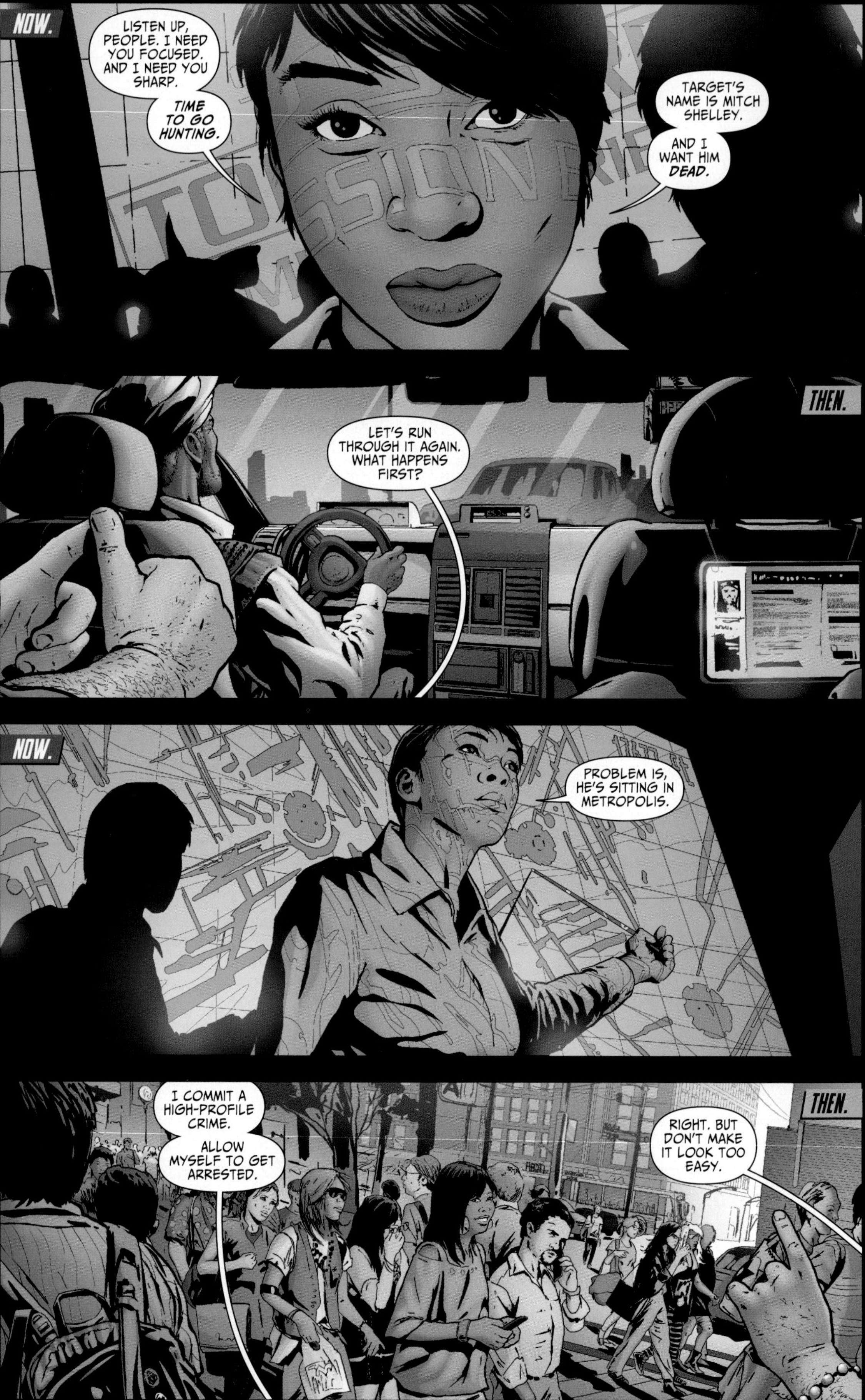
NOW.
LISTEN UP, PEOPLE. I NEED YOU FOCUSED. AND I NEED YOU SHARP.
TIME TO GO HUNTING.
TARGET'S NAME IS MITCH SHELLEY.
AND I WANT HIM DEAD.
THEN.
LET'S RUN THROUGH IT AGAIN. WHAT HAPPENS FIRST?
NOW.
PROBLEM IS, HE'S SITTING IN METROPOLIS.
THEN.
I COMMIT A HIGH-PROFILE CRIME.
ALLOW MYSELF TO GET ARRESTED.
RIGHT. BUT DON'T MAKE IT LOOK TOO EASY.

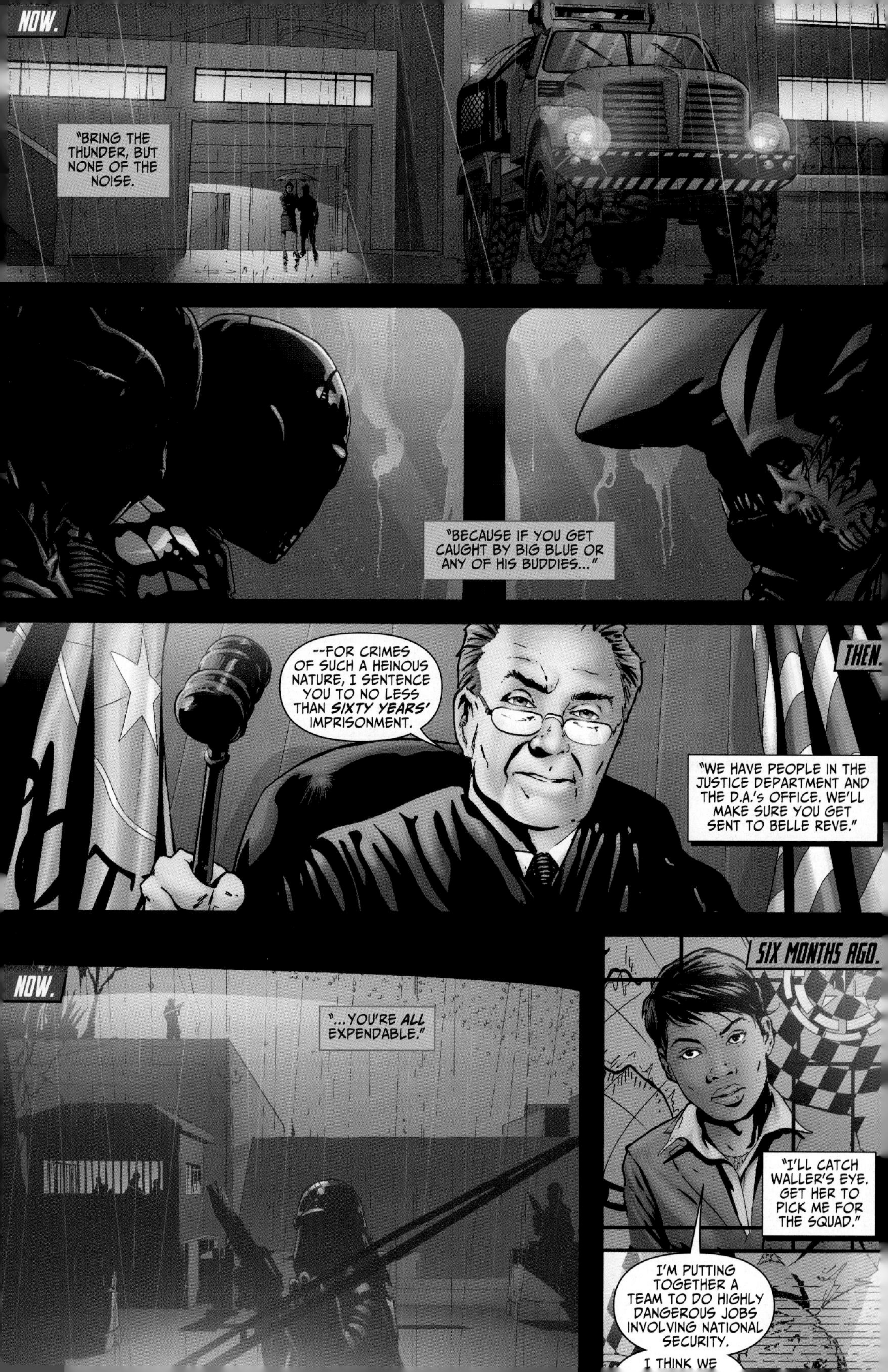

NOW.
"BRING THE THUNDER, BUT NONE OF THE NOISE.
"BECAUSE IF YOU GET CAUGHT BY BIG BLUE OR ANY OF HIS BUDDIES..."
--FOR CRIMES OF SUCH A HEINOUS NATURE, I SENTENCE YOU TO NO LESS THAN SIXTY YEARS' IMPRISONMENT.
THEN.
"WE HAVE PEOPLE IN THE JUSTICE DEPARTMENT AND THE D.A.'s OFFICE. WE'LL MAKE SURE YOU GET SENT TO BELLE REVE."
NOW.
"...YOU'RE ALL EXPENDABLE."
SIX MONTHS AGO.
"I'LL CATCH WALLER'S EYE. GET HER TO PICK ME FOR THE SQUAD."
I'M PUTTING TOGETHER A TEAM TO DO HIGHLY DANGEROUS JOBS INVOLVING NATIONAL SECURITY.
I THINK WE

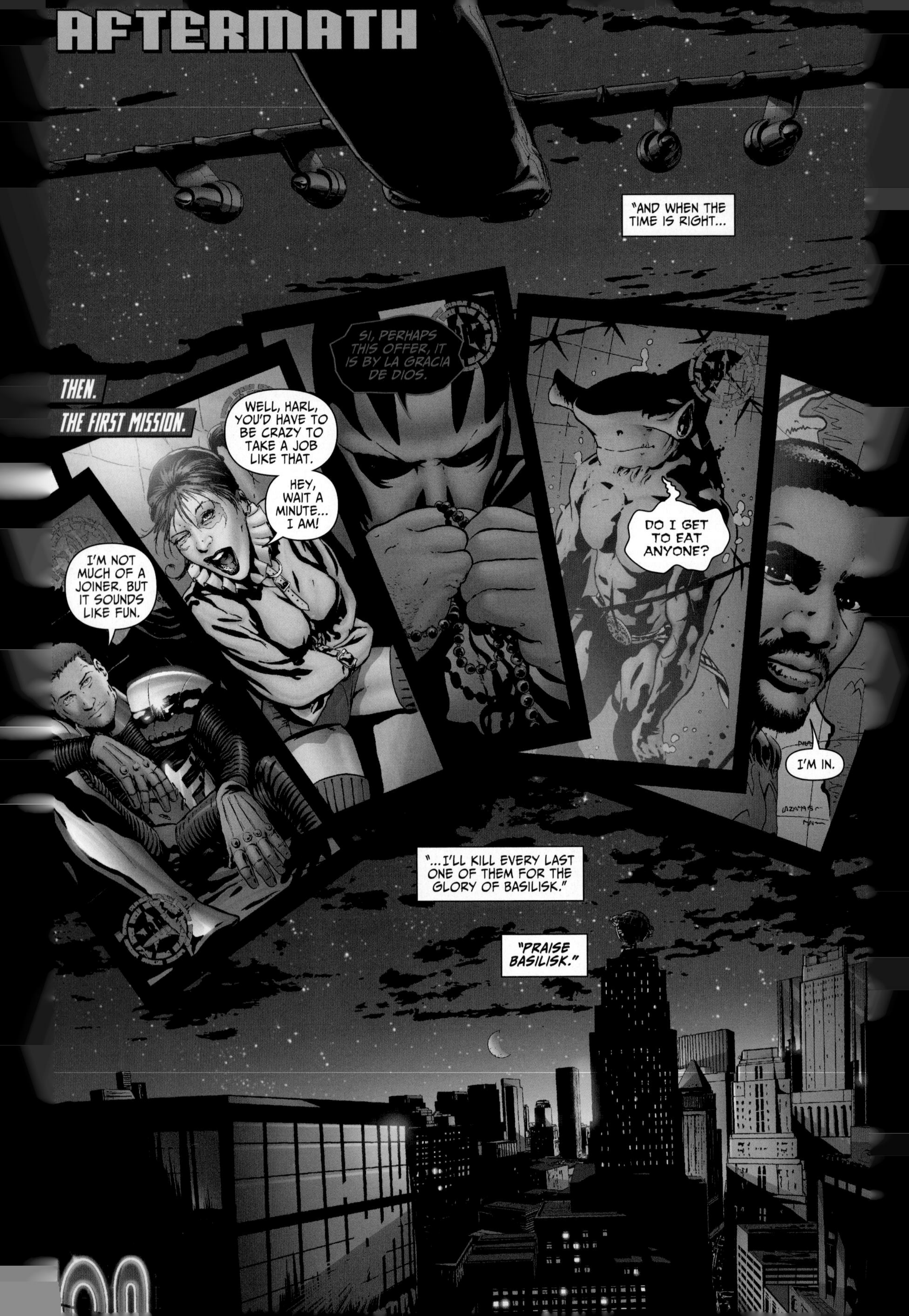
AFTERMATH
"AND WHEN THE TIME IS RIGHT...
THEN.
THE FIRST MISSION.
I'M NOT MUCH OF A JOINER. BUT IT SOUNDS LIKE FUN.
WELL, HARL, YOU'D HAVE TO BE CRAZY TO TAKE A JOB LIKE THAT.
HEY, WAIT A MINUTE... I AM!
SI, PERHAPS THIS OFFER, IT IS BY LA GRACIA DE DIOS.
DO I GET TO EAT ANYONE?
I'M IN.
"...I'LL KILL EVERY LAST ONE OF THEM FOR THE GLORY OF BASILISK."
"PRAISE BASILISK."

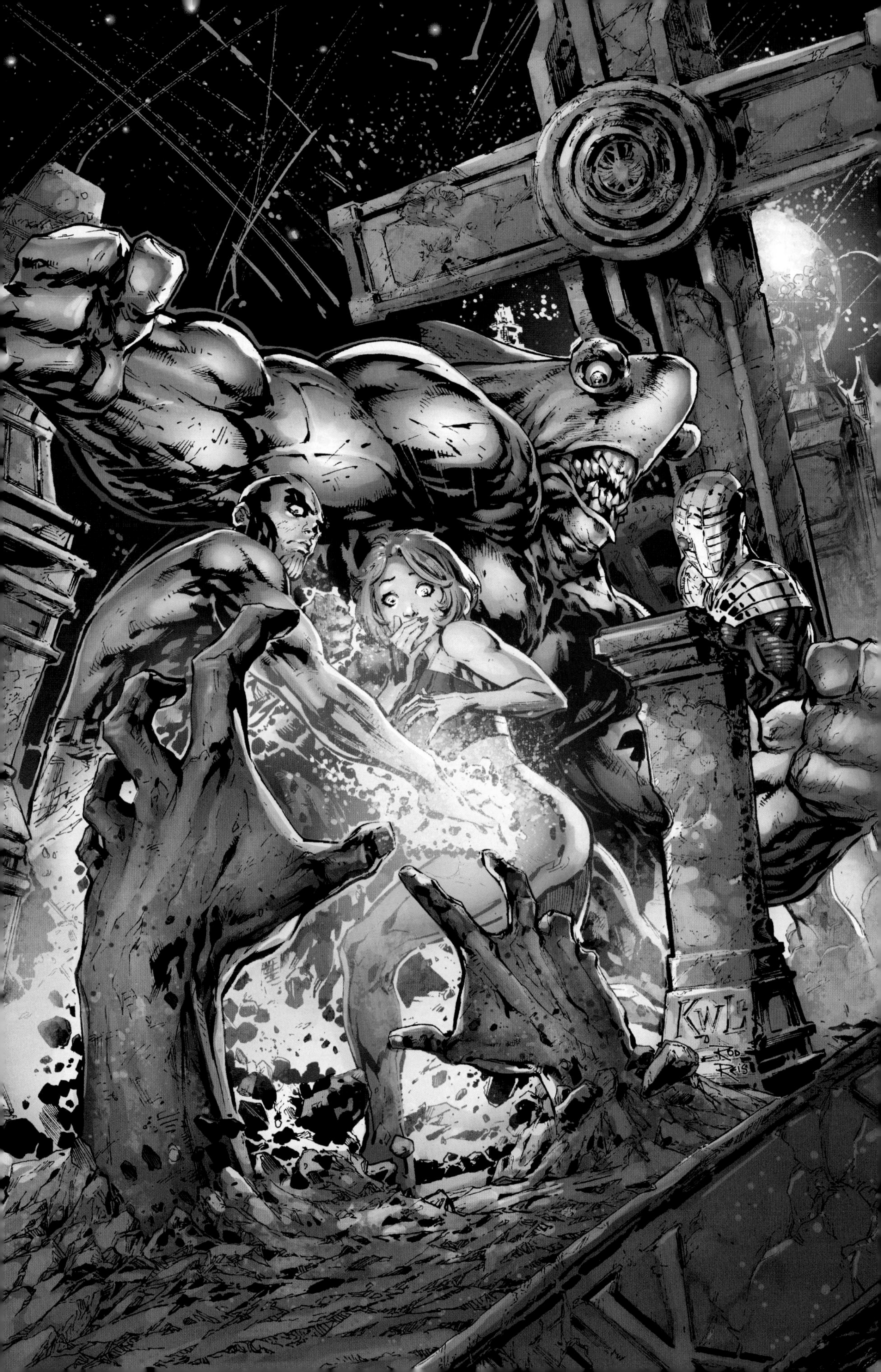
KWL
ROD REIS

DEAD MAN WALKING

ADAM GLASS
writer

FERNANDO DAGNINO
artist

cover art by KEN LASHLEY & ROD REIS

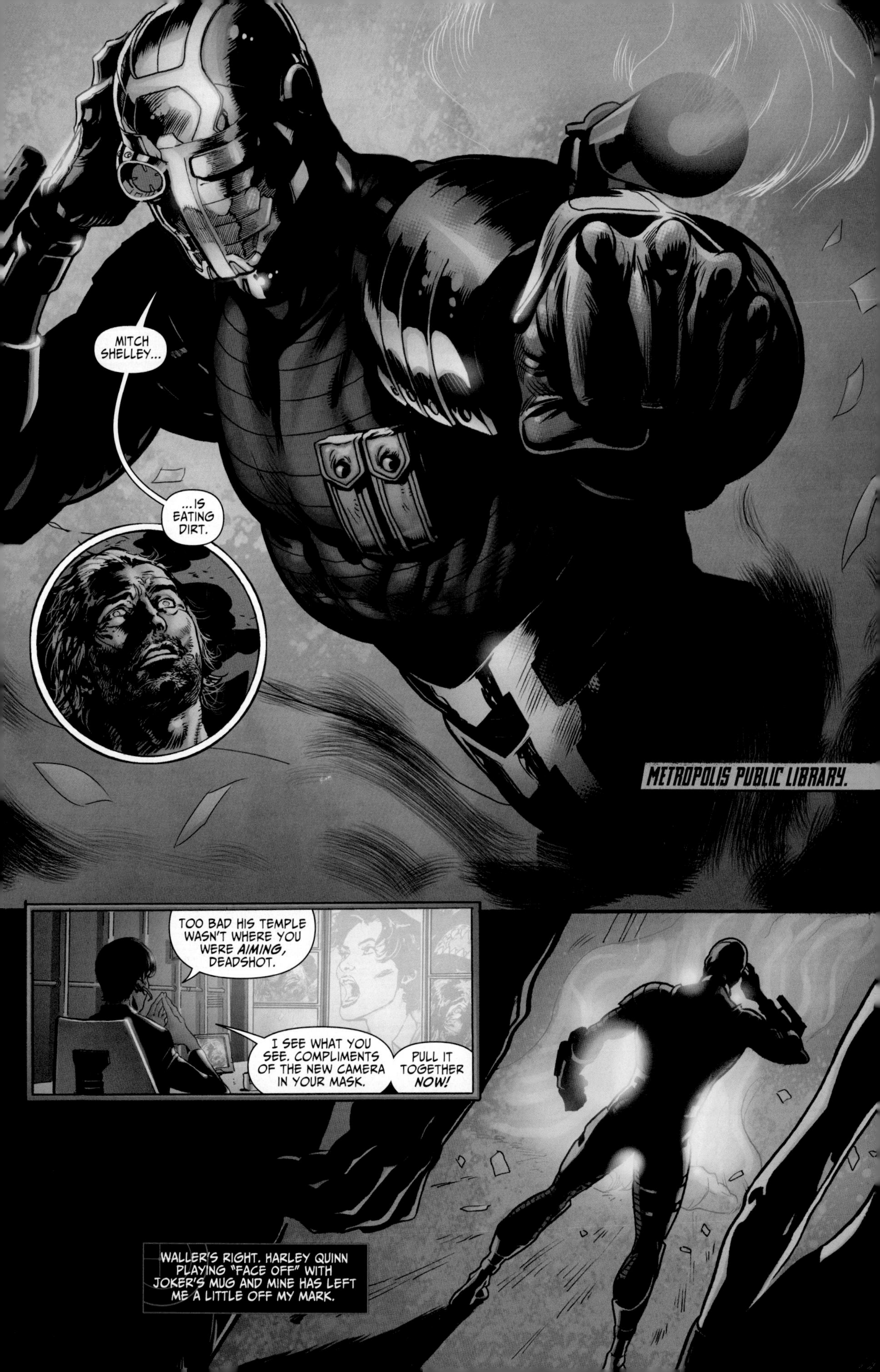
MITCH SHELLEY...
...IS EATING DIRT.
METROPOLIS PUBLIC LIBRARY.
TOO BAD HIS TEMPLE WASN'T WHERE YOU WERE AIMING, DEADSHOT.
I SEE WHAT YOU SEE. COMPLIMENTS OF THE NEW CAMERA IN YOUR MASK.
PULL IT TOGETHER NOW!
WALLER'S RIGHT. HARLEY QUINN PLAYING "FACE OFF" WITH JOKER'S MUG AND MINE HAS LEFT ME A LITTLE OFF MY MARK.

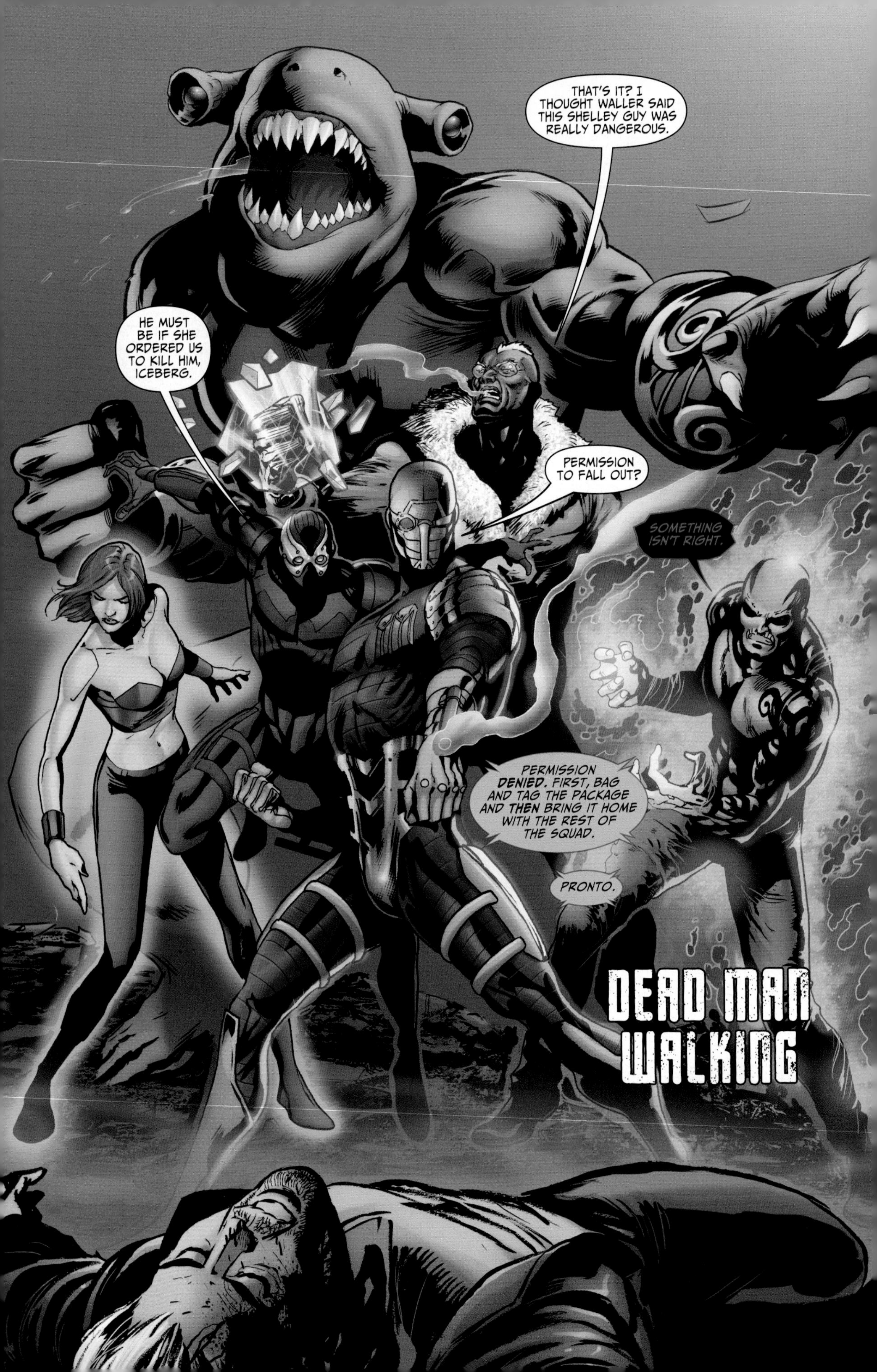
THAT'S IT? I THOUGHT WALLER SAID THIS SHELLEY GUY WAS REALLY DANGEROUS.
HE MUST BE IF SHE ORDERED US TO KILL HIM, ICEBERG.
PERMISSION TO FALL OUT?
SOMETHING ISN'T RIGHT.
PERMISSION DENIED. FIRST, BAG AND TAG THE PACKAGE AND THEN BRING IT HOME WITH THE REST OF THE SQUAD.
PRONTO.
DEAD MAN WALKING

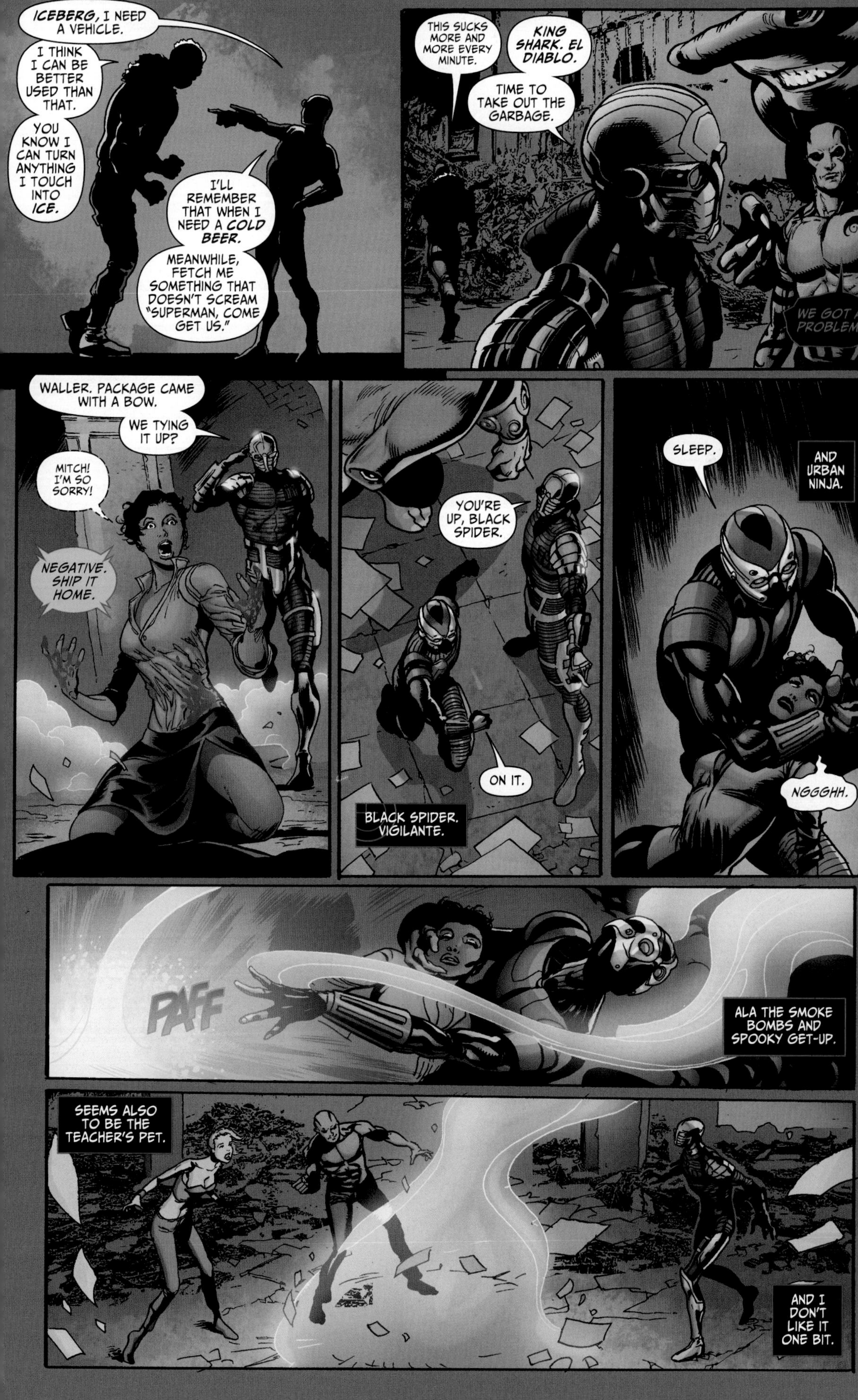
ICEBERG, I NEED A VEHICLE.
I THINK I CAN BE BETTER USED THAN THAT.
YOU KNOW I CAN TURN ANYTHING I TOUCH INTO ICE.
I'LL REMEMBER THAT WHEN I NEED A COLD BEER.
MEANWHILE, FETCH ME SOMETHING THAT DOESN'T SCREAM "SUPERMAN, COME GET US."
THIS SUCKS MORE AND MORE EVERY MINUTE.
KING SHARK. EL DIABLO.
TIME TO TAKE OUT THE GARBAGE.
WE GOT A PROBLEM.
WALLER. PACKAGE CAME WITH A BOW.
WE TYING IT UP?
MITCH! I'M SO SORRY!
NEGATIVE. SHIP IT HOME.
YOU'RE UP, BLACK SPIDER.
ON IT.
BLACK SPIDER. VIGILANTE.
SLEEP.
AND URBAN NINJA.
NGGGHH.
PAFF
ALA THE SMOKE BOMBS AND SPOOKY GET-UP.
SEEMS ALSO TO BE THE TEACHER'S PET.
AND I DON'T LIKE IT ONE BIT.

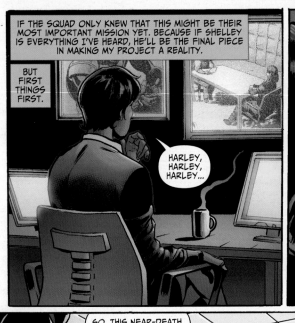

IF THE SQUAD ONLY KNEW THAT THIS MIGHT BE THEIR MOST IMPORTANT MISSION YET. BECAUSE IF SHELLEY IS EVERYTHING I'VE HEARD, HE'LL BE THE FINAL PIECE IN MAKING MY PROJECT A REALITY.

BUT FIRST THINGS FIRST.

HARLEY, HARLEY, HARLEY...

...AFTER THE CRAP STORM YOU RAINED ON ME WITH YOUR LITTLE FIELD TRIP TO GOTHAM, I SHOULD'VE LET DEADSHOT'S *BULLET* DO ITS JOB.

BUT I STILL NEED YOU.

SO, THIS NEAR-DEATH EXPERIENCE HAS CHANGED YOU.

THAT'S ONE WAY TO PUT IT, DOC.

WHAT DO YOU MEAN, HARLEY?

BELLE REVE PENITENTIARY.

WELL, THAT'S THE *THING.*

HARLEY'S NOT HOME ANYMORE.

THEN TO WHO AM I SPEAKING?

DOCTOR HARLEEN QUINZEL.

PLEASURE TO MEET YOU.

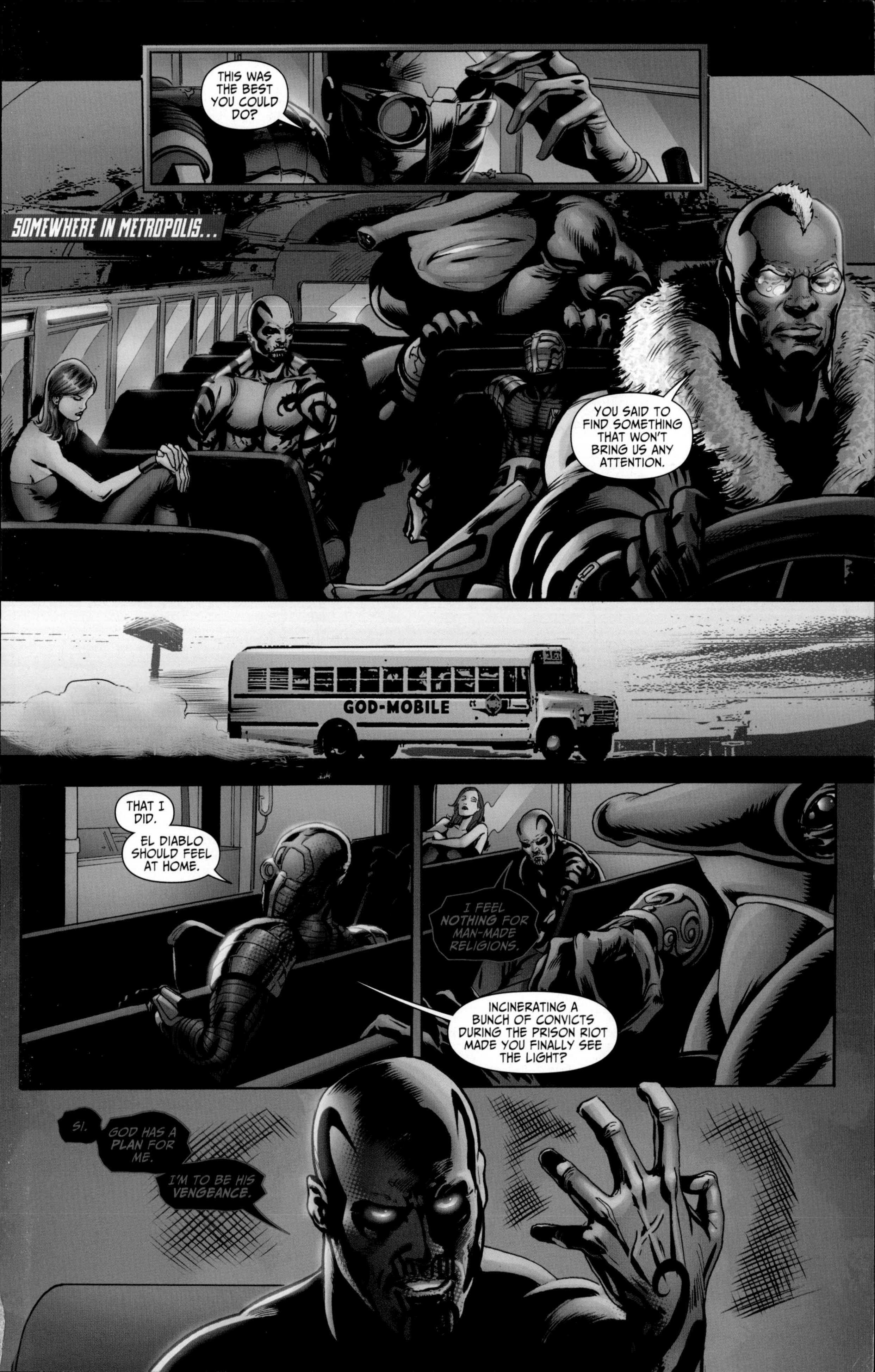
THIS WAS THE BEST YOU COULD DO?
SOMEWHERE IN METROPOLIS...
YOU SAID TO FIND SOMETHING THAT WON'T BRING US ANY ATTENTION.
GOD-MOBILE
THAT I DID.
EL DIABLO SHOULD FEEL AT HOME.
I FEEL NOTHING FOR MAN-MADE RELIGIONS.
INCINERATING A BUNCH OF CONVICTS DURING THE PRISON RIOT MADE YOU FINALLY SEE THE LIGHT?
SI.
GOD HAS A PLAN FOR ME.
I'M TO BE HIS VENGEANCE.

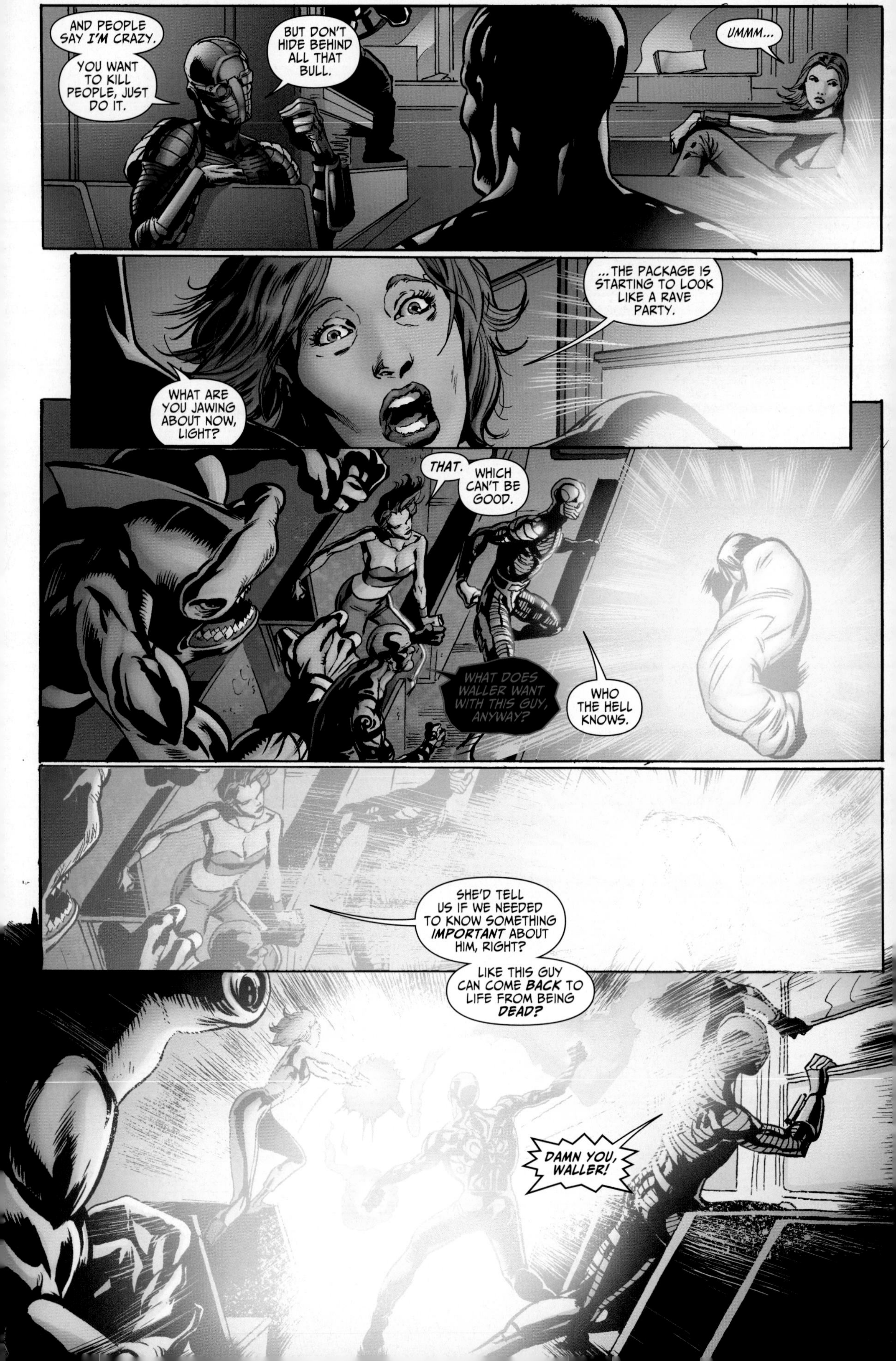
AND PEOPLE SAY I'M CRAZY.
YOU WANT TO KILL PEOPLE, JUST DO IT.
BUT DON'T HIDE BEHIND ALL THAT BULL.
UMMM...
...THE PACKAGE IS STARTING TO LOOK LIKE A RAVE PARTY.
WHAT ARE YOU JAWING ABOUT NOW, LIGHT?
THAT.
WHICH CAN'T BE GOOD.
WHAT DOES WALLER WANT WITH THIS GUY, ANYWAY?
WHO THE HELL KNOWS.
SHE'D TELL US IF WE NEEDED TO KNOW SOMETHING IMPORTANT ABOUT HIM, RIGHT?
LIKE THIS GUY CAN COME BACK TO LIFE FROM BEING DEAD?
DAMN YOU, WALLER!

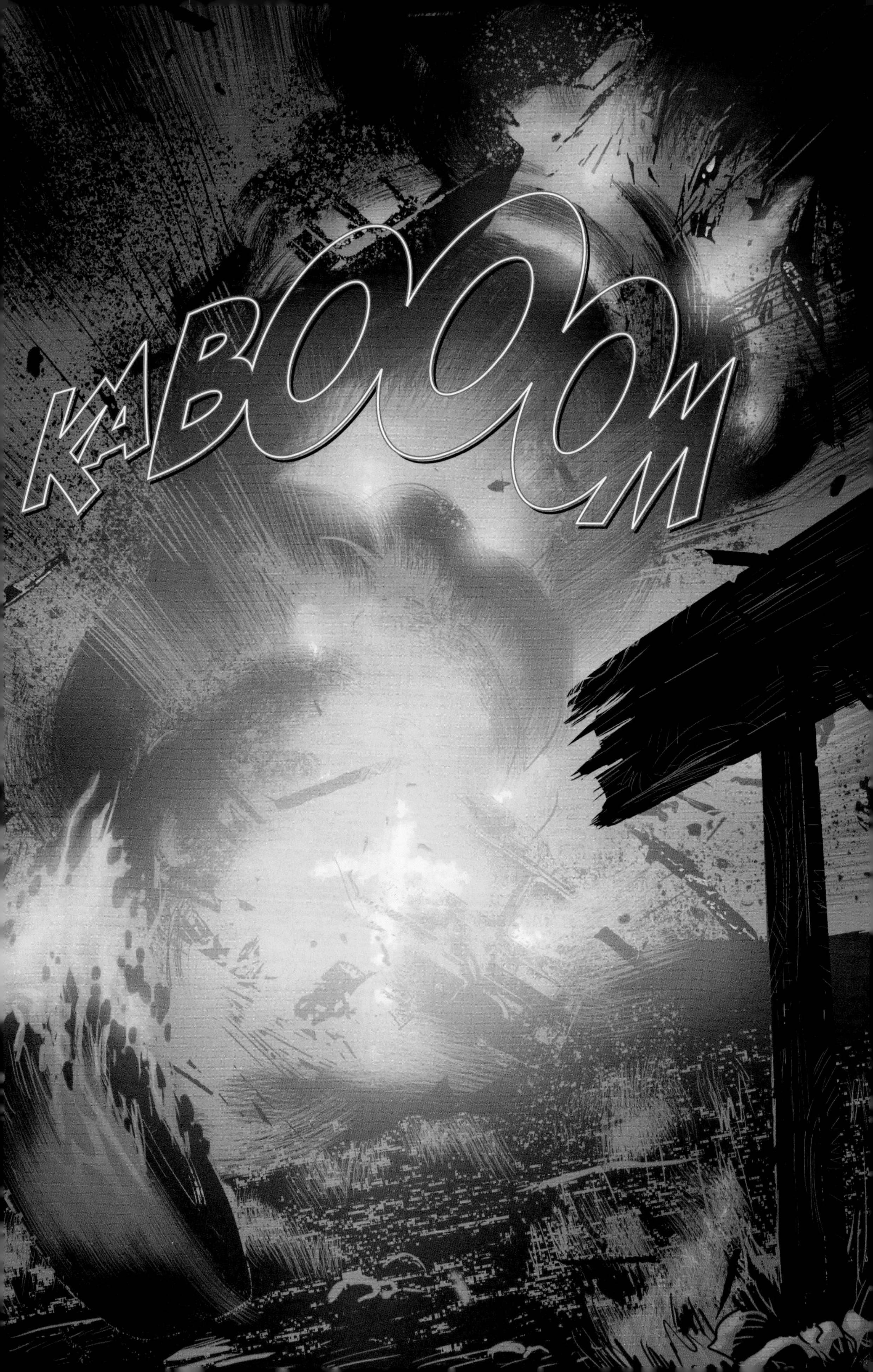
KABOOOM

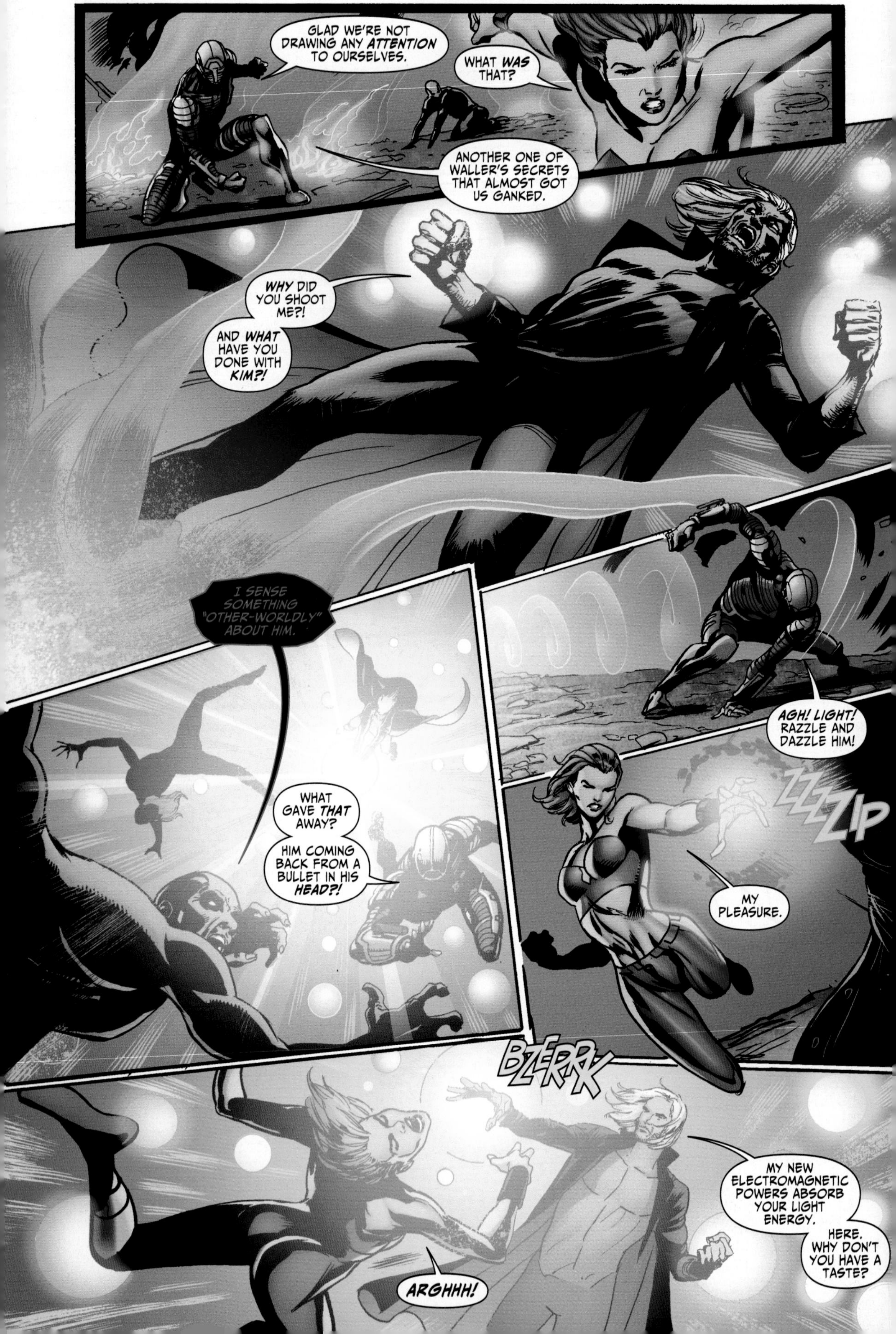
GLAD WE'RE NOT DRAWING ANY ATTENTION TO OURSELVES.
WHAT WAS THAT?
ANOTHER ONE OF WALLER'S SECRETS THAT ALMOST GOT US GANKED.
WHY DID YOU SHOOT ME?!
AND WHAT HAVE YOU DONE WITH KIM?!
I SENSE SOMETHING "OTHER-WORLDLY" ABOUT HIM.
WHAT GAVE THAT AWAY?
HIM COMING BACK FROM A BULLET IN HIS HEAD?!
AGH! LIGHT! RAZZLE AND DAZZLE HIM!
ZZZZIP
MY PLEASURE.
BZERRRK
MY NEW ELECTROMAGNETIC POWERS ABSORB YOUR LIGHT ENERGY.
HERE. WHY DON'T YOU HAVE A TASTE?
ARGHHH!

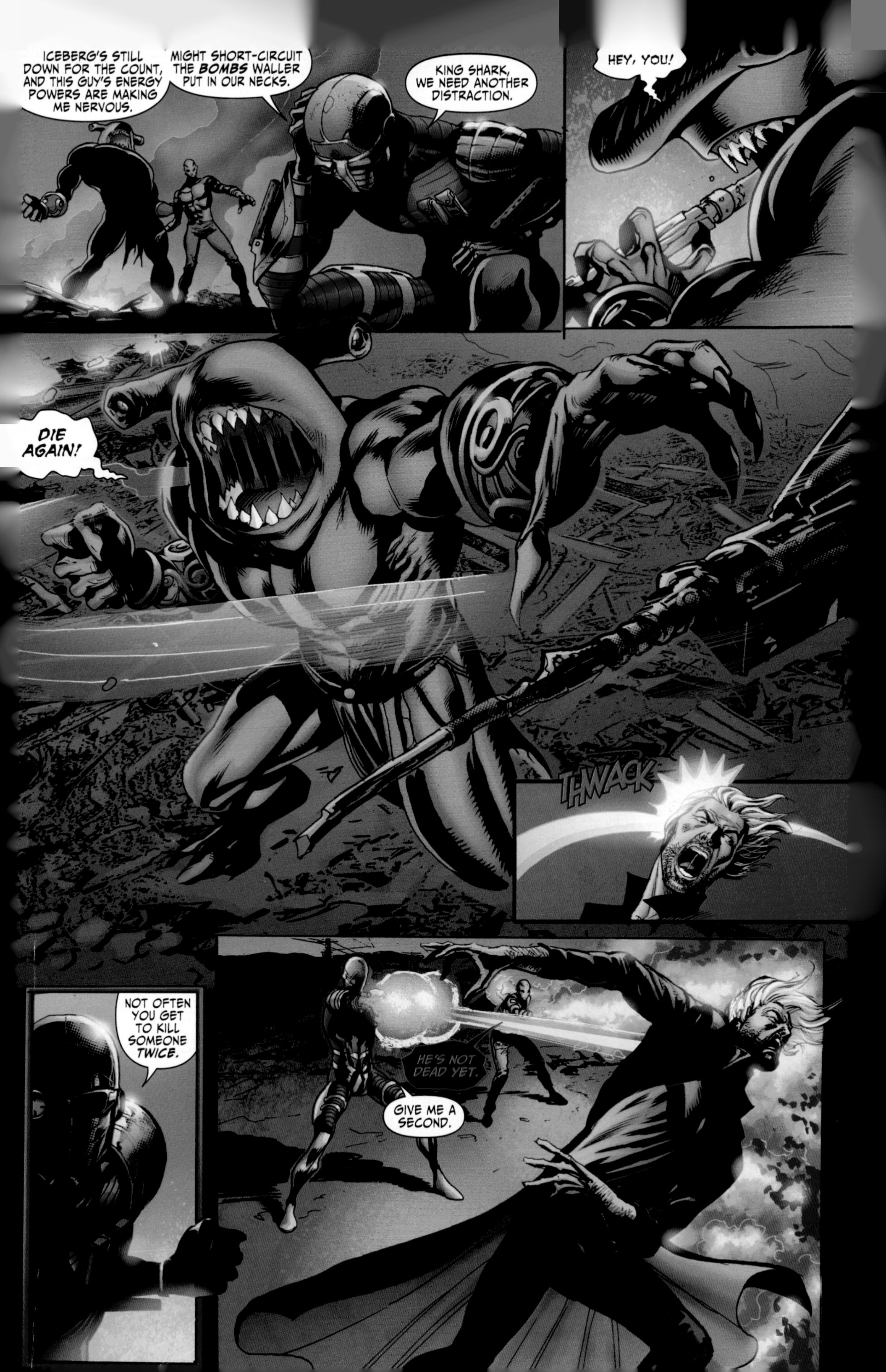
ICEBERG'S STILL DOWN FOR THE COUNT, AND THIS GUY'S ENERGY POWERS ARE MAKING ME NERVOUS.
MIGHT SHORT-CIRCUIT THE BOMBS WALLER PUT IN OUR NECKS.
KING SHARK, WE NEED ANOTHER DISTRACTION.
HEY, YOU!
DIE AGAIN!
THWACK
NOT OFTEN YOU GET TO KILL SOMEONE TWICE.
HE'S NOT DEAD YET.
GIVE ME A SECOND.

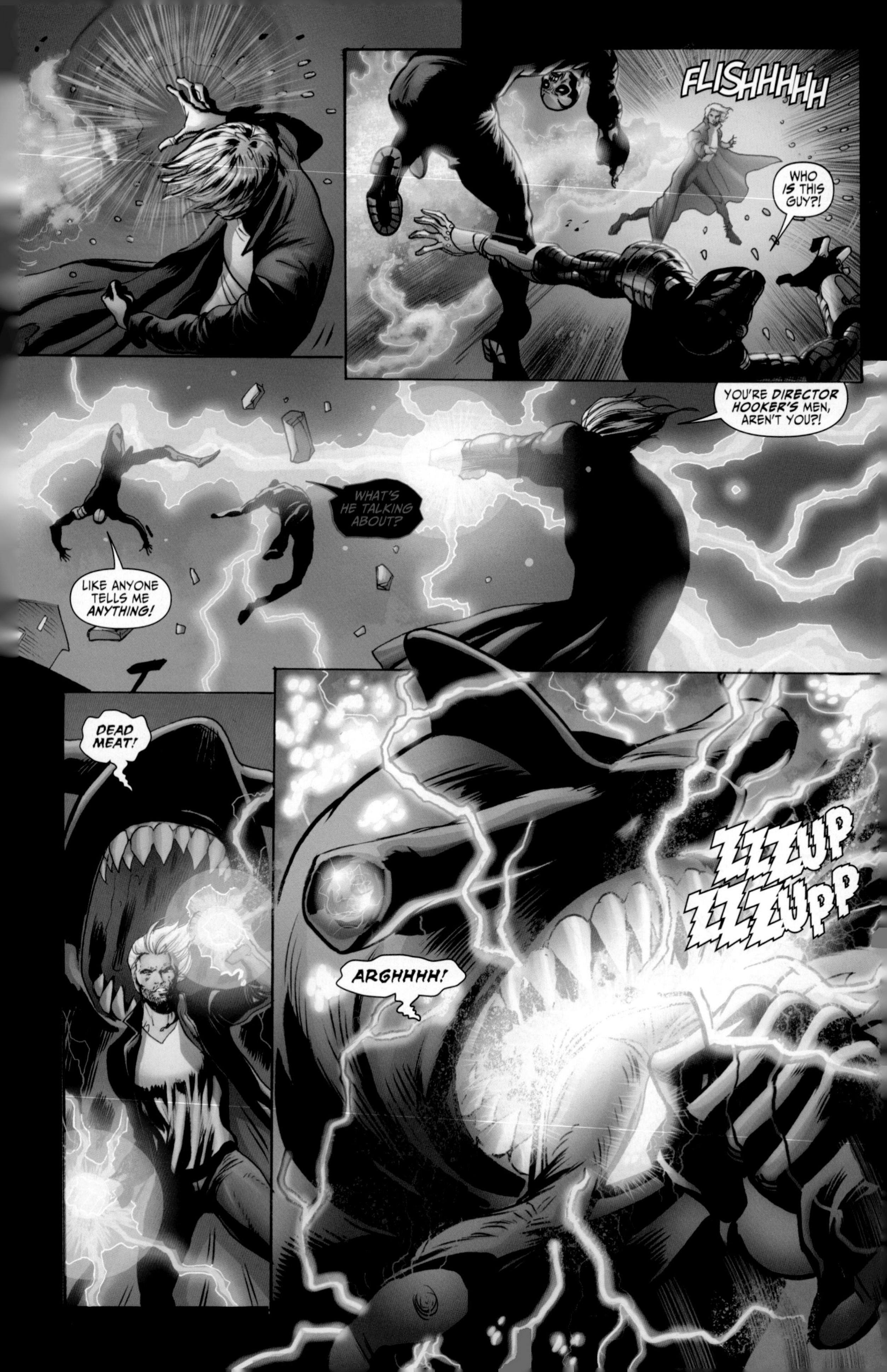
FLISHHHHH
WHO IS THIS GUY?!
YOU'RE DIRECTOR HOOKER'S MEN, AREN'T YOU?!
WHAT'S HE TALKING ABOUT?
LIKE ANYONE TELLS ME ANYTHING!
DEAD MEAT!
ZZZUP
ZZZUPP
ARGHHHH!

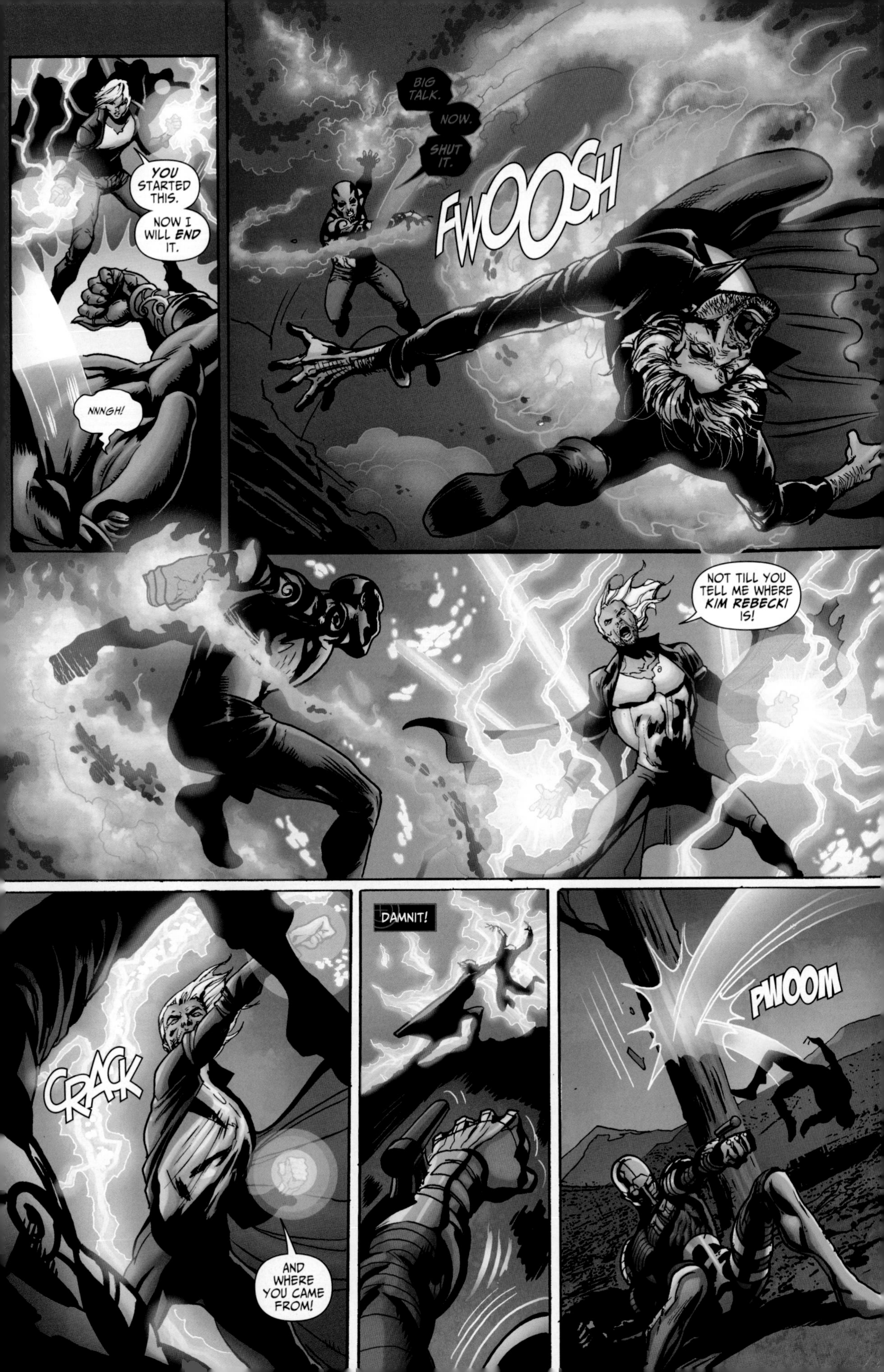
YOU STARTED THIS.
NOW I WILL END IT.
NNNGH!
BIG TALK.
NOW.
SHUT IT.
FWOOSH
NOT TILL YOU TELL ME WHERE KIM REBECKI IS!
CRACK
AND WHERE YOU CAME FROM!
DAMNIT!
PWOOM

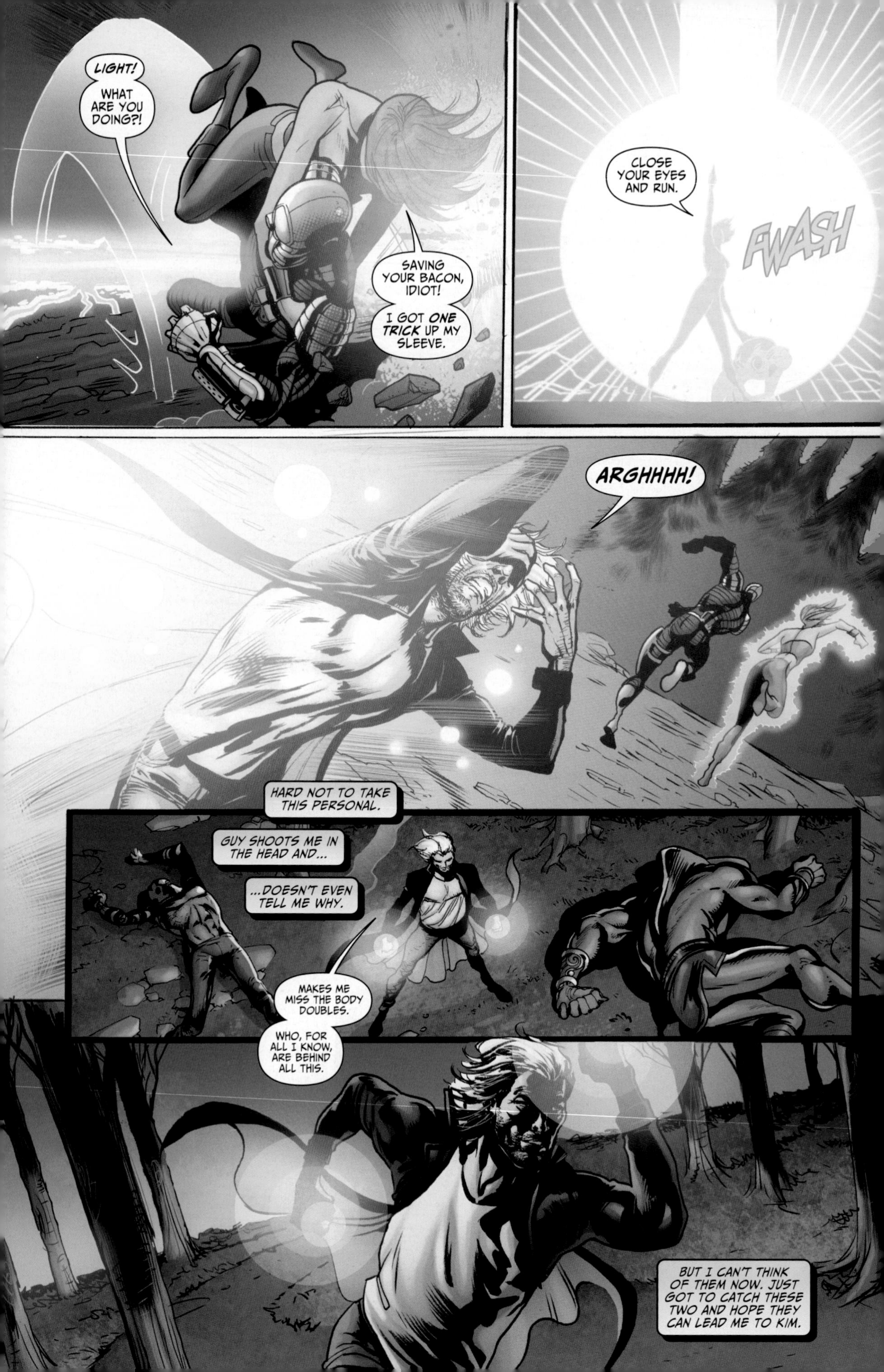
LIGHT!
WHAT ARE YOU DOING?!
SAVING YOUR BACON, IDIOT!
I GOT ONE TRICK UP MY SLEEVE.
CLOSE YOUR EYES AND RUN.
FWASH
ARGHHHH!
HARD NOT TO TAKE THIS PERSONAL.
GUY SHOOTS ME IN THE HEAD AND...
...DOESN'T EVEN TELL ME WHY.
MAKES ME MISS THE BODY DOUBLES.
WHO, FOR ALL I KNOW, ARE BEHIND ALL THIS.
BUT I CAN'T THINK OF THEM NOW. JUST GOT TO CATCH THESE TWO AND HOPE THEY CAN LEAD ME TO KIM.

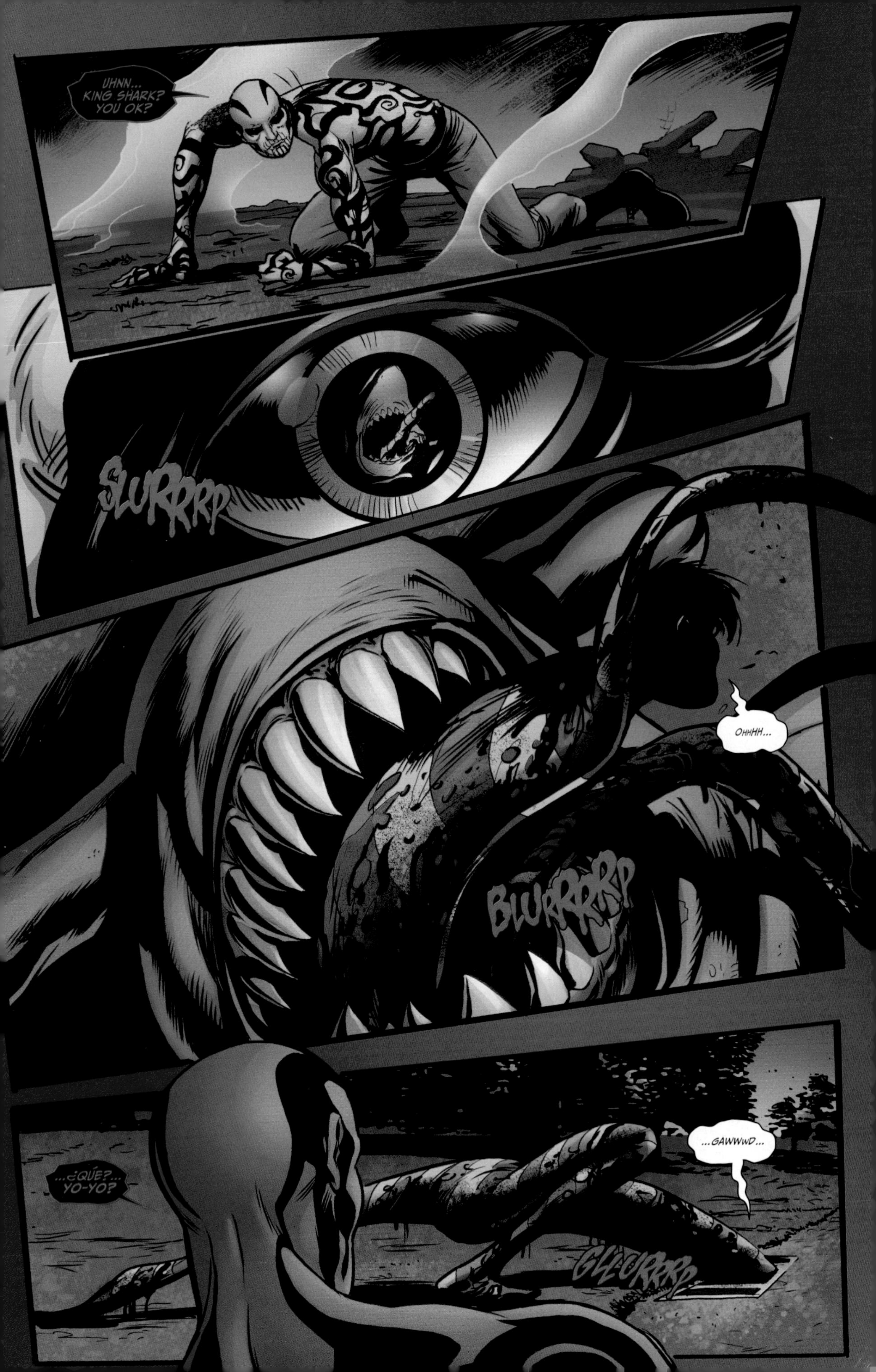
UHNN... KING SHARK? YOU OK?
SLURRRP
OHHHH...
BLURRRP
...¿QUÉ?... YO-YO?
...GAWWWD...
GLLURRRP

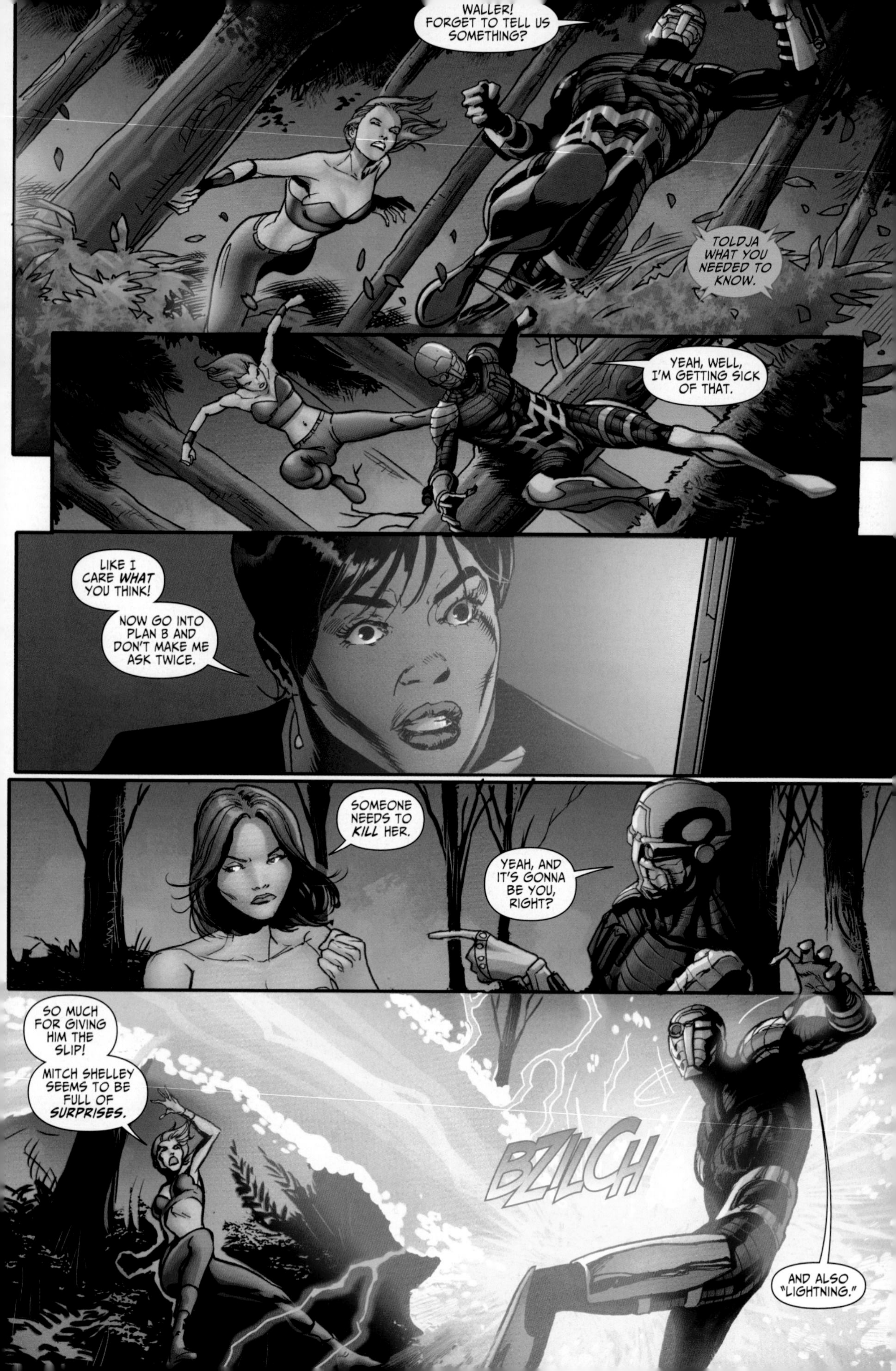
WALLER! FORGET TO TELL US SOMETHING?
TOLDJA WHAT YOU NEEDED TO KNOW.
YEAH, WELL, I'M GETTING SICK OF THAT.
LIKE I CARE *WHAT* YOU THINK!
NOW GO INTO PLAN B AND DON'T MAKE ME ASK TWICE.
SOMEONE NEEDS TO *KILL* HER.
YEAH, AND IT'S GONNA BE YOU, RIGHT?
SO MUCH FOR GIVING HIM THE SLIP!
MITCH SHELLEY SEEMS TO BE FULL OF *SURPRISES.*
BZLCH
AND ALSO "LIGHTNING."

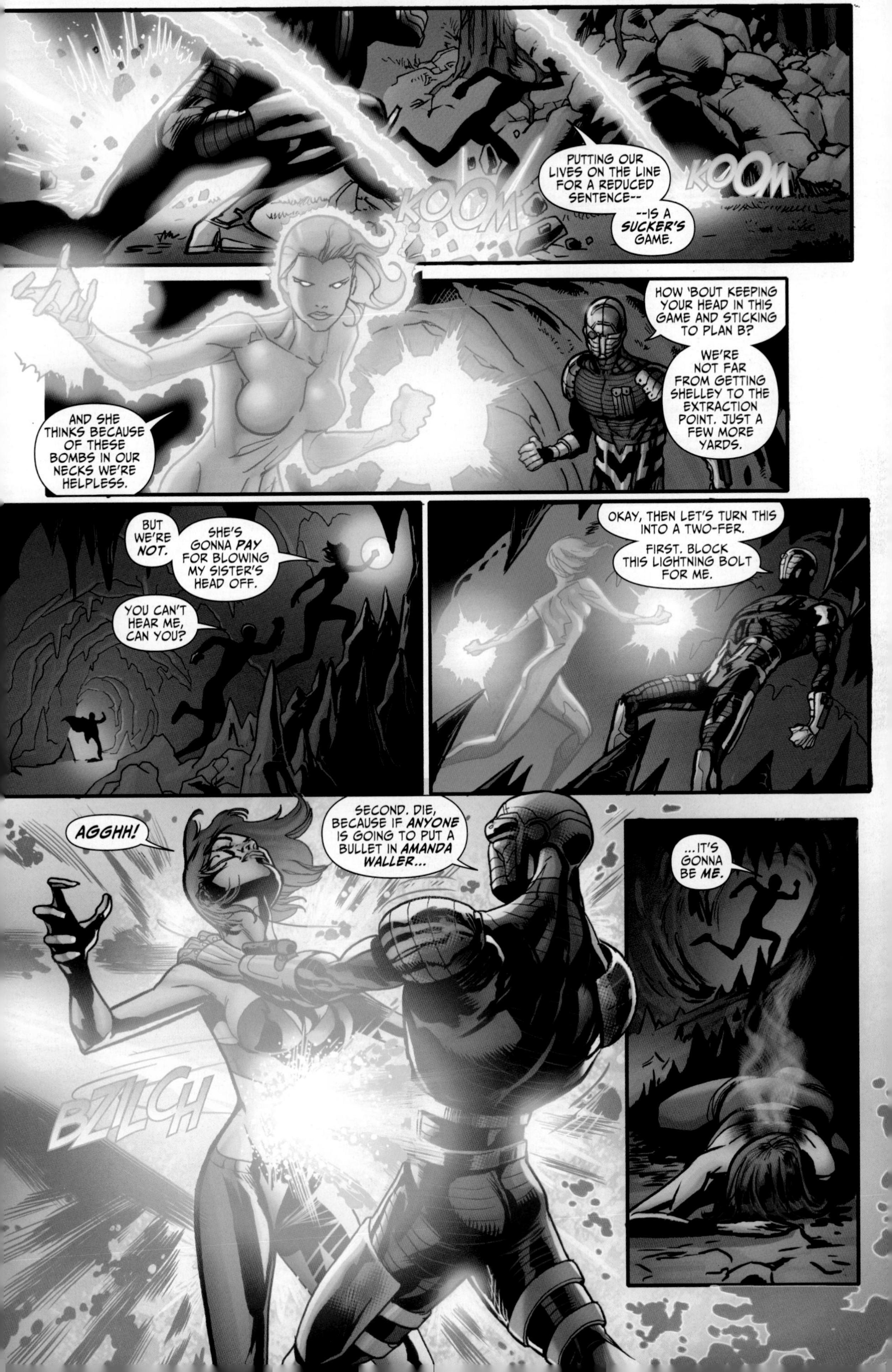
KOOM
KOOM
PUTTING OUR LIVES ON THE LINE FOR A REDUCED SENTENCE--
--IS A SUCKER'S GAME.
HOW 'BOUT KEEPING YOUR HEAD IN THIS GAME AND STICKING TO PLAN B?
WE'RE NOT FAR FROM GETTING SHELLEY TO THE EXTRACTION POINT. JUST A FEW MORE YARDS.
AND SHE THINKS BECAUSE OF THESE BOMBS IN OUR NECKS WE'RE HELPLESS.
BUT WE'RE NOT.
SHE'S GONNA PAY FOR BLOWING MY SISTER'S HEAD OFF.
YOU CAN'T HEAR ME, CAN YOU?
OKAY, THEN LET'S TURN THIS INTO A TWO-FER.
FIRST. BLOCK THIS LIGHTNING BOLT FOR ME.
AGGHH!
SECOND. DIE, BECAUSE IF ANYONE IS GOING TO PUT A BULLET IN AMANDA WALLER...
BZLCH
...IT'S GONNA BE ME.

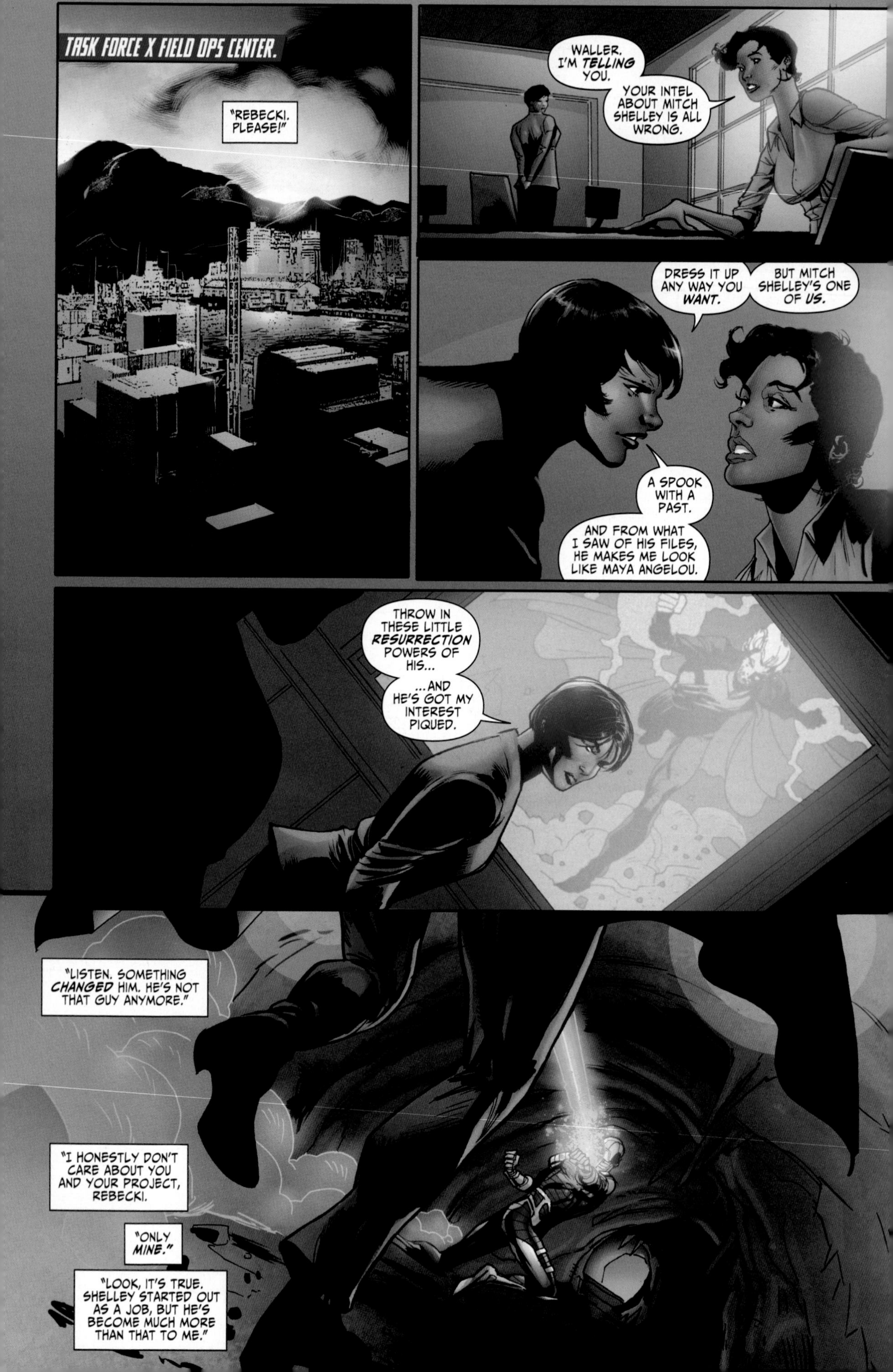
TASK FORCE X FIELD OPS CENTER.
"REBECKI. PLEASE!"
WALLER. I'M TELLING YOU.
YOUR INTEL ABOUT MITCH SHELLEY IS ALL WRONG.
DRESS IT UP ANY WAY YOU WANT.
BUT MITCH SHELLEY'S ONE OF US.
A SPOOK WITH A PAST.
AND FROM WHAT I SAW OF HIS FILES, HE MAKES ME LOOK LIKE MAYA ANGELOU.
THROW IN THESE LITTLE RESURRECTION POWERS OF HIS...
...AND HE'S GOT MY INTEREST PIQUED.
"LISTEN. SOMETHING CHANGED HIM. HE'S NOT THAT GUY ANYMORE."
"I HONESTLY DON'T CARE ABOUT YOU AND YOUR PROJECT, REBECKI.
"ONLY MINE."
"LOOK, IT'S TRUE. SHELLEY STARTED OUT AS A JOB, BUT HE'S BECOME MUCH MORE THAN THAT TO ME."

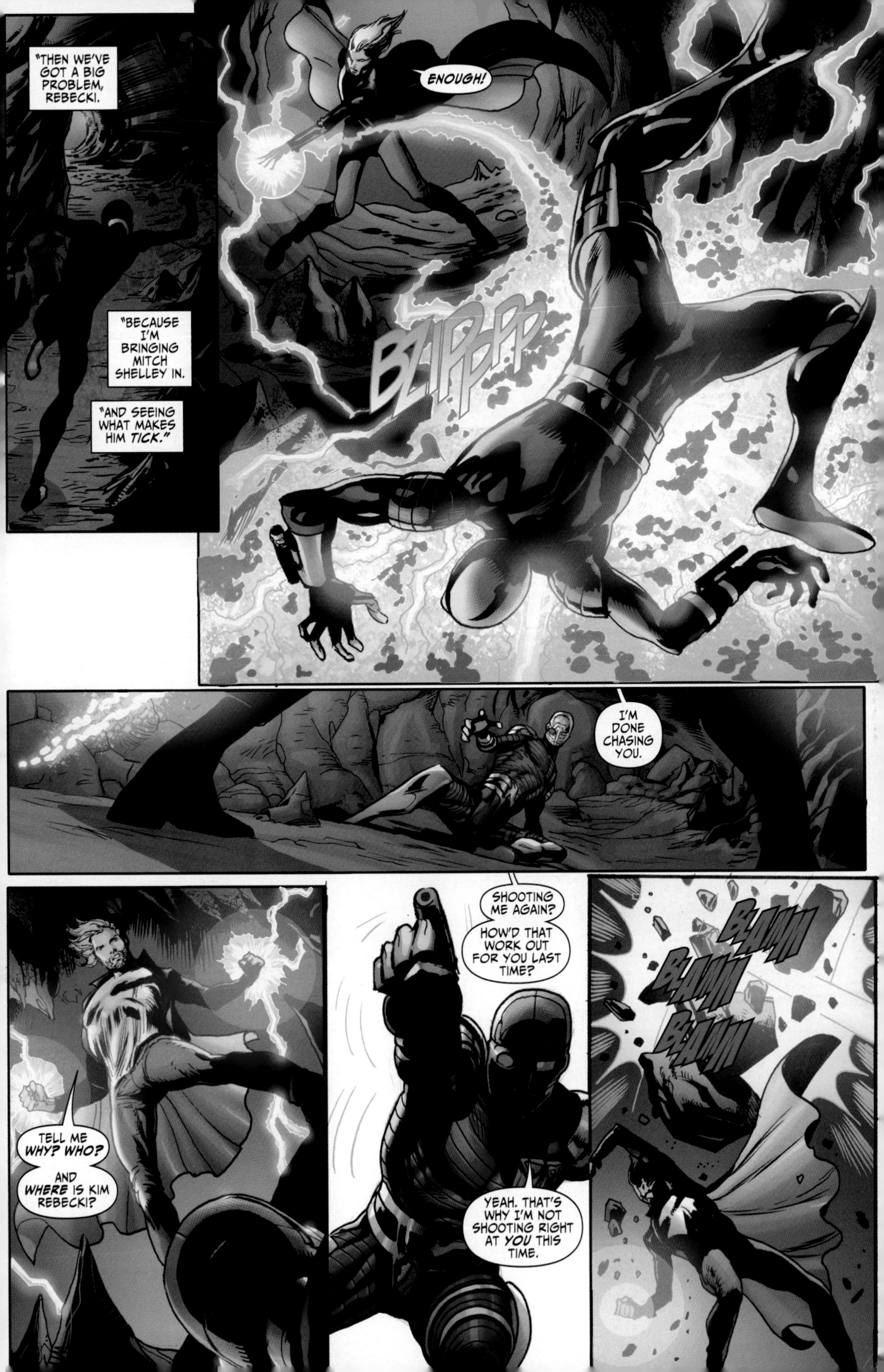
"THEN WE'VE GOT A BIG PROBLEM, REBECKI.
"BECAUSE I'M BRINGING MITCH SHELLEY IN.
"AND SEEING WHAT MAKES HIM TICK."
ENOUGH!
BZIPPPP
I'M DONE CHASING YOU.
TELL ME WHY? WHO?
AND WHERE IS KIM REBECKI?
SHOOTING ME AGAIN?
HOW'D THAT WORK OUT FOR YOU LAST TIME?
YEAH. THAT'S WHY I'M NOT SHOOTING RIGHT AT YOU THIS TIME.
BLAMM
BLAMM
BLAMM

THAT WON'T HOLD HIM FOR LONG.
BUT IT WILL BUY ME SOME TIME.
WALLER'S MEN WILL BE ARRIVING AT THE RENDEZVOUS POINT AS PLANNED.
MY JOB IS TO DELIVER THE PACKAGE.
BUT TO DO THAT, I NEED TO DO SOMETHING CRAZY SO THAT I DON'T GET FRIED BY HIS POWERS.
SPLASH
SO, I DO THE "FUGITIVE JUMP"...

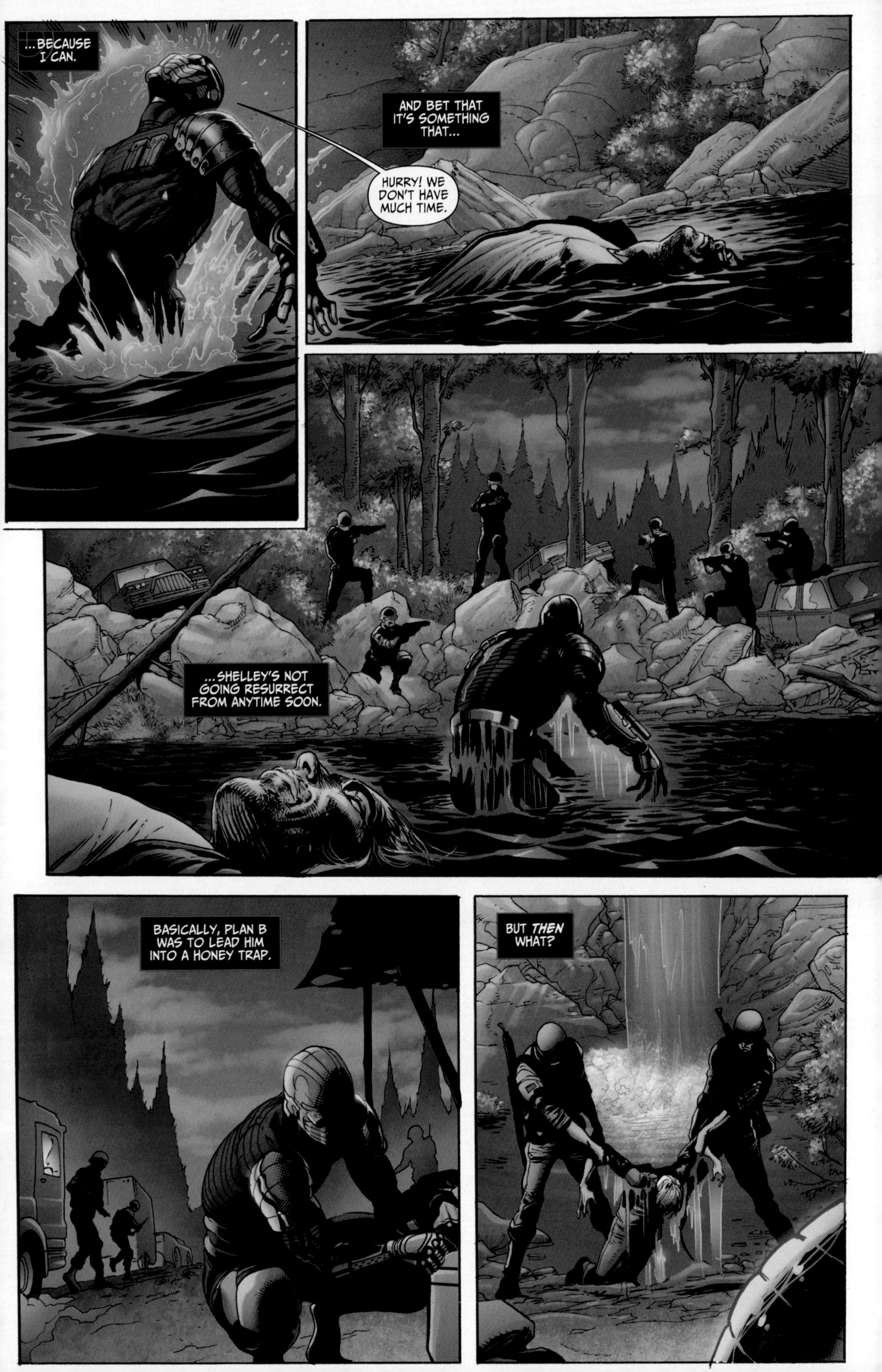
...BECAUSE I CAN.
AND BET THAT IT'S SOMETHING THAT...
HURRY! WE DON'T HAVE MUCH TIME.
...SHELLEY'S NOT GOING RESURRECT FROM ANYTIME SOON.
BASICALLY, PLAN B WAS TO LEAD HIM INTO A HONEY TRAP.
BUT *THEN* WHAT?

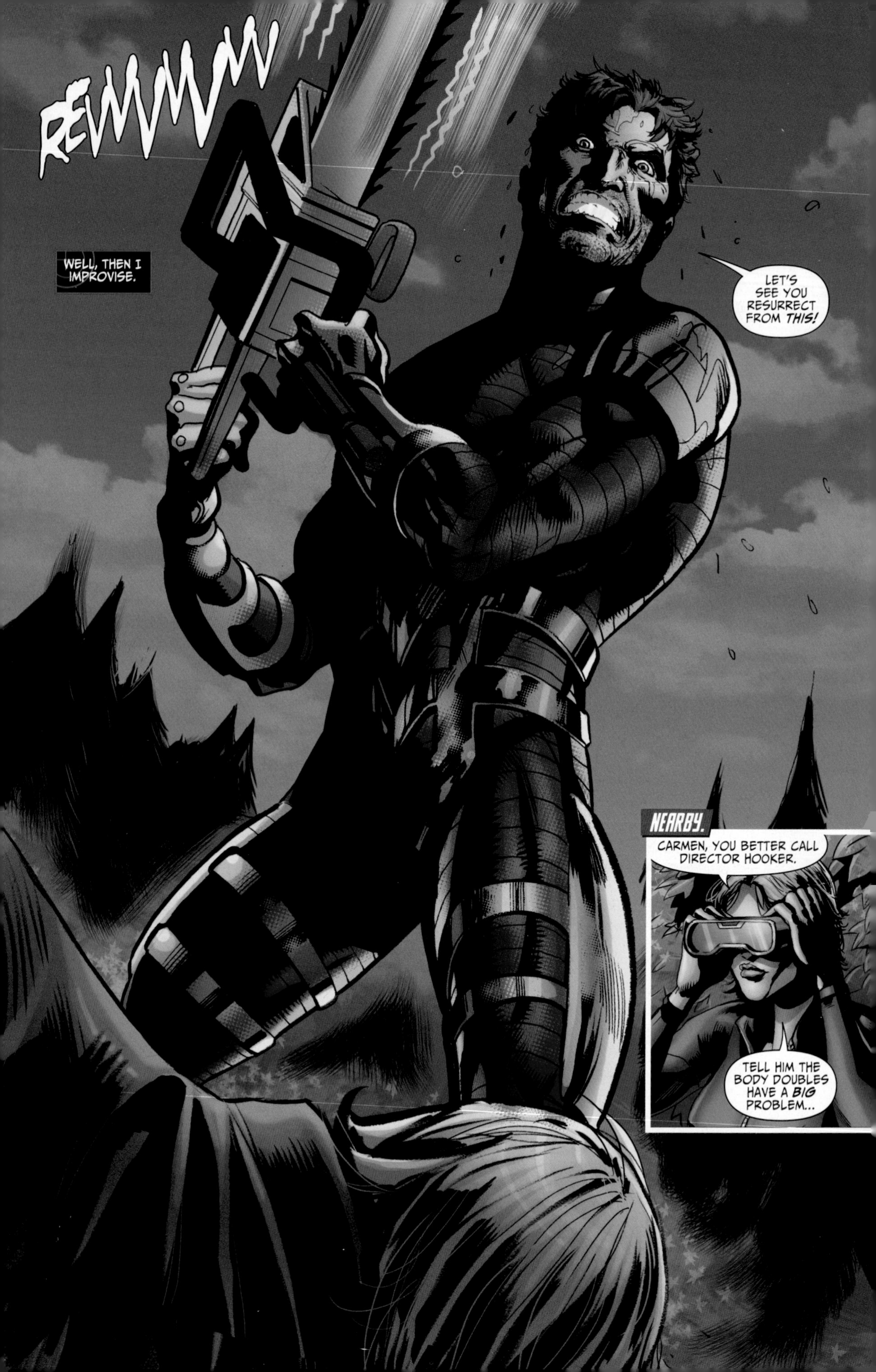
REVVVVVVV
WELL, THEN I IMPROVISE.
LET'S SEE YOU RESURRECT FROM THIS!
NEARBY.
CARMEN, YOU BETTER CALL DIRECTOR HOOKER.
TELL HIM THE BODY DOUBLES HAVE A BIG PROBLEM...

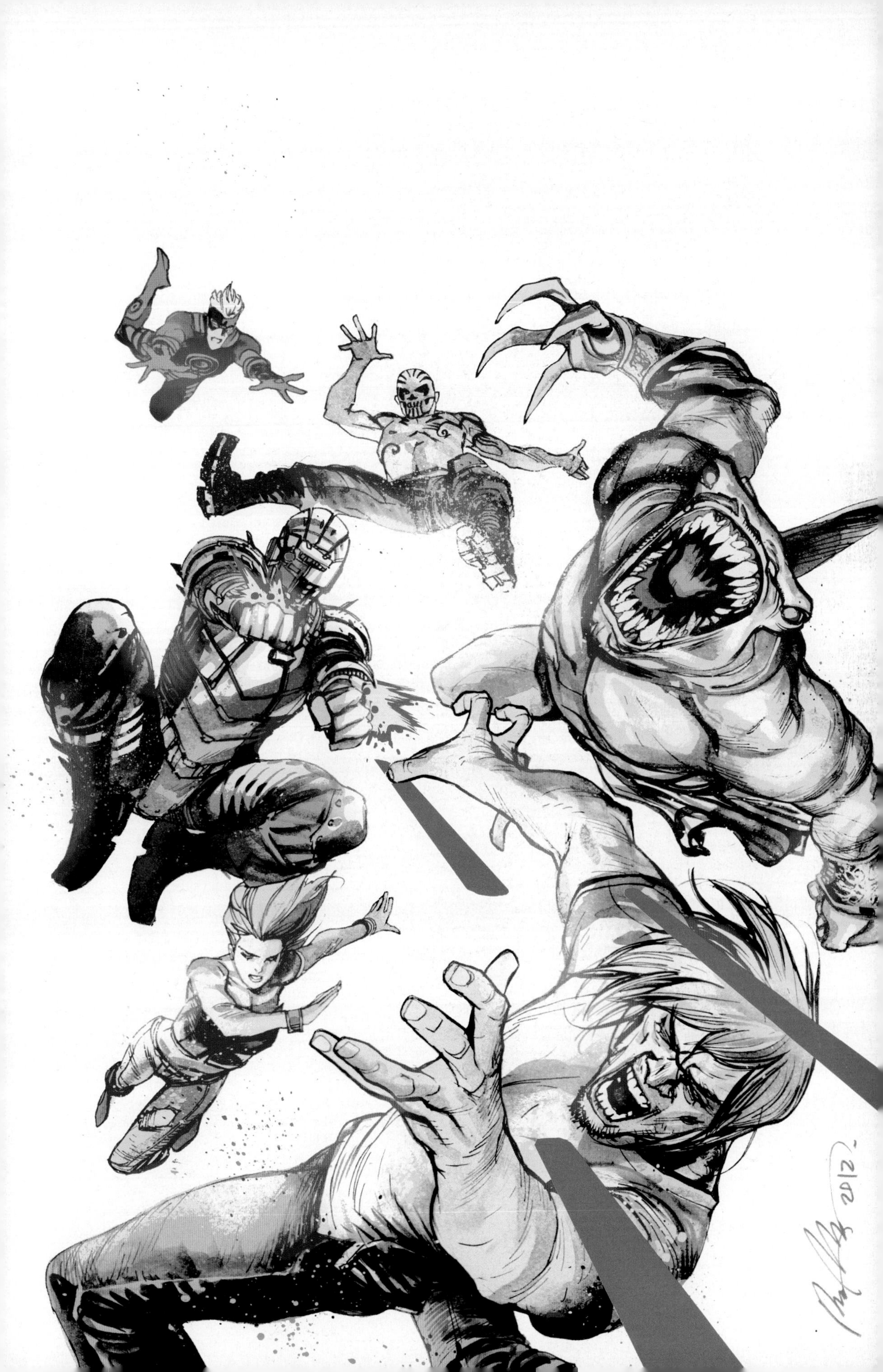
2012

DEAD HEAT

DAN ABNETT & ANDY LANNING
writers

JESUS SAIZ & ANDRES GUINALDO
pencillers

JESUS SAIZ, MARK IRWIN & CHRISTIAN ALAMY
inkers

cover art by RAFAEL ALBUQUERQUE

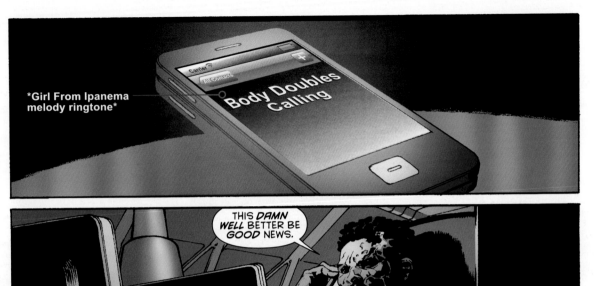

Girl From Ipanema melody ringtone

Body Doubles Calling

THIS *DAMN WELL* BETTER BE *GOOD* NEWS.

WELL, *HALF* OF IT IS, DIRECTOR HOOKER, SO LET'S BE *OPTIMISTS* HERE...

...WE'VE *FOUND* SHELLEY. YOUR HUNCH WAS RIGHT. THAT BLACK OPS GROUP *DID* HAVE A LEAD ON HIM. THEY'VE LED US RIGHT TO HIM.

THE *BAD* NEWS, LENO?

THE BLACK OPS UNIT GOT THERE *FIRST*, DIRECTOR.

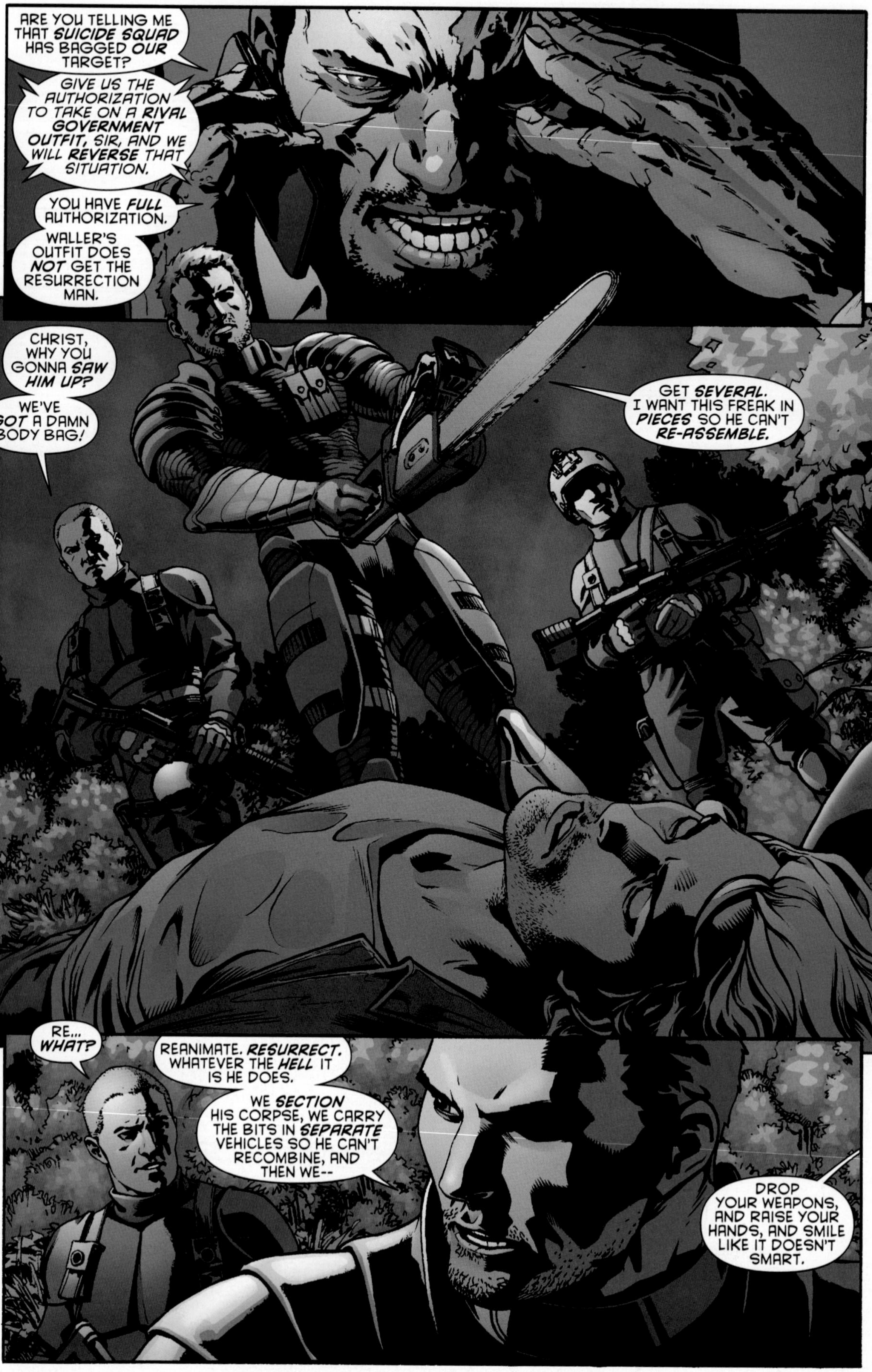
ARE YOU TELLING ME THAT SUICIDE SQUAD HAS BAGGED OUR TARGET?
GIVE US THE AUTHORIZATION TO TAKE ON A RIVAL GOVERNMENT OUTFIT, SIR, AND WE WILL REVERSE THAT SITUATION.
YOU HAVE FULL AUTHORIZATION.
WALLER'S OUTFIT DOES NOT GET THE RESURRECTION MAN.
CHRIST, WHY YOU GONNA SAW HIM UP?
WE'VE GOT A DAMN BODY BAG!
GET SEVERAL. I WANT THIS FREAK IN PIECES SO HE CAN'T RE-ASSEMBLE.
RE... WHAT?
REANIMATE. RESURRECT. WHATEVER THE HELL IT IS HE DOES.
WE SECTION HIS CORPSE, WE CARRY THE BITS IN SEPARATE VEHICLES SO HE CAN'T RECOMBINE, AND THEN WE--
DROP YOUR WEAPONS, AND RAISE YOUR HANDS, AND SMILE LIKE IT DOESN'T SMART.

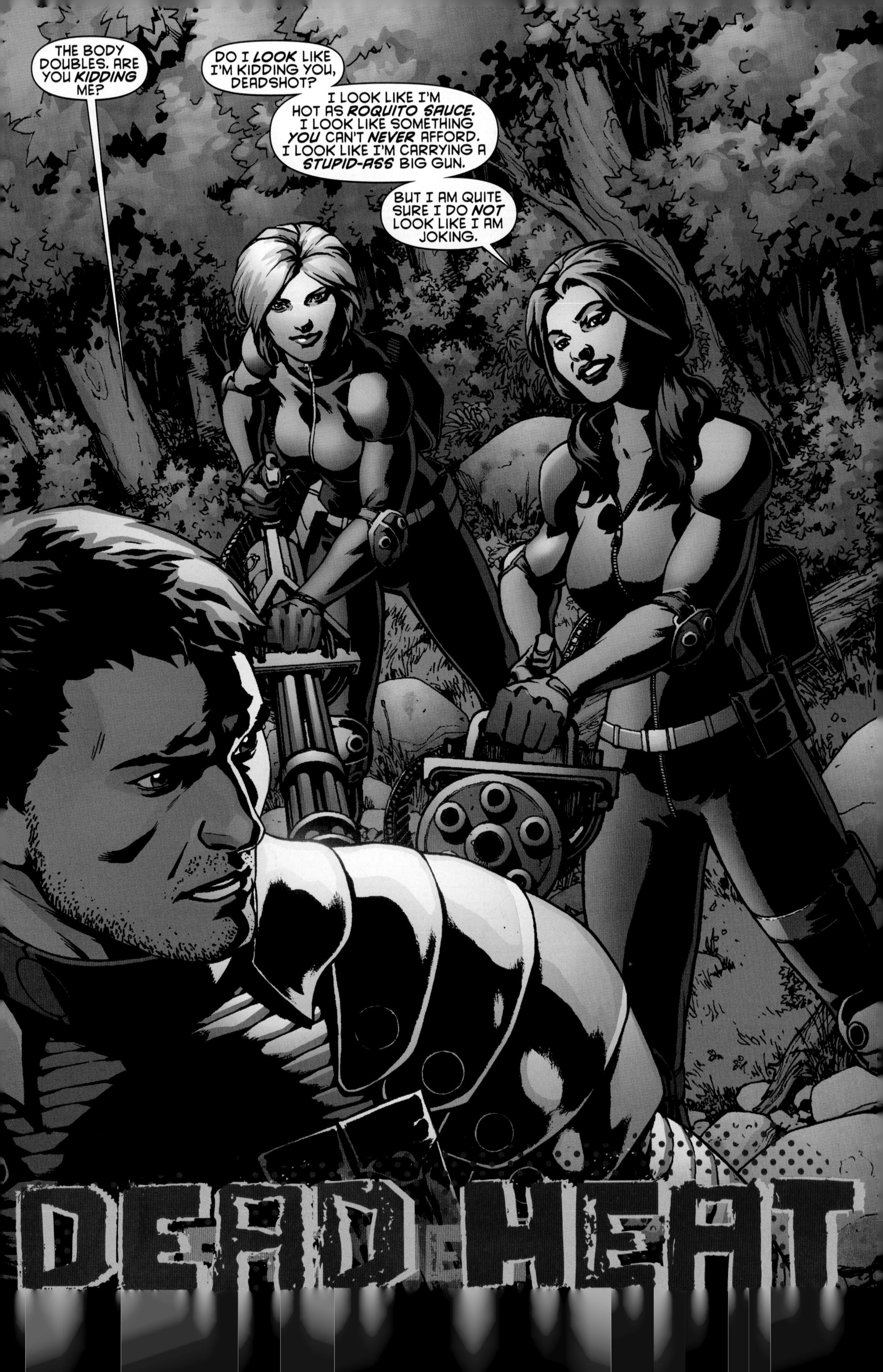
THE BODY DOUBLES. ARE YOU KIDDING ME?
DO I LOOK LIKE I'M KIDDING YOU, DEADSHOT?
I LOOK LIKE I'M HOT AS ROQUITO SAUCE. I LOOK LIKE SOMETHING YOU CAN'T NEVER AFFORD. I LOOK LIKE I'M CARRYING A STUPID-ASS BIG GUN.
BUT I AM QUITE SURE I DO NOT LOOK LIKE I AM JOKING.
DEAD HEAT

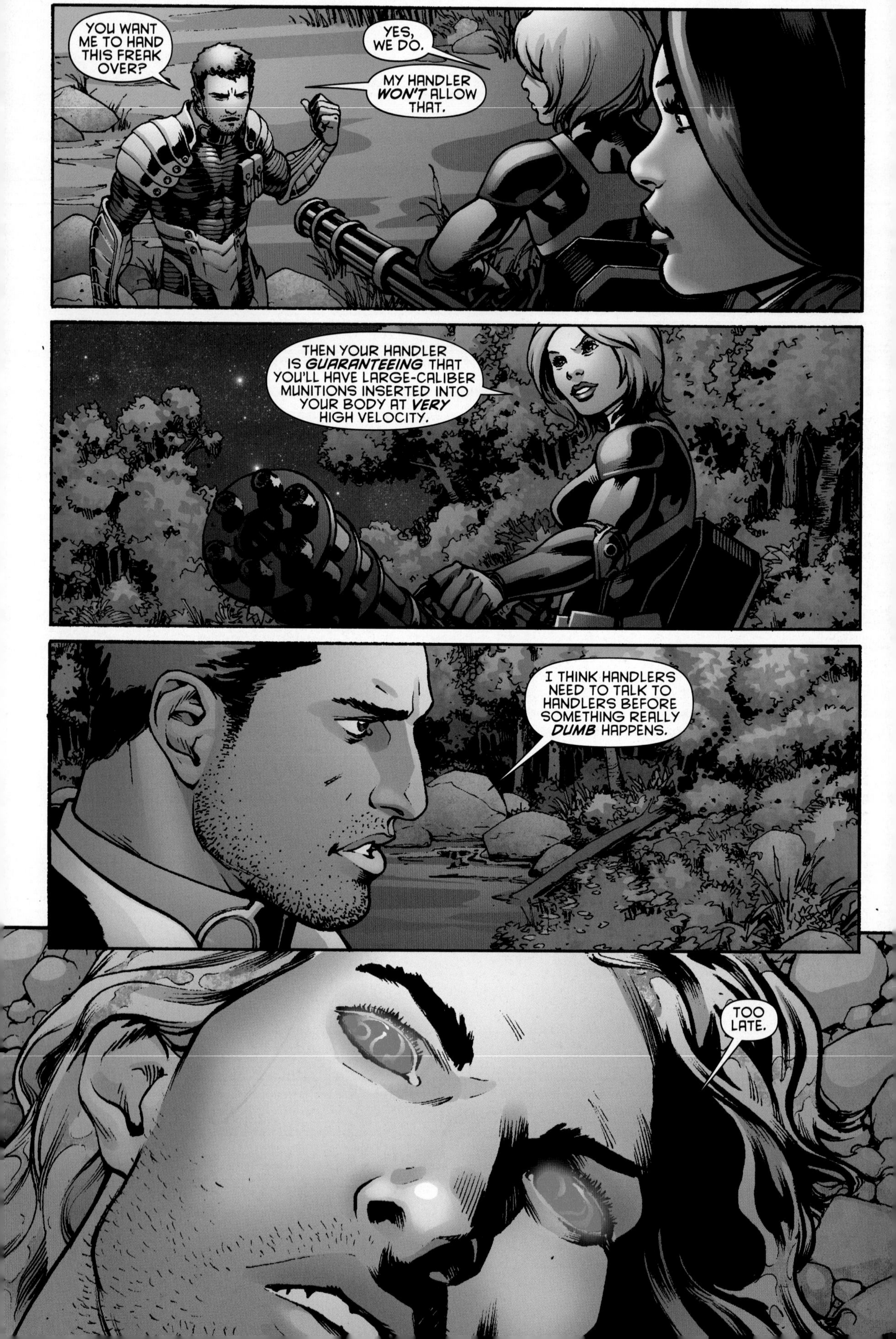
YOU WANT ME TO HAND THIS FREAK OVER?
YES, WE DO.
MY HANDLER WON'T ALLOW THAT.
THEN YOUR HANDLER IS GUARANTEEING THAT YOU'LL HAVE LARGE-CALIBER MUNITIONS INSERTED INTO YOUR BODY AT VERY HIGH VELOCITY.
I THINK HANDLERS NEED TO TALK TO HANDLERS BEFORE SOMETHING REALLY DUMB HAPPENS.
TOO LATE.

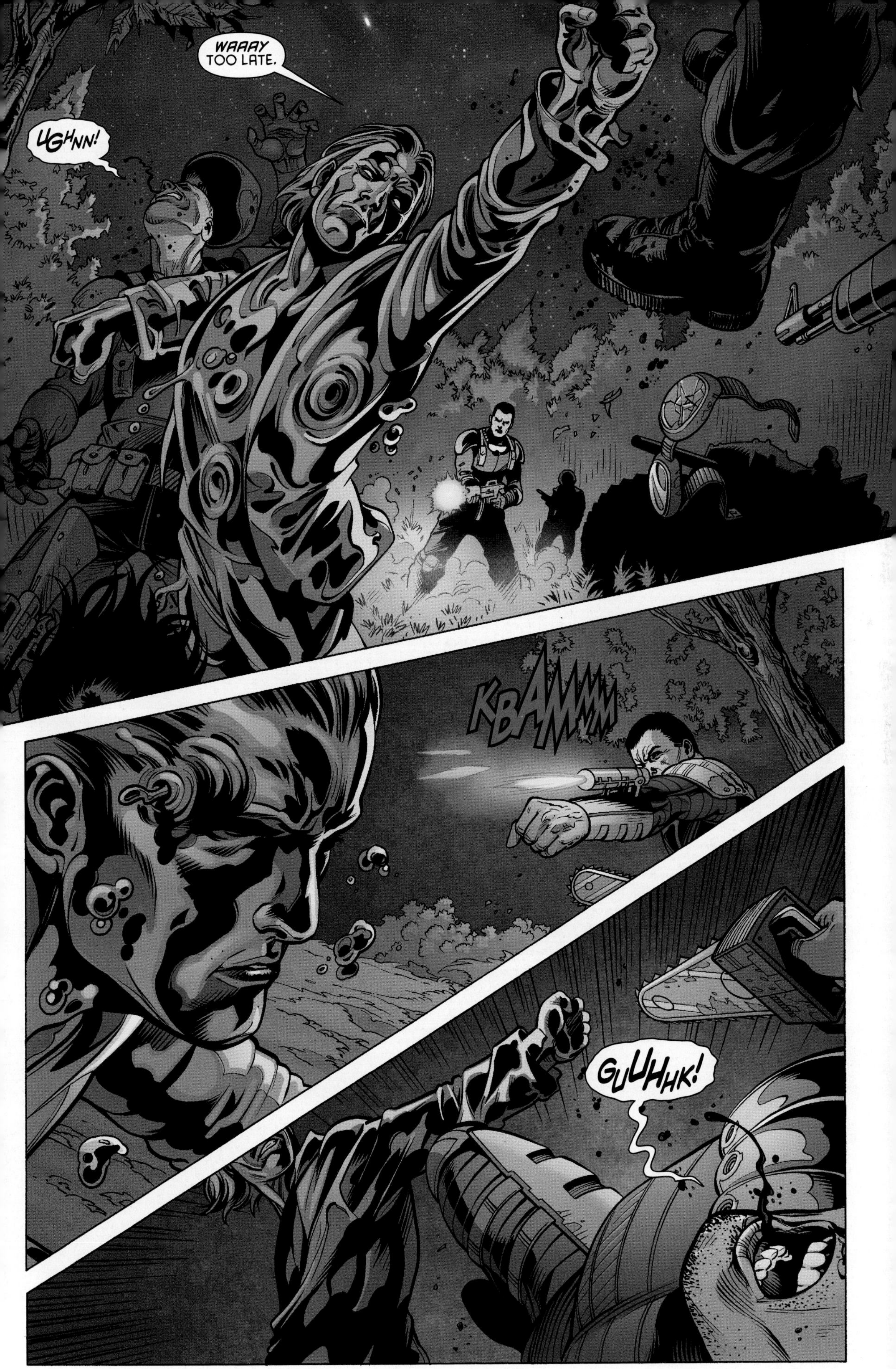
WAAAY TOO LATE.
UGHNN!
KBAMMM
GUUHHK!

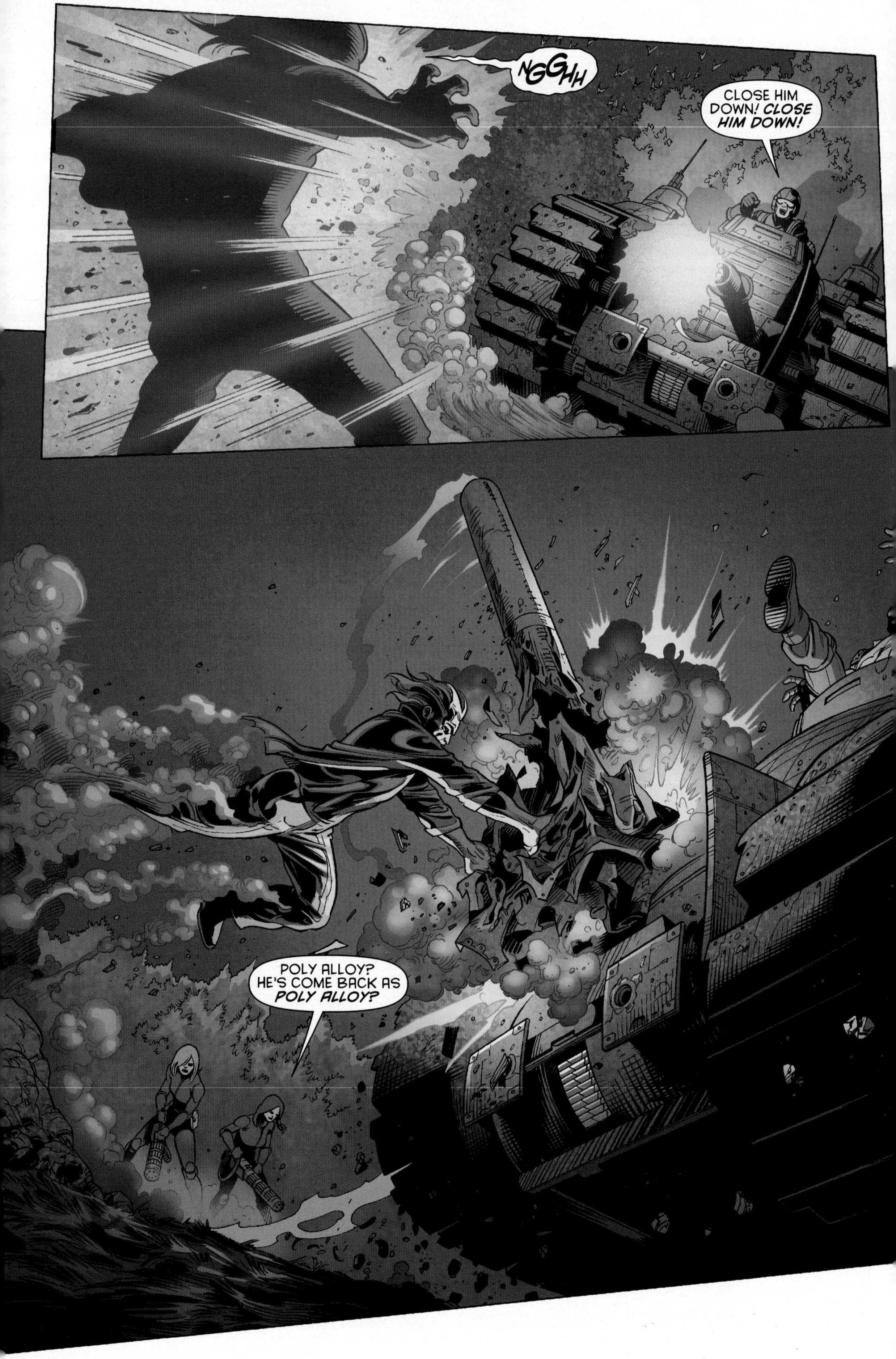
NGGHH
CLOSE HIM DOWN! CLOSE HIM DOWN!
POLY ALLOY? HE'S COME BACK AS POLY ALLOY?

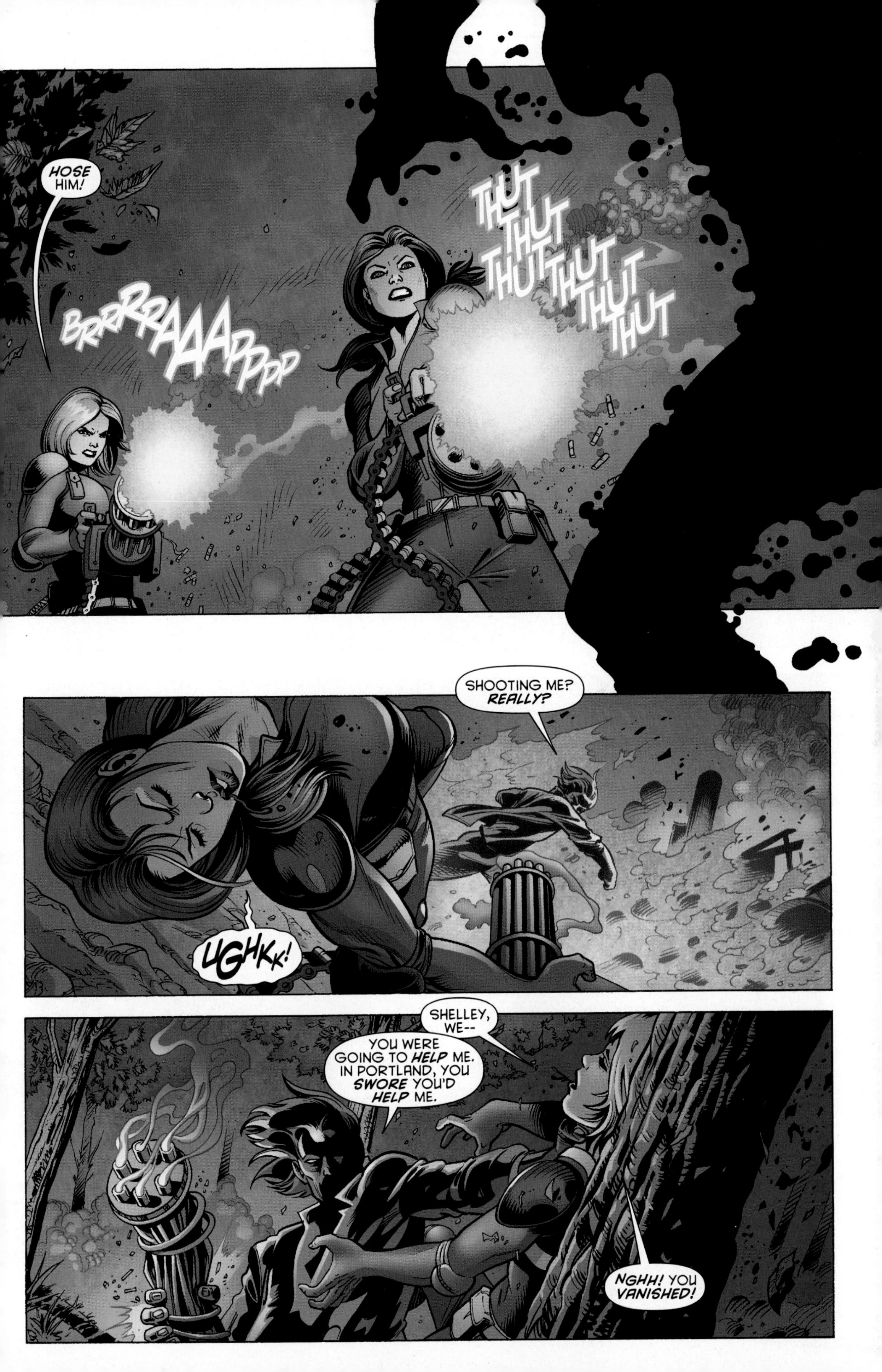
HOSE HIM!
BRRRRAAAPPPP
THUT THUT THUT THUT THUT THUT
SHOOTING ME? REALLY?
UGHKK!
SHELLEY, WE--
YOU WERE GOING TO HELP ME. IN PORTLAND, YOU SWORE YOU'D HELP ME.
NGHH! YOU VANISHED!

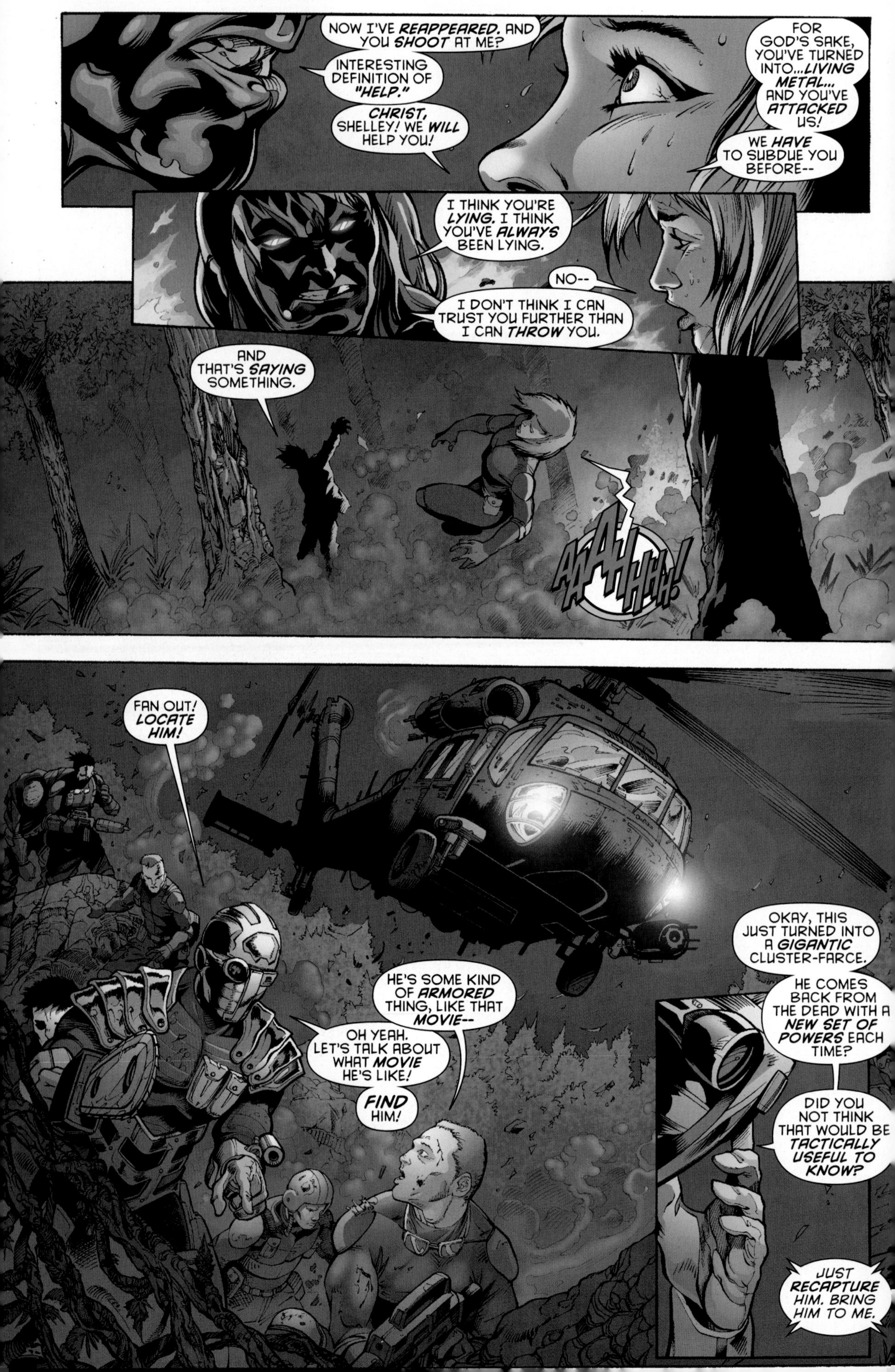
NOW I'VE REAPPEARED. AND YOU SHOOT AT ME?
INTERESTING DEFINITION OF "HELP."
CHRIST, SHELLEY! WE WILL HELP YOU!
FOR GOD'S SAKE, YOU'VE TURNED INTO...LIVING METAL... AND YOU'VE ATTACKED US!
WE HAVE TO SUBDUE YOU BEFORE--
I THINK YOU'RE LYING. I THINK YOU'VE ALWAYS BEEN LYING.
NO--
I DON'T THINK I CAN TRUST YOU FURTHER THAN I CAN THROW YOU.
AND THAT'S SAYING SOMETHING.
AAAHHHH!
FAN OUT! LOCATE HIM!
HE'S SOME KIND OF ARMORED THING, LIKE THAT MOVIE--
OH YEAH. LET'S TALK ABOUT WHAT MOVIE HE'S LIKE!
FIND HIM!
OKAY, THIS JUST TURNED INTO A GIGANTIC CLUSTER-FARCE.
HE COMES BACK FROM THE DEAD WITH A NEW SET OF POWERS EACH TIME?
DID YOU NOT THINK THAT WOULD BE TACTICALLY USEFUL TO KNOW?
JUST RECAPTURE HIM. BRING HIM TO ME.

AND WE'VE GOT A TURF CLASH WITH A *RIVAL OFF-BOOKS* OUTFIT. WE--

I WILL *HANDLE*. JUST *BRING* HIM TO ME.

I'M AT THE *FIELD OPS CENTER* AS AGREED.

BRING HIM TO ME.

UGHNNKK!

DEADSHOT. *DEADSHOT?*

OH GOD. *MITCH.*

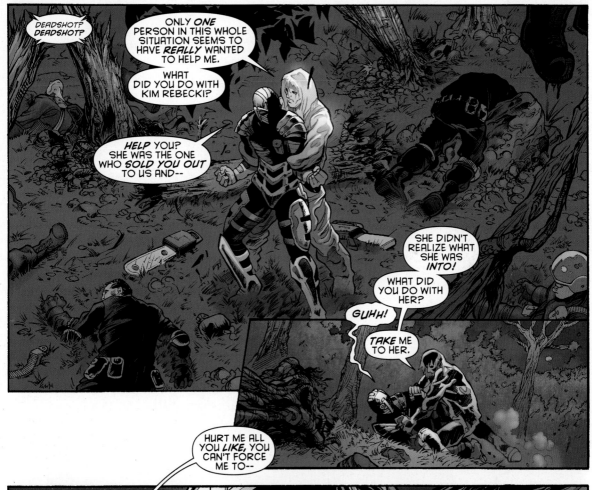

DEADSHOT? DEADSHOT?

ONLY *ONE* PERSON IN THIS WHOLE SITUATION SEEMS TO HAVE *REALLY* WANTED TO HELP ME.

WHAT DID YOU DO WITH KIM REBECKI?

HELP YOU? SHE WAS THE ONE WHO *SOLD YOU OUT* TO US AND--

SHE DIDN'T REALIZE WHAT SHE WAS *INTO!*

WHAT DID YOU DO WITH HER?

GUHH!

TAKE ME TO HER.

HURT ME ALL YOU *LIKE,* YOU CAN'T FORCE ME TO--

WHAT THE *HELL--*

TAKE ME TO HER.

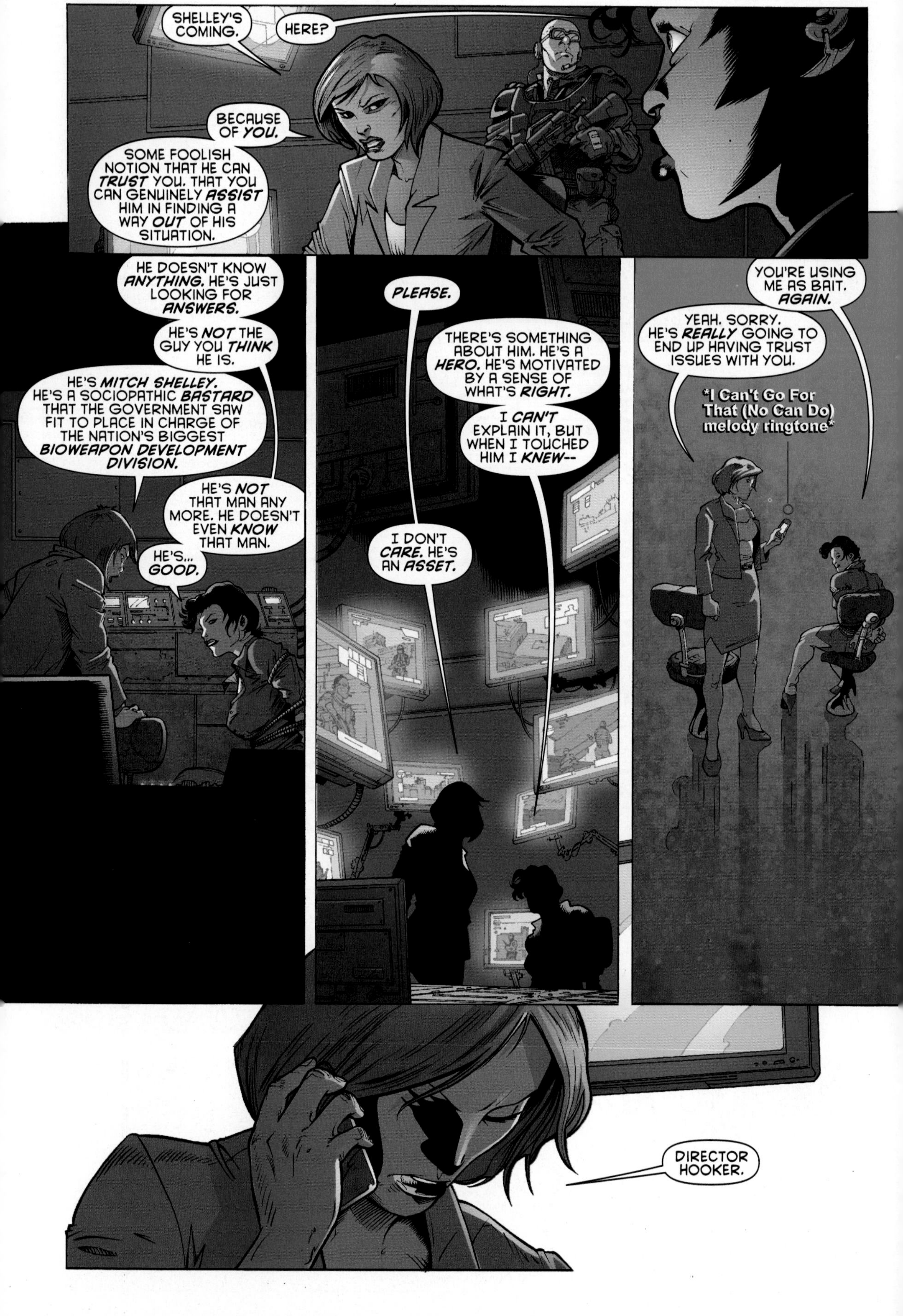
SHELLEY'S COMING.
HERE?
BECAUSE OF YOU.
SOME FOOLISH NOTION THAT HE CAN TRUST YOU. THAT YOU CAN GENUINELY ASSIST HIM IN FINDING A WAY OUT OF HIS SITUATION.
HE DOESN'T KNOW ANYTHING. HE'S JUST LOOKING FOR ANSWERS.
HE'S NOT THE GUY YOU THINK HE IS.
HE'S MITCH SHELLEY. HE'S A SOCIOPATHIC BASTARD THAT THE GOVERNMENT SAW FIT TO PLACE IN CHARGE OF THE NATION'S BIGGEST BIOWEAPON DEVELOPMENT DIVISION.
HE'S NOT THAT MAN ANY MORE. HE DOESN'T EVEN KNOW THAT MAN.
HE'S... GOOD.
PLEASE.
THERE'S SOMETHING ABOUT HIM. HE'S A HERO. HE'S MOTIVATED BY A SENSE OF WHAT'S RIGHT.
I CAN'T EXPLAIN IT, BUT WHEN I TOUCHED HIM I KNEW--
I DON'T CARE. HE'S AN ASSET.
YOU'RE USING ME AS BAIT. AGAIN.
YEAH. SORRY. HE'S REALLY GOING TO END UP HAVING TRUST ISSUES WITH YOU.
I Can't Go For That (No Can Do) melody ringtone
DIRECTOR HOOKER.

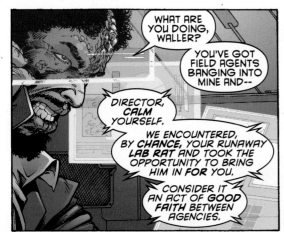

WHAT ARE YOU DOING, WALLER?

YOU'VE GOT FIELD AGENTS BANGING INTO MINE AND--

DIRECTOR, *CALM* YOURSELF.

WE ENCOUNTERED, BY *CHANCE*, YOUR RUNAWAY *LAB RAT* AND TOOK THE OPPORTUNITY TO BRING HIM IN FOR YOU.

CONSIDER IT AN ACT OF *GOOD FAITH* BETWEEN AGENCIES.

YOU'RE NOT EVEN CONVINCING *YOURSELF*.

AU CONTRAIRE. WE'RE *RETURNING* YOUR ASSET TO YOU. WE'RE DOING *YOUR* DIRTY WORK FOR YOU.

YOU OUGHT TO BE *GRATEFUL*.

AND *YET*...

CALL YOUR *GIRLS* OFF, DIRECTOR. I WILL DELIVER *MITCHELL SHELLEY* TO YOU BEFORE *DAY'S END*.

Call ended

Girl From Ipanema melody ringtone

Carrier

All Contacts

Body Doubles Calling

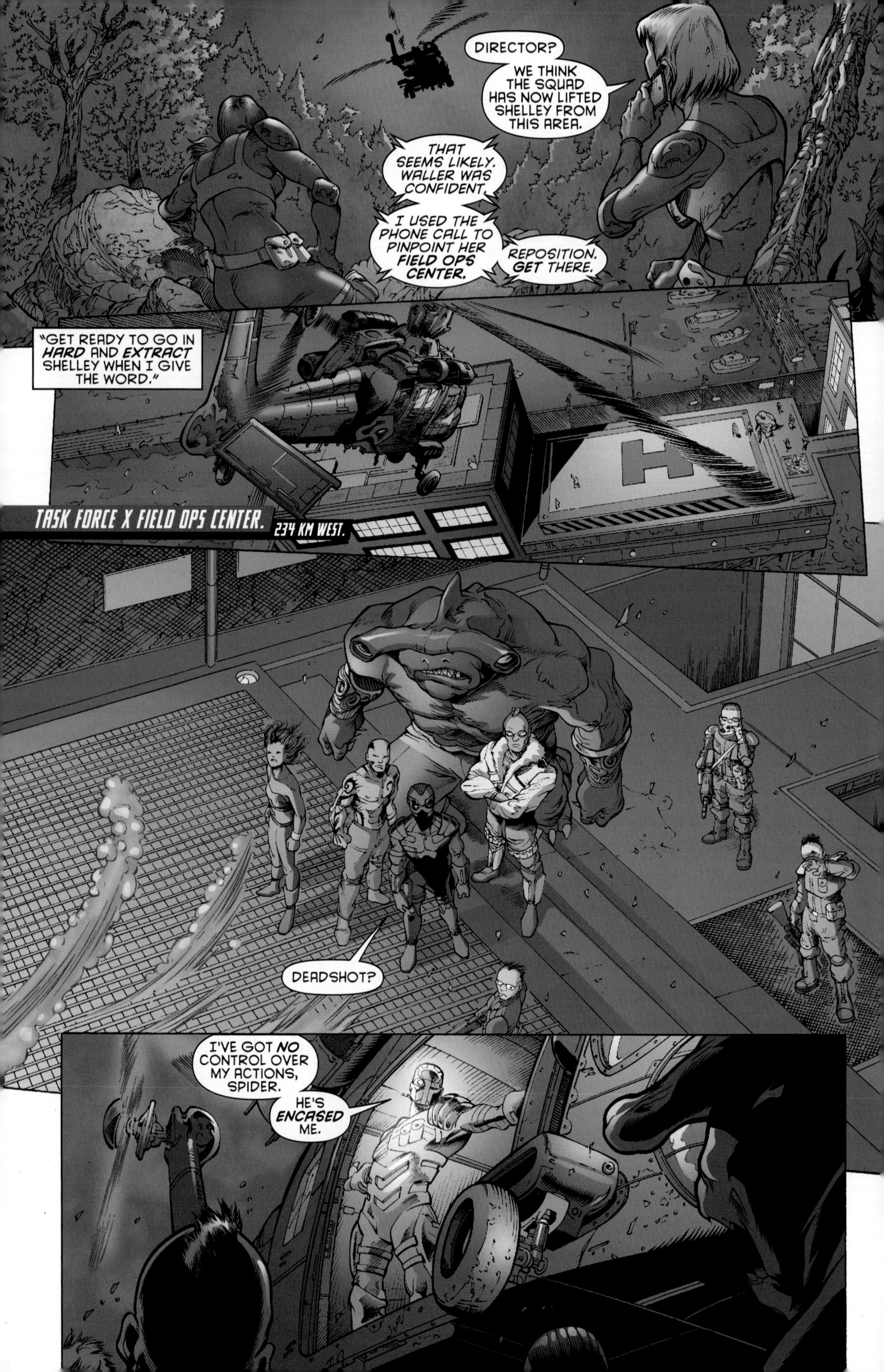
DIRECTOR?
WE THINK THE SQUAD HAS NOW LIFTED SHELLEY FROM THIS AREA.
THAT SEEMS LIKELY. WALLER WAS CONFIDENT.
I USED THE PHONE CALL TO PINPOINT HER FIELD OPS CENTER.
REPOSITION. GET THERE.
"GET READY TO GO IN HARD AND EXTRACT SHELLEY WHEN I GIVE THE WORD."
TASK FORCE X FIELD OPS CENTER.
234 KM WEST.
DEADSHOT?
I'VE GOT NO CONTROL OVER MY ACTIONS, SPIDER.
HE'S ENCASED ME.

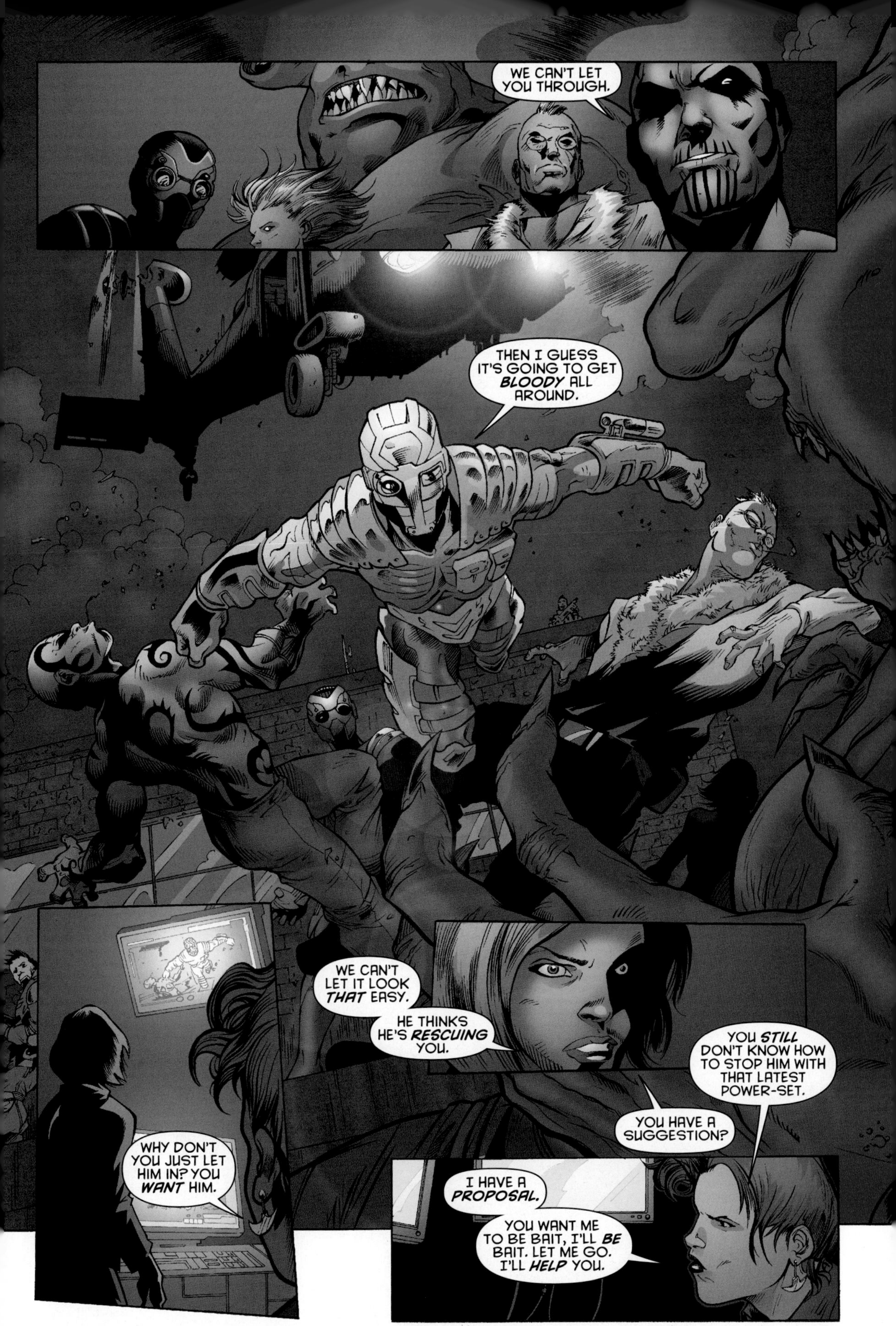
WE CAN'T LET YOU THROUGH.
THEN I GUESS IT'S GOING TO GET BLOODY ALL AROUND.
WHY DON'T YOU JUST LET HIM IN? YOU WANT HIM.
WE CAN'T LET IT LOOK THAT EASY.
HE THINKS HE'S RESCUING YOU.
YOU STILL DON'T KNOW HOW TO STOP HIM WITH THAT LATEST POWER-SET.
YOU HAVE A SUGGESTION?
I HAVE A PROPOSAL.
YOU WANT ME TO BE BAIT, I'LL BE BAIT. LET ME GO. I'LL HELP YOU.

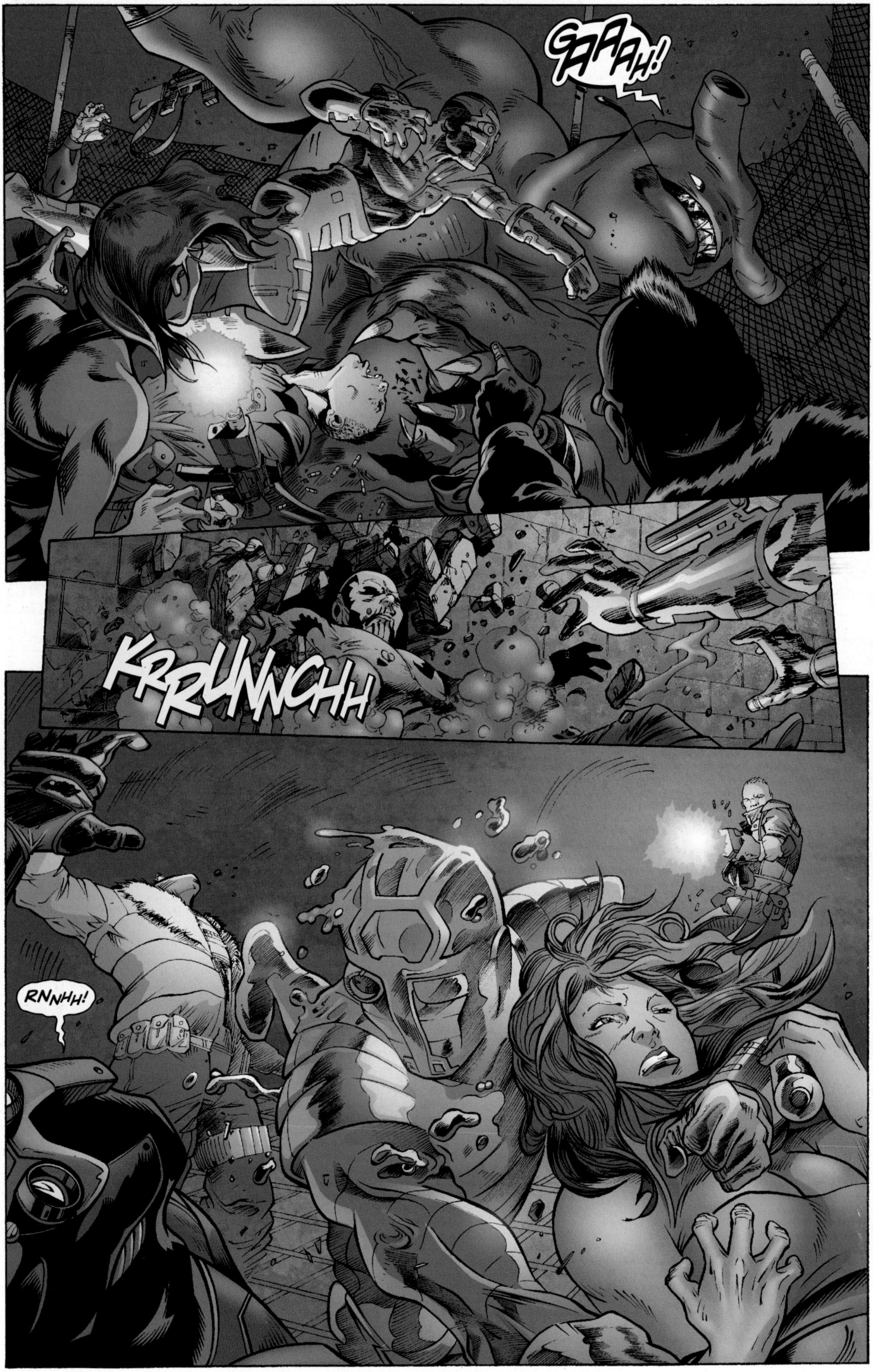
GAAAAH!
KRRUNNCHH
RNHH!

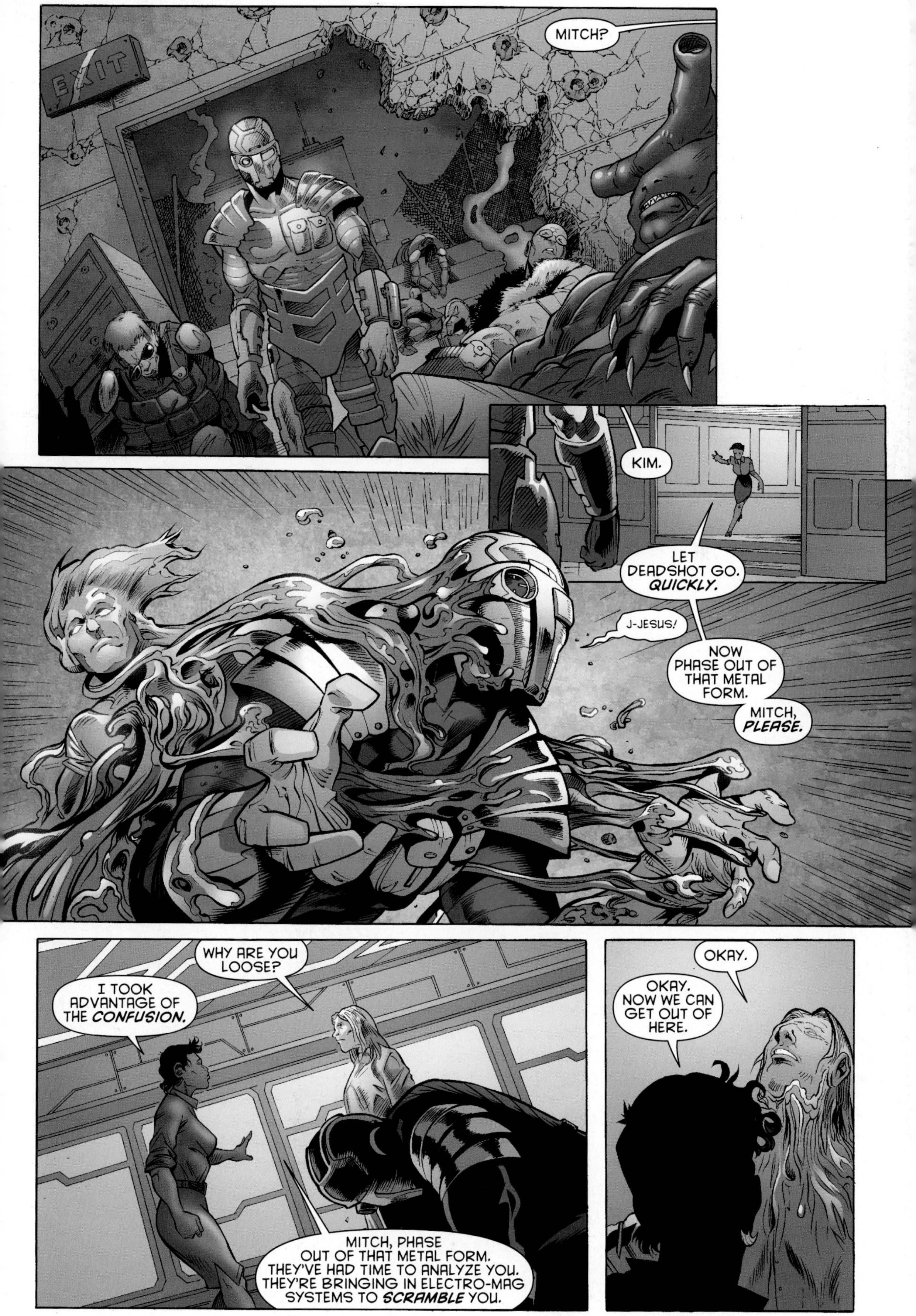
MITCH?
KIM.
LET DEADSHOT GO. QUICKLY.
J-JESUS!
NOW PHASE OUT OF THAT METAL FORM.
MITCH, PLEASE.
WHY ARE YOU LOOSE?
I TOOK ADVANTAGE OF THE CONFUSION.
MITCH, PHASE OUT OF THAT METAL FORM. THEY'VE HAD TIME TO ANALYZE YOU. THEY'RE BRINGING IN ELECTRO-MAG SYSTEMS TO SCRAMBLE YOU.
OKAY.
OKAY. NOW WE CAN GET OUT OF HERE.

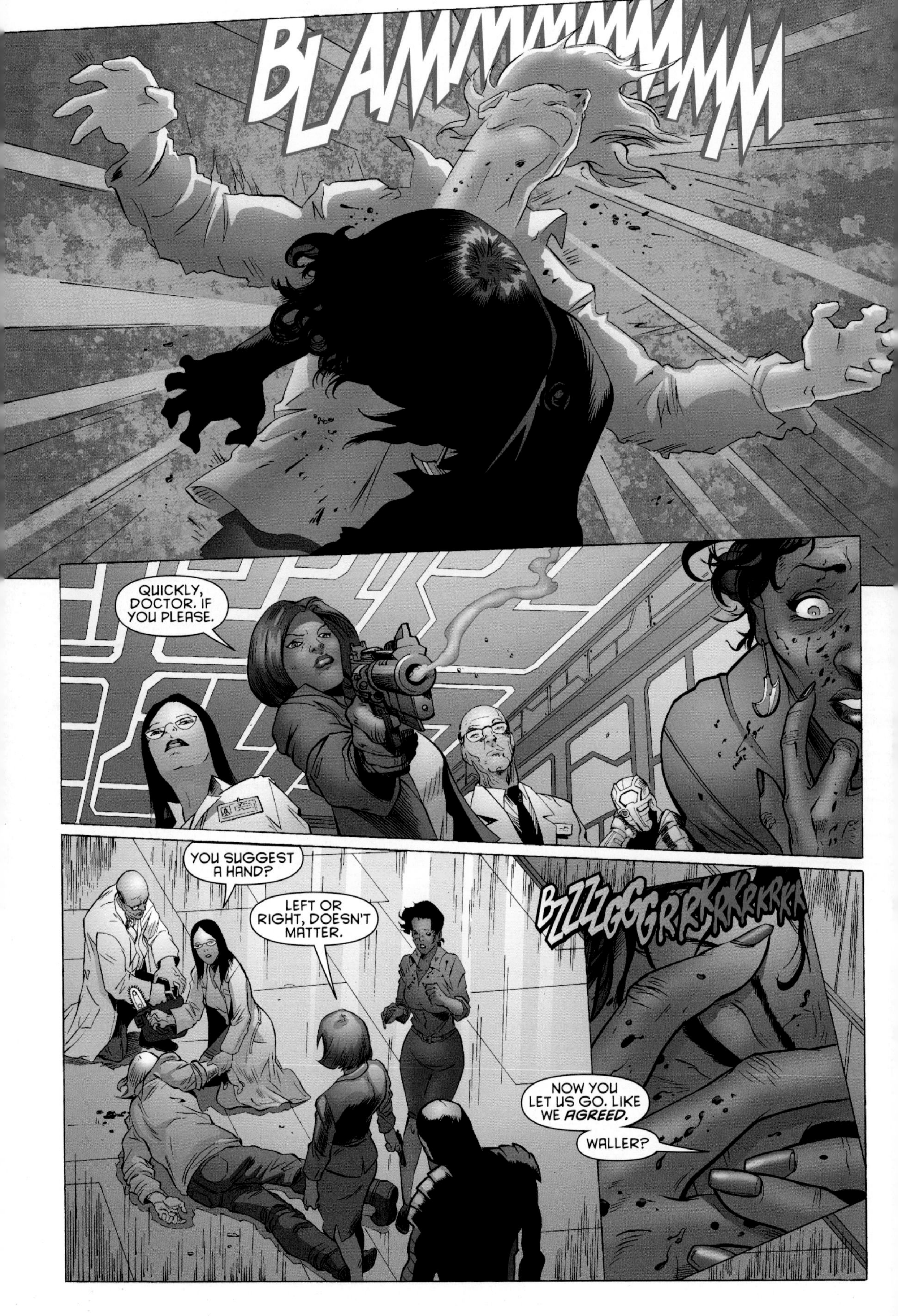

BLAMMMMMMM
QUICKLY, DOCTOR. IF YOU PLEASE.
YOU SUGGEST A HAND?
LEFT OR RIGHT, DOESN'T MATTER.
BZZZZGGGRRKRKRKRKRK
NOW YOU LET US GO. LIKE WE *AGREED.*
WALLER?

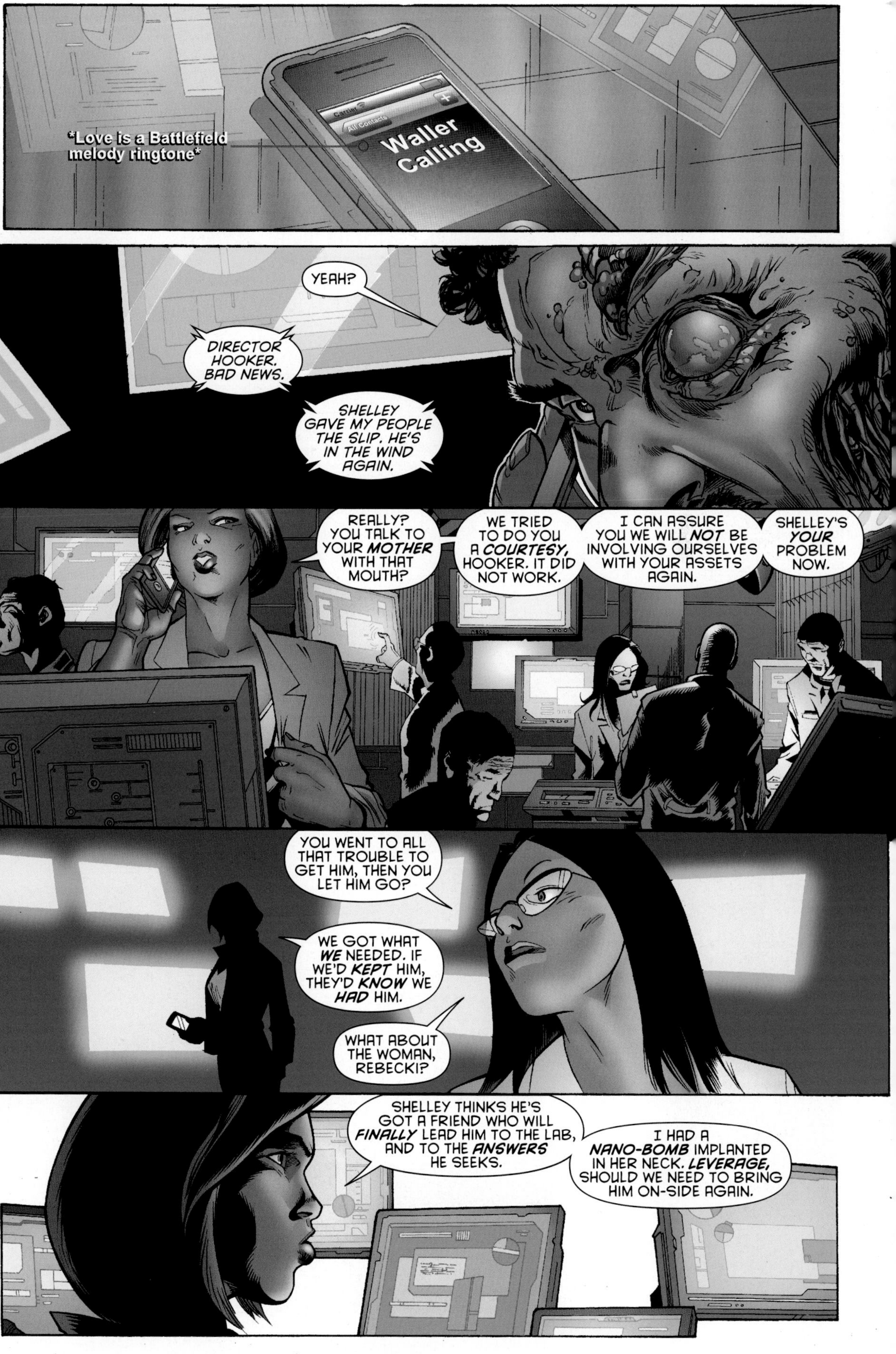
Love is a Battlefield melody ringtone
Waller Calling
YEAH?
DIRECTOR HOOKER. BAD NEWS.
SHELLEY GAVE MY PEOPLE THE SLIP. HE'S IN THE WIND AGAIN.
REALLY? YOU TALK TO YOUR MOTHER WITH THAT MOUTH?
WE TRIED TO DO YOU A COURTESY, HOOKER. IT DID NOT WORK.
I CAN ASSURE YOU WE WILL NOT BE INVOLVING OURSELVES WITH YOUR ASSETS AGAIN.
SHELLEY'S YOUR PROBLEM NOW.
YOU WENT TO ALL THAT TROUBLE TO GET HIM, THEN YOU LET HIM GO?
WE GOT WHAT WE NEEDED. IF WE'D KEPT HIM, THEY'D KNOW WE HAD HIM.
WHAT ABOUT THE WOMAN, REBECKI?
SHELLEY THINKS HE'S GOT A FRIEND WHO WILL FINALLY LEAD HIM TO THE LAB, AND TO THE ANSWERS HE SEEKS.
I HAD A NANO-BOMB IMPLANTED IN HER NECK. LEVERAGE, SHOULD WE NEED TO BRING HIM ON-SIDE AGAIN.

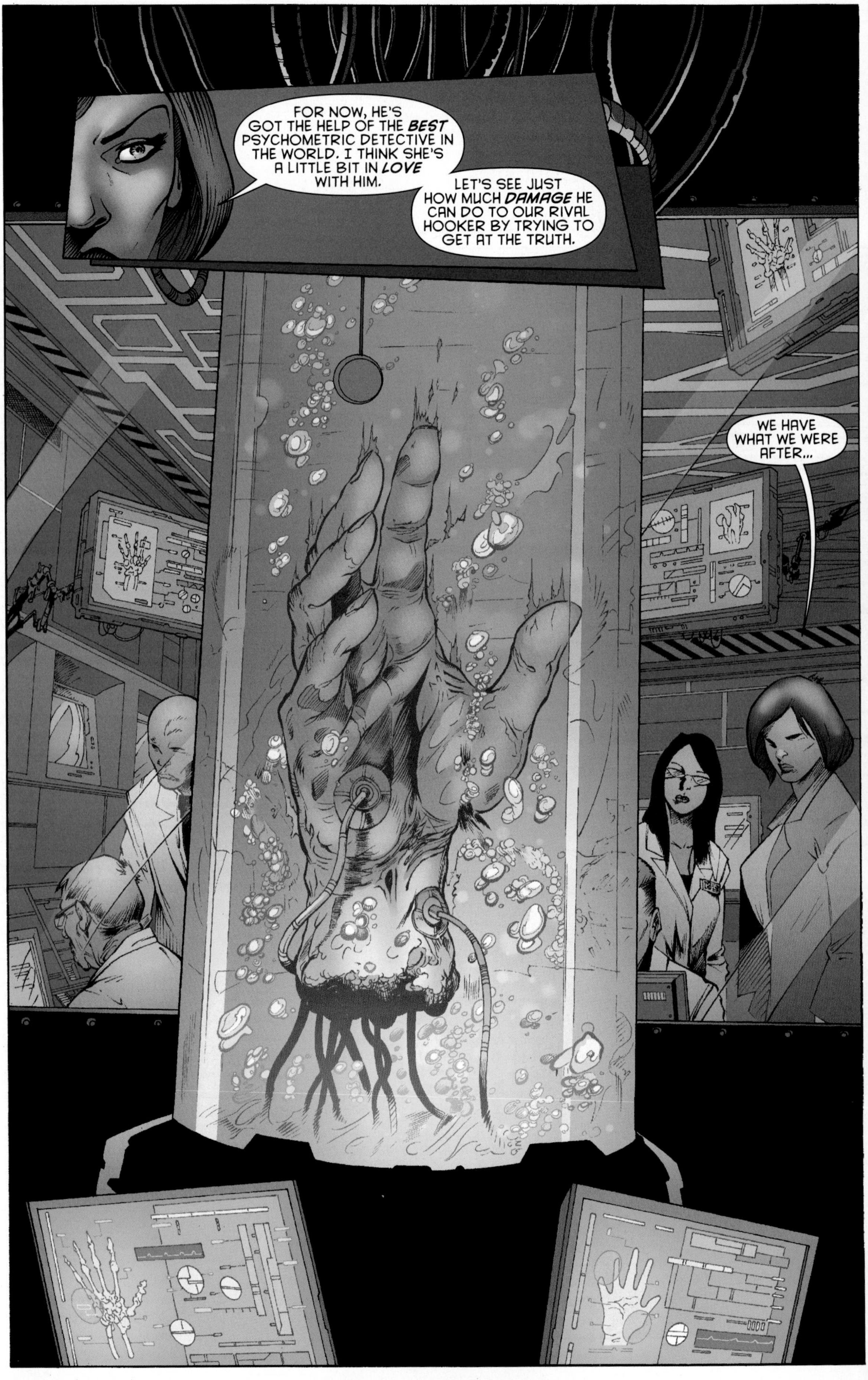
FOR NOW, HE'S GOT THE HELP OF THE BEST PSYCHOMETRIC DETECTIVE IN THE WORLD. I THINK SHE'S A LITTLE BIT IN LOVE WITH HIM.
LET'S SEE JUST HOW MUCH DAMAGE HE CAN DO TO OUR RIVAL HOOKER BY TRYING TO GET AT THE TRUTH.
WE HAVE WHAT WE WERE AFTER...

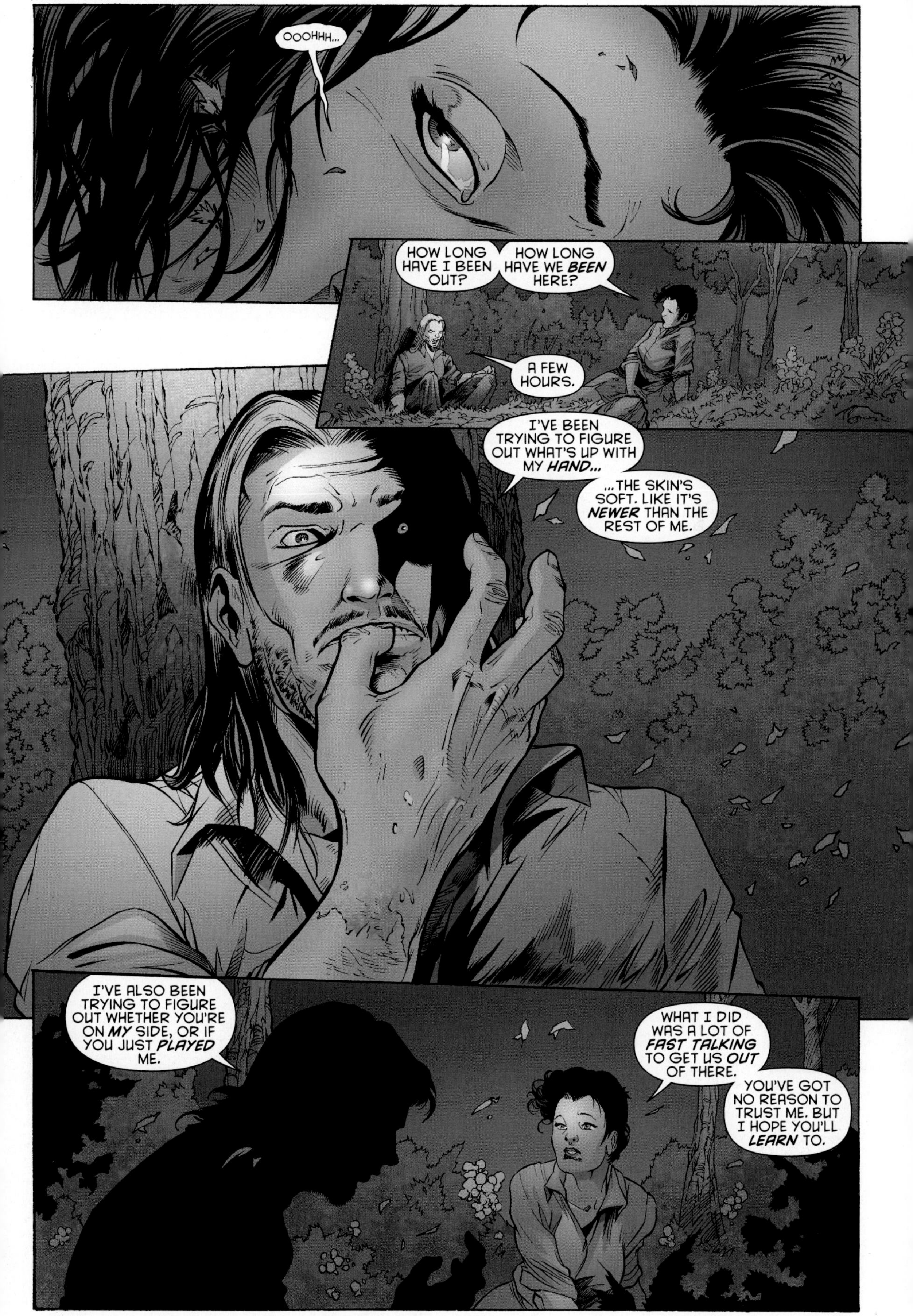
OOOHHH...
HOW LONG HAVE I BEEN OUT?
HOW LONG HAVE WE *BEEN* HERE?
A FEW HOURS.
I'VE BEEN TRYING TO FIGURE OUT WHAT'S UP WITH MY *HAND*...
...THE SKIN'S SOFT. LIKE IT'S *NEWER* THAN THE REST OF ME.
I'VE ALSO BEEN TRYING TO FIGURE OUT WHETHER YOU'RE ON *MY* SIDE, OR IF YOU JUST *PLAYED* ME.
WHAT I DID WAS A LOT OF *FAST TALKING* TO GET US *OUT* OF THERE.
YOU'VE GOT NO REASON TO TRUST ME. BUT I HOPE YOU'LL *LEARN* TO.

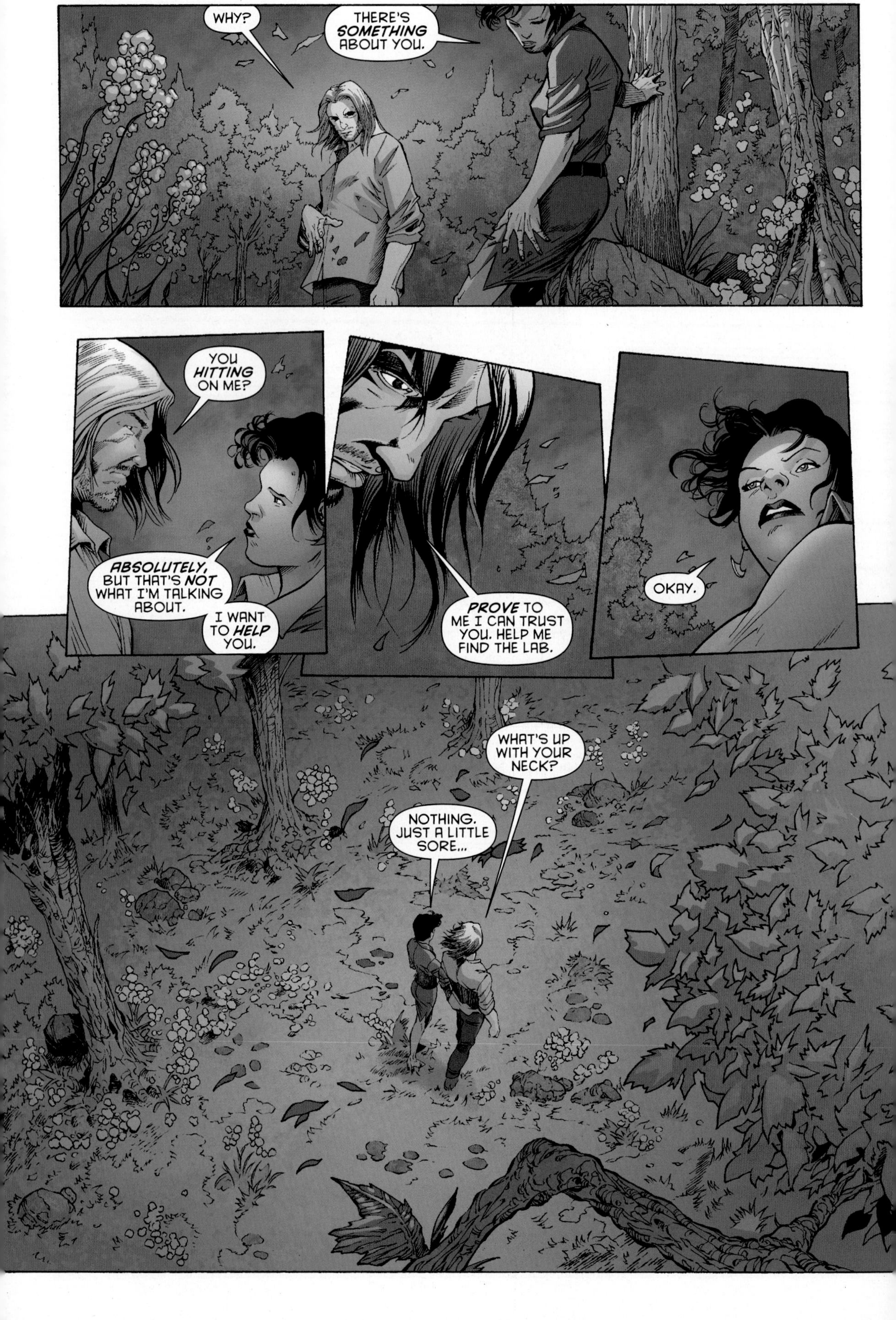
WHY?
THERE'S SOMETHING ABOUT YOU.
YOU HITTING ON ME?
ABSOLUTELY, BUT THAT'S NOT WHAT I'M TALKING ABOUT.
I WANT TO HELP YOU.
PROVE TO ME I CAN TRUST YOU. HELP ME FIND THE LAB.
OKAY.
WHAT'S UP WITH YOUR NECK?
NOTHING. JUST A LITTLE SORE...

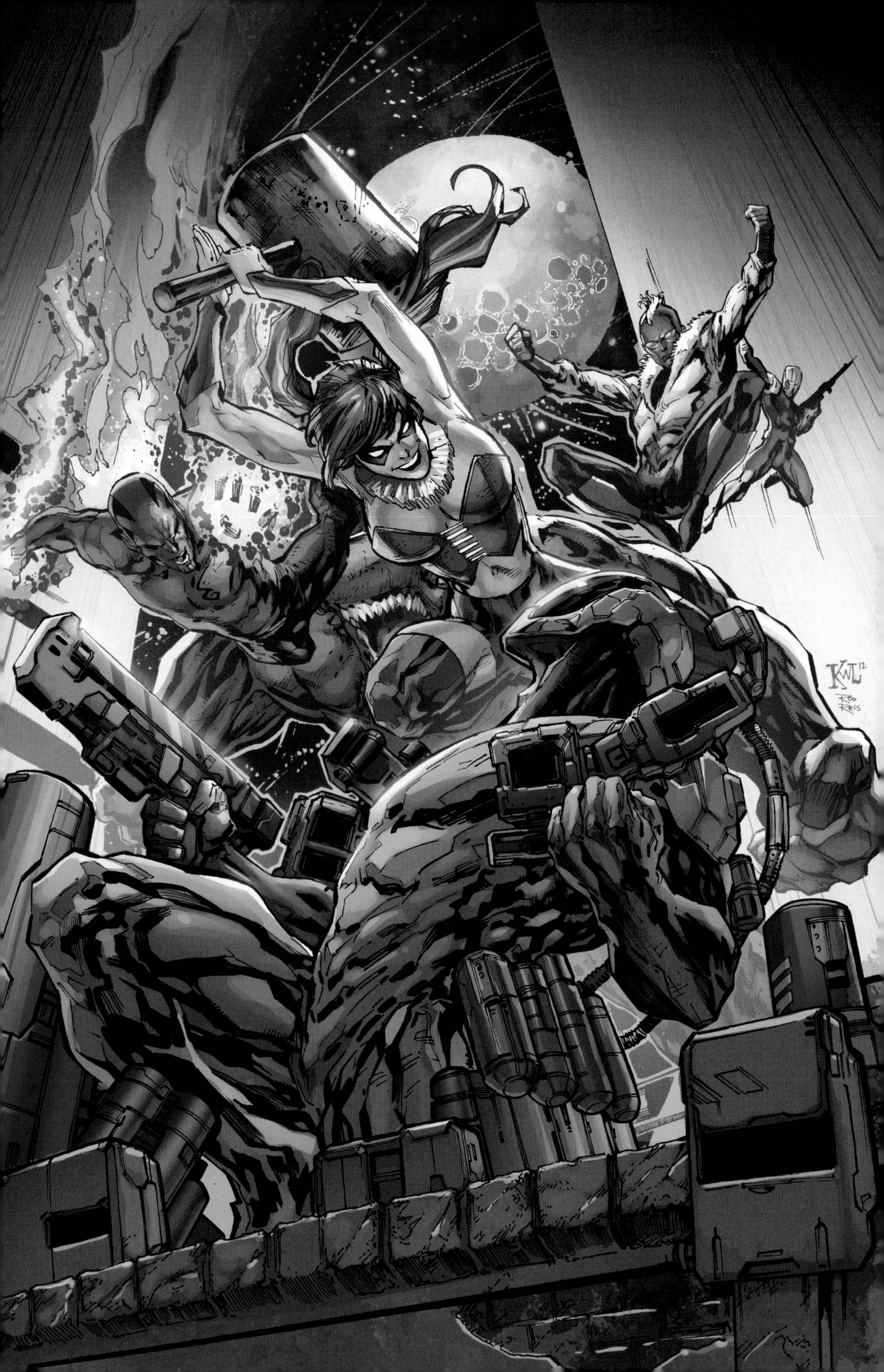
KNL 12
ROD REIS

JUDAS RISING

ADAM GLASS
writer

FERNANDO DAGNINO
artist

cover art by KEN LASHLEY & ROD REIS

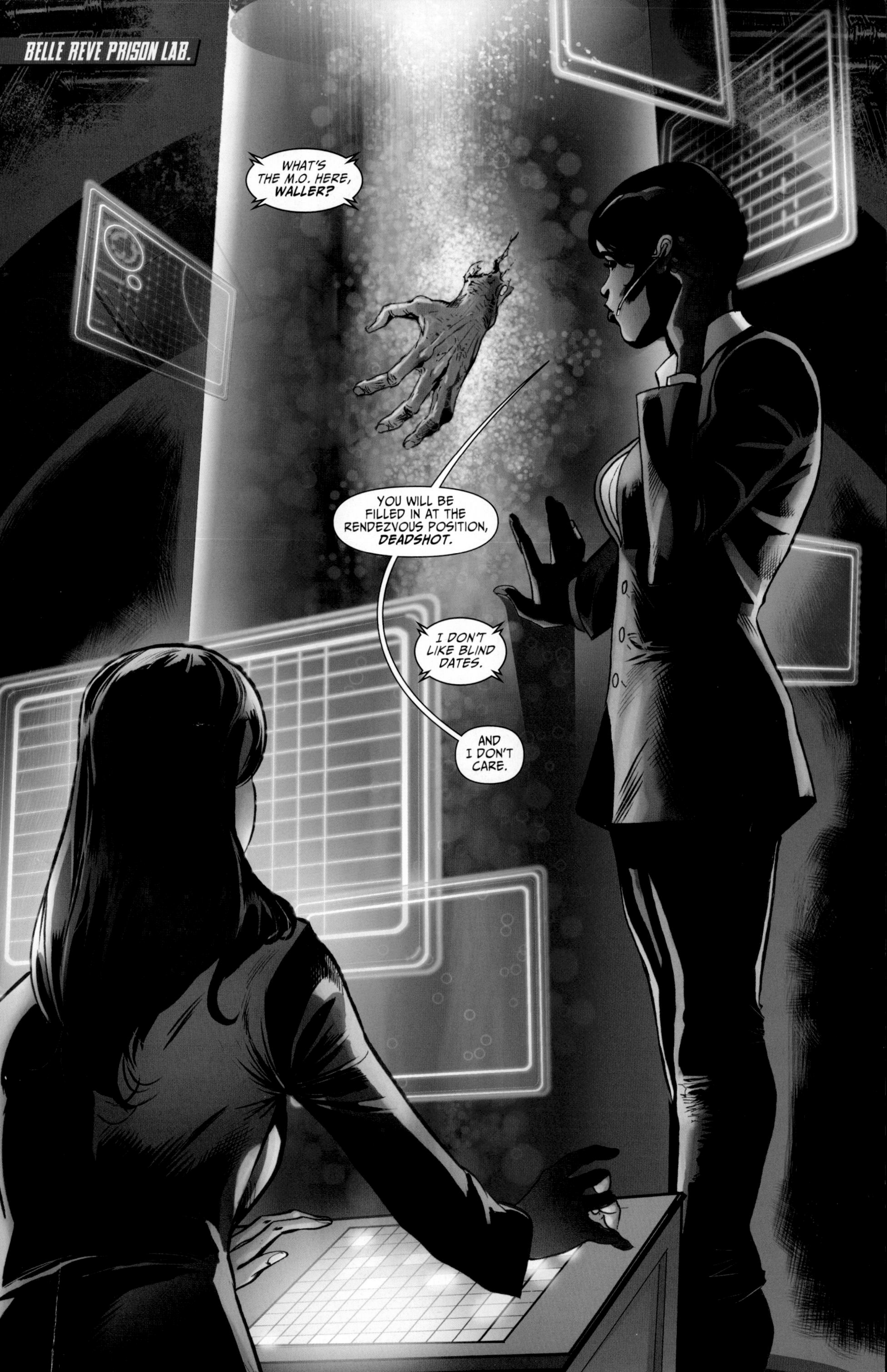
BELLE REVE PRISON LAB.
WHAT'S THE M.O. HERE, WALLER?
YOU WILL BE FILLED IN AT THE RENDEZVOUS POSITION, DEADSHOT.
I DON'T LIKE BLIND DATES.
AND I DON'T CARE.

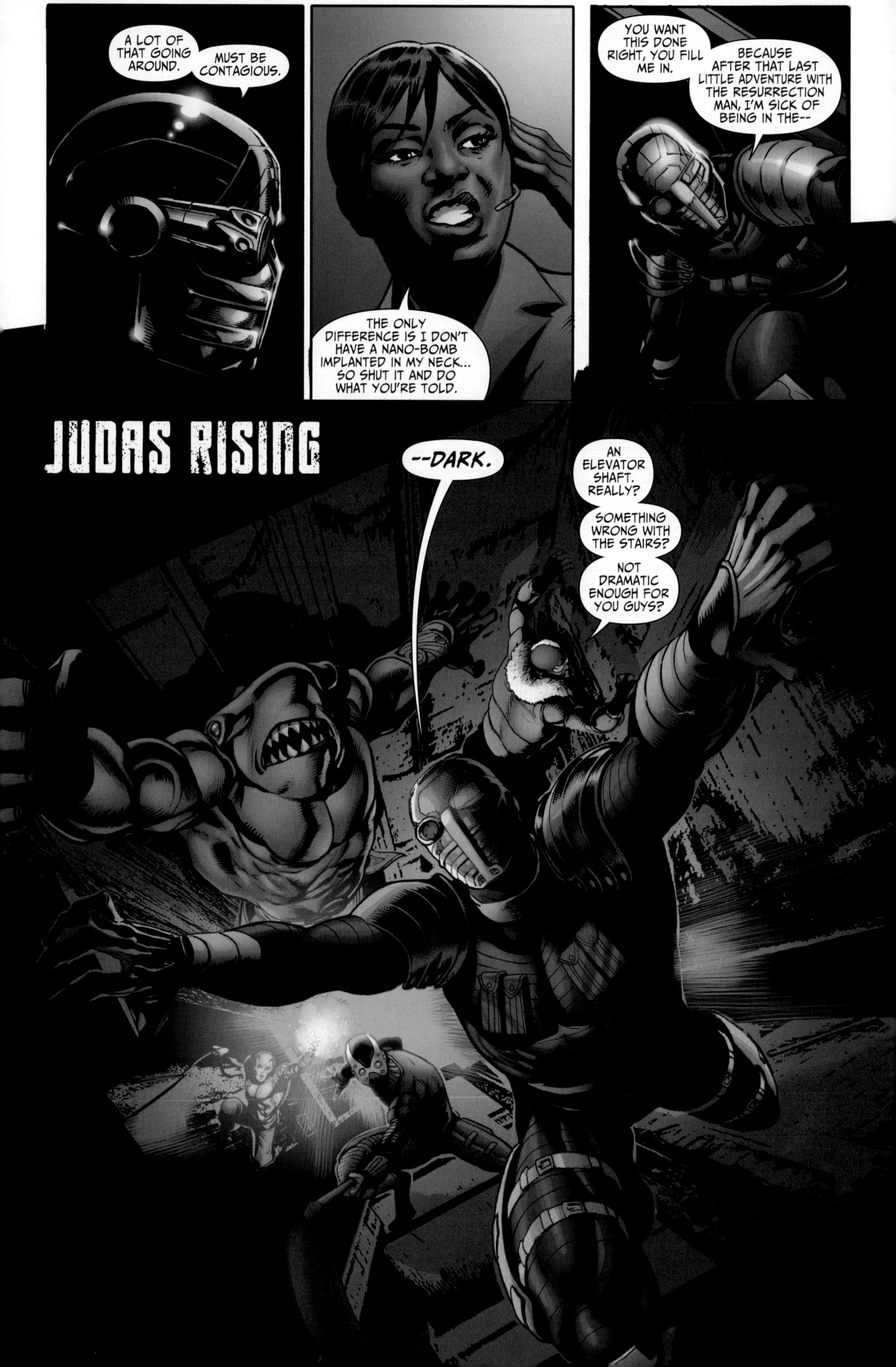

A LOT OF THAT GOING AROUND.
MUST BE CONTAGIOUS.
THE ONLY DIFFERENCE IS I DON'T HAVE A NANO-BOMB IMPLANTED IN MY NECK... SO SHUT IT AND DO WHAT YOU'RE TOLD.
YOU WANT THIS DONE RIGHT, YOU FILL ME IN.
BECAUSE AFTER THAT LAST LITTLE ADVENTURE WITH THE RESURRECTION MAN, I'M SICK OF BEING IN THE--
JUDAS RISING
--DARK.
AN ELEVATOR SHAFT. REALLY?
SOMETHING WRONG WITH THE STAIRS?
NOT DRAMATIC ENOUGH FOR YOU GUYS?

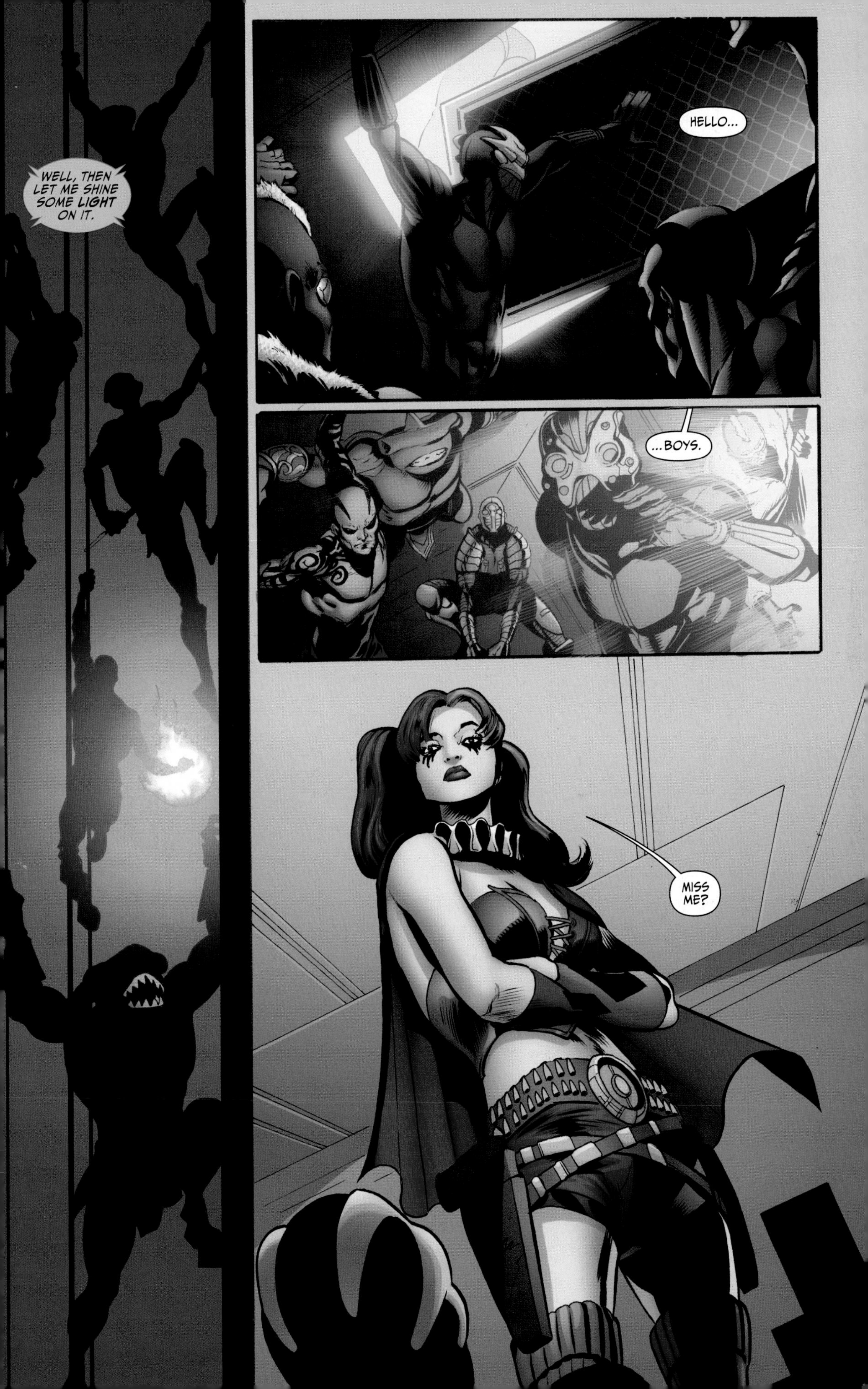
WELL, THEN LET ME SHINE SOME LIGHT ON IT.
HELLO...
...BOYS.
MISS ME?

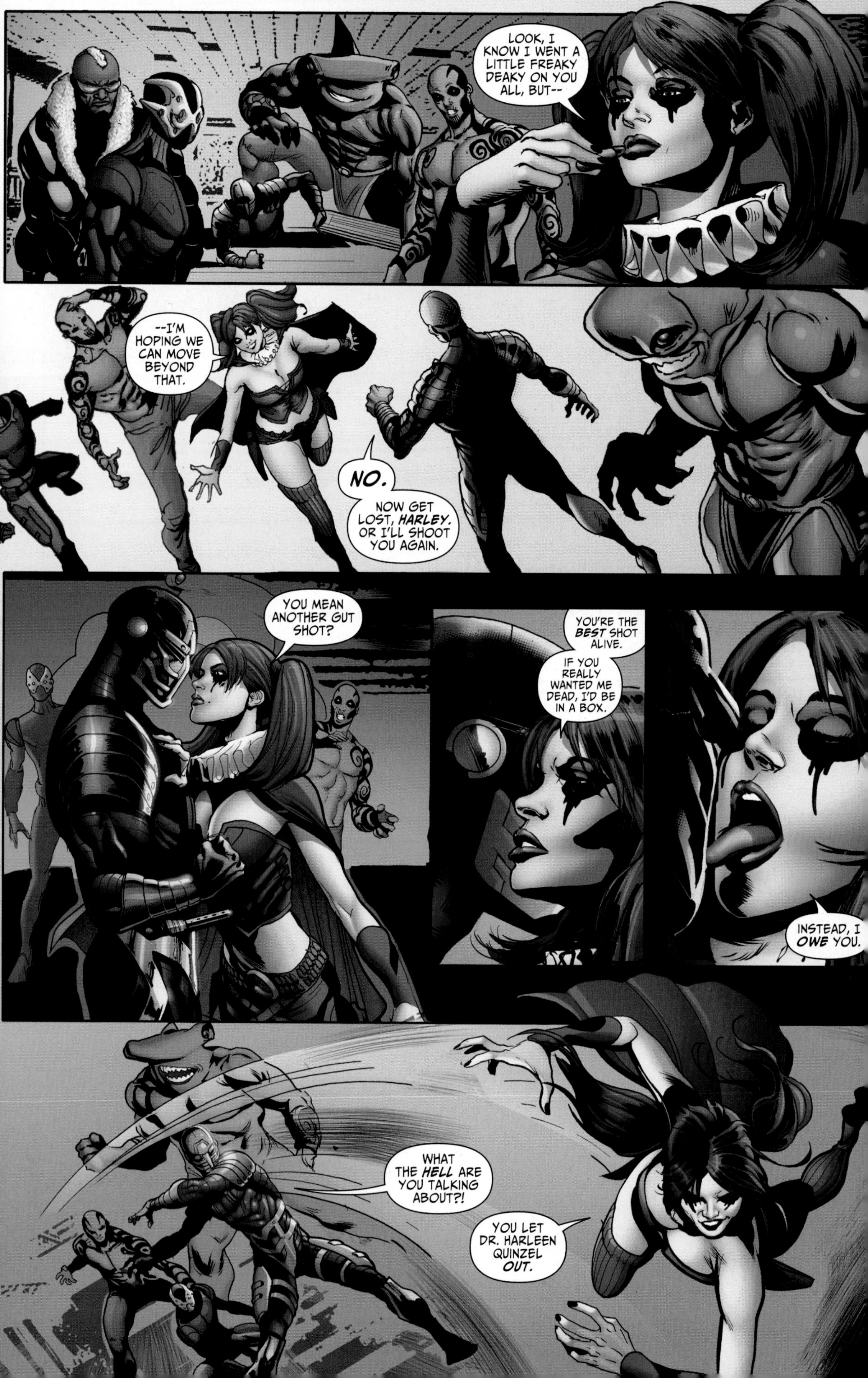
LOOK, I KNOW I WENT A LITTLE FREAKY DEAKY ON YOU ALL, BUT--
--I'M HOPING WE CAN MOVE BEYOND THAT.
NO.
NOW GET LOST, HARLEY. OR I'LL SHOOT YOU AGAIN.
YOU MEAN ANOTHER GUT SHOT?
YOU'RE THE BEST SHOT ALIVE.
IF YOU REALLY WANTED ME DEAD, I'D BE IN A BOX.
INSTEAD, I OWE YOU.
WHAT THE HELL ARE YOU TALKING ABOUT?!
YOU LET DR. HARLEEN QUINZEL OUT.

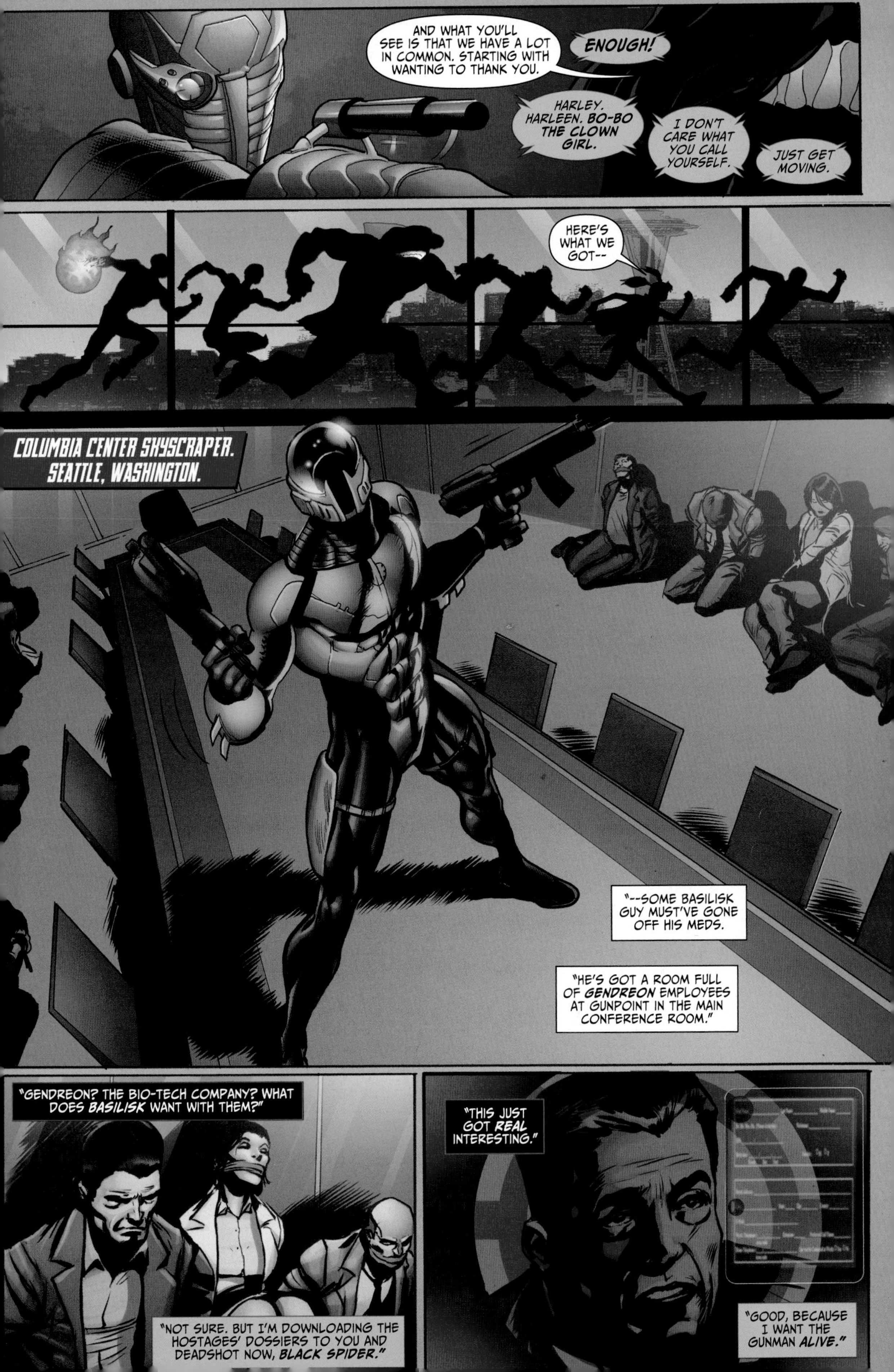
AND WHAT YOU'LL SEE IS THAT WE HAVE A LOT IN COMMON. STARTING WITH WANTING TO THANK YOU.
ENOUGH!
HARLEY. HARLEEN. BO-BO THE CLOWN GIRL.
I DON'T CARE WHAT YOU CALL YOURSELF.
JUST GET MOVING.
HERE'S WHAT WE GOT--
COLUMBIA CENTER SKYSCRAPER. SEATTLE, WASHINGTON.
"--SOME BASILISK GUY MUST'VE GONE OFF HIS MEDS.
"HE'S GOT A ROOM FULL OF GENDREON EMPLOYEES AT GUNPOINT IN THE MAIN CONFERENCE ROOM."
"GENDREON? THE BIO-TECH COMPANY? WHAT DOES BASILISK WANT WITH THEM?"
"NOT SURE. BUT I'M DOWNLOADING THE HOSTAGES' DOSSIERS TO YOU AND DEADSHOT NOW, BLACK SPIDER."
"THIS JUST GOT REAL INTERESTING."
"GOOD, BECAUSE I WANT THE GUNMAN ALIVE."

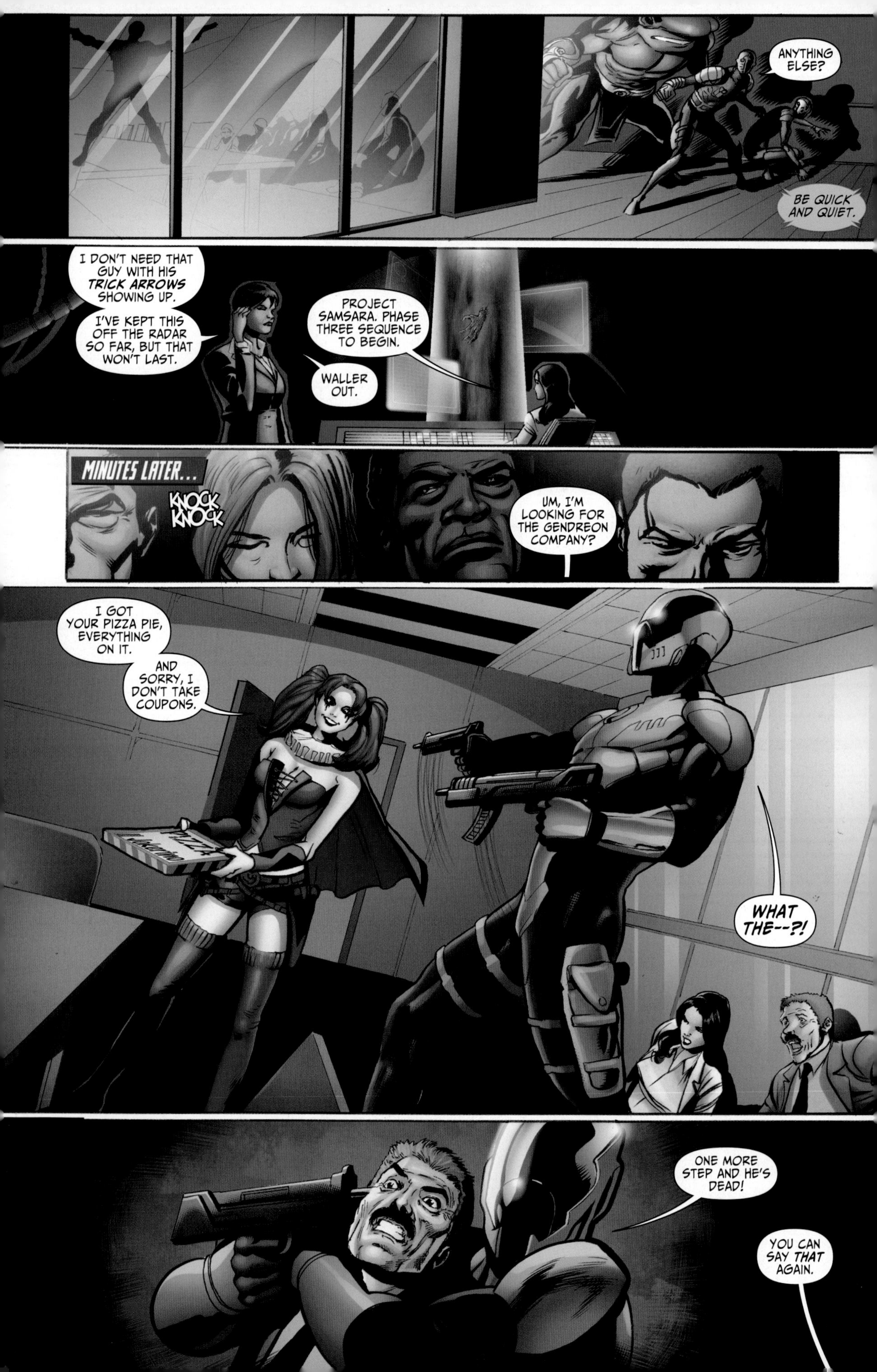

ANYTHING ELSE?
BE QUICK AND QUIET.
I DON'T NEED THAT GUY WITH HIS TRICK ARROWS SHOWING UP.
I'VE KEPT THIS OFF THE RADAR SO FAR, BUT THAT WON'T LAST.
PROJECT SAMSARA. PHASE THREE SEQUENCE TO BEGIN.
WALLER OUT.
MINUTES LATER...
KNOCK KNOCK
UM, I'M LOOKING FOR THE GENDREON COMPANY?
I GOT YOUR PIZZA PIE, EVERYTHING ON IT.
AND SORRY, I DON'T TAKE COUPONS.
PIZZA
WHAT THE--?!
ONE MORE STEP AND HE'S DEAD!
YOU CAN SAY THAT AGAIN.

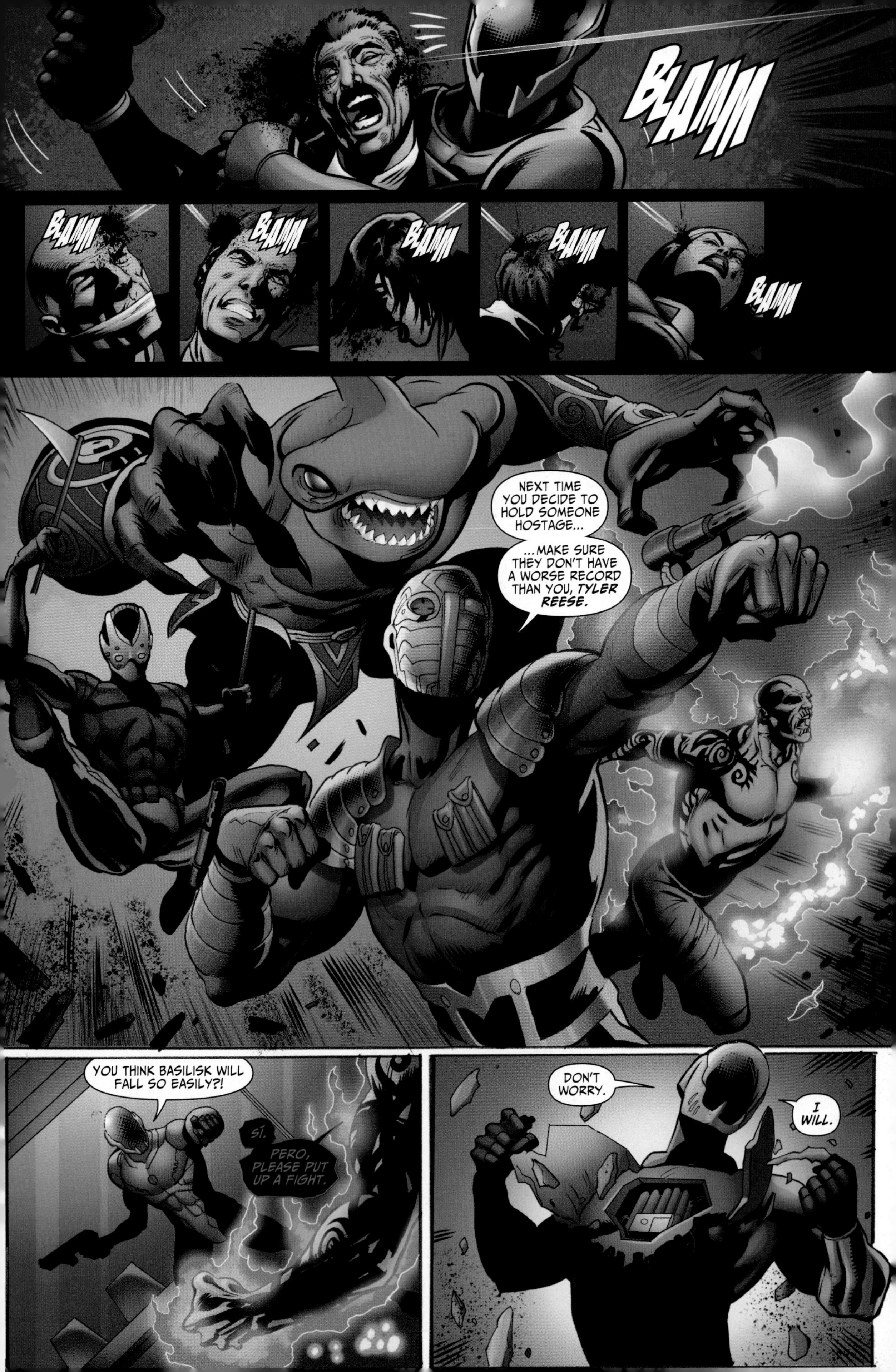
BLAMM
BLAMM
BLAMM
BLAMM
BLAMM
BLAMM
NEXT TIME YOU DECIDE TO HOLD SOMEONE HOSTAGE...
...MAKE SURE THEY DON'T HAVE A WORSE RECORD THAN YOU, TYLER REESE.
YOU THINK BASILISK WILL FALL SO EASILY?!
SÍ.
PERO, PLEASE PUT UP A FIGHT.
DON'T WORRY.
I WILL.

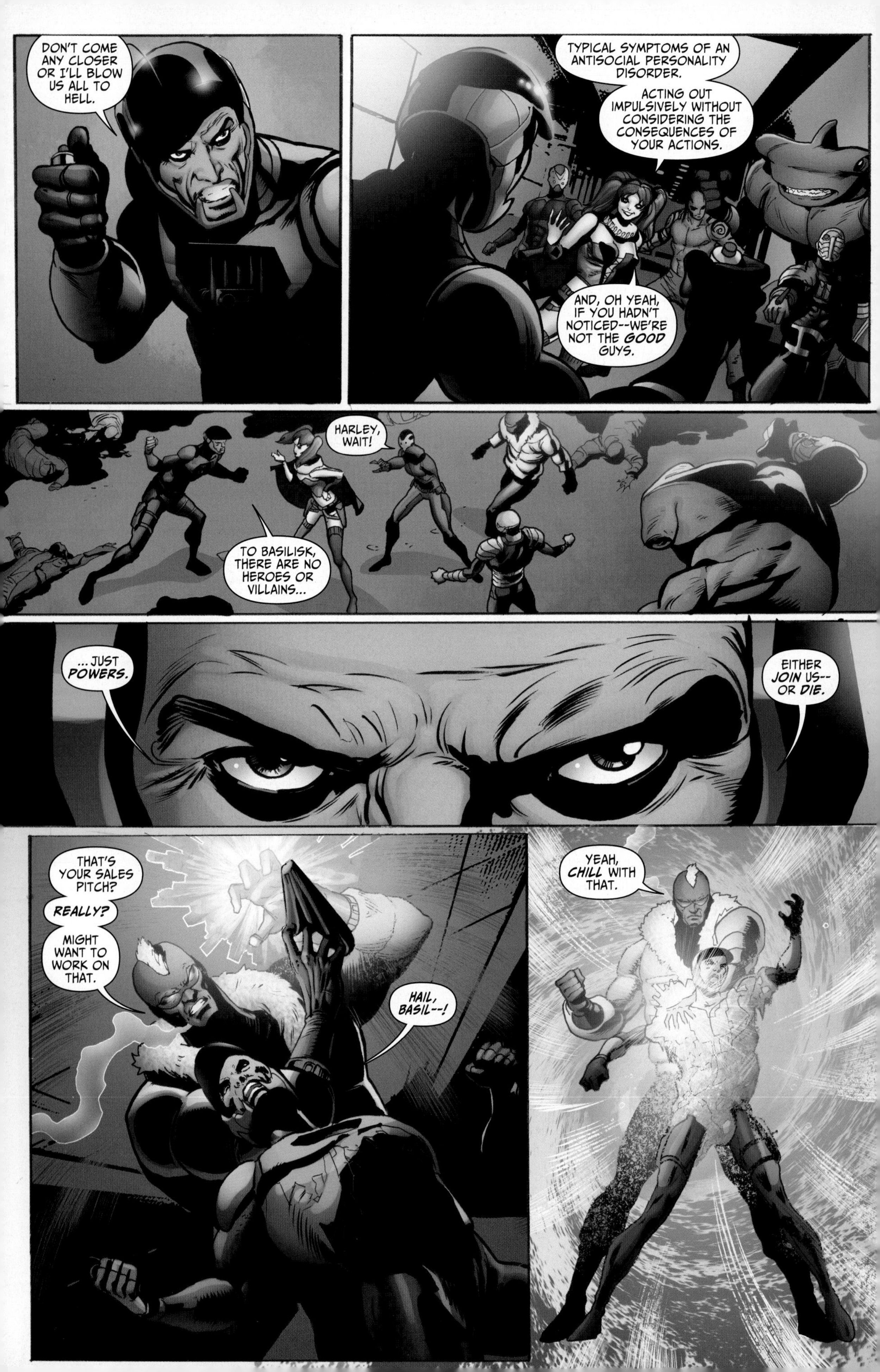
DON'T COME ANY CLOSER OR I'LL BLOW US ALL TO HELL.
TYPICAL SYMPTOMS OF AN ANTISOCIAL PERSONALITY DISORDER.
ACTING OUT IMPULSIVELY WITHOUT CONSIDERING THE CONSEQUENCES OF YOUR ACTIONS.
AND, OH YEAH, IF YOU HADN'T NOTICED--WE'RE NOT THE GOOD GUYS.
HARLEY, WAIT!
TO BASILISK, THERE ARE NO HEROES OR VILLAINS...
...JUST POWERS.
EITHER JOIN US-- OR DIE.
THAT'S YOUR SALES PITCH?
REALLY?
MIGHT WANT TO WORK ON THAT.
HAIL, BASIL--!
YEAH, CHILL WITH THAT.

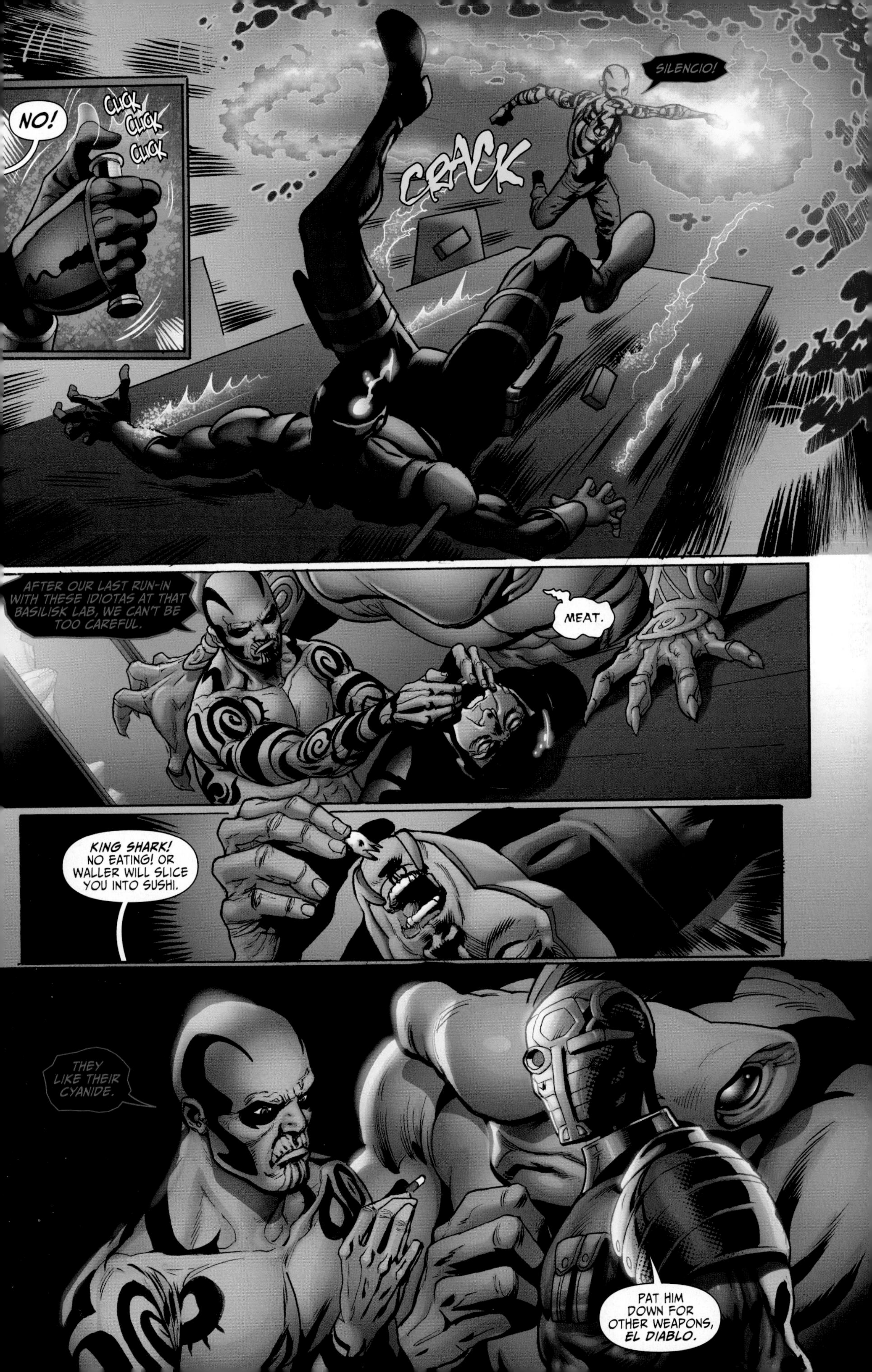
NO!
CLICK
CLICK
CLICK
SILENCIO!
CRACK
AFTER OUR LAST RUN-IN WITH THESE IDIOTAS AT THAT BASILISK LAB, WE CAN'T BE TOO CAREFUL.
MEAT.
KING SHARK! NO EATING! OR WALLER WILL SLICE YOU INTO SUSHI.
THEY LIKE THEIR CYANIDE.
PAT HIM DOWN FOR OTHER WEAPONS, EL DIABLO.

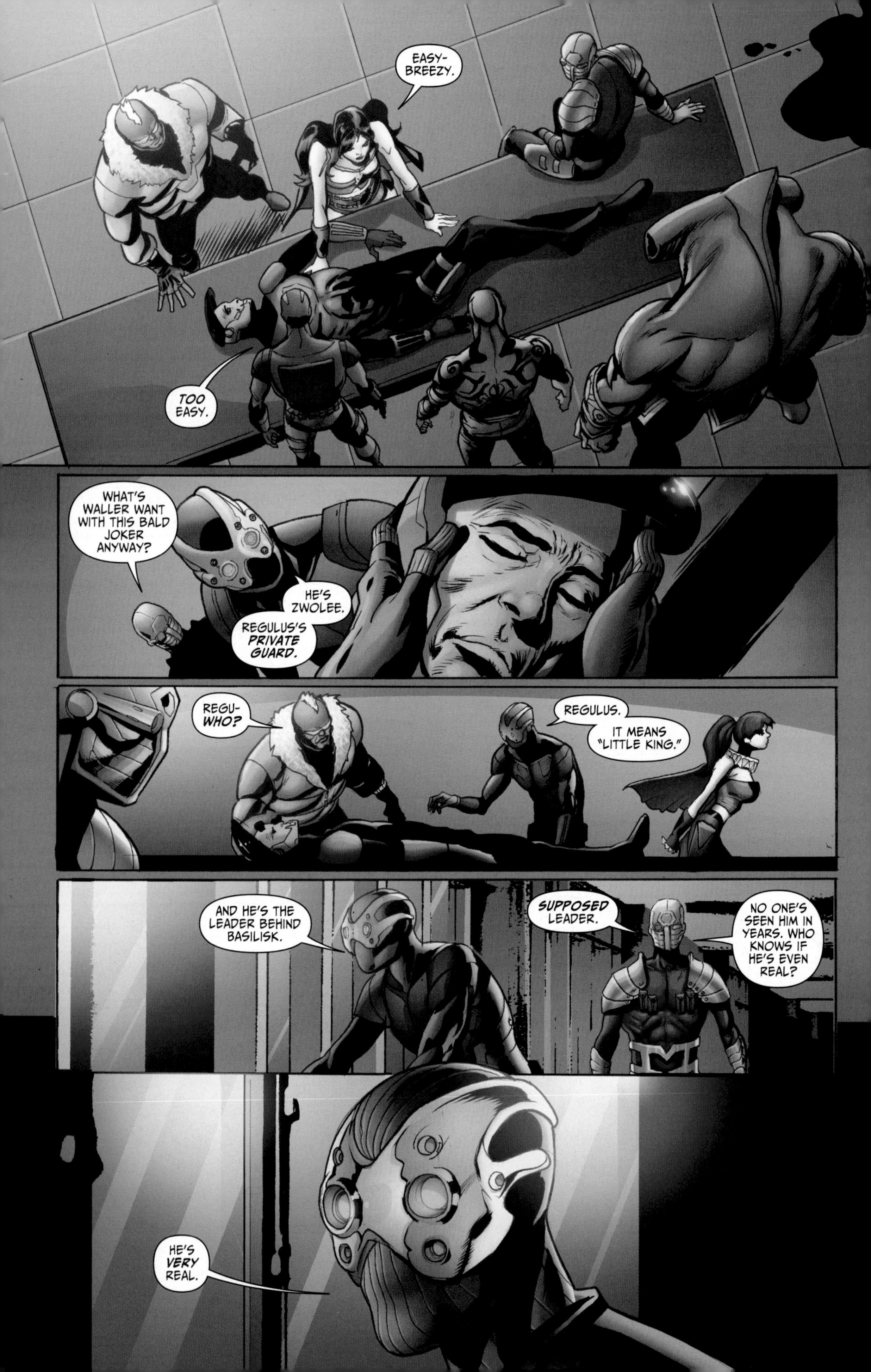
EASY-BREEZY.
TOO EASY.
WHAT'S WALLER WANT WITH THIS BALD JOKER ANYWAY?
HE'S ZWOLEE.
REGULUS'S PRIVATE GUARD.
REGU-WHO?
REGULUS.
IT MEANS "LITTLE KING."
AND HE'S THE LEADER BEHIND BASILISK.
SUPPOSED LEADER.
NO ONE'S SEEN HIM IN YEARS. WHO KNOWS IF HE'S EVEN REAL?
HE'S VERY REAL.

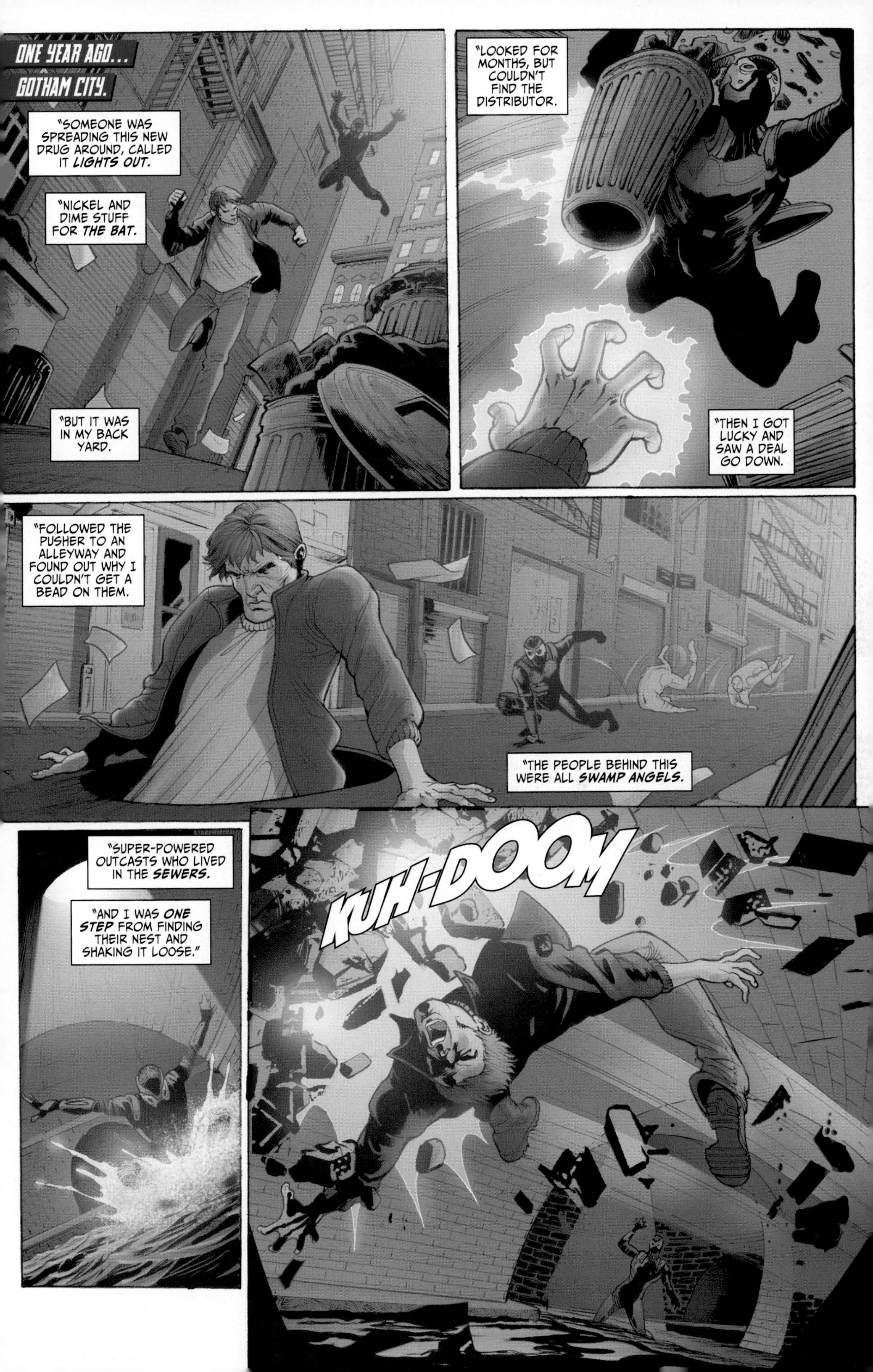
ONE YEAR AGO...
GOTHAM CITY.
"SOMEONE WAS SPREADING THIS NEW DRUG AROUND, CALLED IT LIGHTS OUT.
"NICKEL AND DIME STUFF FOR THE BAT.
"BUT IT WAS IN MY BACK YARD.
"LOOKED FOR MONTHS, BUT COULDN'T FIND THE DISTRIBUTOR.
"THEN I GOT LUCKY AND SAW A DEAL GO DOWN.
"FOLLOWED THE PUSHER TO AN ALLEYWAY AND FOUND OUT WHY I COULDN'T GET A BEAD ON THEM.
"THE PEOPLE BEHIND THIS WERE ALL SWAMP ANGELS.
"SUPER-POWERED OUTCASTS WHO LIVED IN THE SEWERS.
"AND I WAS ONE STEP FROM FINDING THEIR NEST AND SHAKING IT LOOSE."
KUH-DOOM

"BUT SOMEONE *BEAT* ME THERE.

SLINK

SLINK

BLACK *SPIDER.*

YEAH. AND YOU *ARE?!*

DEATH.

"LIKE TO SAY IT WAS A FIGHT.

"BUT IT WAS MORE OF AN *ASS-KICKING.*

"I COULDN'T *TOUCH* THE GUY.

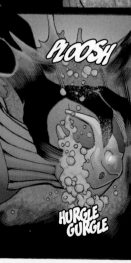

PLOOSH

HURGLE GURGLE

"THEN DUMB LUCK *SAVED* ME."

FOOOOOSH

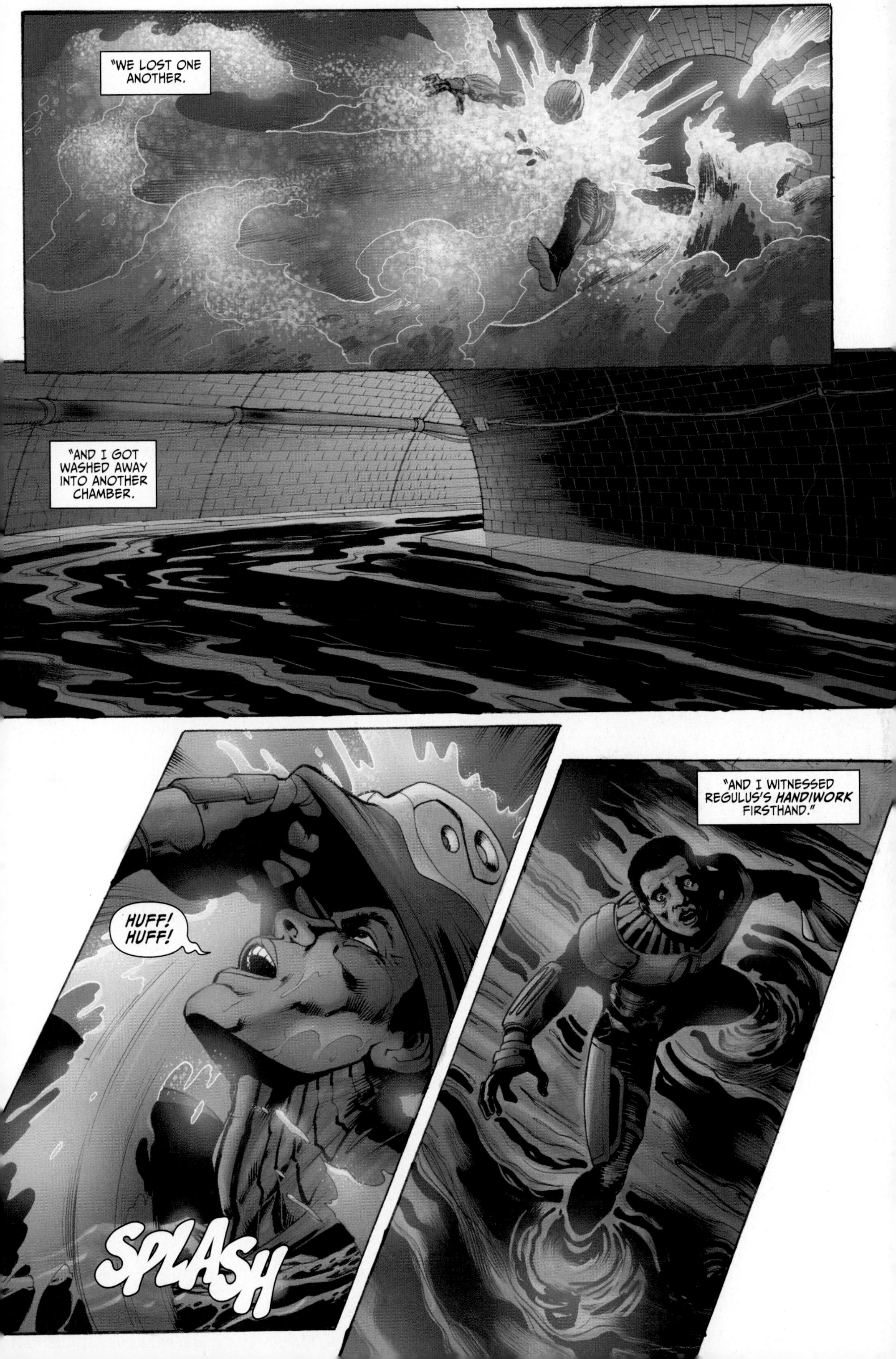
"WE LOST ONE ANOTHER.
"AND I GOT WASHED AWAY INTO ANOTHER CHAMBER.
HUFF! HUFF!
SPLASH
"AND I WITNESSED REGULUS'S *HANDIWORK* FIRSTHAND."

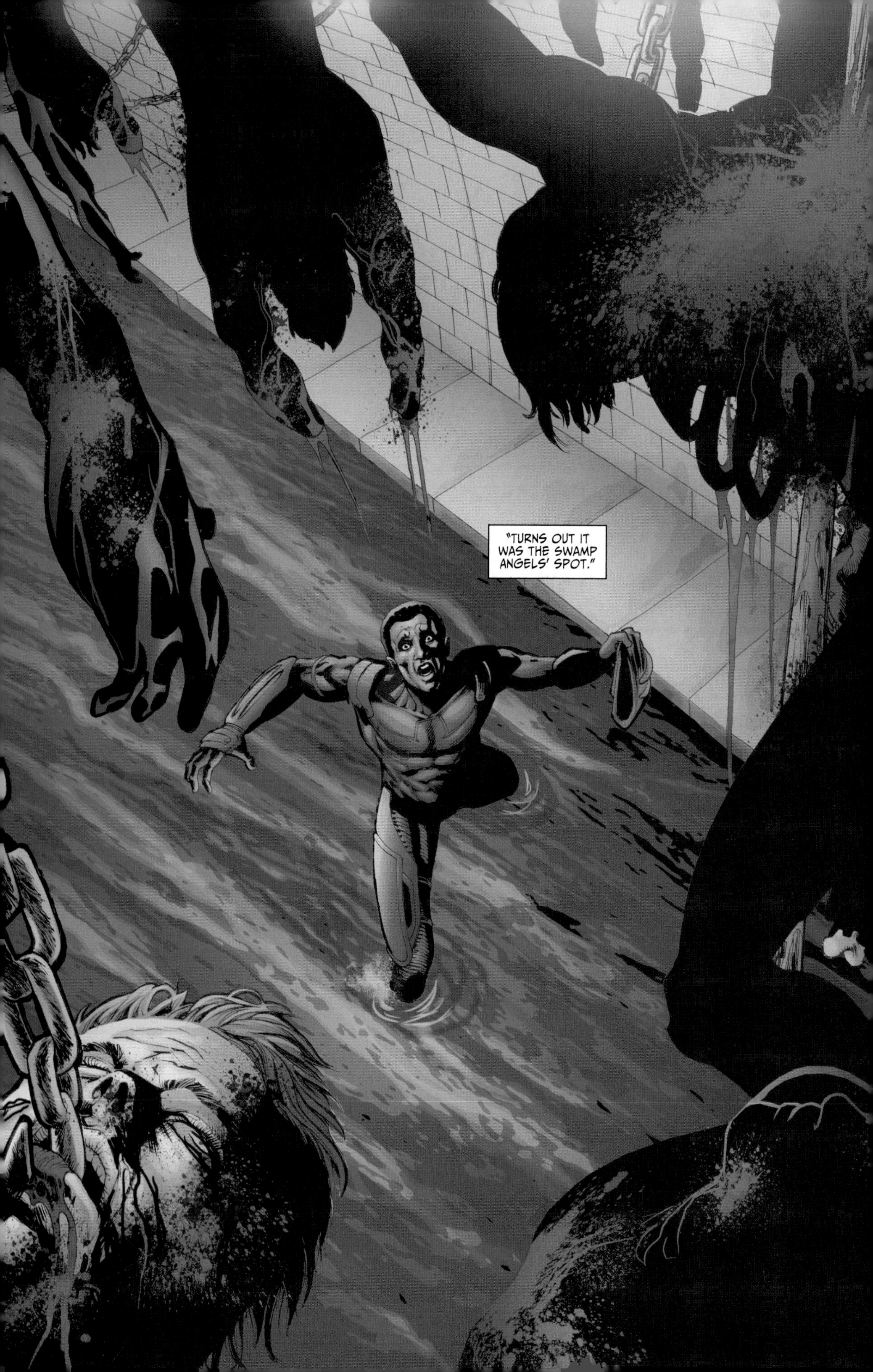
"TURNS OUT IT WAS THE SWAMP ANGELS' SPOT."

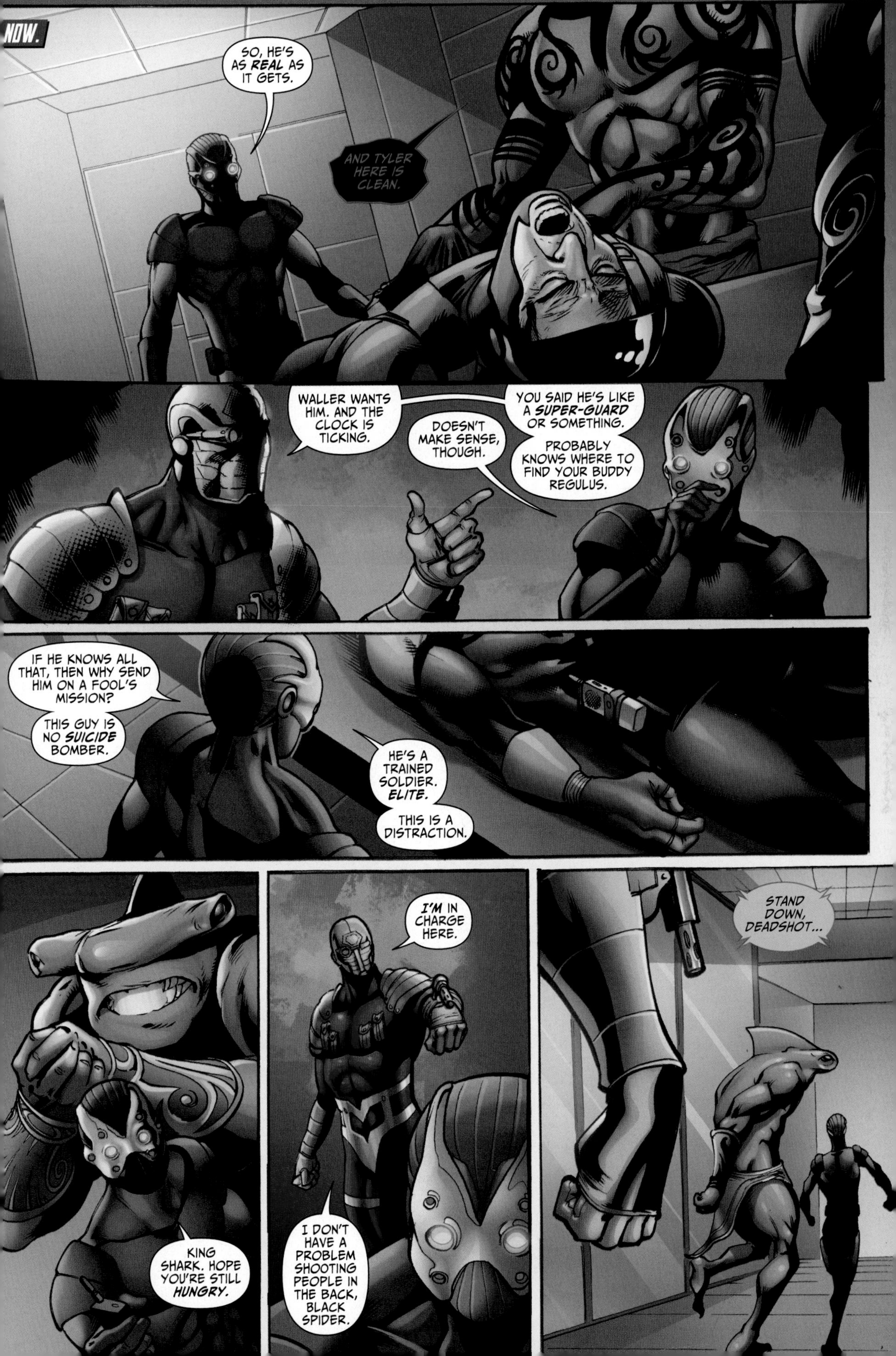
NOW.
SO, HE'S AS **REAL** AS IT GETS.
AND TYLER HERE IS CLEAN.
WALLER WANTS HIM. AND THE CLOCK IS TICKING.
YOU SAID HE'S LIKE A **SUPER-GUARD** OR SOMETHING.
DOESN'T MAKE SENSE, THOUGH.
PROBABLY KNOWS WHERE TO FIND YOUR BUDDY REGULUS.
IF HE KNOWS ALL THAT, THEN WHY SEND HIM ON A FOOL'S MISSION?
THIS GUY IS NO **SUICIDE** BOMBER.
HE'S A TRAINED SOLDIER. **ELITE.**
THIS IS A DISTRACTION.
KING SHARK. HOPE YOU'RE STILL **HUNGRY.**
I'M IN CHARGE HERE.
I DON'T HAVE A PROBLEM SHOOTING PEOPLE IN THE BACK, BLACK SPIDER.
STAND DOWN, DEADSHOT...

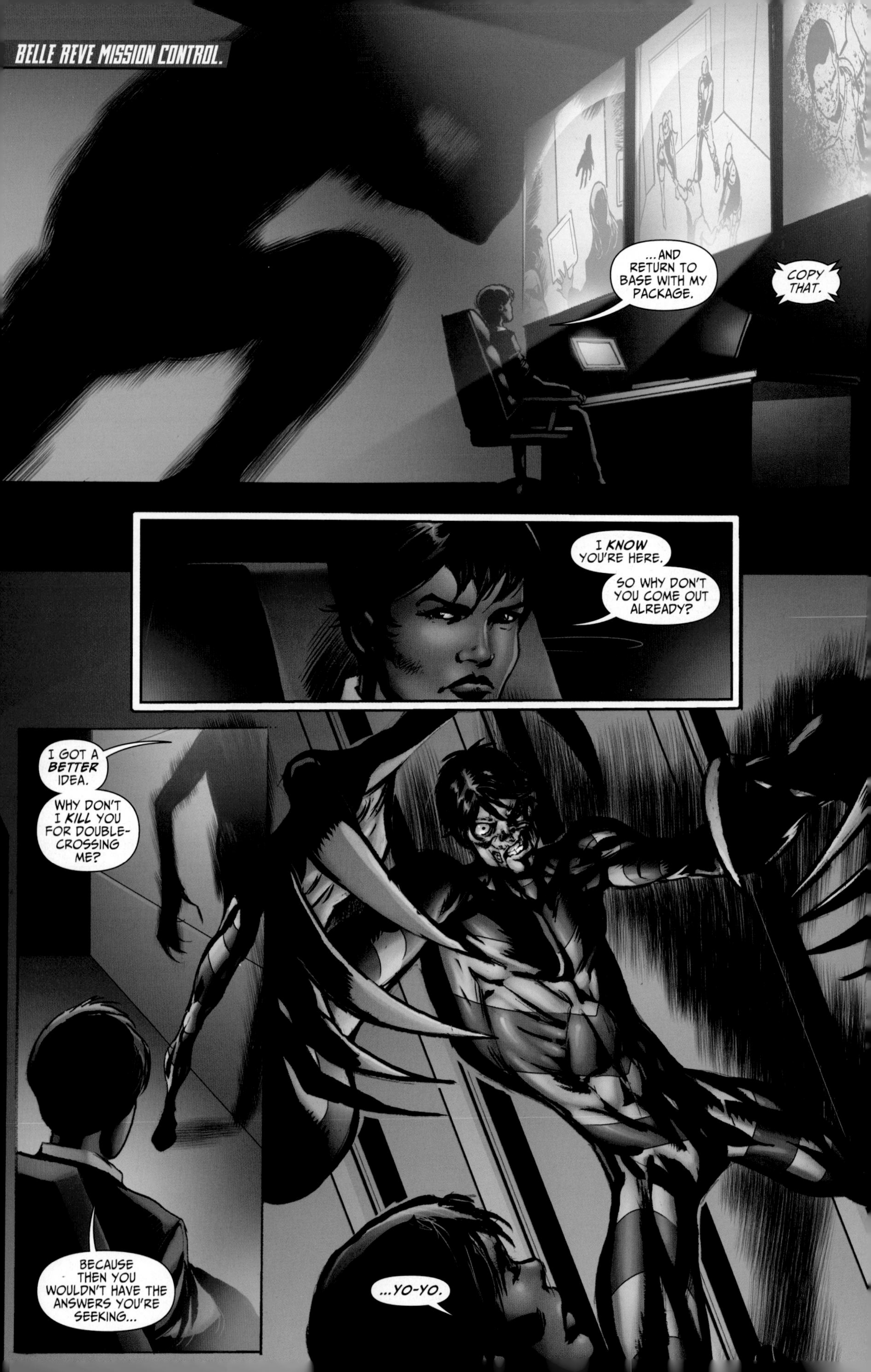
BELLE REVE MISSION CONTROL.
...AND RETURN TO BASE WITH MY PACKAGE.
COPY THAT.
I KNOW YOU'RE HERE.
SO WHY DON'T YOU COME OUT ALREADY?
I GOT A BETTER IDEA.
WHY DON'T I KILL YOU FOR DOUBLE-CROSSING ME?
BECAUSE THEN YOU WOULDN'T HAVE THE ANSWERS YOU'RE SEEKING...
...YO-YO.

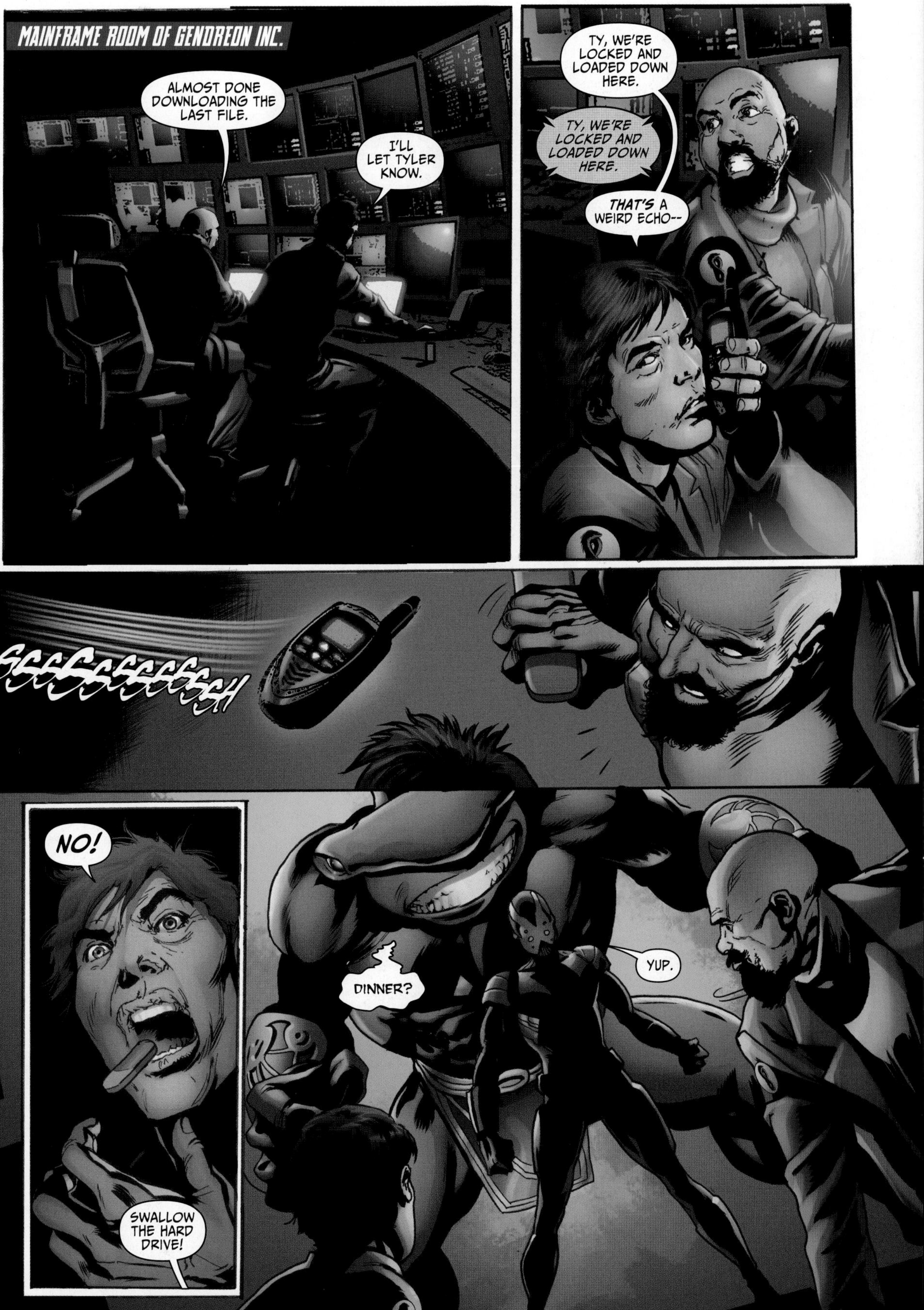
MAINFRAME ROOM OF GENDREON INC.
ALMOST DONE DOWNLOADING THE LAST FILE.
I'LL LET TYLER KNOW.
TY, WE'RE LOCKED AND LOADED DOWN HERE.
TY, WE'RE LOCKED AND LOADED DOWN HERE.
THAT'S A WEIRD ECHO--
SSSSSSSSSSSSCH
NO!
SWALLOW THE HARD DRIVE!
DINNER?
YUP.

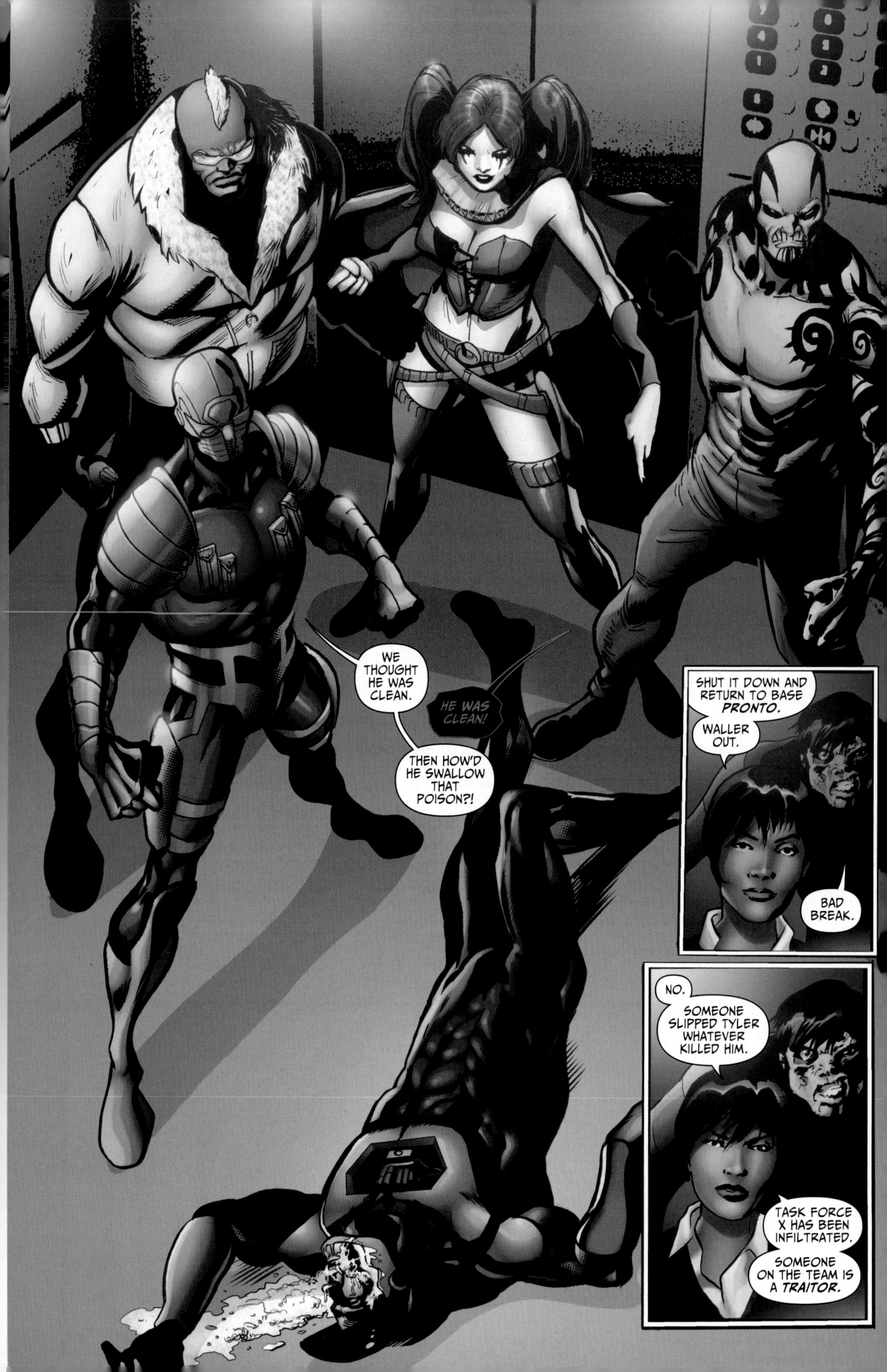
WE THOUGHT HE WAS CLEAN.
HE WAS CLEAN!
THEN HOW'D HE SWALLOW THAT POISON?!
SHUT IT DOWN AND RETURN TO BASE PRONTO.
WALLER OUT.
BAD BREAK.
NO.
SOMEONE SLIPPED TYLER WHATEVER KILLED HIM.
TASK FORCE X HAS BEEN INFILTRATED.
SOMEONE ON THE TEAM IS A TRAITOR.

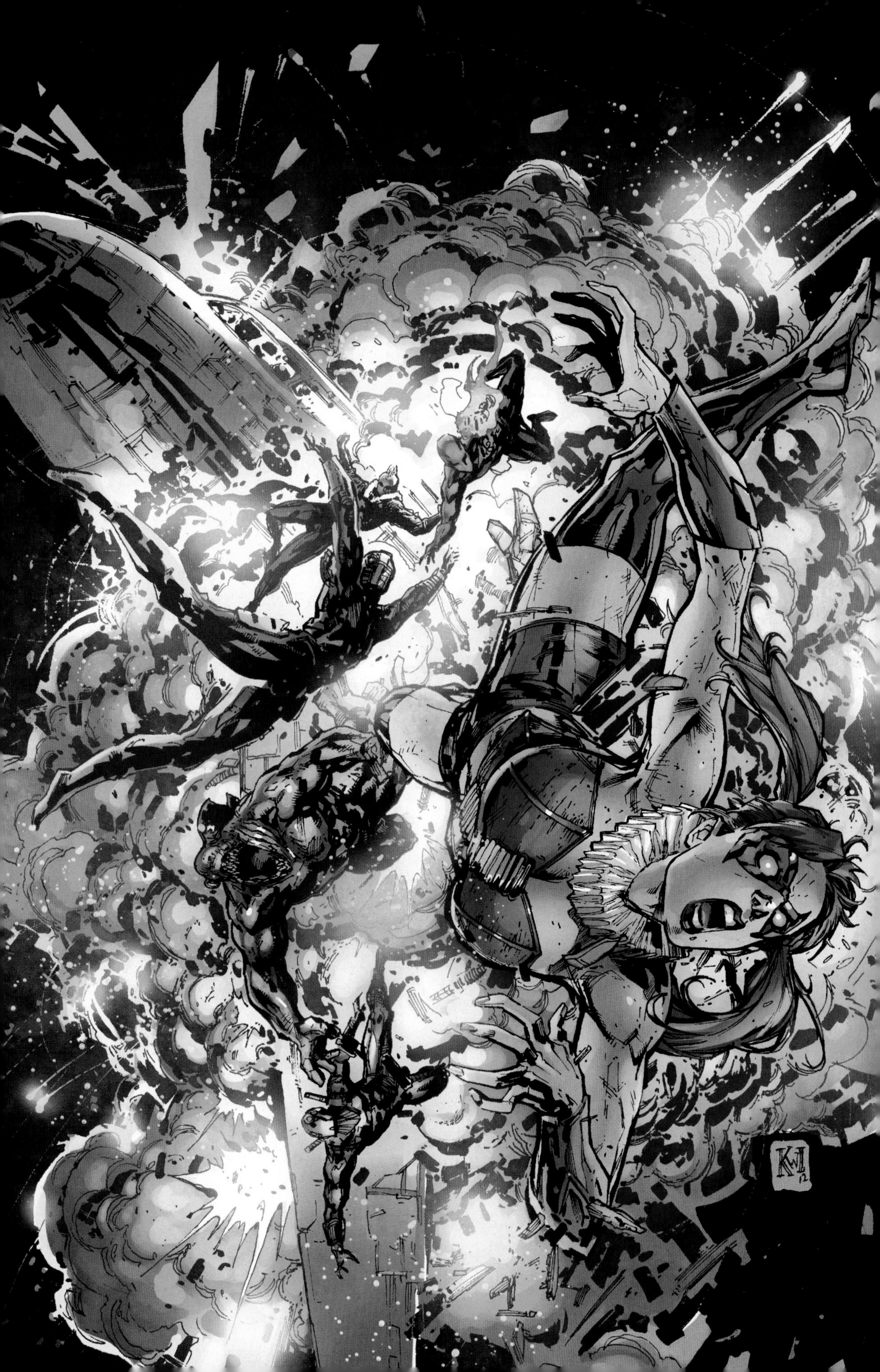

COMMUNICATION BREAKDOWN

ADAM GLASS
writer

CARLOS RODRIGUEZ
artist

cover art by KEN LASHLEY & ROD REIS

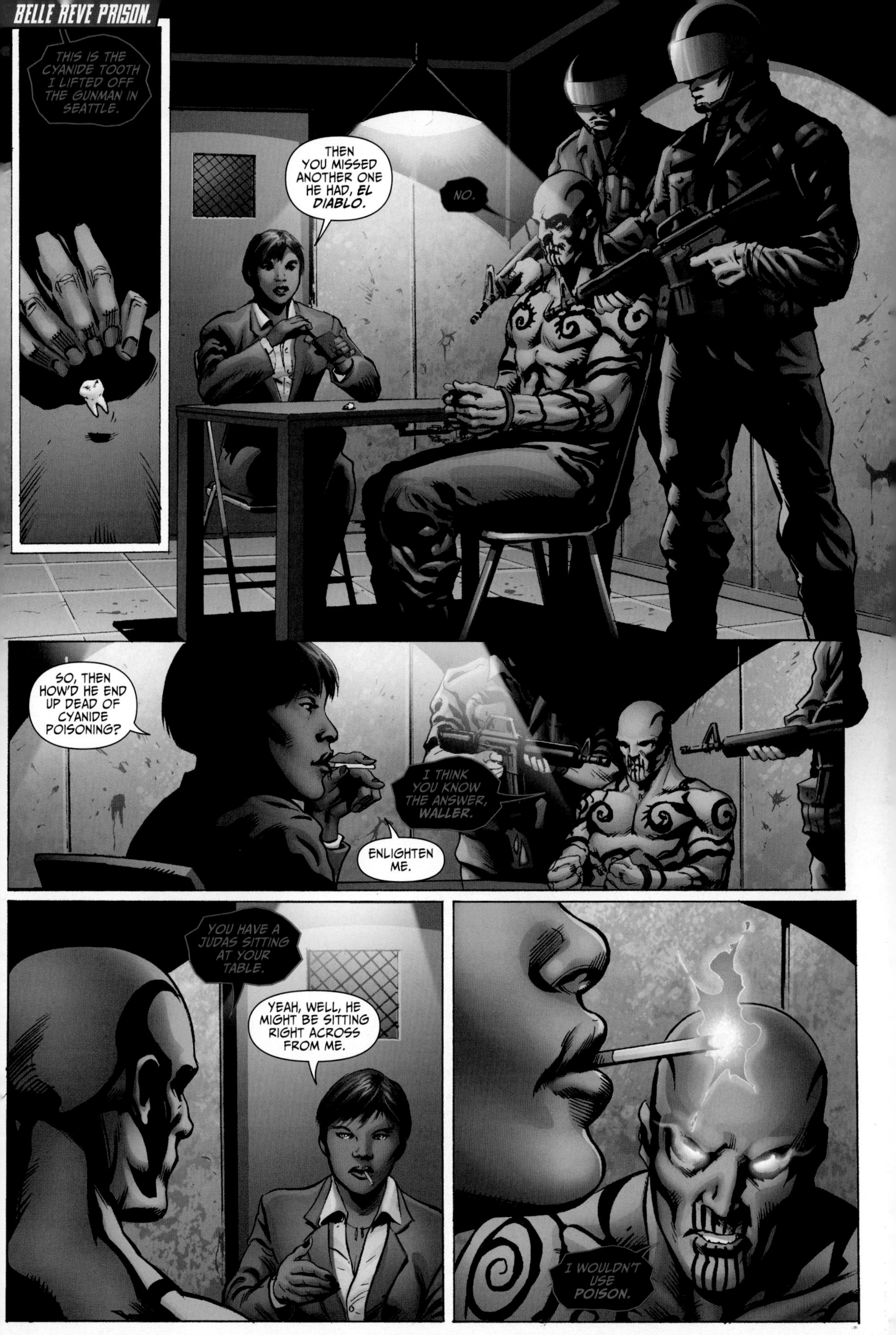
BELLE REVE PRISON.
THIS IS THE CYANIDE TOOTH I LIFTED OFF THE GUNMAN IN SEATTLE.
THEN YOU MISSED ANOTHER ONE HE HAD, EL DIABLO.
NO.
SO, THEN HOW'D HE END UP DEAD OF CYANIDE POISONING?
I THINK YOU KNOW THE ANSWER, WALLER.
ENLIGHTEN ME.
YOU HAVE A JUDAS SITTING AT YOUR TABLE.
YEAH, WELL, HE MIGHT BE SITTING RIGHT ACROSS FROM ME.
I WOULDN'T USE POISON.

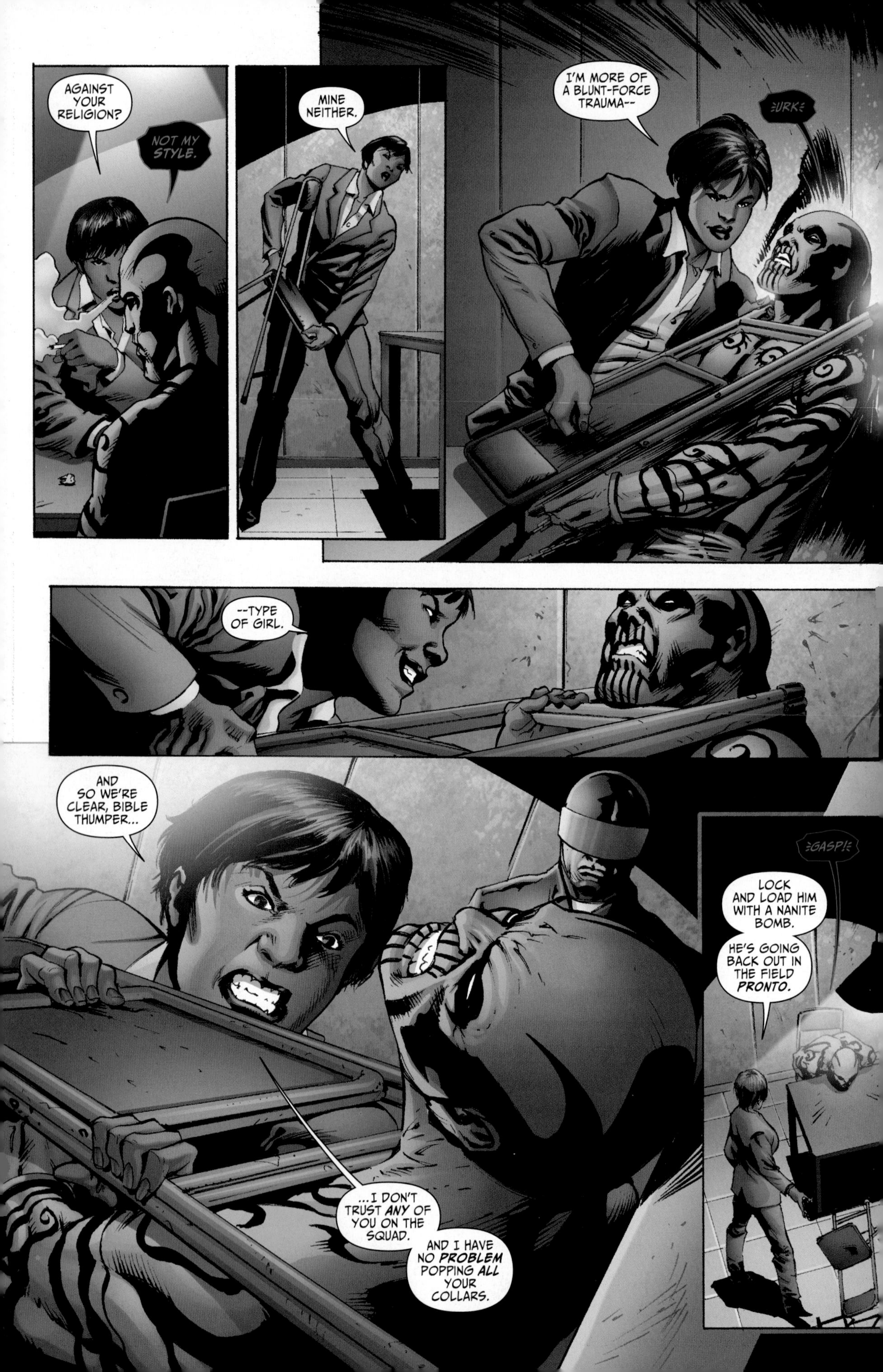
AGAINST YOUR RELIGION?
NOT MY STYLE.
MINE NEITHER.
I'M MORE OF A BLUNT-FORCE TRAUMA--
URK
--TYPE OF GIRL.
AND SO WE'RE CLEAR, BIBLE THUMPER...
...I DON'T TRUST ANY OF YOU ON THE SQUAD.
AND I HAVE NO PROBLEM POPPING ALL YOUR COLLARS.
GASP!
LOCK AND LOAD HIM WITH A NANITE BOMB.
HE'S GOING BACK OUT IN THE FIELD PRONTO.

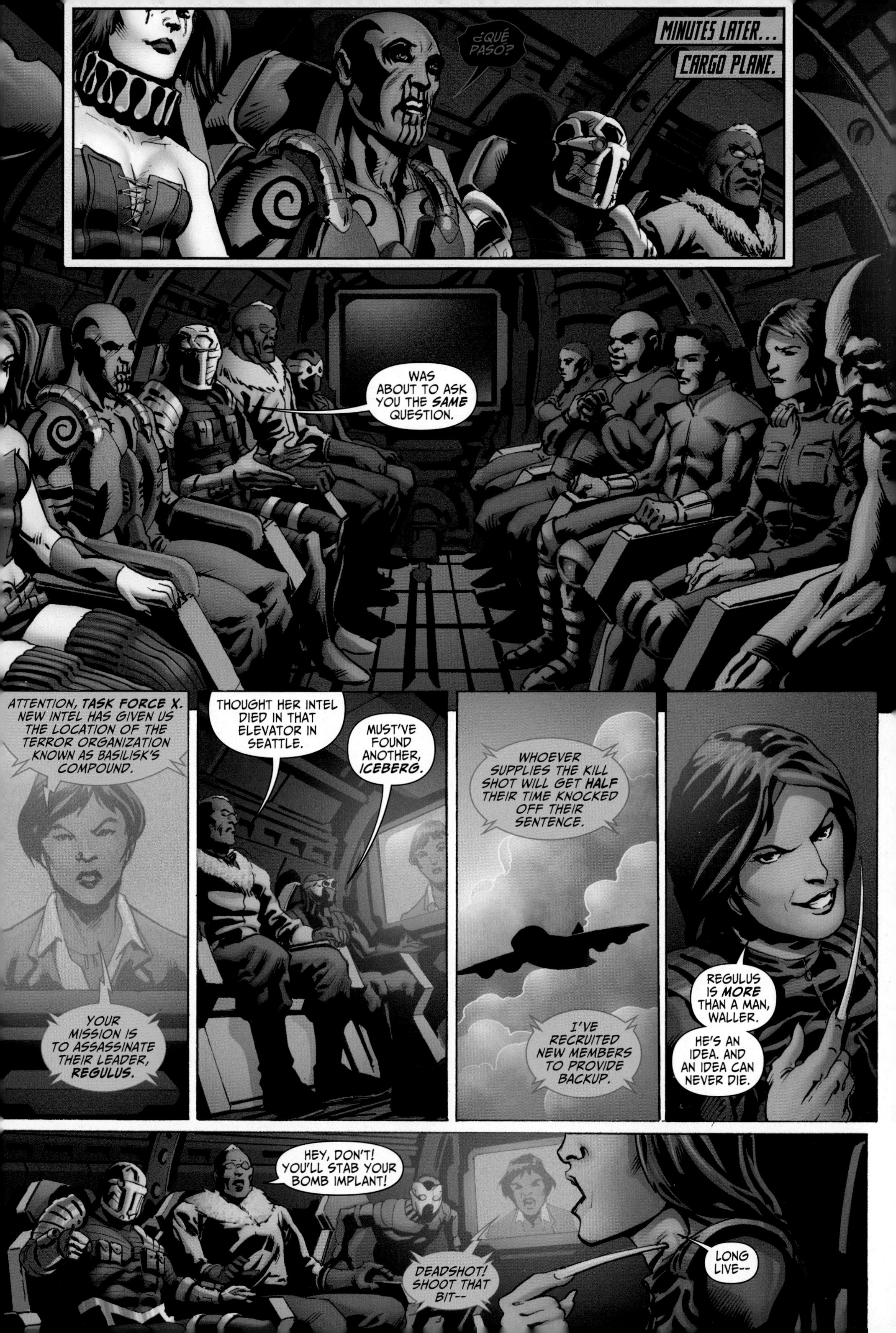
MINUTES LATER...
CARGO PLANE.
¿QUÉ PASO?
WAS ABOUT TO ASK YOU THE SAME QUESTION.
ATTENTION, TASK FORCE X. NEW INTEL HAS GIVEN US THE LOCATION OF THE TERROR ORGANIZATION KNOWN AS BASILISK'S COMPOUND.
YOUR MISSION IS TO ASSASSINATE THEIR LEADER, REGULUS.
THOUGHT HER INTEL DIED IN THAT ELEVATOR IN SEATTLE.
MUST'VE FOUND ANOTHER, ICEBERG.
WHOEVER SUPPLIES THE KILL SHOT WILL GET HALF THEIR TIME KNOCKED OFF THEIR SENTENCE.
I'VE RECRUITED NEW MEMBERS TO PROVIDE BACKUP.
REGULUS IS MORE THAN A MAN, WALLER.
HE'S AN IDEA. AND AN IDEA CAN NEVER DIE.
HEY, DON'T! YOU'LL STAB YOUR BOMB IMPLANT!
DEADSHOT! SHOOT THAT BIT--
LONG LIVE--

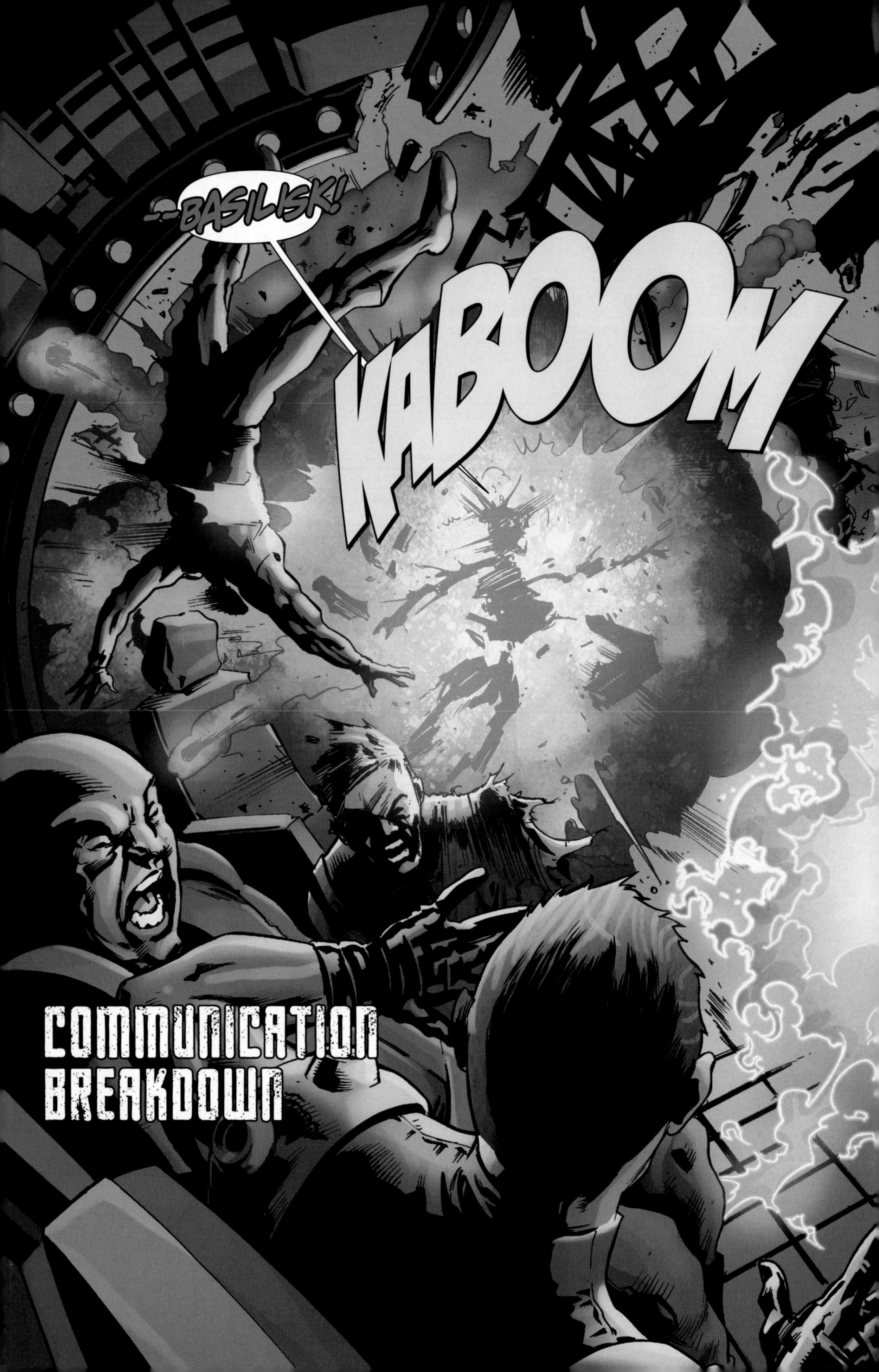
--BASILISK!
KABOOM
COMMUNICATION BREAKDOWN

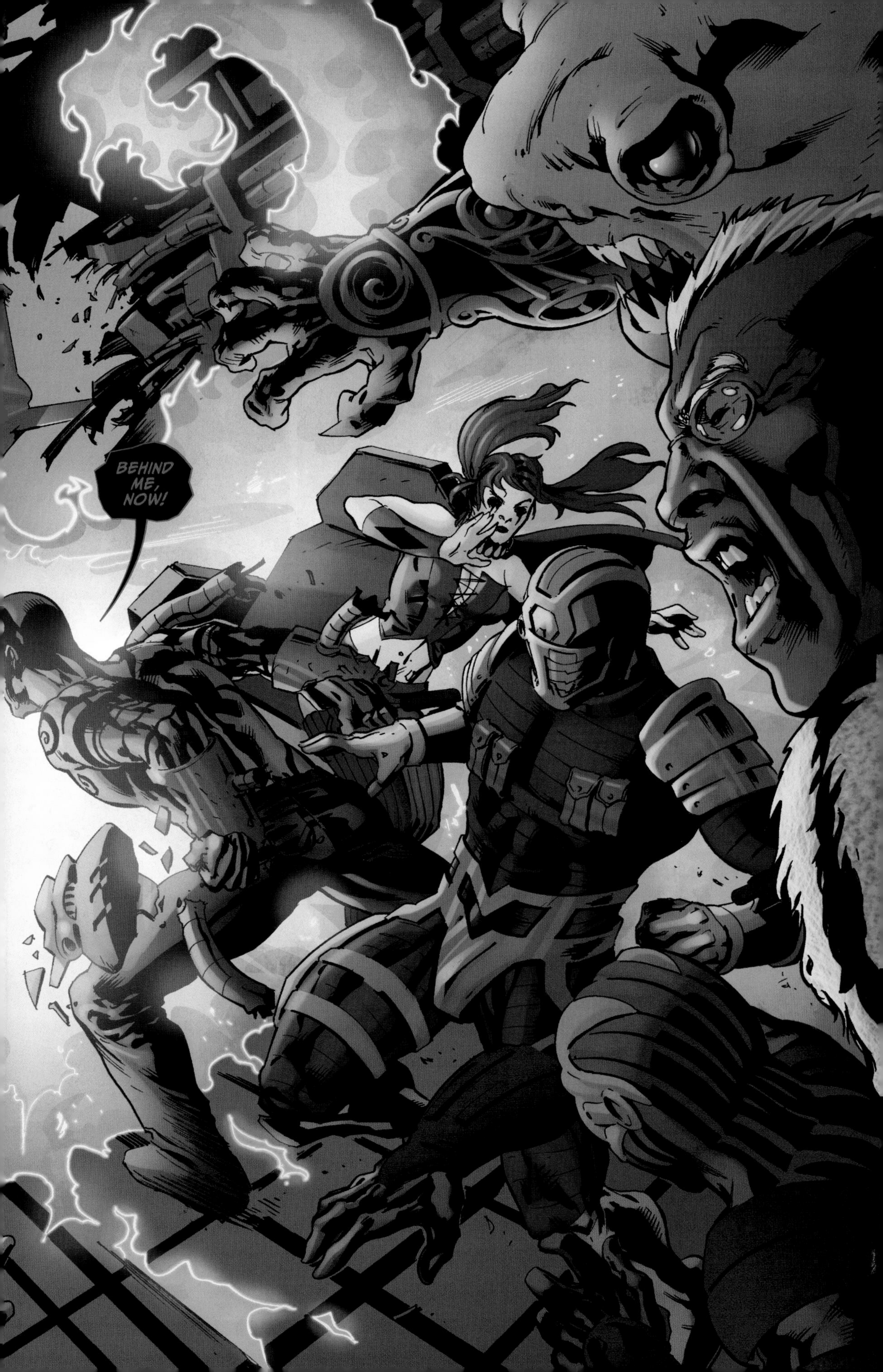
BEHIND ME, NOW!

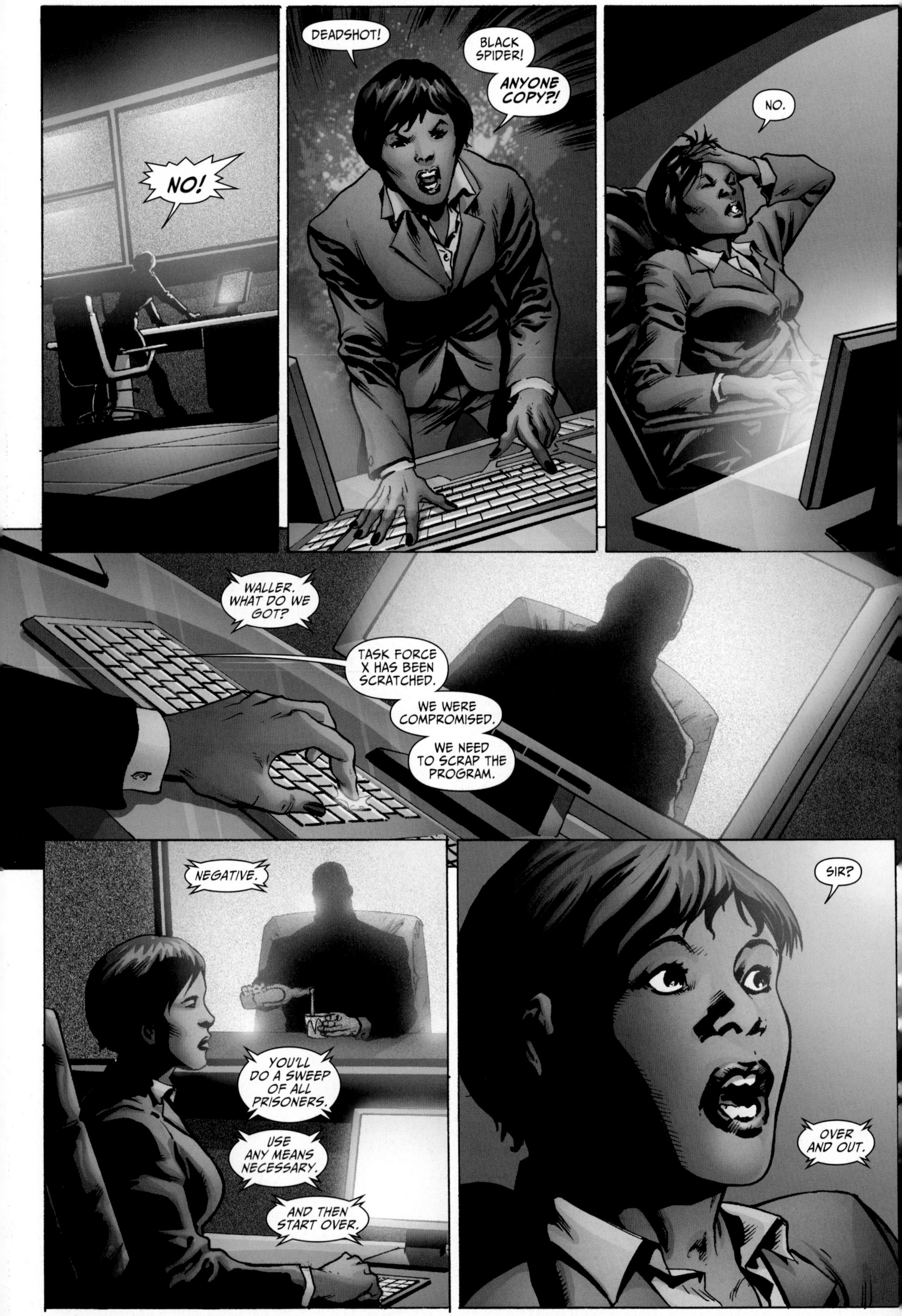
NO!
DEADSHOT!
BLACK SPIDER!
ANYONE COPY?!
NO.
WALLER. WHAT DO WE GOT?
TASK FORCE X HAS BEEN SCRATCHED.
WE WERE COMPROMISED.
WE NEED TO SCRAP THE PROGRAM.
NEGATIVE.
YOU'LL DO A SWEEP OF ALL PRISONERS.
USE ANY MEANS NECESSARY.
AND THEN START OVER.
SIR?
OVER AND OUT.

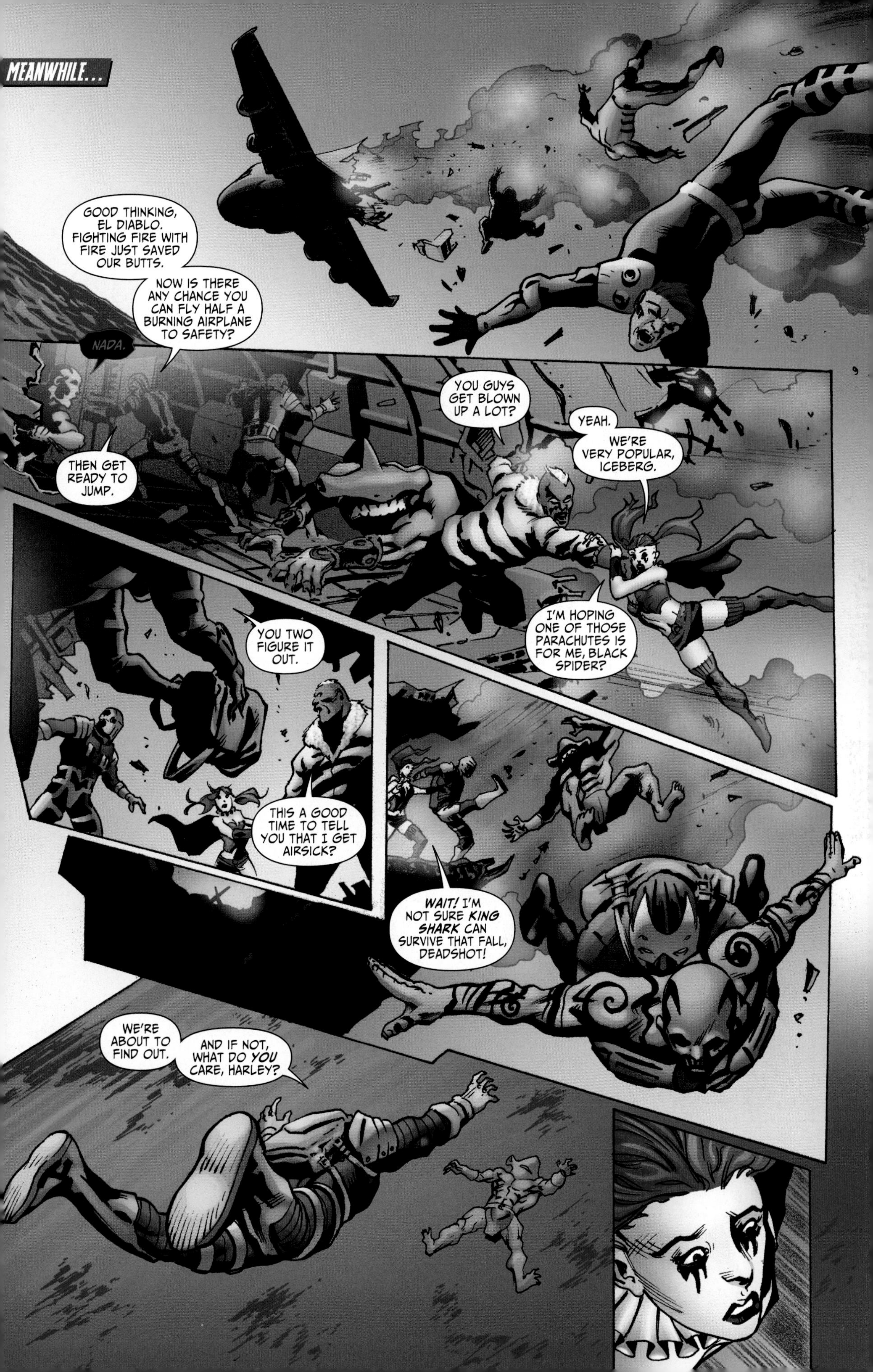
MEANWHILE...
GOOD THINKING, EL DIABLO. FIGHTING FIRE WITH FIRE JUST SAVED OUR BUTTS.
NOW IS THERE ANY CHANCE YOU CAN FLY HALF A BURNING AIRPLANE TO SAFETY?
NADA.
THEN GET READY TO JUMP.
YOU GUYS GET BLOWN UP A LOT?
YEAH.
WE'RE VERY POPULAR, ICEBERG.
I'M HOPING ONE OF THOSE PARACHUTES IS FOR ME, BLACK SPIDER?
YOU TWO FIGURE IT OUT.
THIS A GOOD TIME TO TELL YOU THAT I GET AIRSICK?
WAIT! I'M NOT SURE KING SHARK CAN SURVIVE THAT FALL, DEADSHOT!
WE'RE ABOUT TO FIND OUT.
AND IF NOT, WHAT DO YOU CARE, HARLEY?

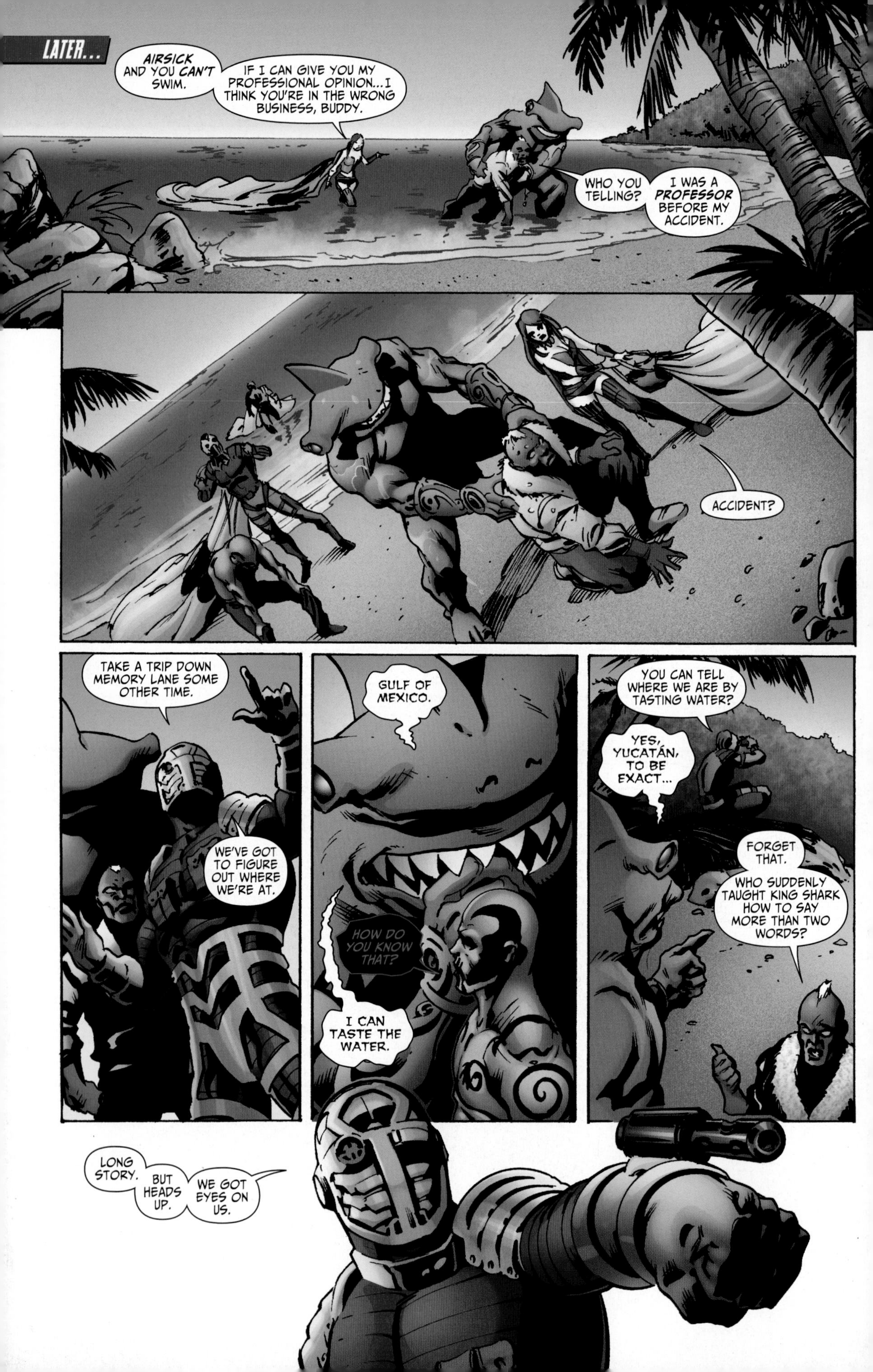
LATER...
AIRSICK AND YOU CAN'T SWIM.
IF I CAN GIVE YOU MY PROFESSIONAL OPINION...I THINK YOU'RE IN THE WRONG BUSINESS, BUDDY.
WHO YOU TELLING?
I WAS A PROFESSOR BEFORE MY ACCIDENT.
ACCIDENT?
TAKE A TRIP DOWN MEMORY LANE SOME OTHER TIME.
WE'VE GOT TO FIGURE OUT WHERE WE'RE AT.
GULF OF MEXICO.
HOW DO YOU KNOW THAT?
I CAN TASTE THE WATER.
YOU CAN TELL WHERE WE ARE BY TASTING WATER?
YES, YUCATÁN, TO BE EXACT...
FORGET THAT.
WHO SUDDENLY TAUGHT KING SHARK HOW TO SAY MORE THAN TWO WORDS?
LONG STORY.
BUT HEADS UP.
WE GOT EYES ON US.

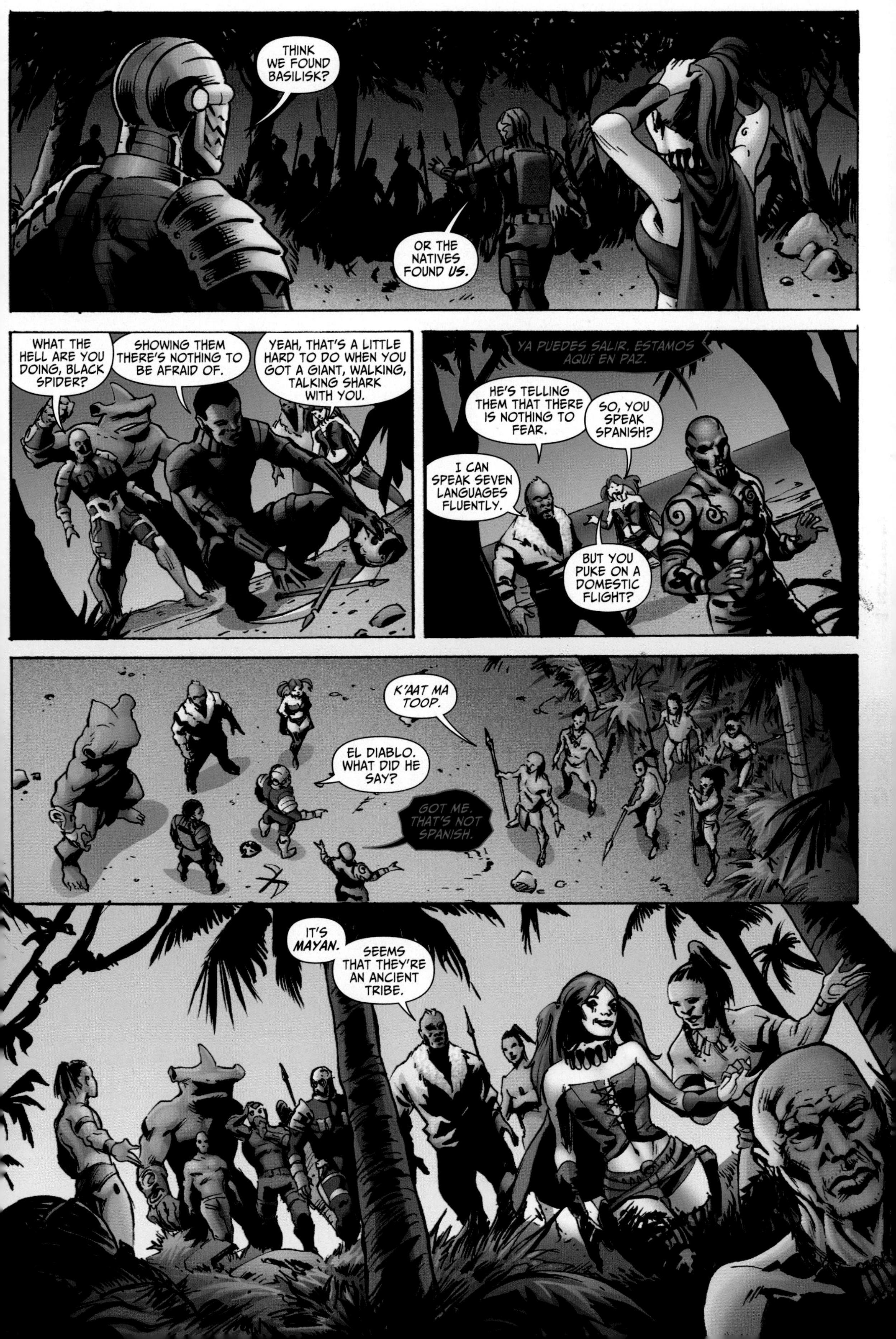
THINK WE FOUND BASILISK?
OR THE NATIVES FOUND *US.*
WHAT THE HELL ARE YOU DOING, BLACK SPIDER?
SHOWING THEM THERE'S NOTHING TO BE AFRAID OF.
YEAH, THAT'S A LITTLE HARD TO DO WHEN YOU GOT A GIANT, WALKING, TALKING SHARK WITH YOU.
YA PUEDES SALIR. ESTAMOS AQUÍ EN PAZ.
HE'S TELLING THEM THAT THERE IS NOTHING TO FEAR.
SO, YOU SPEAK SPANISH?
I CAN SPEAK SEVEN LANGUAGES FLUENTLY.
BUT YOU PUKE ON A DOMESTIC FLIGHT?
K'AAT MA TOOP.
EL DIABLO. WHAT DID HE SAY?
GOT ME. THAT'S NOT SPANISH.
IT'S *MAYAN.*
SEEMS THAT THEY'RE AN ANCIENT TRIBE.

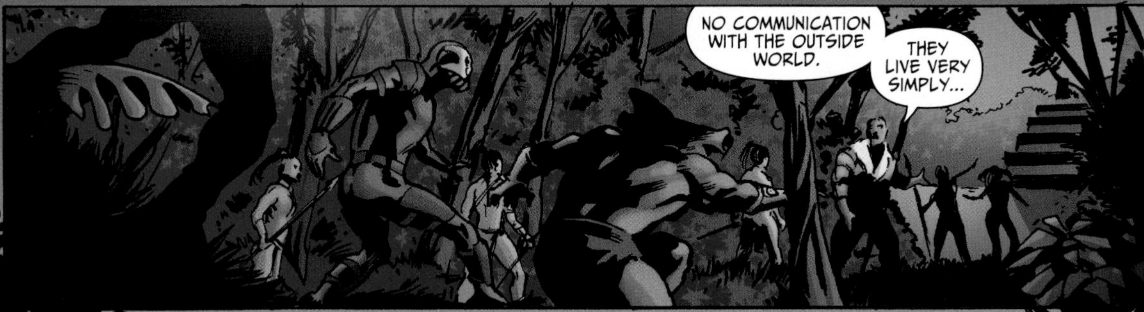
NO COMMUNICATION WITH THE OUTSIDE WORLD.
THEY LIVE VERY SIMPLY...

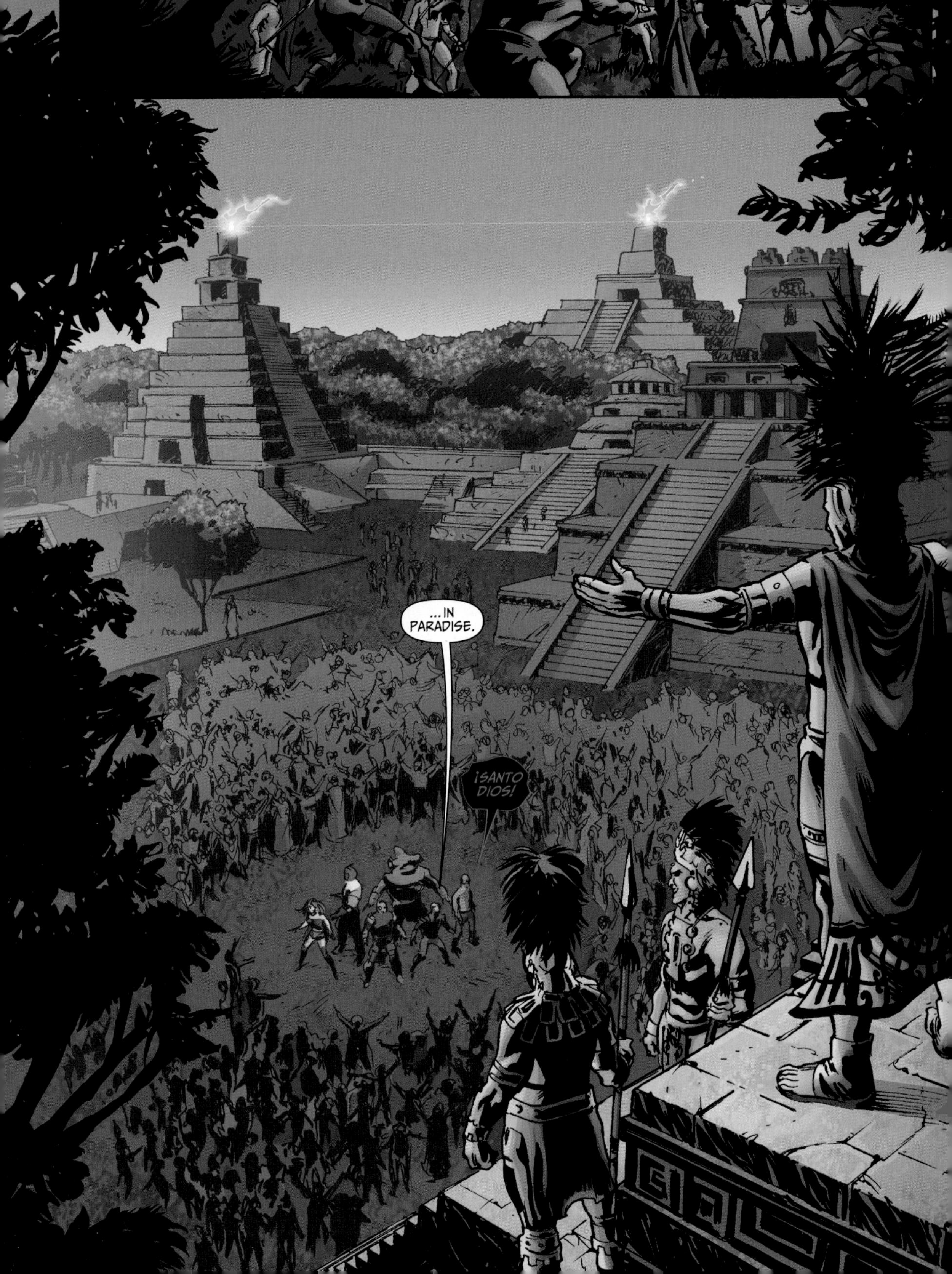
...IN PARADISE.
¡SANTO DIOS!

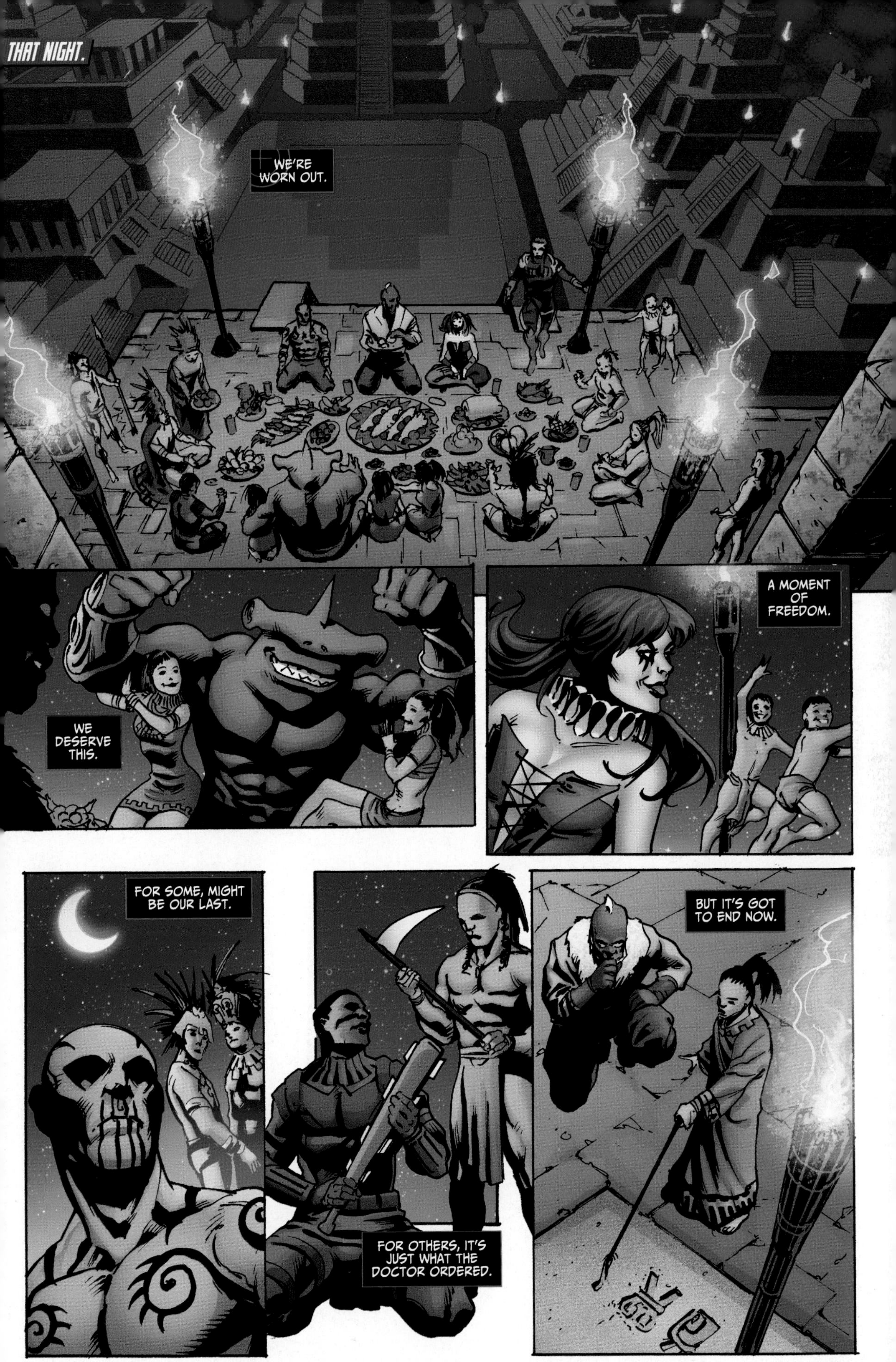
THAT NIGHT.
WE'RE WORN OUT.
WE DESERVE THIS.
A MOMENT OF FREEDOM.
FOR SOME, MIGHT BE OUR LAST.
FOR OTHERS, IT'S JUST WHAT THE DOCTOR ORDERED.
BUT IT'S GOT TO END NOW.

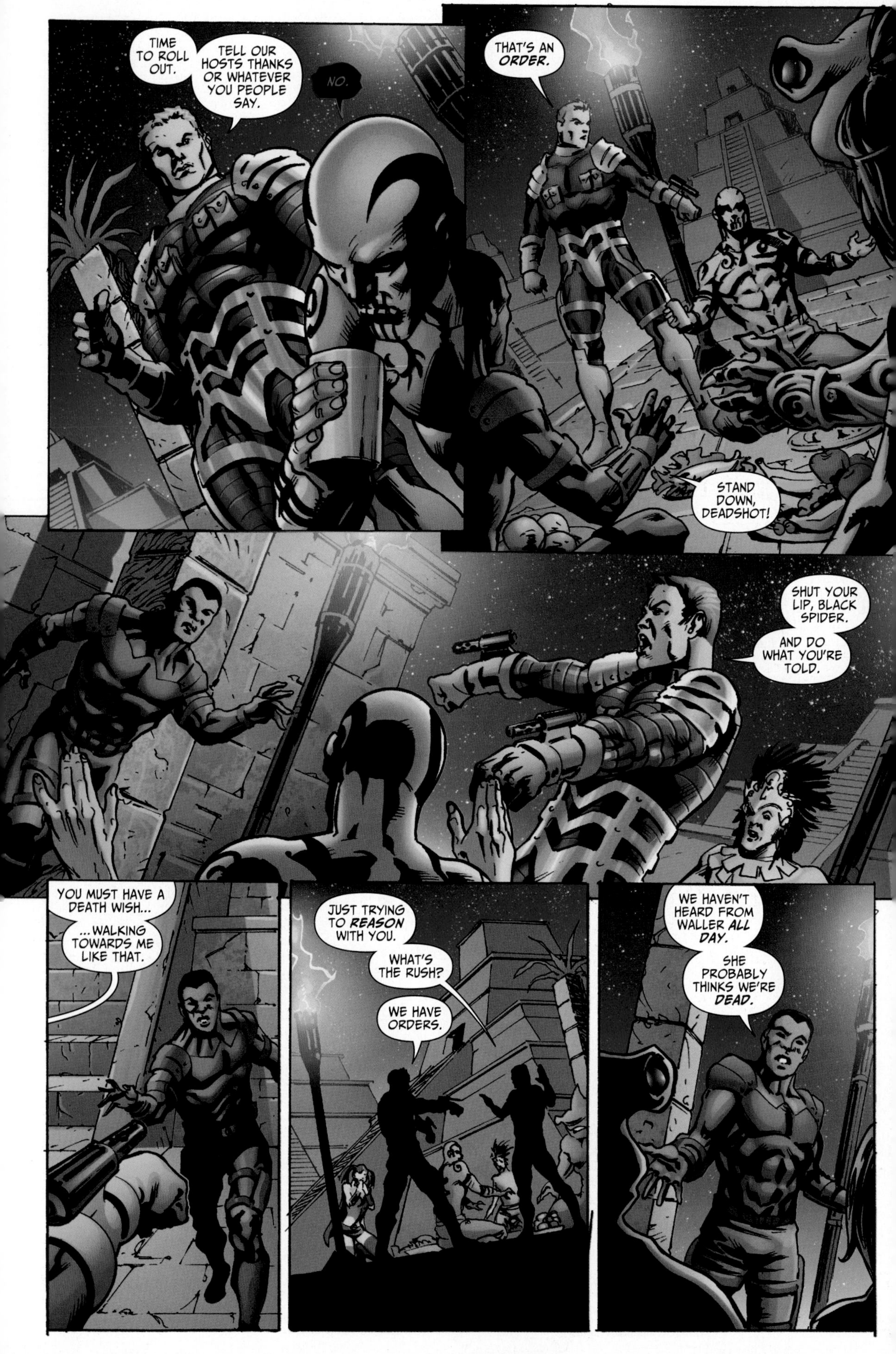
TIME TO ROLL OUT.
TELL OUR HOSTS THANKS OR WHATEVER YOU PEOPLE SAY.
NO.
THAT'S AN ORDER.
STAND DOWN, DEADSHOT!
SHUT YOUR LIP, BLACK SPIDER.
AND DO WHAT YOU'RE TOLD.
YOU MUST HAVE A DEATH WISH...
...WALKING TOWARDS ME LIKE THAT.
JUST TRYING TO REASON WITH YOU.
WHAT'S THE RUSH?
WE HAVE ORDERS.
WE HAVEN'T HEARD FROM WALLER ALL DAY.
SHE PROBABLY THINKS WE'RE DEAD.

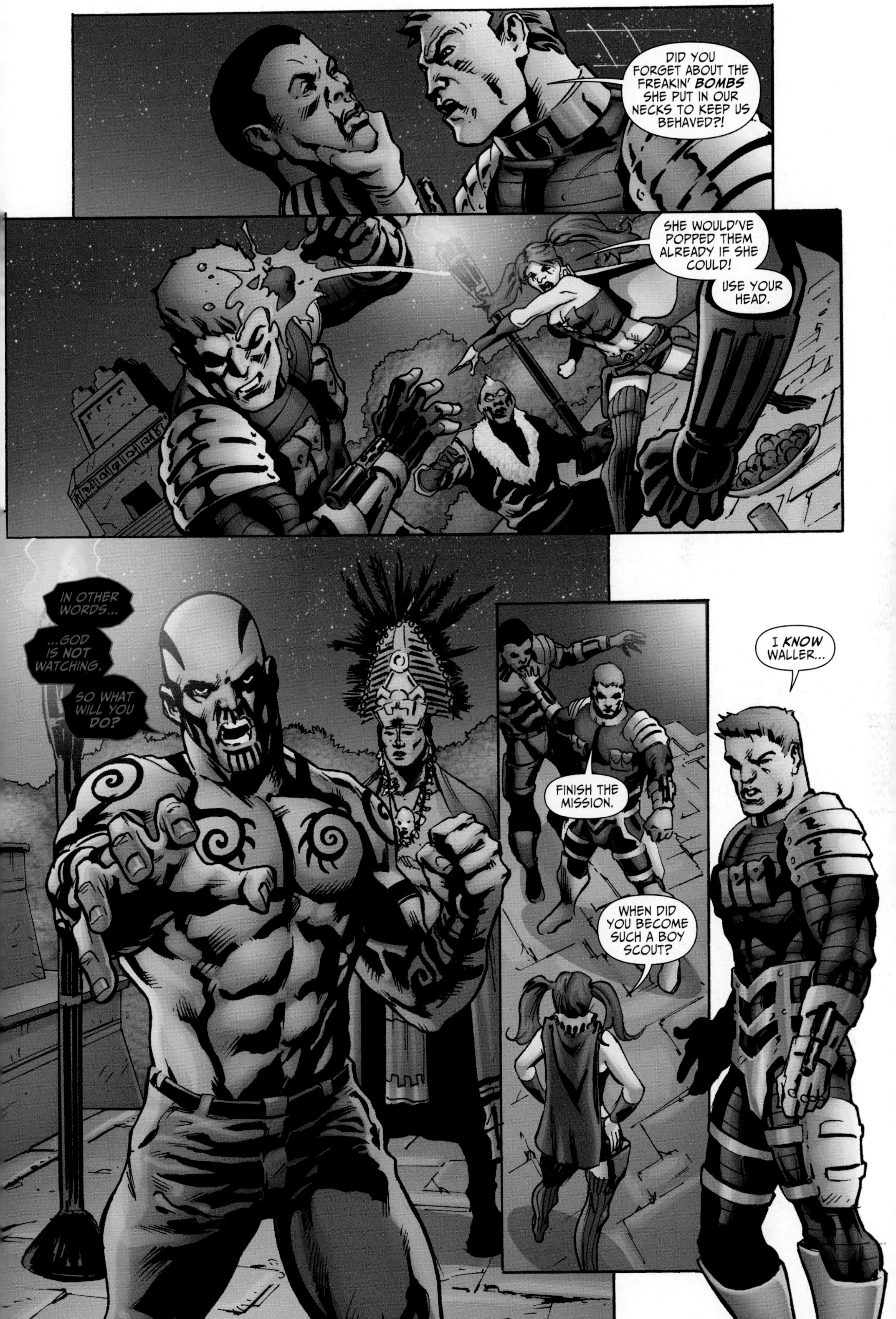
DID YOU FORGET ABOUT THE FREAKIN' BOMBS SHE PUT IN OUR NECKS TO KEEP US BEHAVED?!
SHE WOULD'VE POPPED THEM ALREADY IF SHE COULD!
USE YOUR HEAD.
IN OTHER WORDS...
...GOD IS NOT WATCHING.
SO WHAT WILL YOU DO?
FINISH THE MISSION.
WHEN DID YOU BECOME SUCH A BOY SCOUT?
I KNOW WALLER...

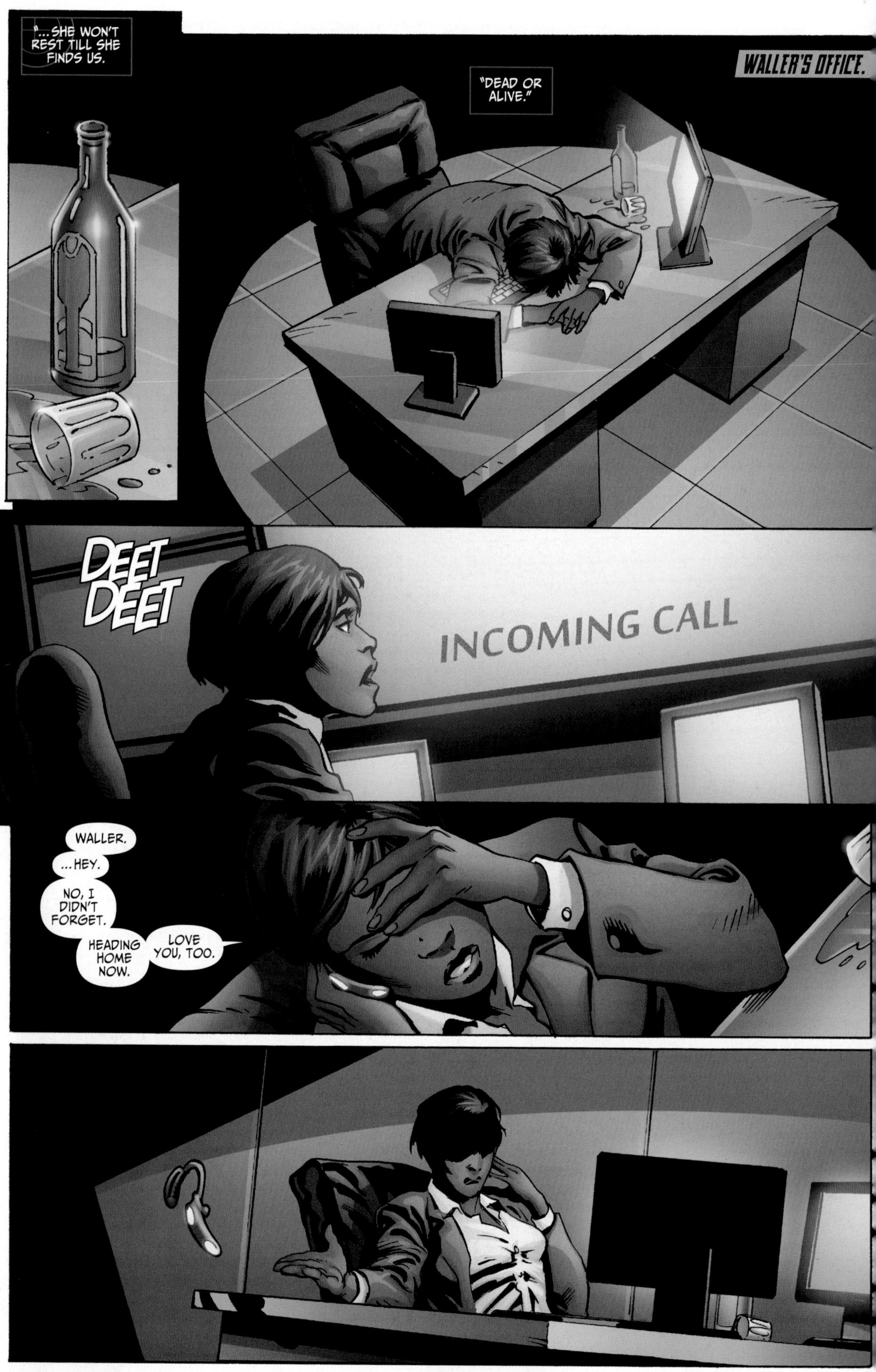
"...SHE WON'T REST TILL SHE FINDS US.
WALLER'S OFFICE.
"DEAD OR ALIVE."
DEET DEET
INCOMING CALL
WALLER.
...HEY.
NO, I DIDN'T FORGET.
HEADING HOME NOW.
LOVE YOU, TOO.

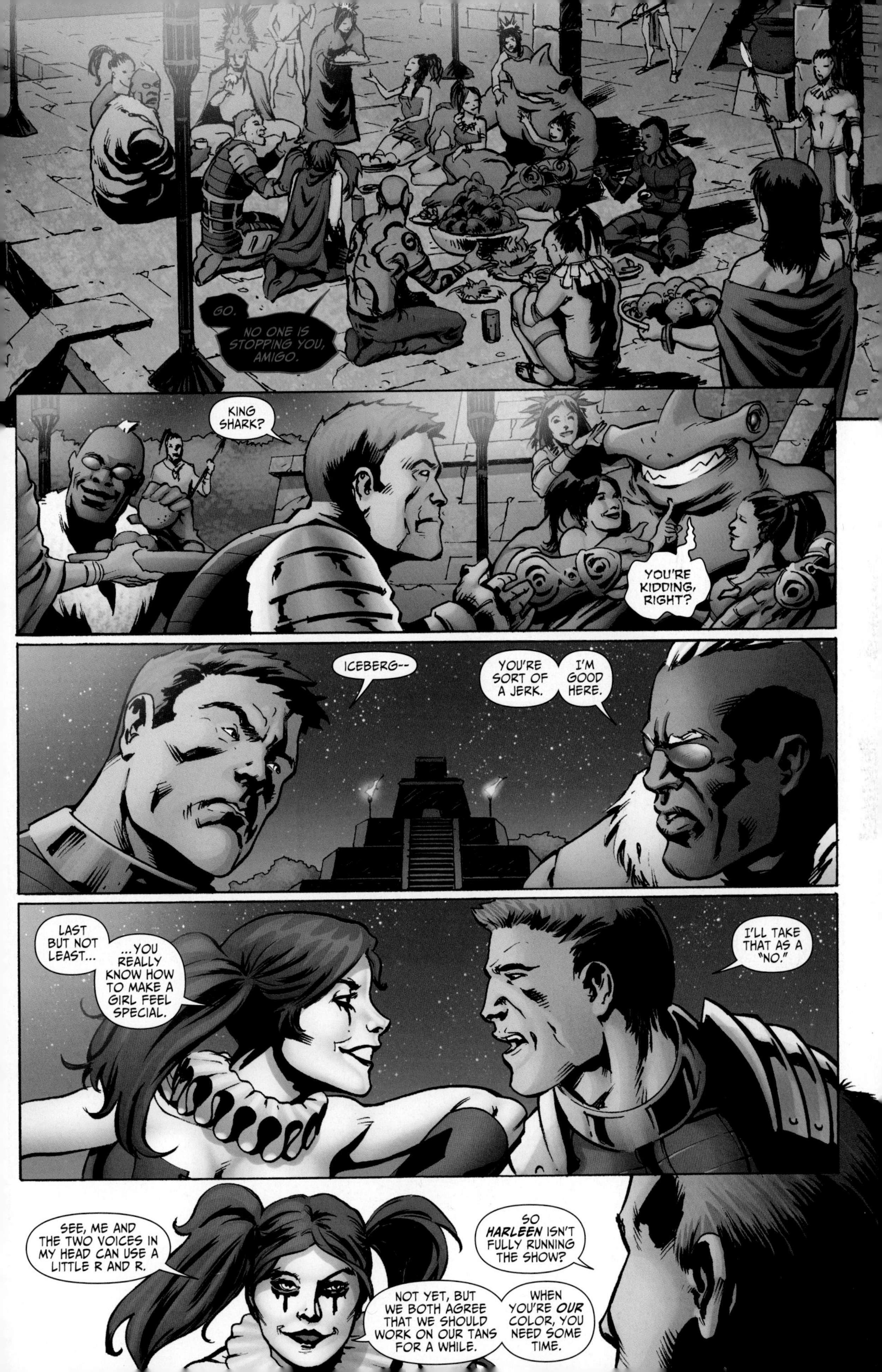
GO.
NO ONE IS STOPPING YOU, AMIGO.
KING SHARK?
YOU'RE KIDDING, RIGHT?
ICEBERG--
YOU'RE SORT OF A JERK.
I'M GOOD HERE.
LAST BUT NOT LEAST...
...YOU REALLY KNOW HOW TO MAKE A GIRL FEEL SPECIAL.
I'LL TAKE THAT AS A "NO."
SEE, ME AND THE TWO VOICES IN MY HEAD CAN USE A LITTLE R AND R.
SO *HARLEEN* ISN'T FULLY RUNNING THE SHOW?
NOT YET, BUT WE BOTH AGREE THAT WE SHOULD WORK ON OUR TANS FOR A WHILE.
WHEN YOU'RE *OUR* COLOR, YOU NEED SOME TIME.

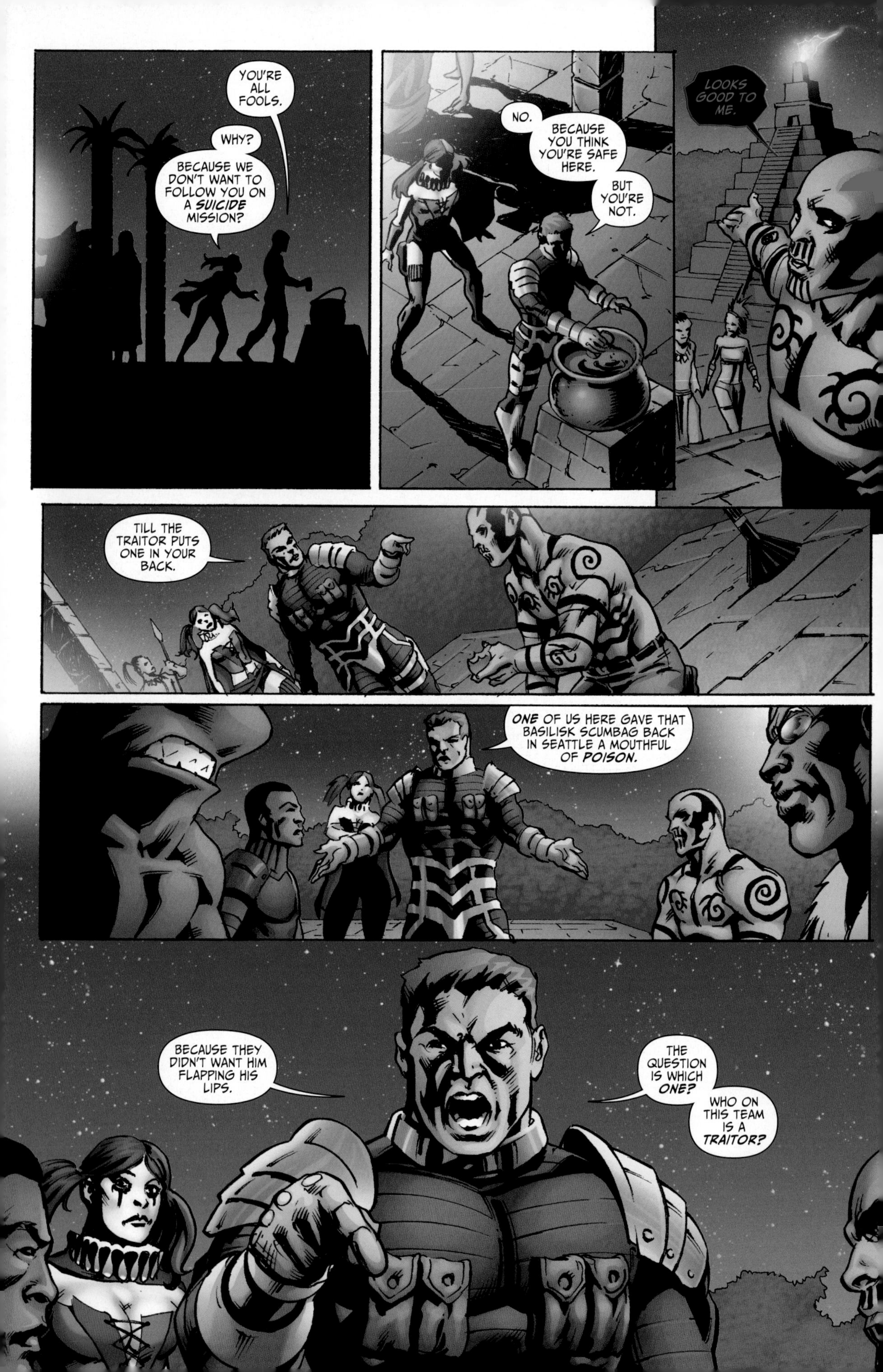
YOU'RE ALL FOOLS.
WHY?
BECAUSE WE DON'T WANT TO FOLLOW YOU ON A SUICIDE MISSION?
NO.
BECAUSE YOU THINK YOU'RE SAFE HERE.
BUT YOU'RE NOT.
LOOKS GOOD TO ME.
TILL THE TRAITOR PUTS ONE IN YOUR BACK.
ONE OF US HERE GAVE THAT BASILISK SCUMBAG BACK IN SEATTLE A MOUTHFUL OF POISON.
BECAUSE THEY DIDN'T WANT HIM FLAPPING HIS LIPS.
THE QUESTION IS WHICH ONE?
WHO ON THIS TEAM IS A TRAITOR?

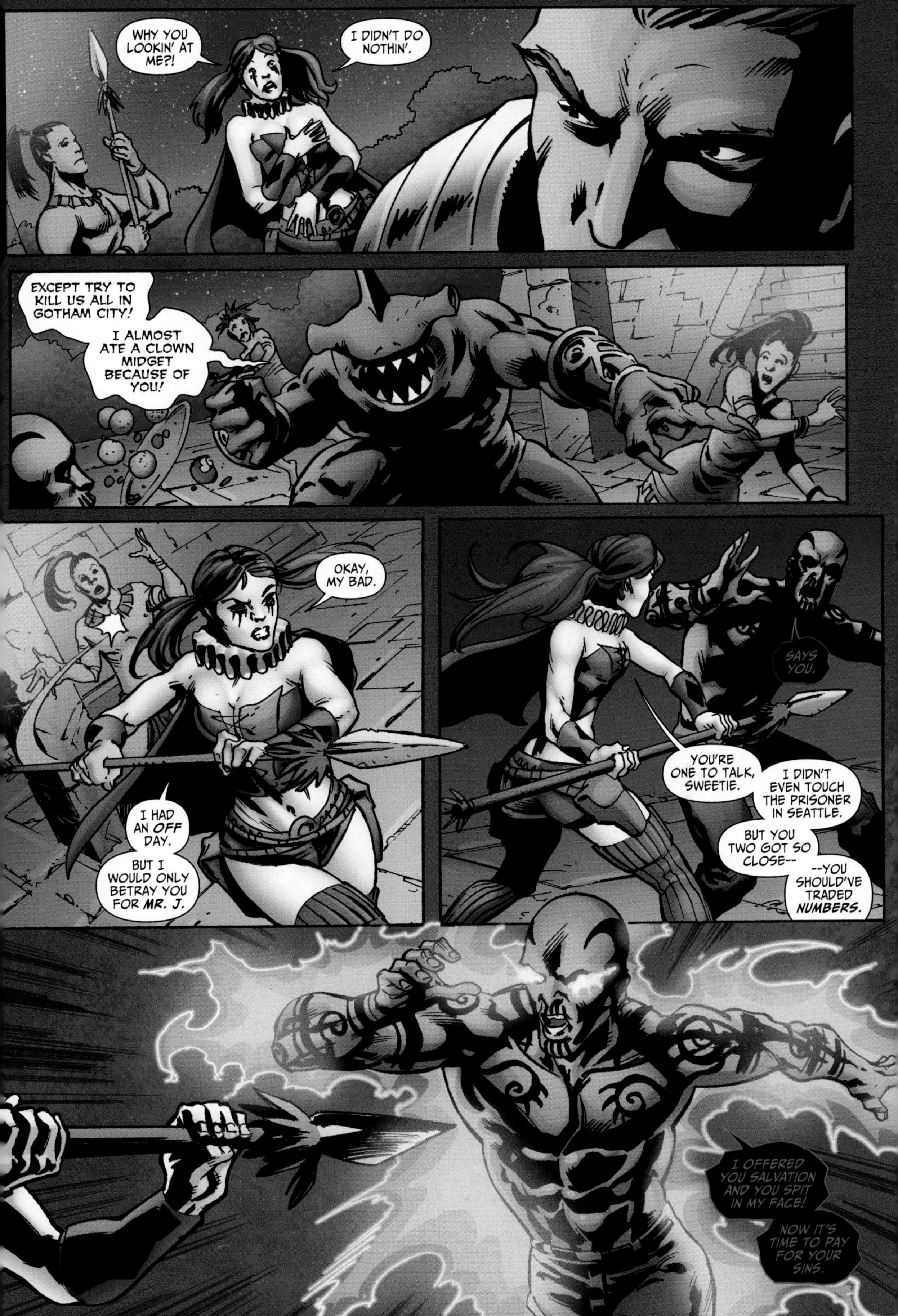

WHY YOU LOOKIN' AT ME?!
I DIDN'T DO NOTHIN'.
EXCEPT TRY TO KILL US ALL IN GOTHAM CITY!
I ALMOST ATE A CLOWN MIDGET BECAUSE OF YOU!
OKAY, MY BAD.
I HAD AN OFF DAY.
BUT I WOULD ONLY BETRAY YOU FOR MR. J.
SAYS YOU.
YOU'RE ONE TO TALK, SWEETIE.
I DIDN'T EVEN TOUCH THE PRISONER IN SEATTLE.
BUT YOU TWO GOT SO CLOSE--
--YOU SHOULD'VE TRADED NUMBERS.
I OFFERED YOU SALVATION AND YOU SPIT IN MY FACE!
NOW IT'S TIME TO PAY FOR YOUR SINS.

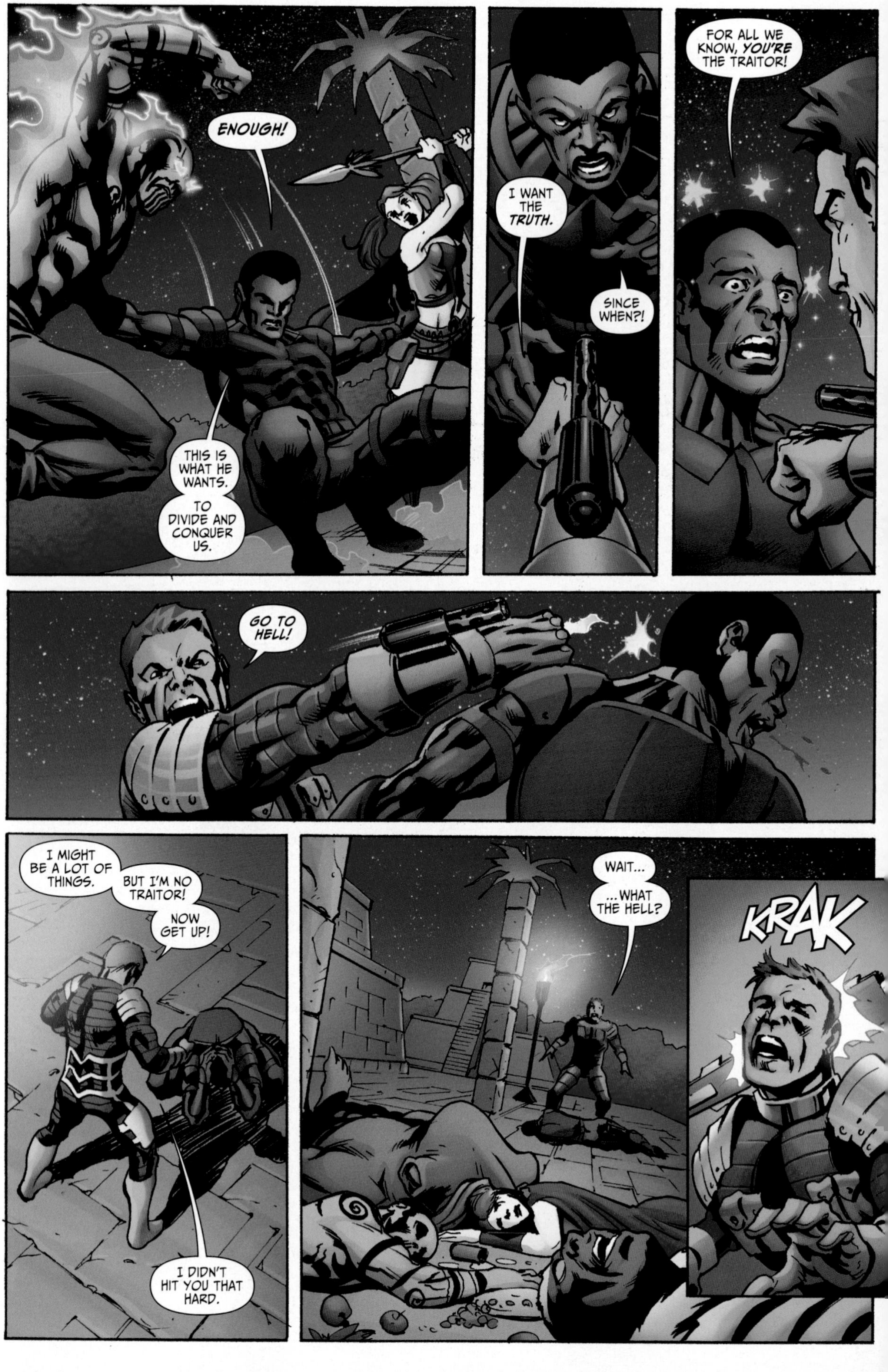
ENOUGH!
THIS IS WHAT HE WANTS.
TO DIVIDE AND CONQUER US.
I WANT THE TRUTH.
SINCE WHEN?!
FOR ALL WE KNOW, YOU'RE THE TRAITOR!
GO TO HELL!
I MIGHT BE A LOT OF THINGS.
BUT I'M NO TRAITOR!
NOW GET UP!
I DIDN'T HIT YOU THAT HARD.
WAIT...
...WHAT THE HELL?
KRAK

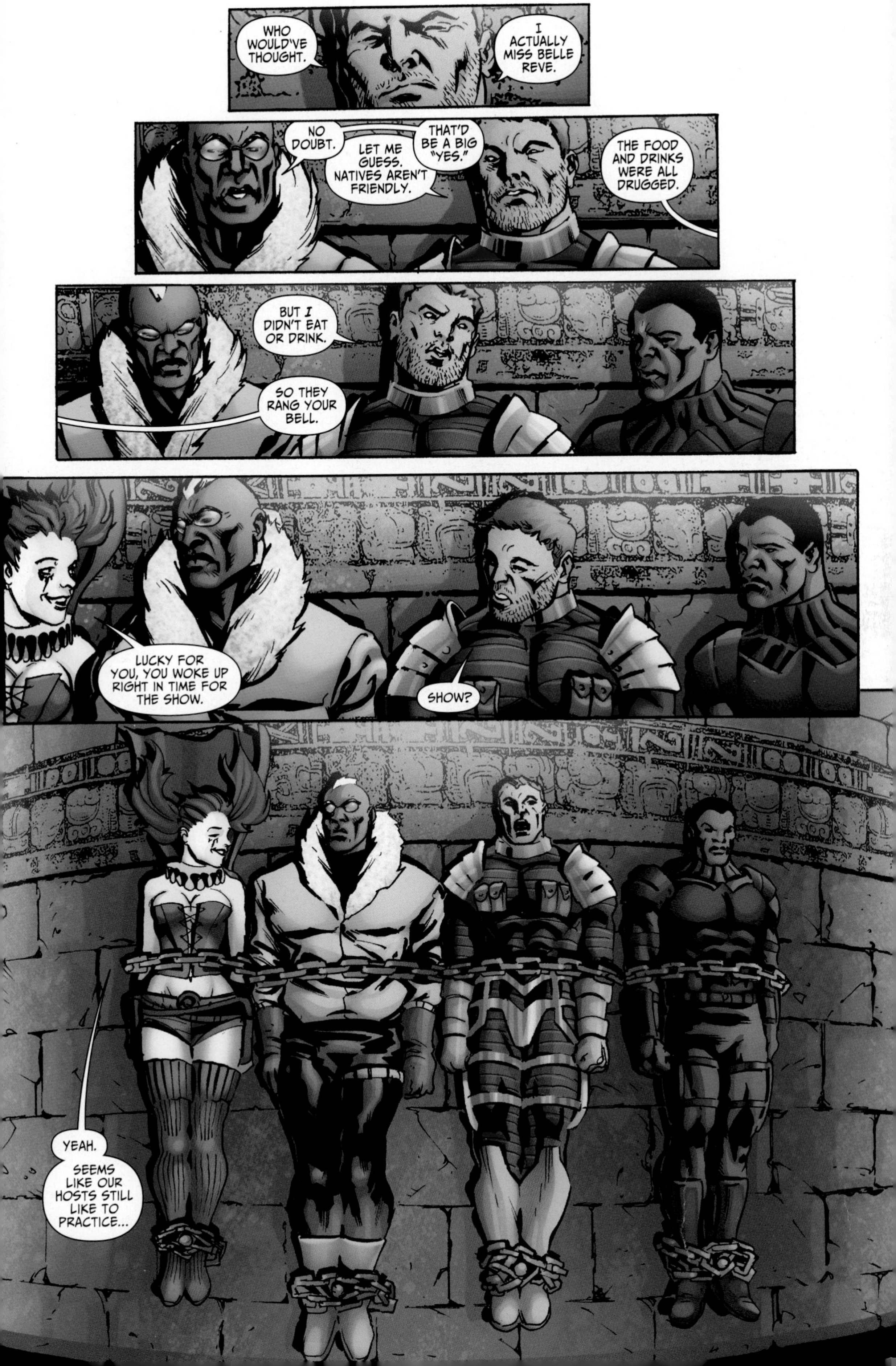
WHO WOULD'VE THOUGHT.
I ACTUALLY MISS BELLE REVE.
NO DOUBT.
LET ME GUESS. NATIVES AREN'T FRIENDLY.
THAT'D BE A BIG "YES."
THE FOOD AND DRINKS WERE ALL DRUGGED.
BUT I DIDN'T EAT OR DRINK.
SO THEY RANG YOUR BELL.
LUCKY FOR YOU, YOU WOKE UP RIGHT IN TIME FOR THE SHOW.
SHOW?
YEAH.
SEEMS LIKE OUR HOSTS STILL LIKE TO PRACTICE...

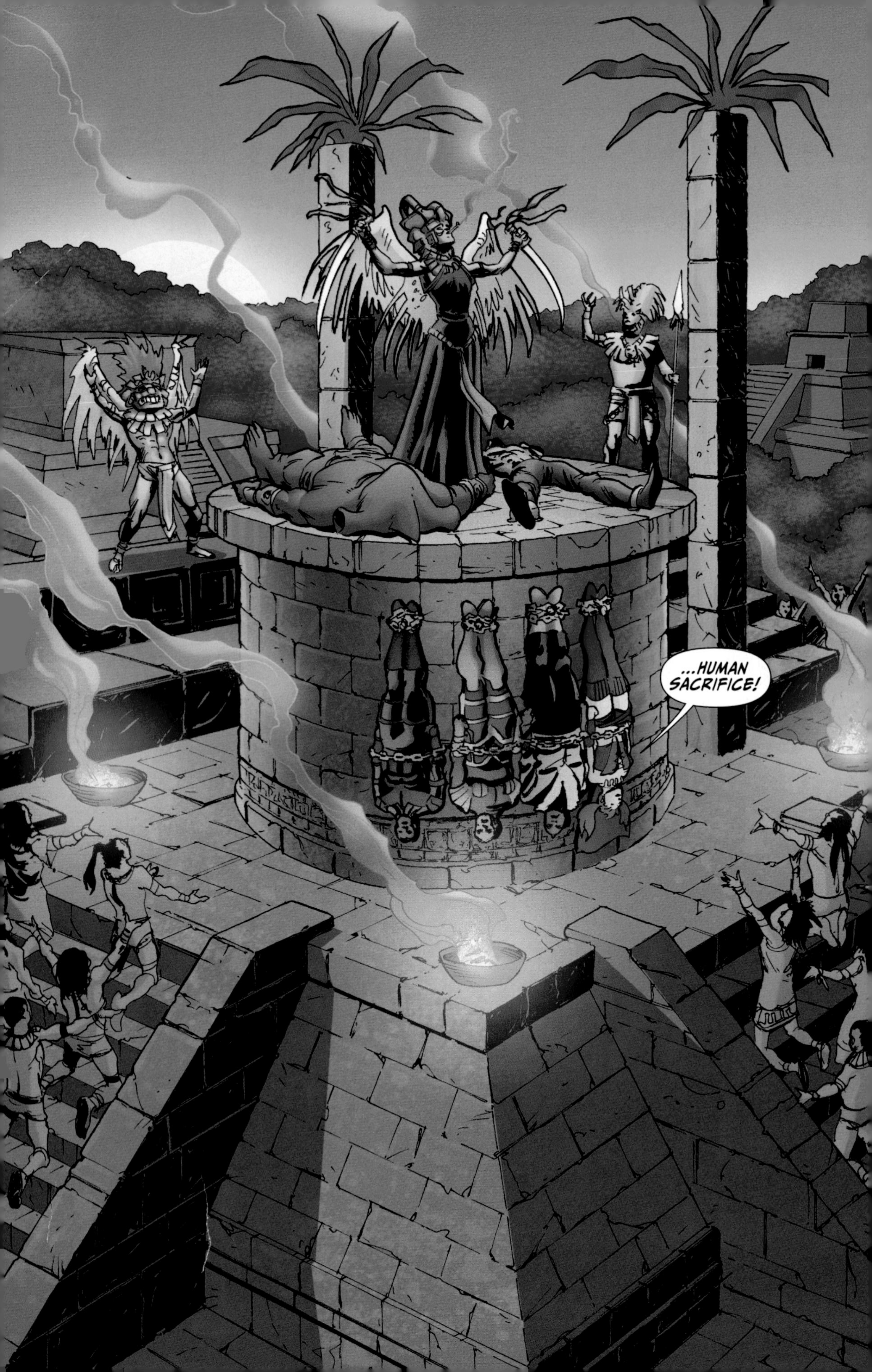
...HUMAN SACRIFICE!

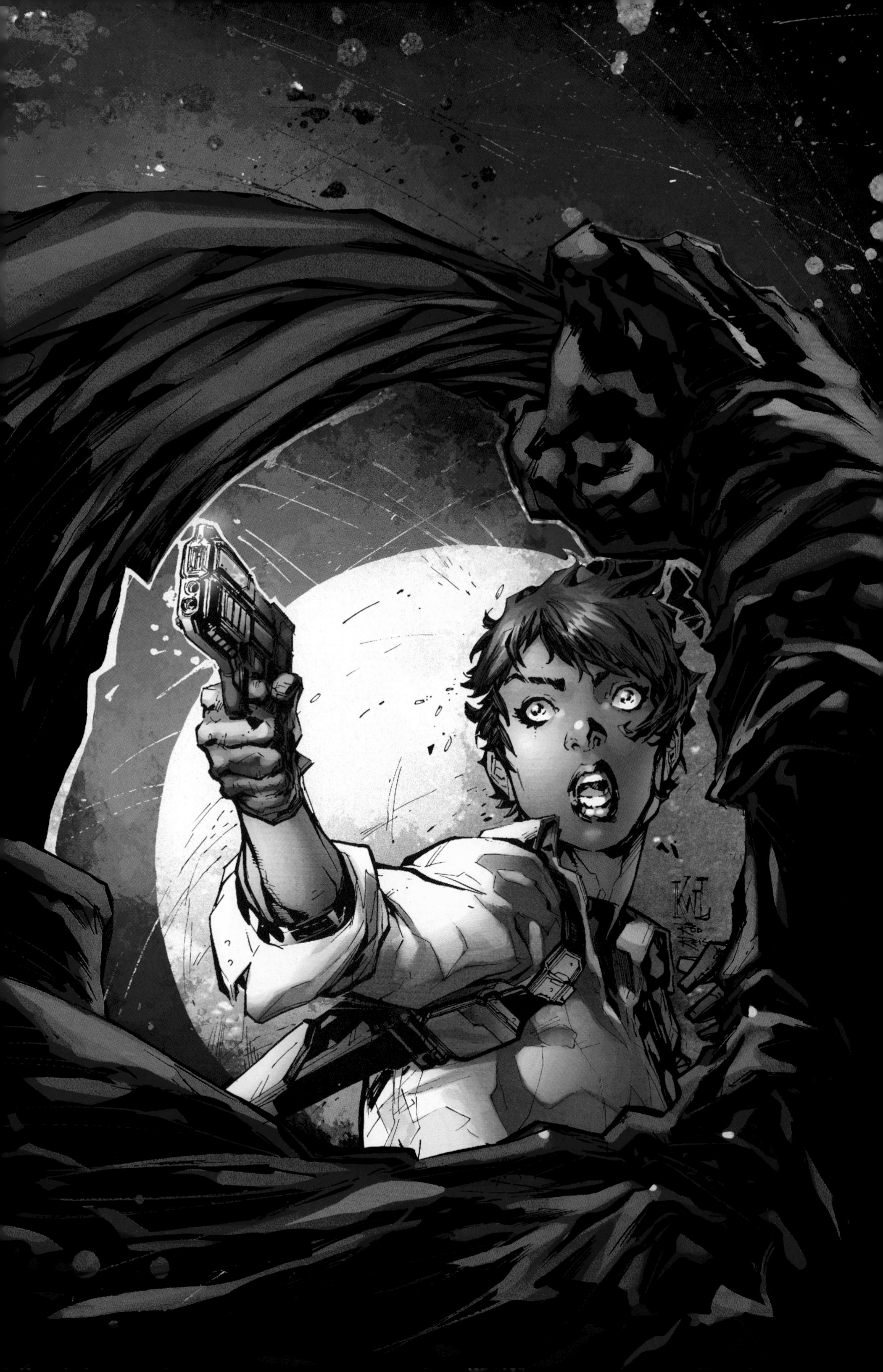

KILLIN' TIME

ADAM GLASS
writer

FERNANDO DAGNINO
artist

cover art by KEN LASHLEY & ROD REIS

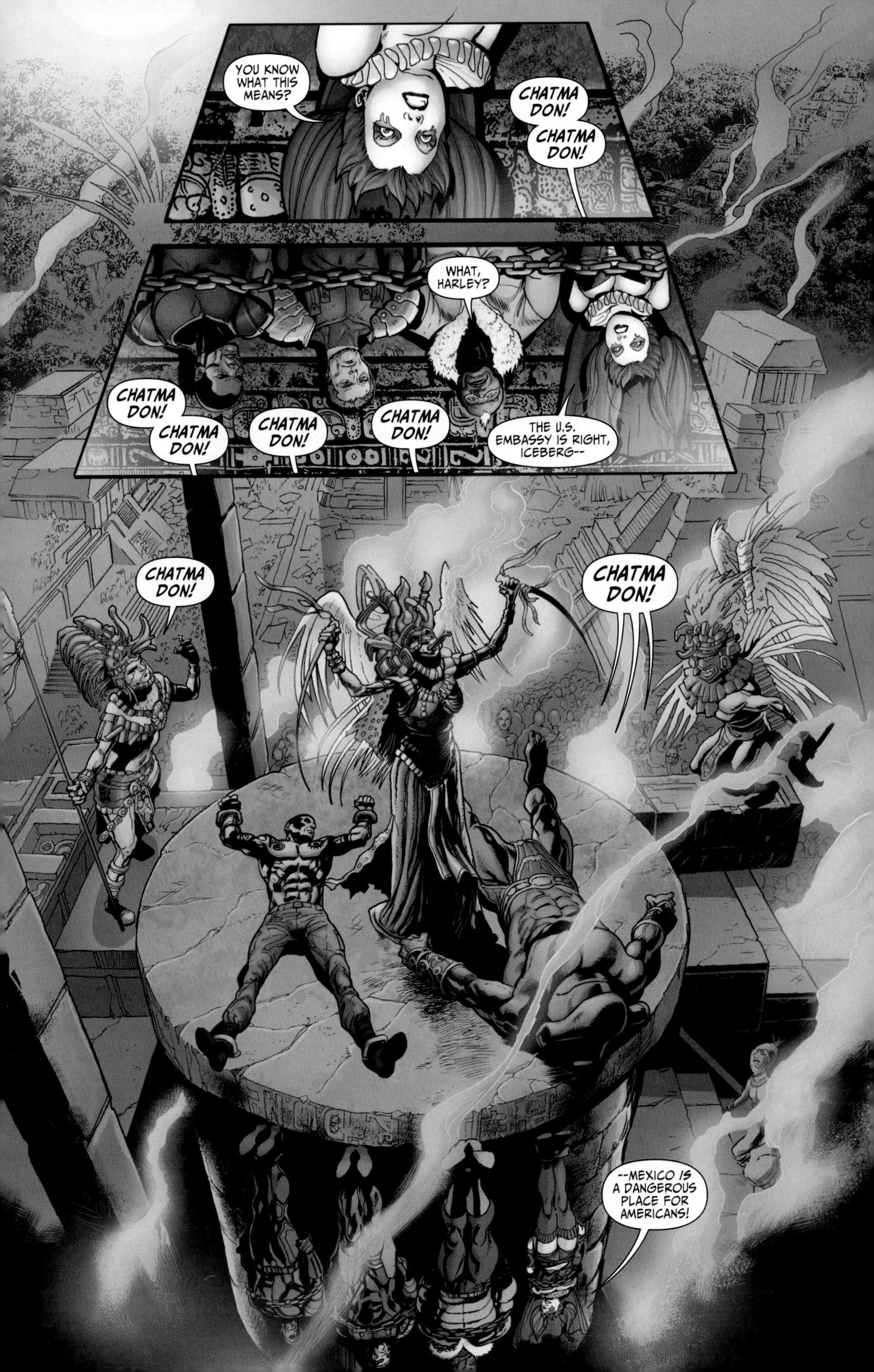
YOU KNOW WHAT THIS MEANS?
CHATMA DON!
CHATMA DON!
WHAT, HARLEY?
CHATMA DON!
CHATMA DON!
CHATMA DON!
CHATMA DON!
THE U.S. EMBASSY IS RIGHT, ICEBERG--
CHATMA DON!
CHATMA DON!
--MEXICO IS A DANGEROUS PLACE FOR AMERICANS!

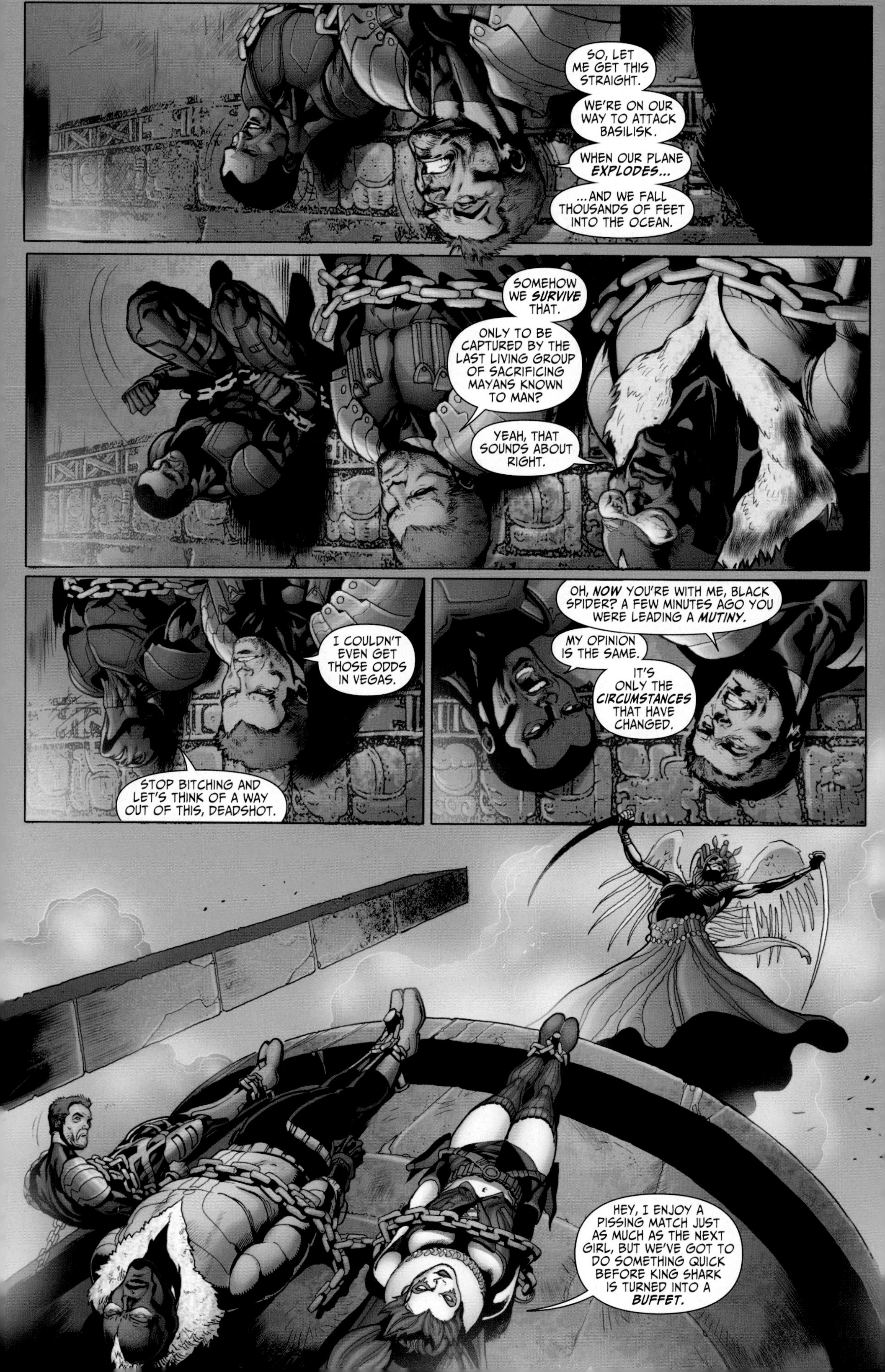
SO, LET ME GET THIS STRAIGHT.
WE'RE ON OUR WAY TO ATTACK BASILISK.
WHEN OUR PLANE EXPLODES...
...AND WE FALL THOUSANDS OF FEET INTO THE OCEAN.
SOMEHOW WE SURVIVE THAT.
ONLY TO BE CAPTURED BY THE LAST LIVING GROUP OF SACRIFICING MAYANS KNOWN TO MAN?
YEAH, THAT SOUNDS ABOUT RIGHT.
I COULDN'T EVEN GET THOSE ODDS IN VEGAS.
STOP BITCHING AND LET'S THINK OF A WAY OUT OF THIS, DEADSHOT.
OH, NOW YOU'RE WITH ME, BLACK SPIDER? A FEW MINUTES AGO YOU WERE LEADING A MUTINY.
MY OPINION IS THE SAME.
IT'S ONLY THE CIRCUMSTANCES THAT HAVE CHANGED.
HEY, I ENJOY A PISSING MATCH JUST AS MUCH AS THE NEXT GIRL, BUT WE'VE GOT TO DO SOMETHING QUICK BEFORE KING SHARK IS TURNED INTO A BUFFET.

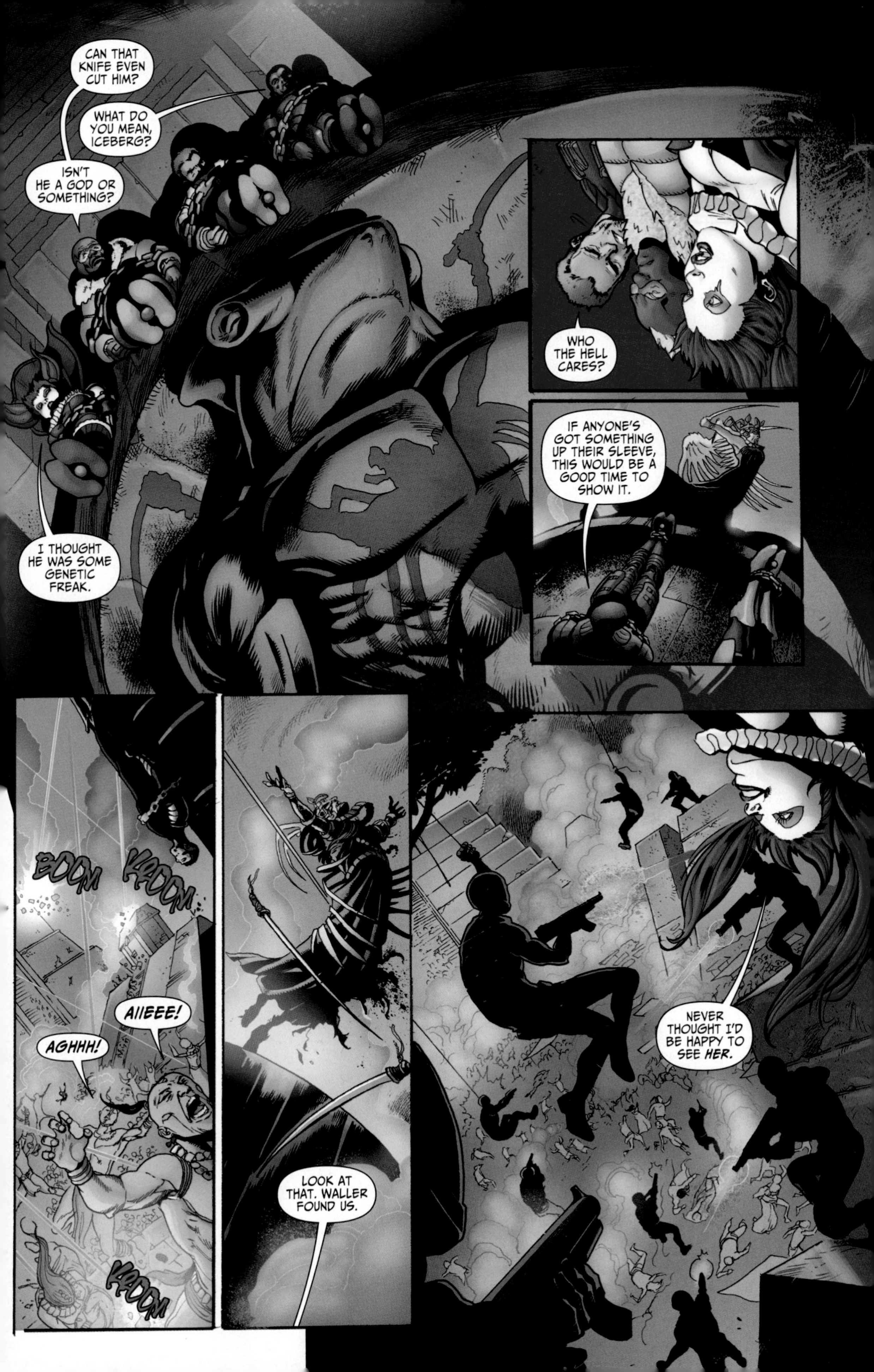
CAN THAT KNIFE EVEN CUT HIM?
WHAT DO YOU MEAN, ICEBERG?
ISN'T HE A GOD OR SOMETHING?
I THOUGHT HE WAS SOME GENETIC FREAK.
WHO THE HELL CARES?
IF ANYONE'S GOT SOMETHING UP THEIR SLEEVE, THIS WOULD BE A GOOD TIME TO SHOW IT.
BOOM
KROOM
AIIEEE!
AGHHH!
KROOM
LOOK AT THAT. WALLER FOUND US.
NEVER THOUGHT I'D BE HAPPY TO SEE *HER*.

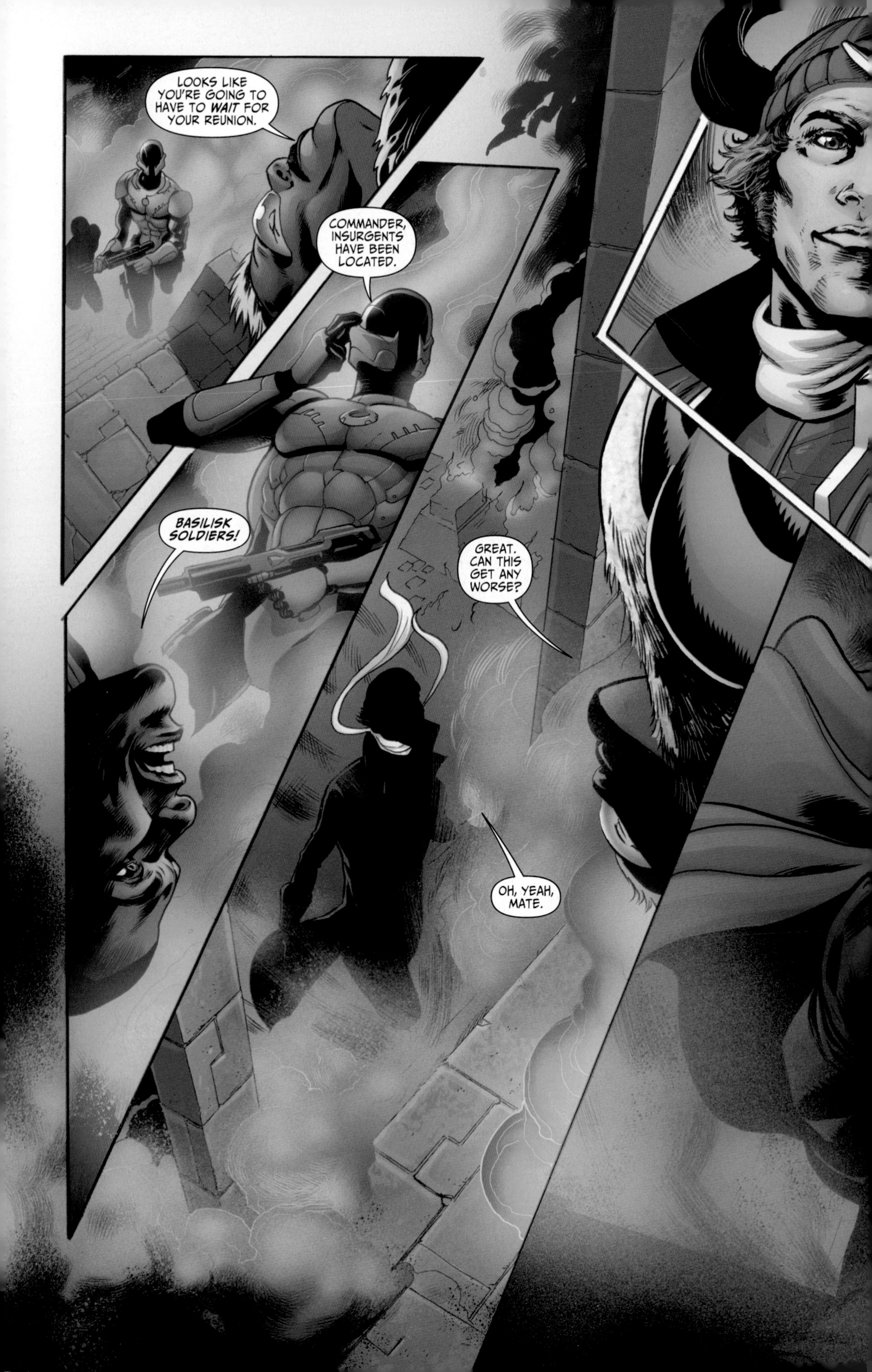
LOOKS LIKE YOU'RE GOING TO HAVE TO *WAIT* FOR YOUR REUNION.
COMMANDER, INSURGENTS HAVE BEEN LOCATED.
BASILISK SOLDIERS!
GREAT. CAN THIS GET ANY WORSE?
OH, YEAH, MATE.

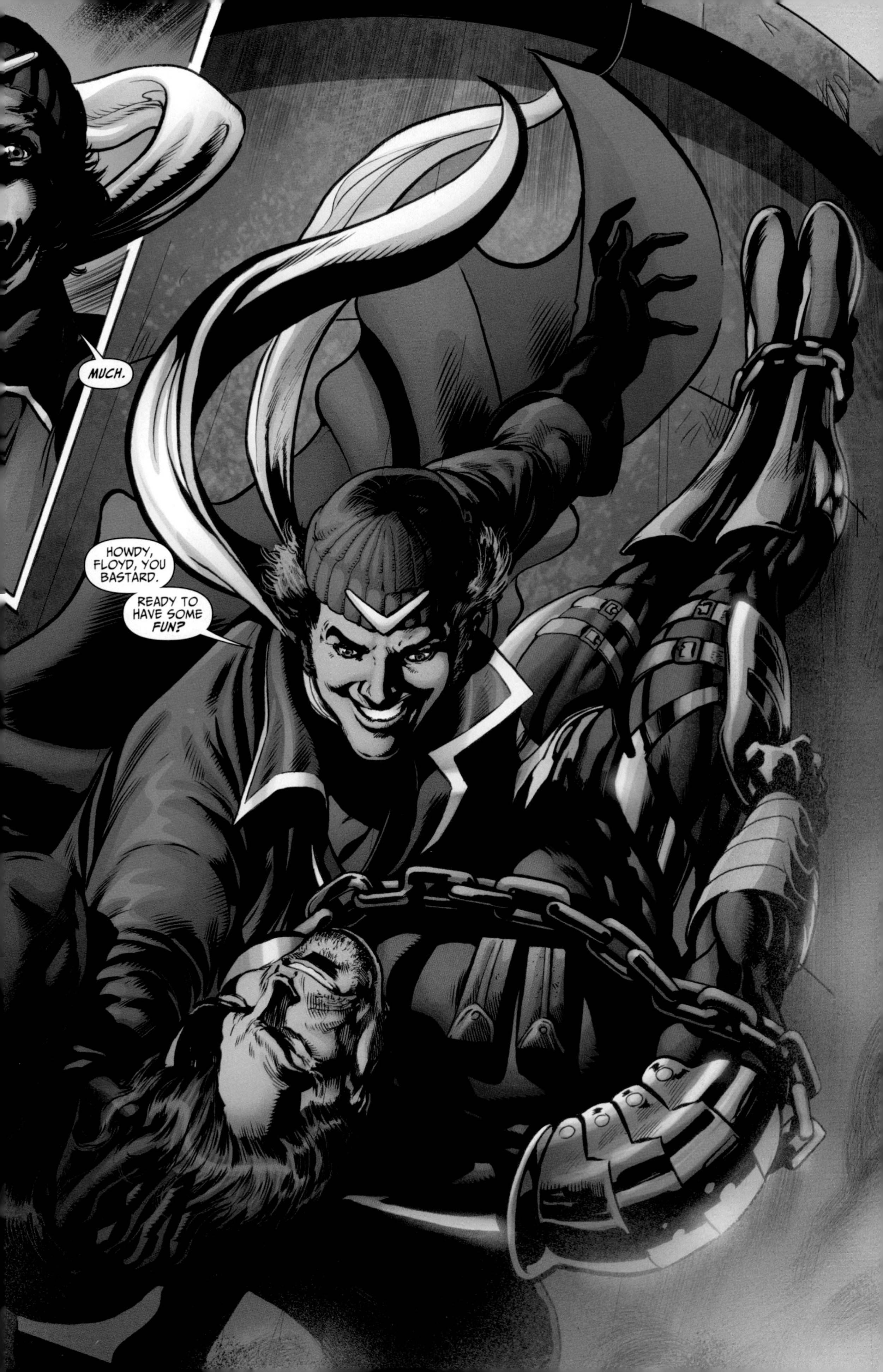
MUCH.
HOWDY, FLOYD, YOU BASTARD.
READY TO HAVE SOME *FUN?*

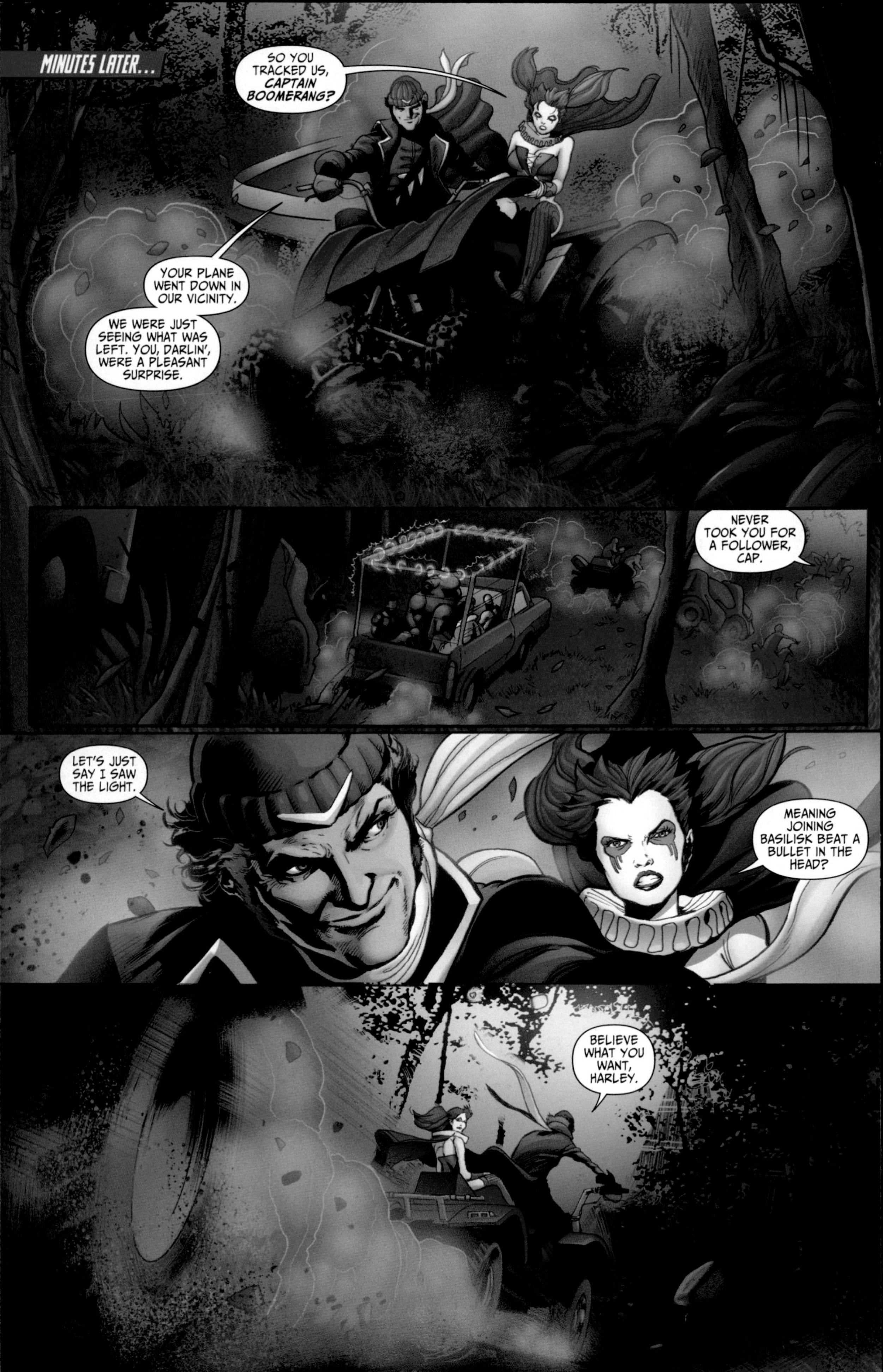
MINUTES LATER...
SO YOU TRACKED US, CAPTAIN BOOMERANG?
YOUR PLANE WENT DOWN IN OUR VICINITY.
WE WERE JUST SEEING WHAT WAS LEFT. YOU, DARLIN', WERE A PLEASANT SURPRISE.
NEVER TOOK YOU FOR A FOLLOWER, CAP.
LET'S JUST SAY I SAW THE LIGHT.
MEANING JOINING BASILISK BEAT A BULLET IN THE HEAD?
BELIEVE WHAT YOU WANT, HARLEY.

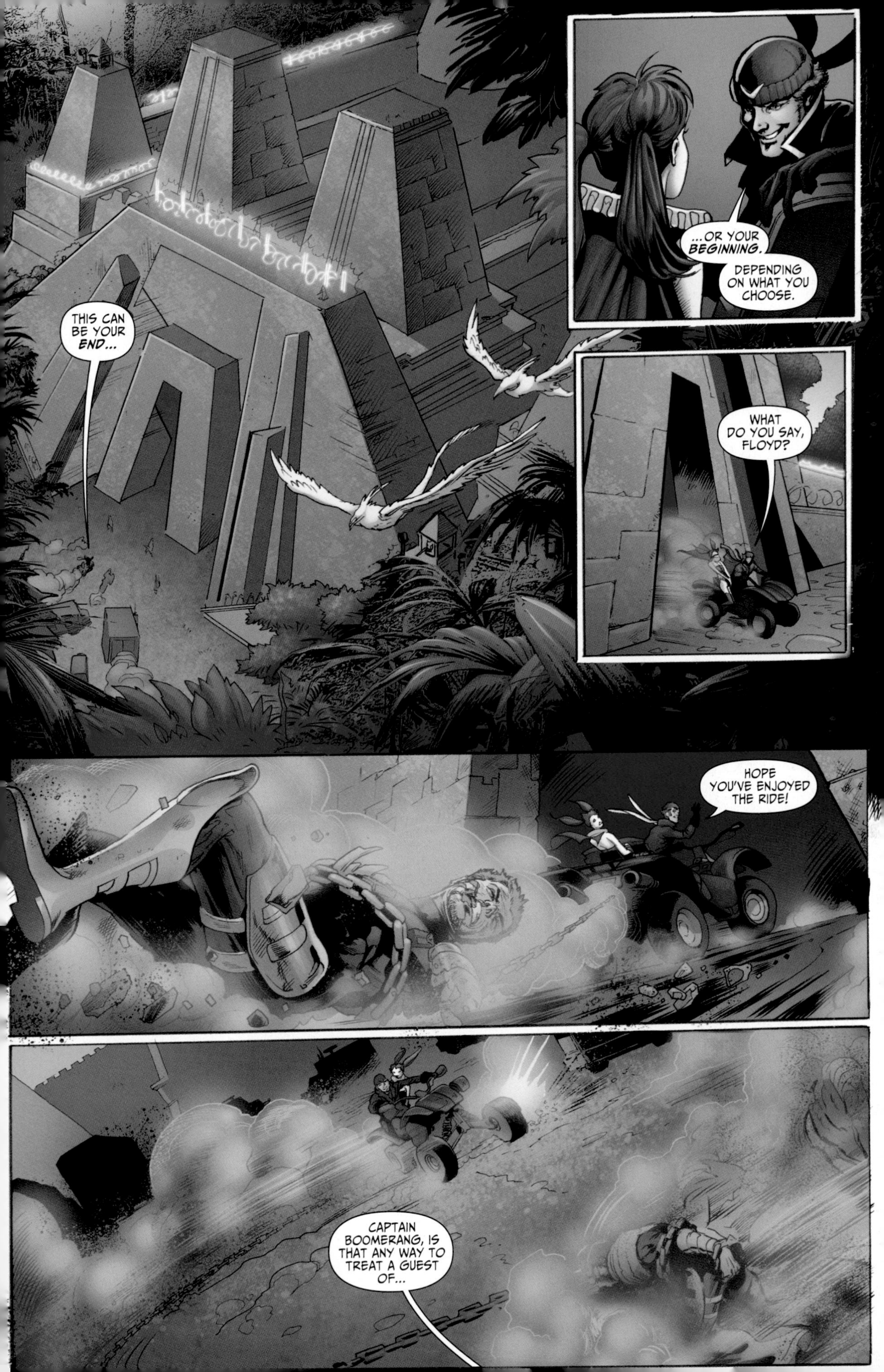
THIS CAN BE YOUR END...
...OR YOUR BEGINNING.
DEPENDING ON WHAT YOU CHOOSE.
WHAT DO YOU SAY, FLOYD?
HOPE YOU'VE ENJOYED THE RIDE!
CAPTAIN BOOMERANG, IS THAT ANY WAY TO TREAT A GUEST OF...

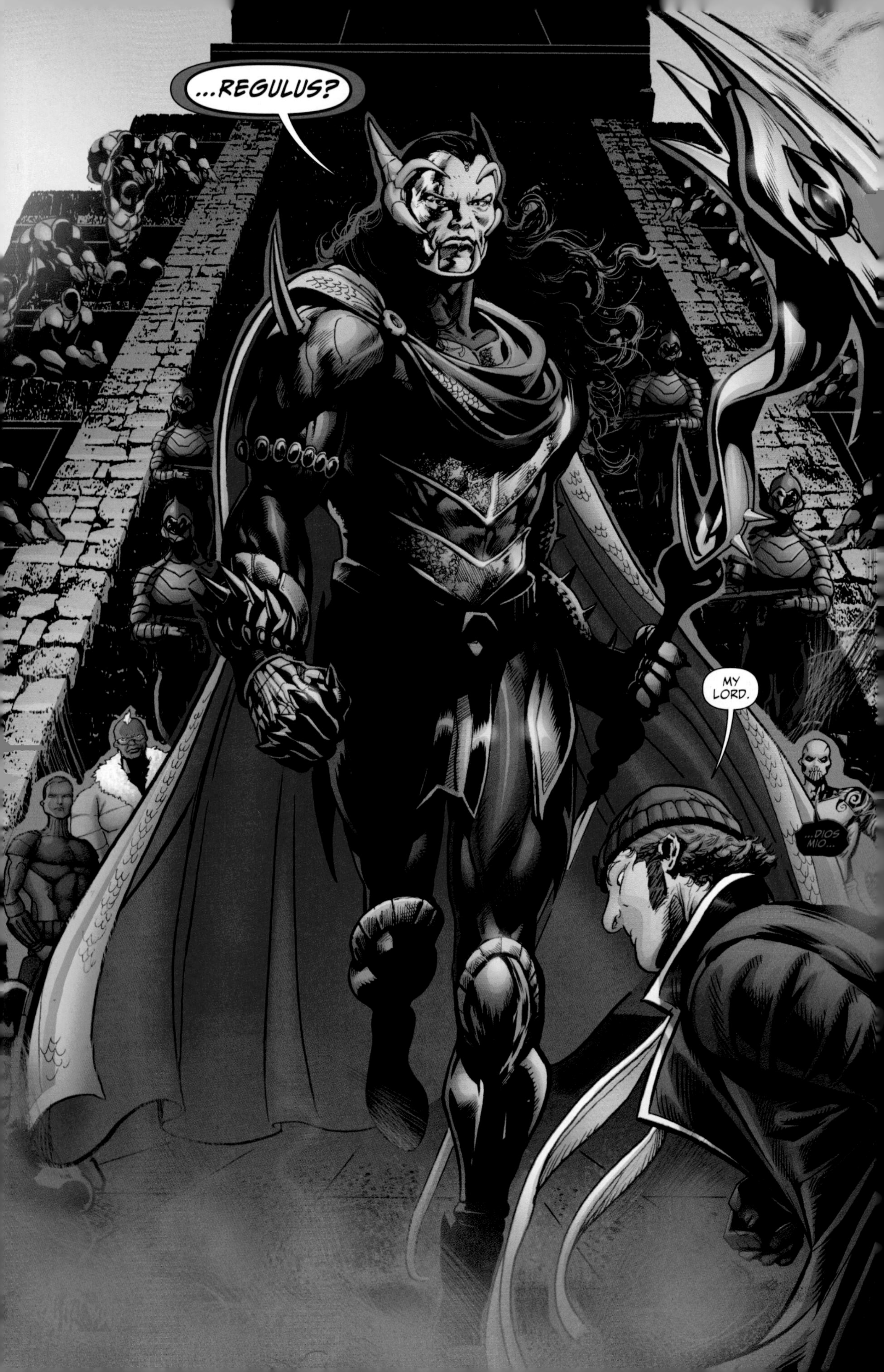
...REGULUS?
MY LORD.
...DIOS MIO...

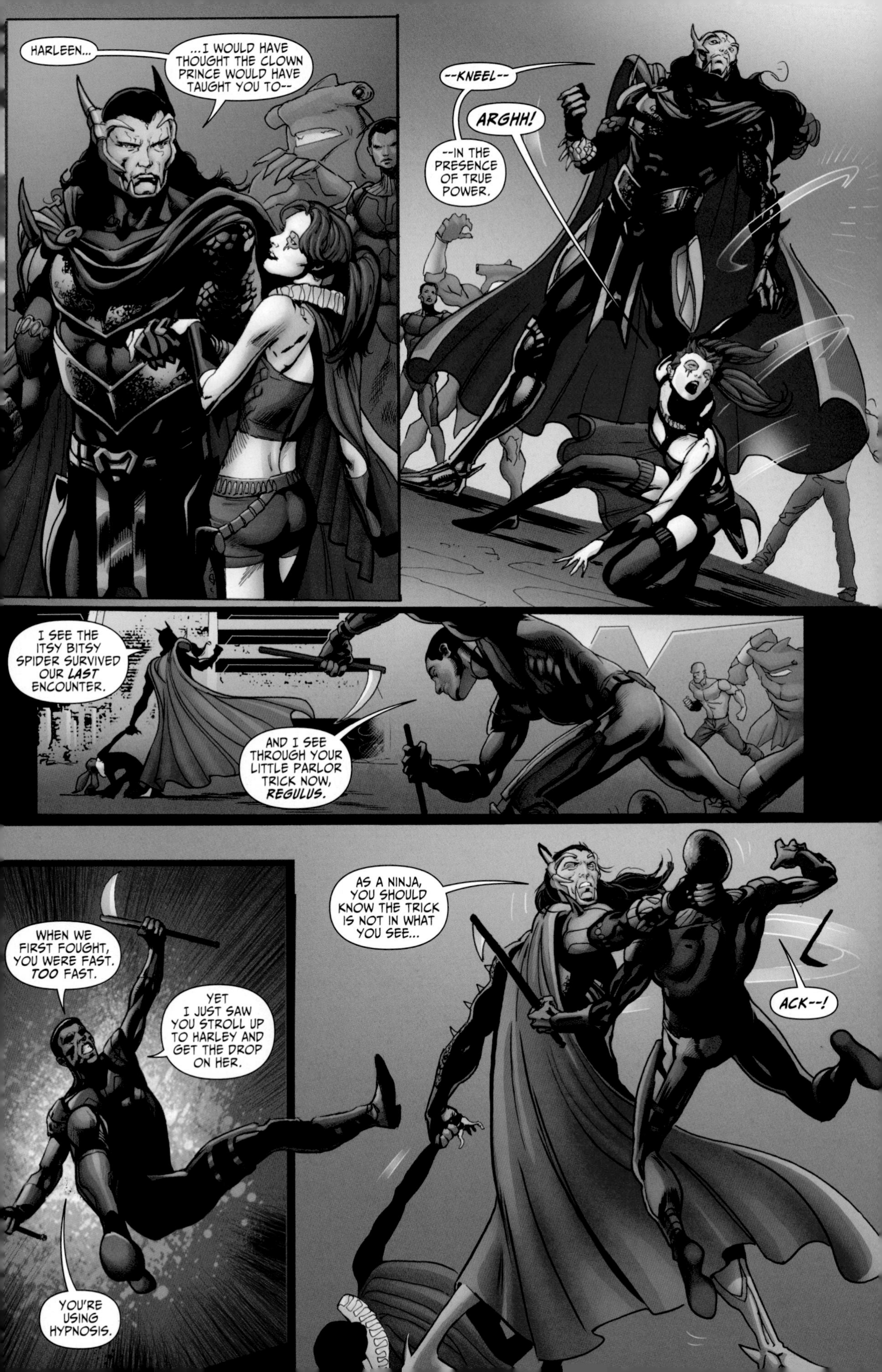
HARLEEN...
...I WOULD HAVE THOUGHT THE CLOWN PRINCE WOULD HAVE TAUGHT YOU TO--
--KNEEL--
ARGHH!
--IN THE PRESENCE OF TRUE POWER.
I SEE THE ITSY BITSY SPIDER SURVIVED OUR LAST ENCOUNTER.
AND I SEE THROUGH YOUR LITTLE PARLOR TRICK NOW, REGULUS.
WHEN WE FIRST FOUGHT, YOU WERE FAST. TOO FAST.
YET I JUST SAW YOU STROLL UP TO HARLEY AND GET THE DROP ON HER.
YOU'RE USING HYPNOSIS.
AS A NINJA, YOU SHOULD KNOW THE TRICK IS NOT IN WHAT YOU SEE...
ACK--!

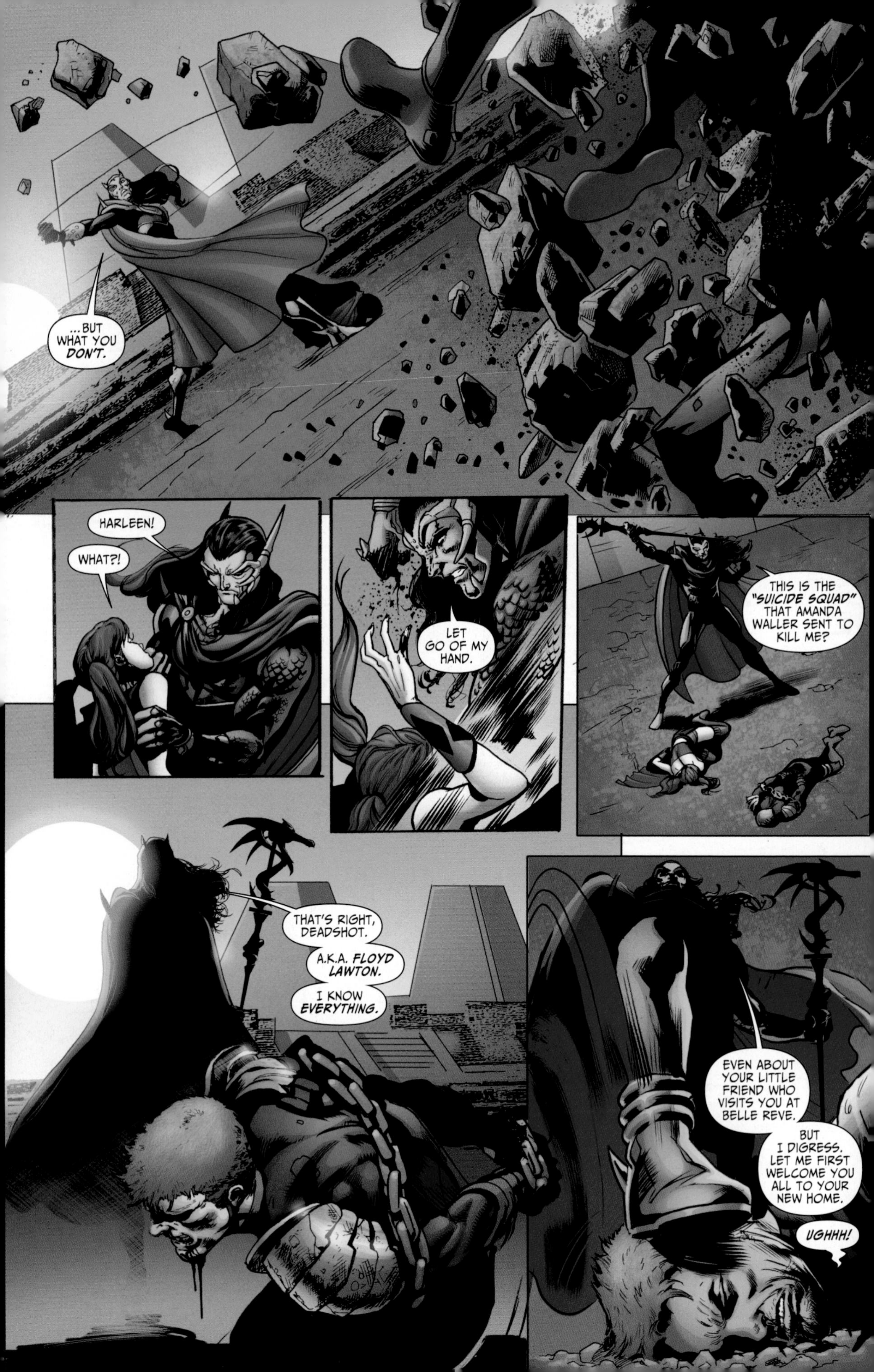
...BUT WHAT YOU *DON'T.*
HARLEEN!
WHAT?!
LET GO OF MY HAND.
THIS IS THE *"SUICIDE SQUAD"* THAT AMANDA WALLER SENT TO KILL ME?
THAT'S RIGHT, DEADSHOT.
A.K.A. *FLOYD LAWTON.*
I KNOW *EVERYTHING.*
EVEN ABOUT YOUR LITTLE FRIEND WHO VISITS YOU AT BELLE REVE.
BUT I DIGRESS. LET ME FIRST WELCOME YOU ALL TO YOUR NEW HOME.
UGHHH!

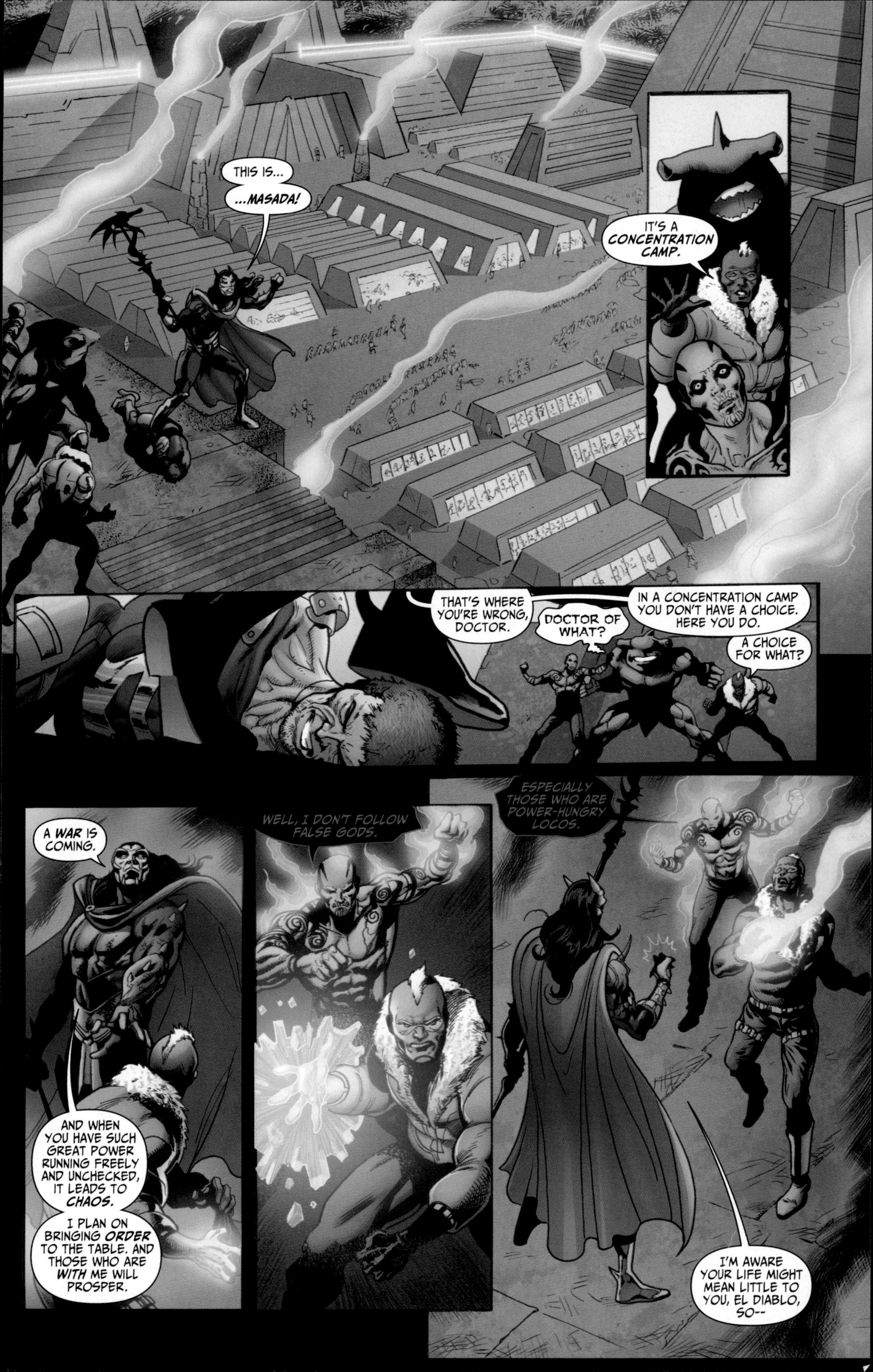
THIS IS...
...MASADA!
IT'S A CONCENTRATION CAMP.
THAT'S WHERE YOU'RE WRONG, DOCTOR.
DOCTOR OF WHAT?
IN A CONCENTRATION CAMP YOU DON'T HAVE A CHOICE. HERE YOU DO.
A CHOICE FOR WHAT?
A WAR IS COMING.
AND WHEN YOU HAVE SUCH GREAT POWER RUNNING FREELY AND UNCHECKED, IT LEADS TO CHAOS.
I PLAN ON BRINGING ORDER TO THE TABLE. AND THOSE WHO ARE WITH ME WILL PROSPER.
WELL, I DON'T FOLLOW FALSE GODS.
ESPECIALLY THOSE WHO ARE POWER-HUNGRY LOCOS.
I'M AWARE YOUR LIFE MIGHT MEAN LITTLE TO YOU, EL DIABLO, SO--

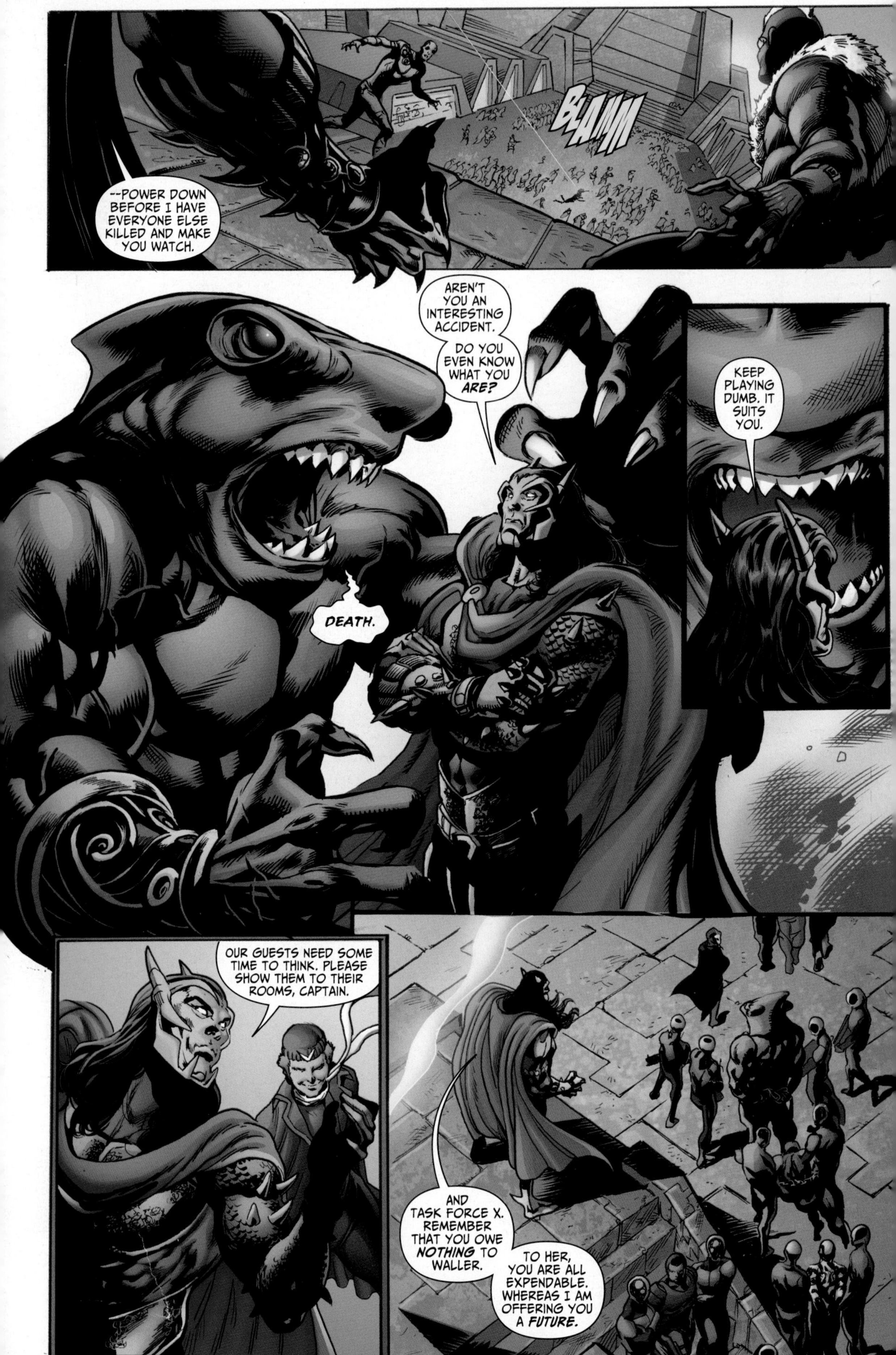
BLAMM
--POWER DOWN BEFORE I HAVE EVERYONE ELSE KILLED AND MAKE YOU WATCH.
AREN'T YOU AN INTERESTING ACCIDENT.
DO YOU EVEN KNOW WHAT YOU *ARE?*
DEATH.
KEEP PLAYING DUMB. IT SUITS YOU.
OUR GUESTS NEED SOME TIME TO THINK. PLEASE SHOW THEM TO THEIR ROOMS, CAPTAIN.
AND TASK FORCE X. REMEMBER THAT YOU OWE *NOTHING* TO WALLER.
TO HER, YOU ARE ALL EXPENDABLE. WHEREAS I AM OFFERING YOU A *FUTURE.*

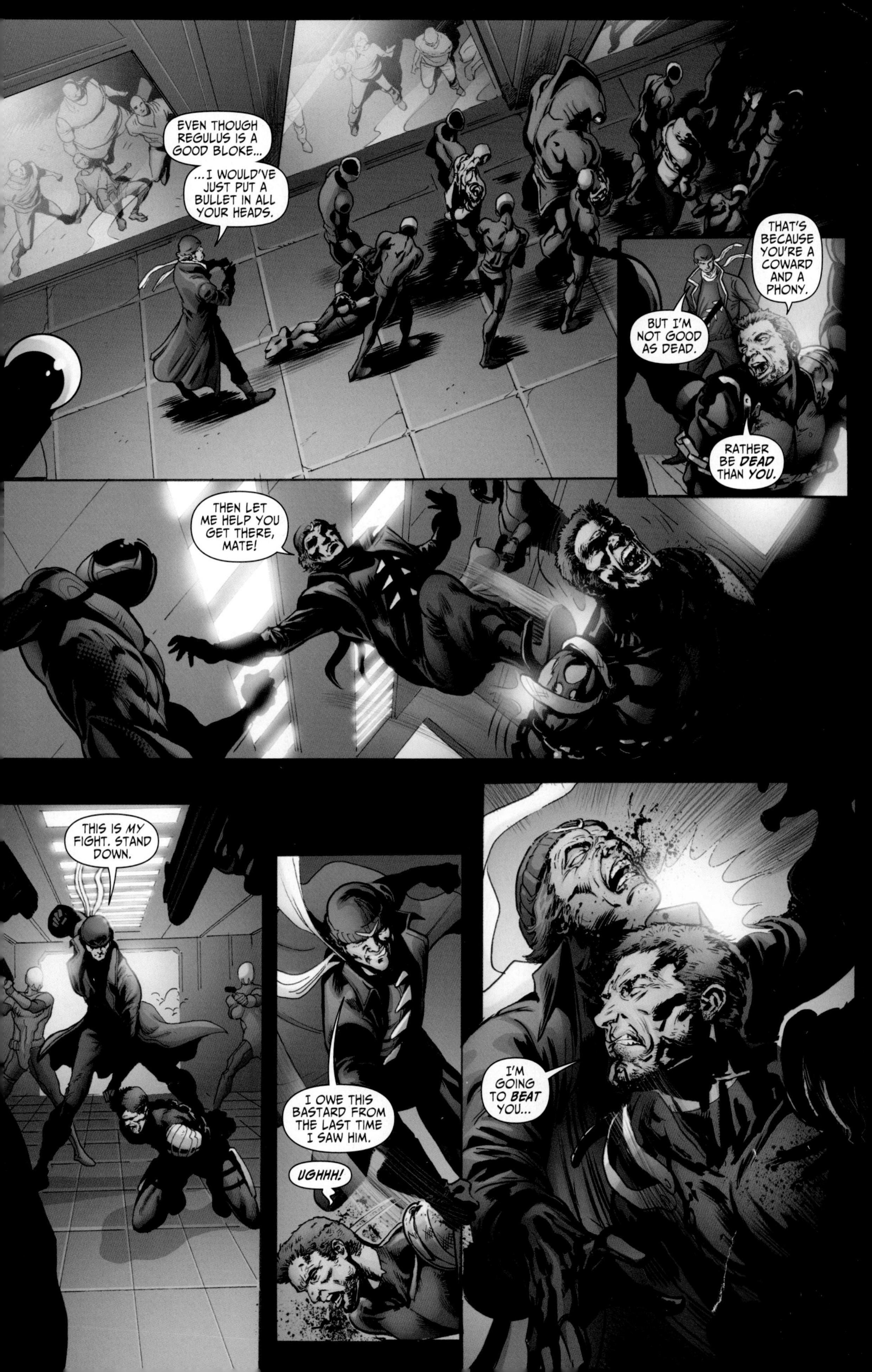
EVEN THOUGH REGULUS IS A GOOD BLOKE...
...I WOULD'VE JUST PUT A BULLET IN ALL YOUR HEADS.
BUT I'M NOT GOOD AS DEAD.
THAT'S BECAUSE YOU'RE A COWARD AND A PHONY.
RATHER BE DEAD THAN YOU.
THEN LET ME HELP YOU GET THERE, MATE!
THIS IS MY FIGHT. STAND DOWN.
I OWE THIS BASTARD FROM THE LAST TIME I SAW HIM.
UGHHH!
I'M GOING TO BEAT YOU...

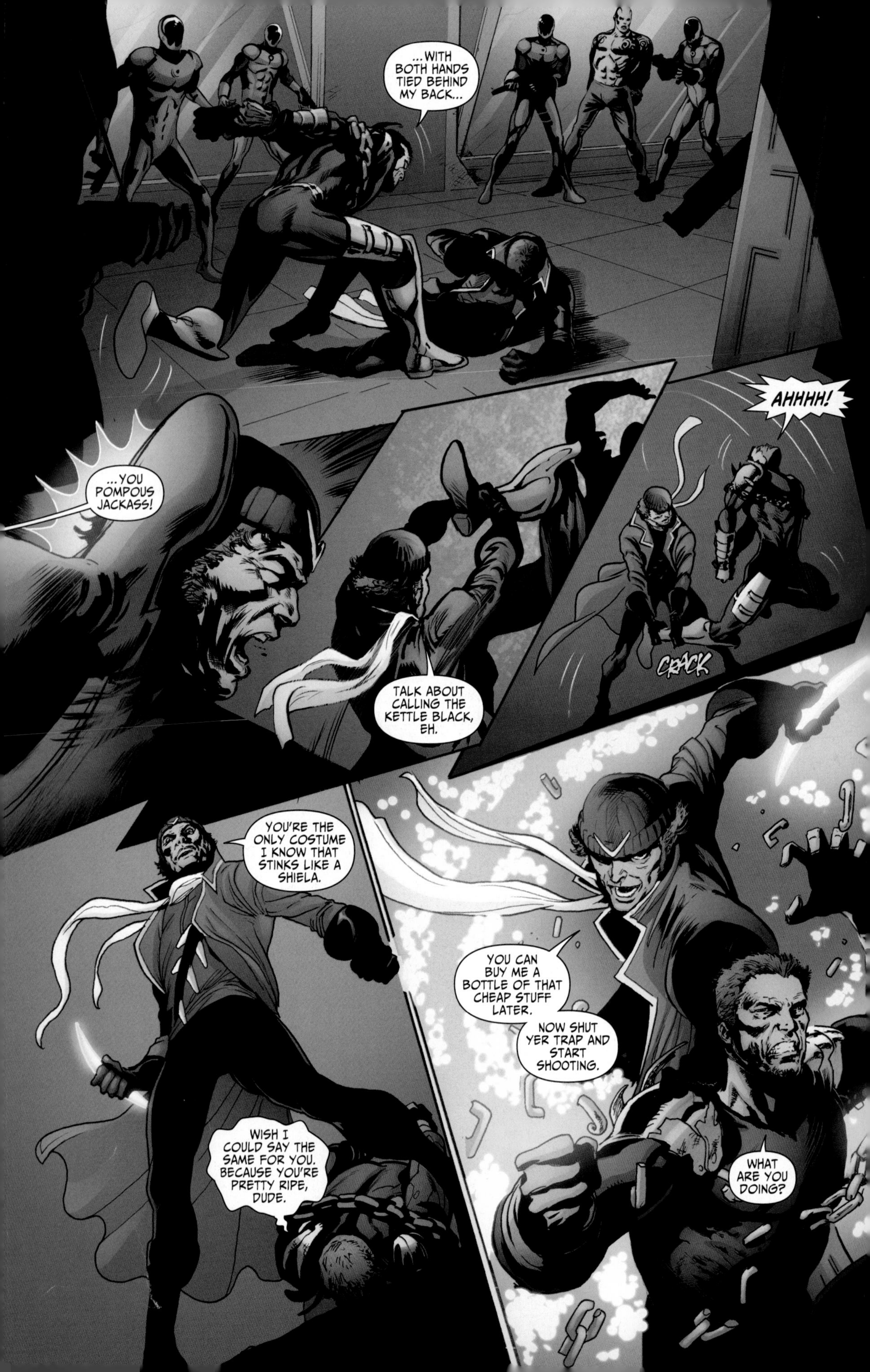
...WITH BOTH HANDS TIED BEHIND MY BACK...
...YOU POMPOUS JACKASS!
TALK ABOUT CALLING THE KETTLE BLACK, EH.
AHHHH!
CRACK
YOU'RE THE ONLY COSTUME I KNOW THAT STINKS LIKE A SHIELA.
WISH I COULD SAY THE SAME FOR YOU. BECAUSE YOU'RE PRETTY RIPE, DUDE.
YOU CAN BUY ME A BOTTLE OF THAT CHEAP STUFF LATER.
NOW SHUT YER TRAP AND START SHOOTING.
WHAT ARE YOU DOING?

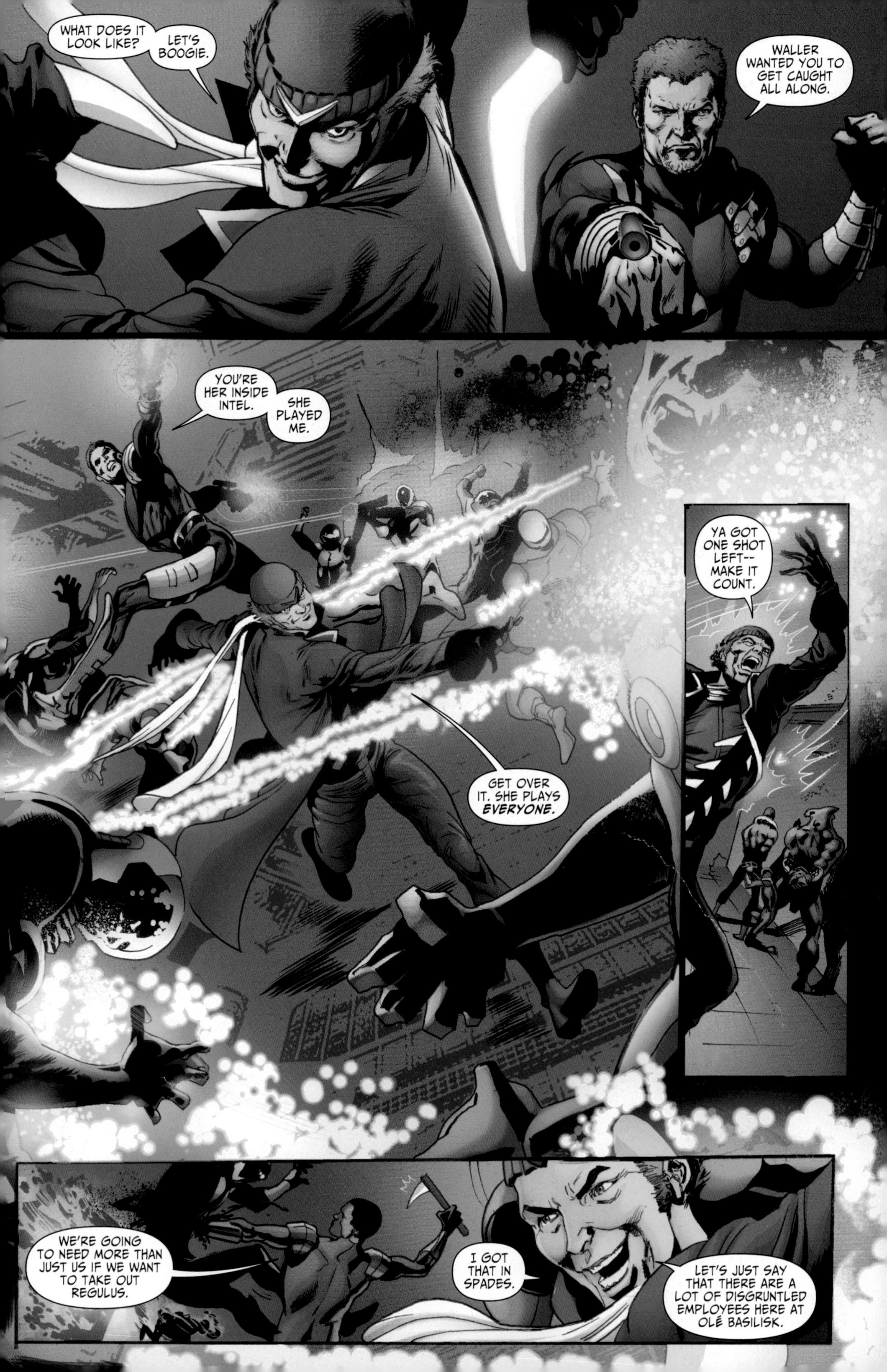
WHAT DOES IT LOOK LIKE?
LET'S BOOGIE.
WALLER WANTED YOU TO GET CAUGHT ALL ALONG.
YOU'RE HER INSIDE INTEL.
SHE PLAYED ME.
GET OVER IT. SHE PLAYS *EVERYONE*.
YA GOT ONE SHOT LEFT-- MAKE IT COUNT.
WE'RE GOING TO NEED MORE THAN JUST US IF WE WANT TO TAKE OUT REGULUS.
I GOT THAT IN SPADES.
LET'S JUST SAY THAT THERE ARE A LOT OF DISGRUNTLED EMPLOYEES HERE AT OLÉ BASILISK.

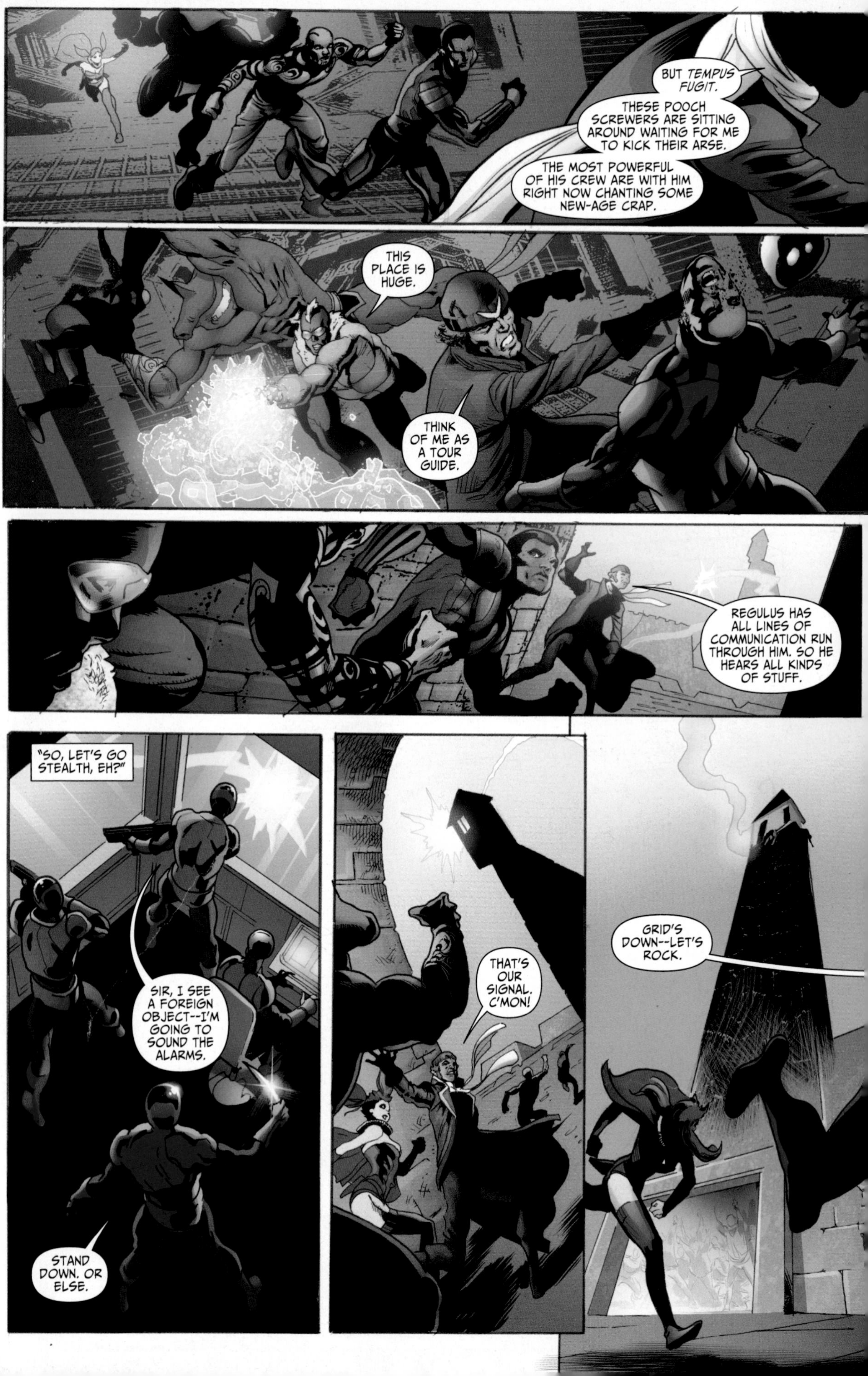
BUT *TEMPUS FUGIT.*
THESE POOCH SCREWERS ARE SITTING AROUND WAITING FOR ME TO KICK THEIR ARSE.
THE MOST POWERFUL OF HIS CREW ARE WITH HIM RIGHT NOW CHANTING SOME NEW-AGE CRAP.
THIS PLACE IS HUGE.
THINK OF ME AS A TOUR GUIDE.
REGULUS HAS ALL LINES OF COMMUNICATION RUN THROUGH HIM. SO HE HEARS ALL KINDS OF STUFF.
"SO, LET'S GO STEALTH, EH?"
SIR, I SEE A FOREIGN OBJECT--I'M GOING TO SOUND THE ALARMS.
STAND DOWN. OR ELSE.
THAT'S OUR SIGNAL. C'MON!
GRID'S DOWN--LET'S ROCK.

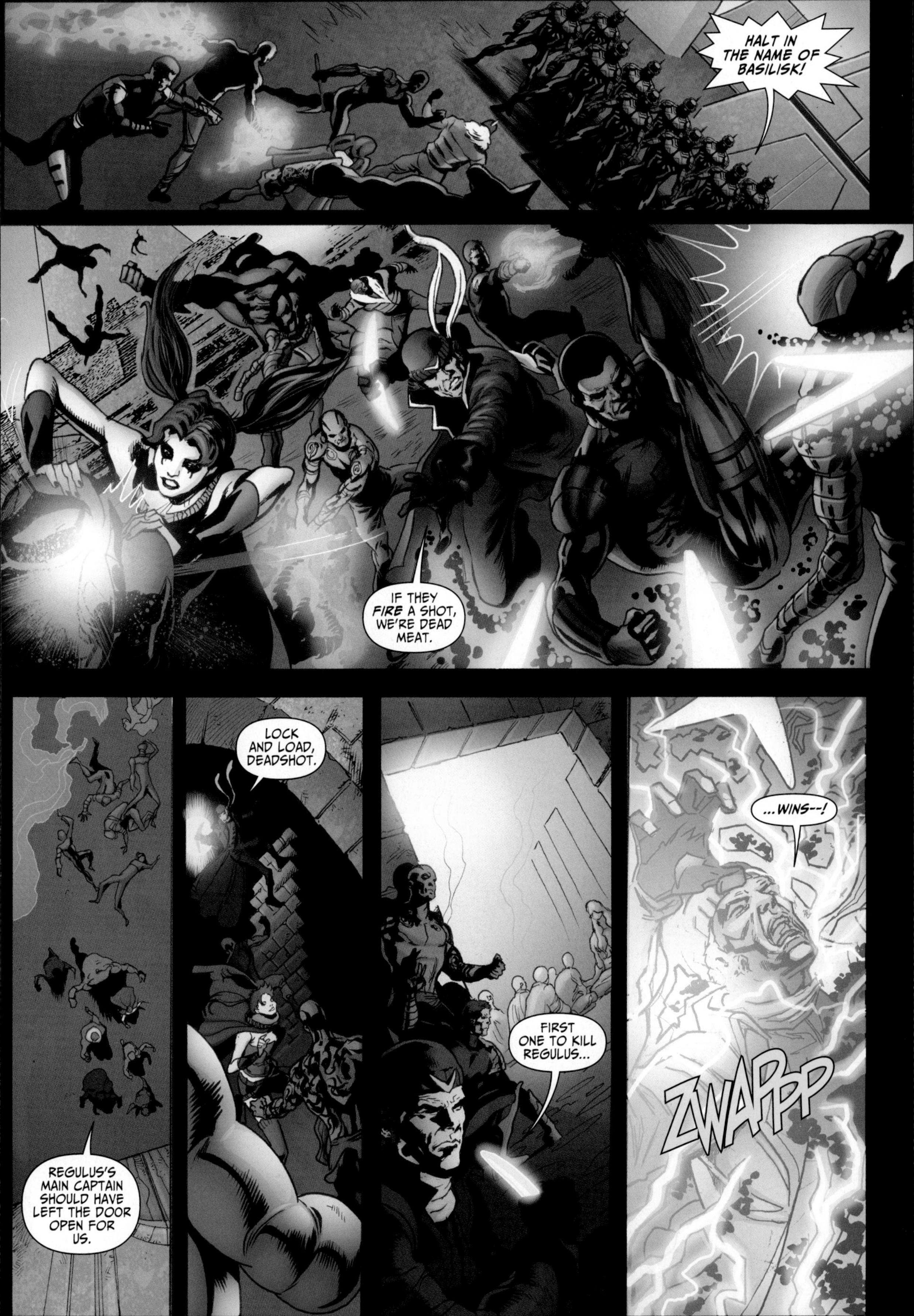
HALT IN THE NAME OF BASILISK!
IF THEY FIRE A SHOT, WE'RE DEAD MEAT.
REGULUS'S MAIN CAPTAIN SHOULD HAVE LEFT THE DOOR OPEN FOR US.
LOCK AND LOAD, DEADSHOT.
FIRST ONE TO KILL REGULUS...
...WINS--!
ZWAPPP

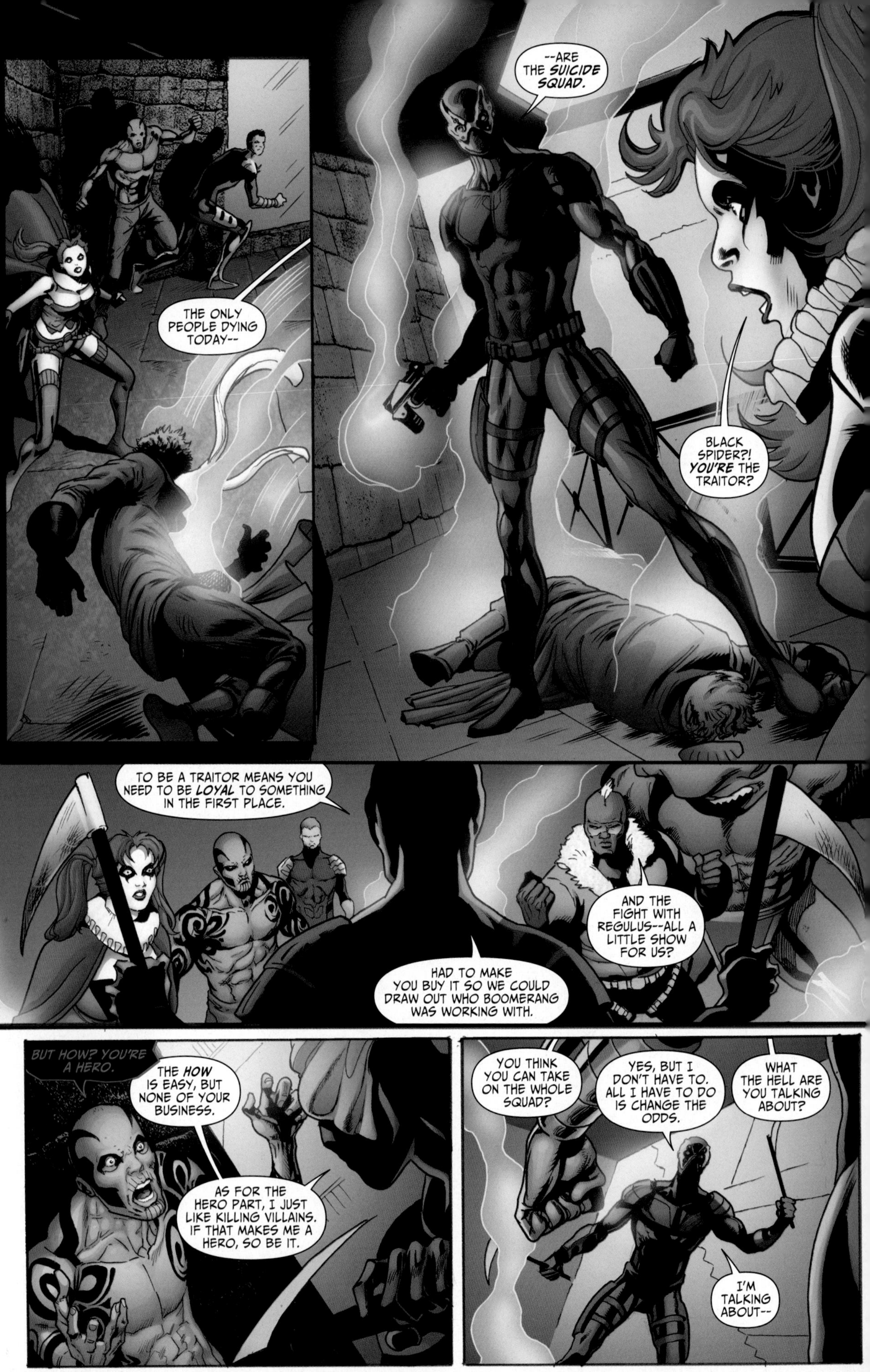
THE ONLY PEOPLE DYING TODAY--
--ARE THE SUICIDE SQUAD.
BLACK SPIDER?! YOU'RE THE TRAITOR?
TO BE A TRAITOR MEANS YOU NEED TO BE LOYAL TO SOMETHING IN THE FIRST PLACE.
AND THE FIGHT WITH REGULUS--ALL A LITTLE SHOW FOR US?
HAD TO MAKE YOU BUY IT SO WE COULD DRAW OUT WHO BOOMERANG WAS WORKING WITH.
BUT HOW? YOU'RE A HERO.
THE HOW IS EASY, BUT NONE OF YOUR BUSINESS.
AS FOR THE HERO PART, I JUST LIKE KILLING VILLAINS. IF THAT MAKES ME A HERO, SO BE IT.
YOU THINK YOU CAN TAKE ON THE WHOLE SQUAD?
YES, BUT I DON'T HAVE TO. ALL I HAVE TO DO IS CHANGE THE ODDS.
WHAT THE HELL ARE YOU TALKING ABOUT?
I'M TALKING ABOUT--

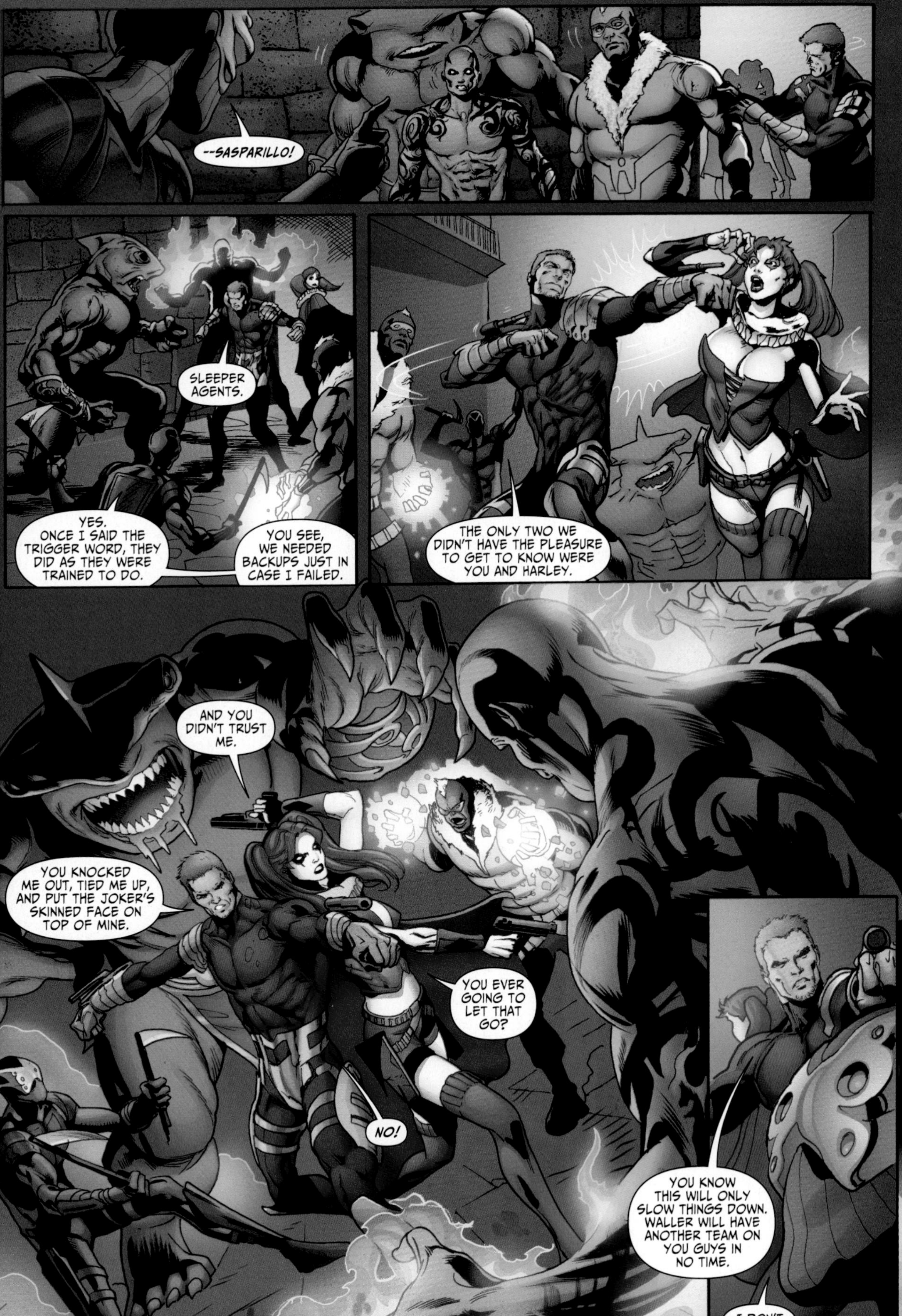
--SASPARILLO!
SLEEPER AGENTS.
YES. ONCE I SAID THE TRIGGER WORD, THEY DID AS THEY WERE TRAINED TO DO.
YOU SEE, WE NEEDED BACKUPS JUST IN CASE I FAILED.
THE ONLY TWO WE DIDN'T HAVE THE PLEASURE TO GET TO KNOW WERE YOU AND HARLEY.
AND YOU DIDN'T TRUST ME.
YOU KNOCKED ME OUT, TIED ME UP, AND PUT THE JOKER'S SKINNED FACE ON TOP OF MINE.
YOU EVER GOING TO LET THAT GO?
NO!
YOU KNOW THIS WILL ONLY SLOW THINGS DOWN. WALLER WILL HAVE ANOTHER TEAM ON YOU GUYS IN NO TIME.
I DON'T THINK SO.

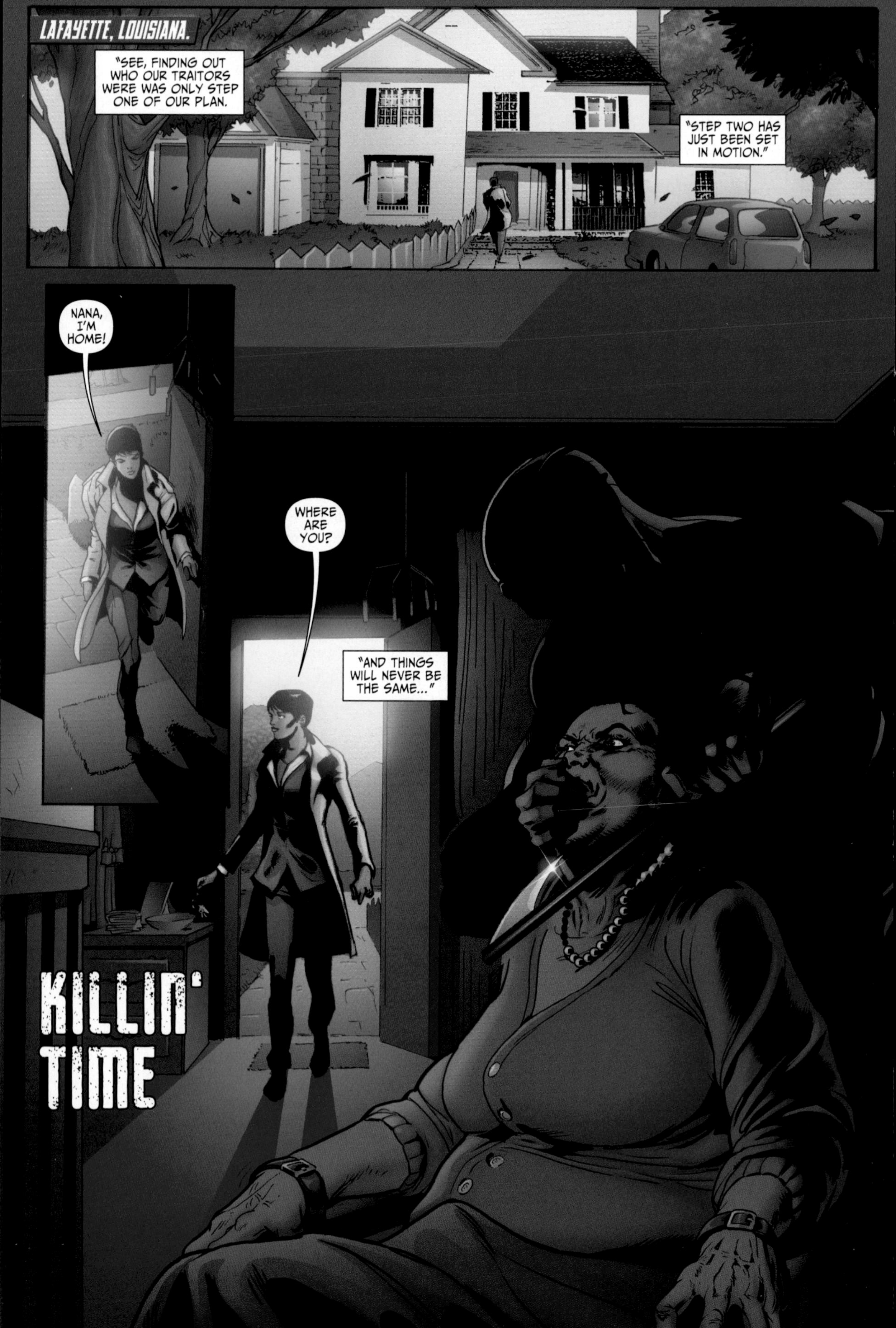
LAFAYETTE, LOUISIANA.
"SEE, FINDING OUT WHO OUR TRAITORS WERE WAS ONLY STEP ONE OF OUR PLAN.
"STEP TWO HAS JUST BEEN SET IN MOTION."
NANA, I'M HOME!
WHERE ARE YOU?
"AND THINGS WILL NEVER BE THE SAME..."
KILLIN' TIME

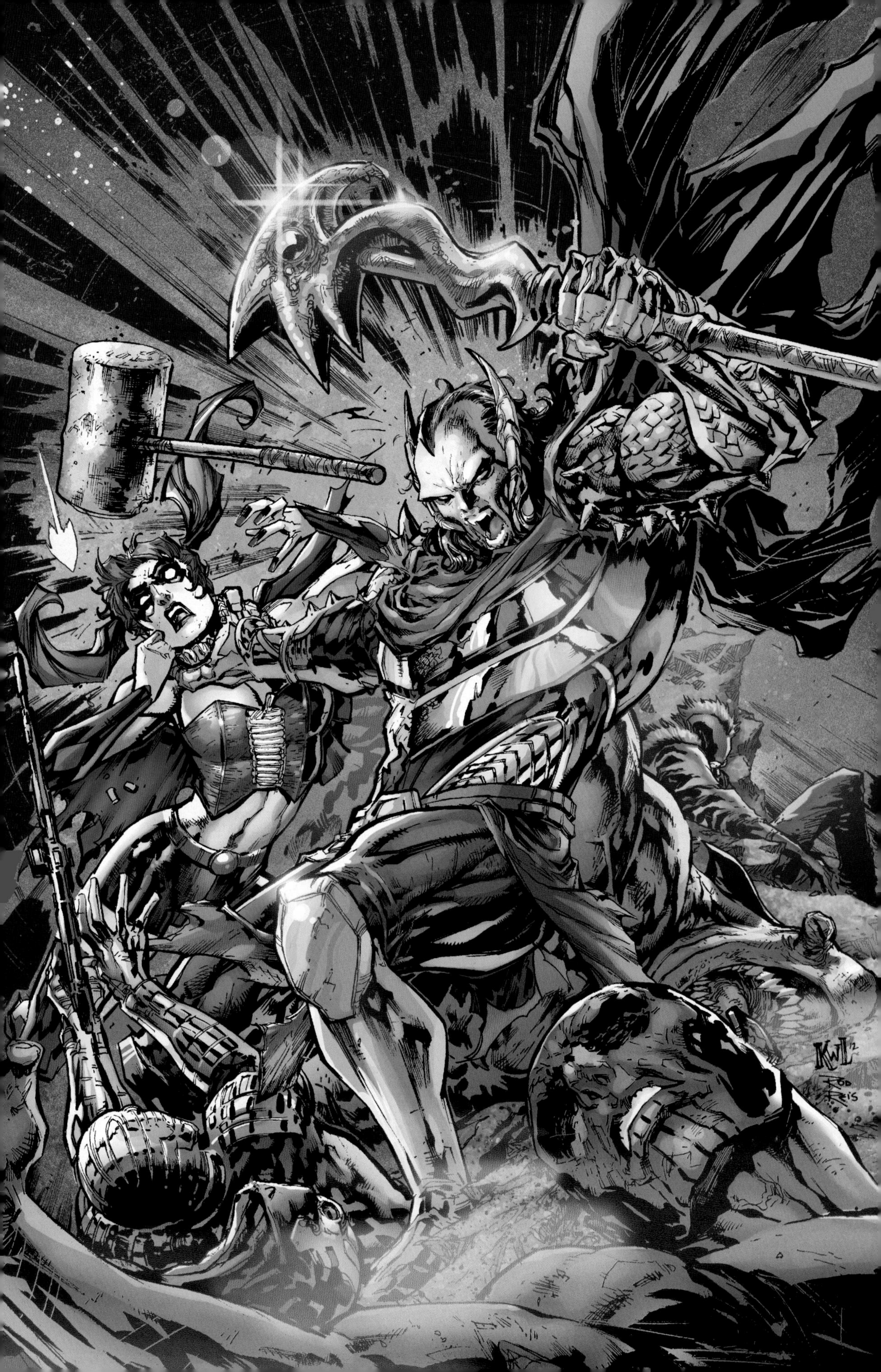
KWL 12
ROD REIS

DEAD END

ADAM GLASS
writer

CLIFF RICHARDS
artist

cover art by KEN LASHLEY & ROD REIS

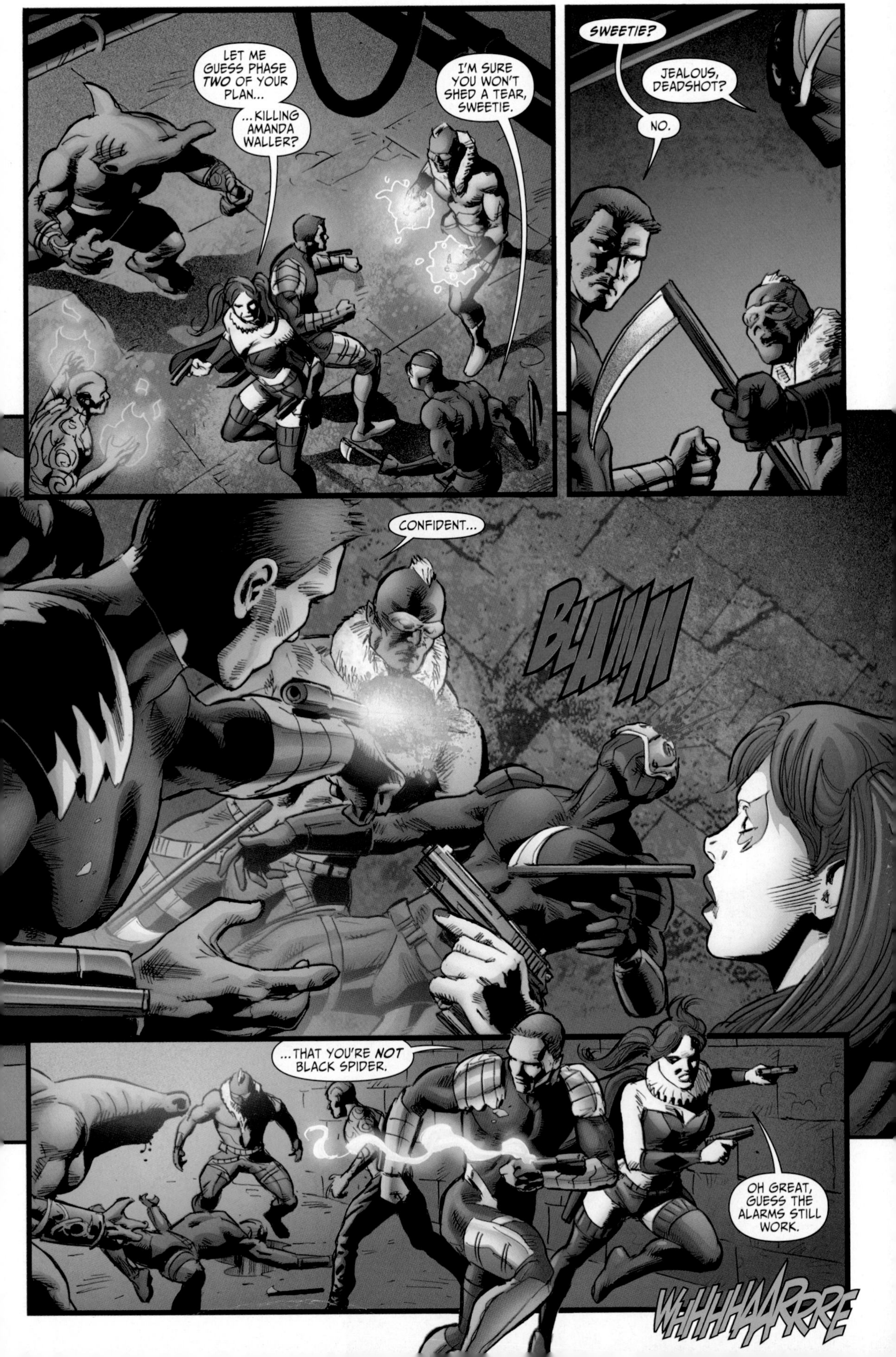
LET ME GUESS PHASE TWO OF YOUR PLAN...
...KILLING AMANDA WALLER?
I'M SURE YOU WON'T SHED A TEAR, SWEETIE.
SWEETIE?
JEALOUS, DEADSHOT?
NO.
CONFIDENT...
BLAMMM
...THAT YOU'RE NOT BLACK SPIDER.
OH GREAT, GUESS THE ALARMS STILL WORK.
WHHHHAARRRE

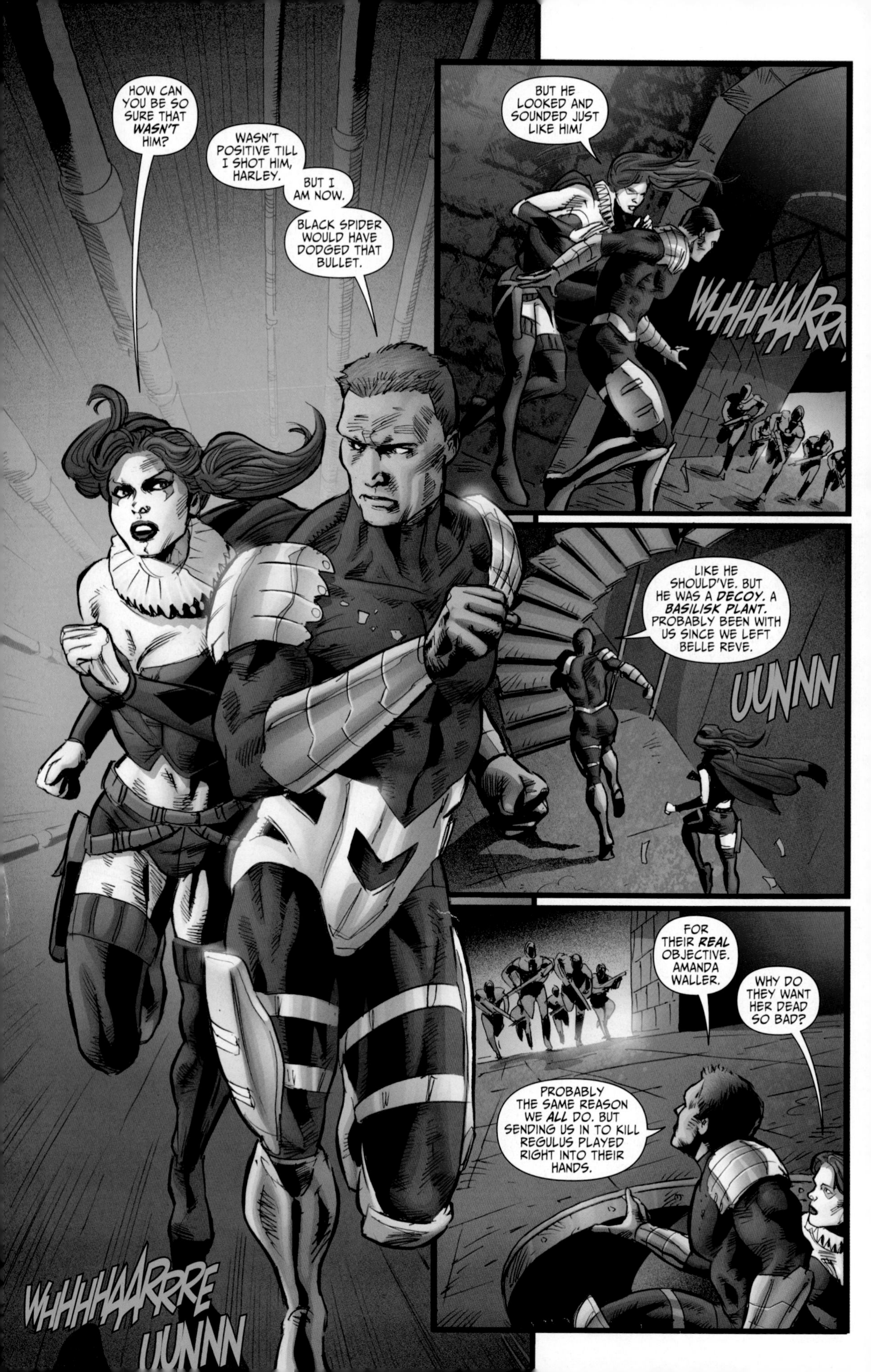
HOW CAN YOU BE SO SURE THAT WASN'T HIM?
WASN'T POSITIVE TILL I SHOT HIM, HARLEY.
BUT I AM NOW.
BLACK SPIDER WOULD HAVE DODGED THAT BULLET.
WHHHHAARRRE
UUNNN
BUT HE LOOKED AND SOUNDED JUST LIKE HIM!
WHHHHAARRR
LIKE HE SHOULD'VE. BUT HE WAS A DECOY. A BASILISK PLANT. PROBABLY BEEN WITH US SINCE WE LEFT BELLE REVE.
UUNNN
FOR THEIR REAL OBJECTIVE. AMANDA WALLER.
WHY DO THEY WANT HER DEAD SO BAD?
PROBABLY THE SAME REASON WE ALL DO. BUT SENDING US IN TO KILL REGULUS PLAYED RIGHT INTO THEIR HANDS.

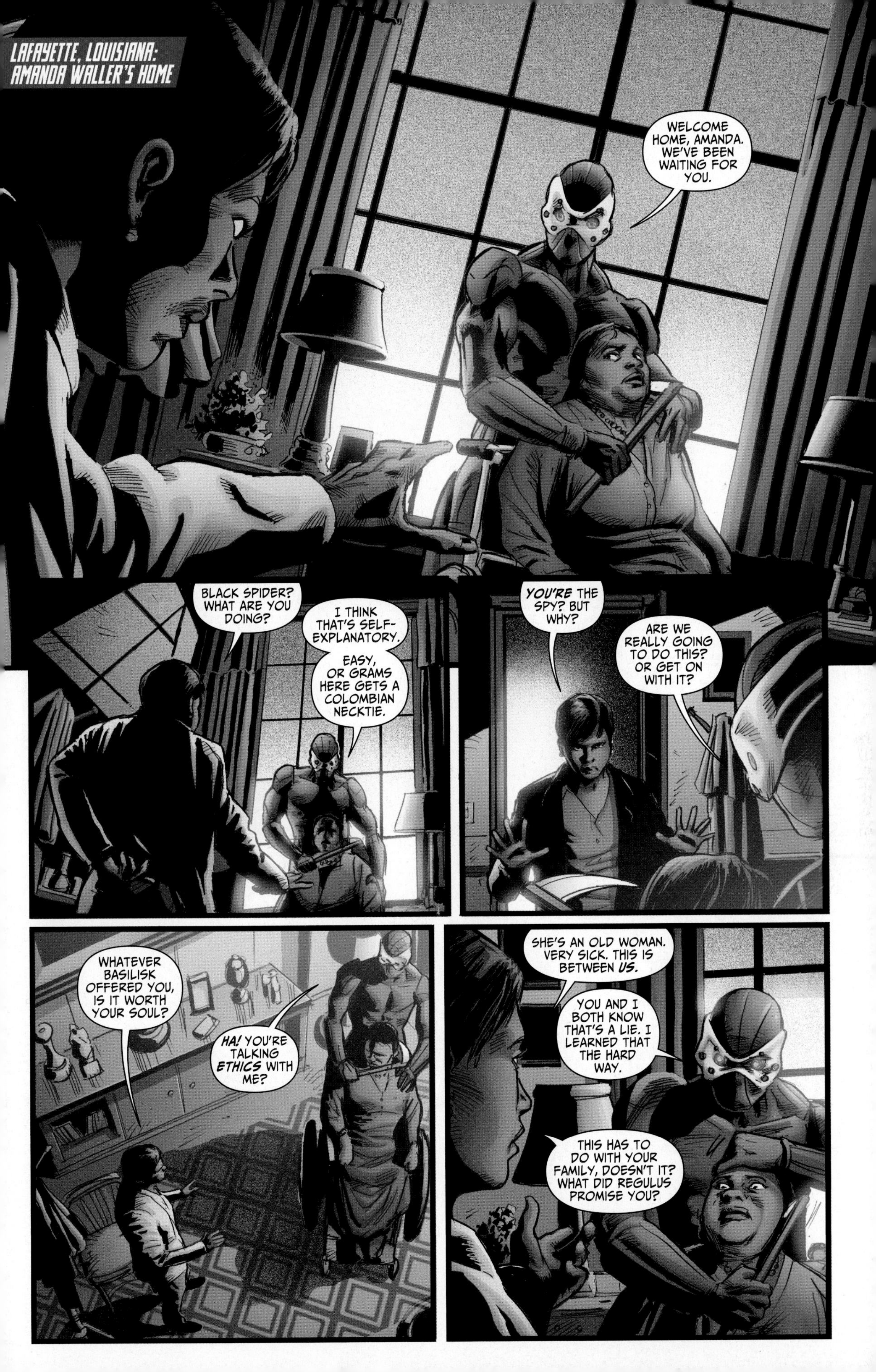

LAFAYETTE, LOUISIANA: AMANDA WALLER'S HOME
WELCOME HOME, AMANDA. WE'VE BEEN WAITING FOR YOU.
BLACK SPIDER? WHAT ARE YOU DOING?
I THINK THAT'S SELF-EXPLANATORY.
EASY, OR GRAMS HERE GETS A COLOMBIAN NECKTIE.
YOU'RE THE SPY? BUT WHY?
ARE WE REALLY GOING TO DO THIS? OR GET ON WITH IT?
WHATEVER BASILISK OFFERED YOU, IS IT WORTH YOUR SOUL?
HA! YOU'RE TALKING ETHICS WITH ME?
SHE'S AN OLD WOMAN. VERY SICK. THIS IS BETWEEN US.
YOU AND I BOTH KNOW THAT'S A LIE. I LEARNED THAT THE HARD WAY.
THIS HAS TO DO WITH YOUR FAMILY, DOESN'T IT? WHAT DID REGULUS PROMISE YOU?

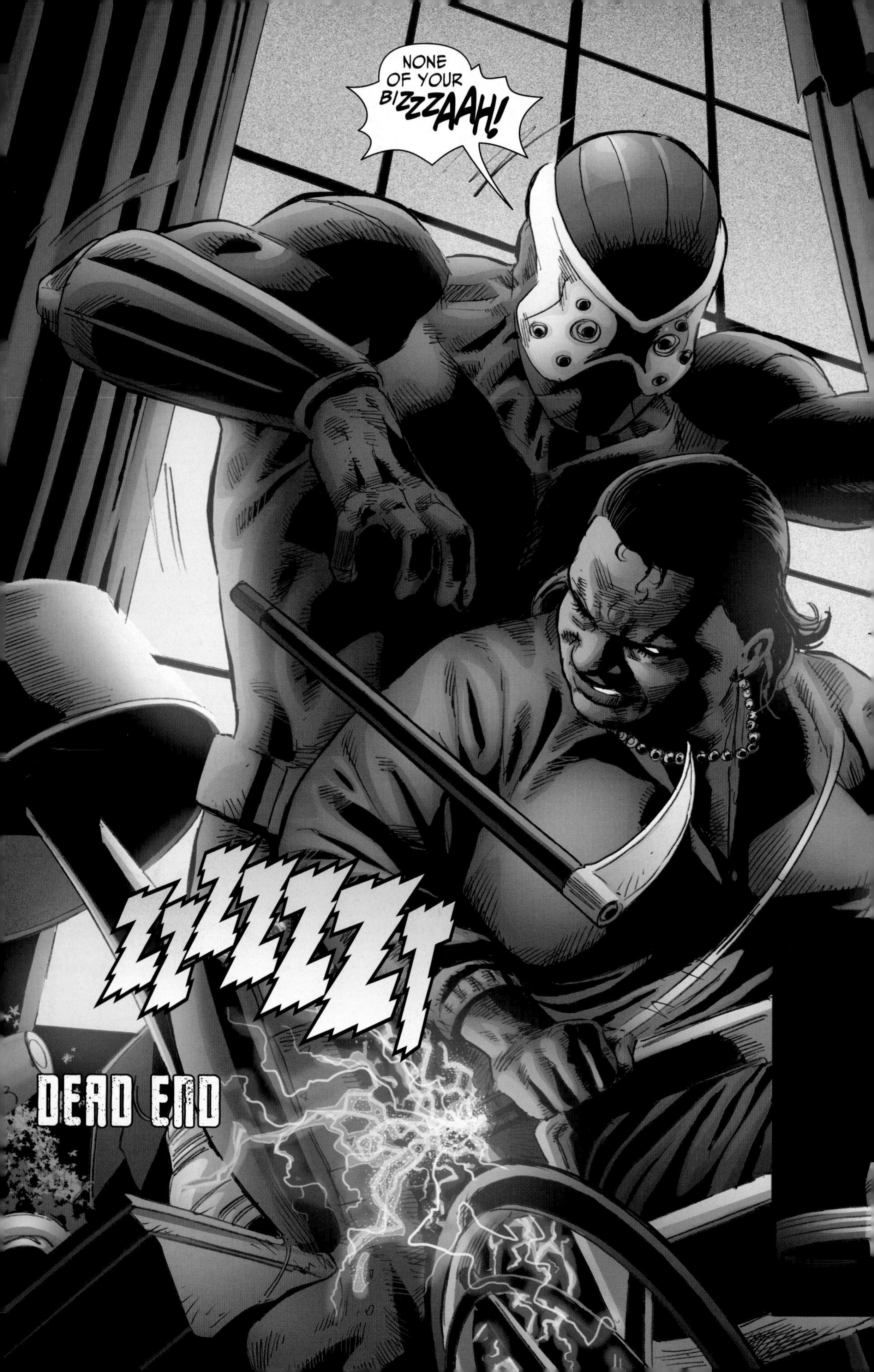
NONE OF YOUR BIZZZAAH!
ZZZZZT
DEAD END

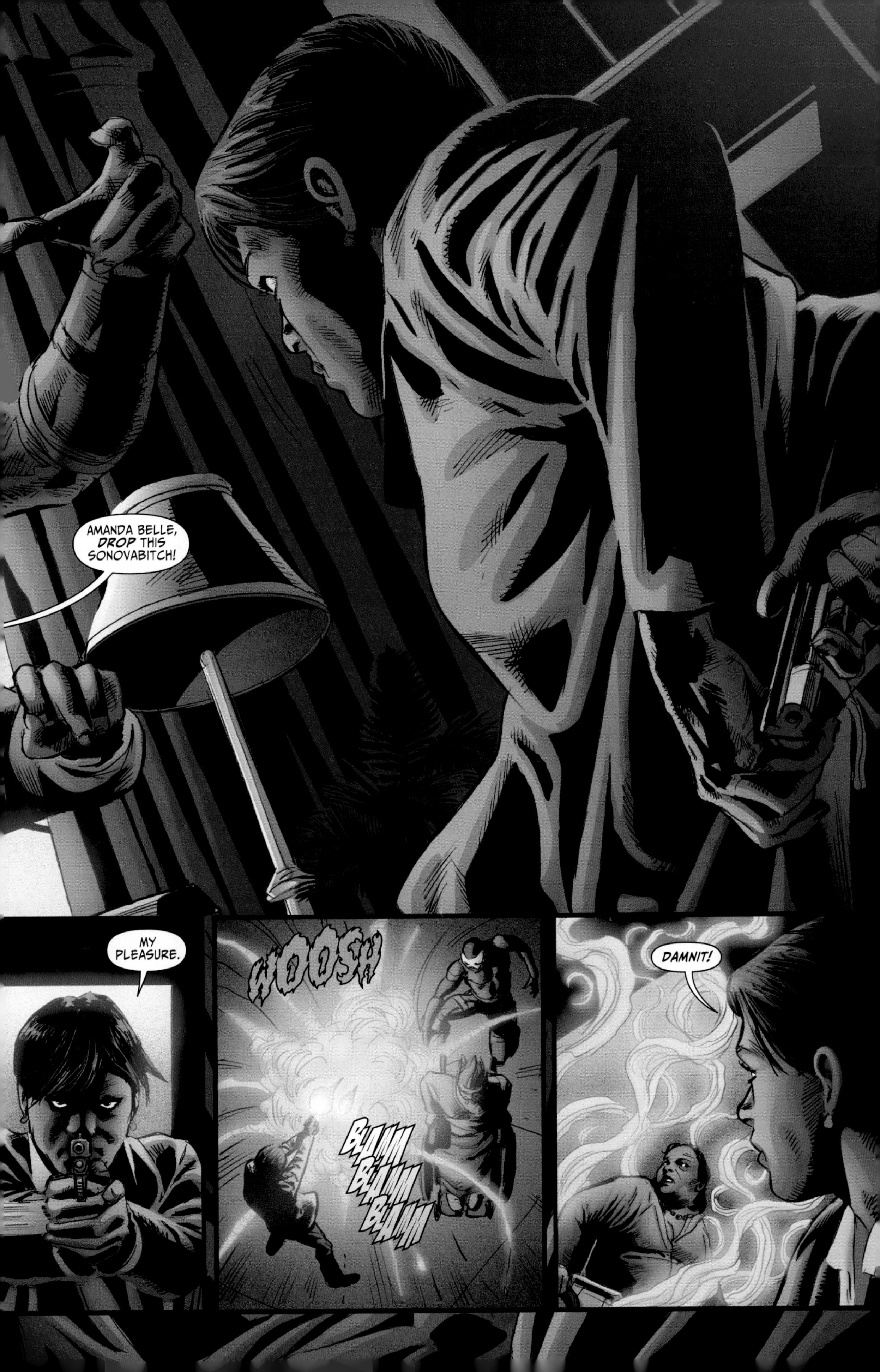
AMANDA BELLE, DROP THIS SONOVABITCH!
MY PLEASURE.
WOOSH
BLAMM BLAMM BLAMM
DAMNIT!

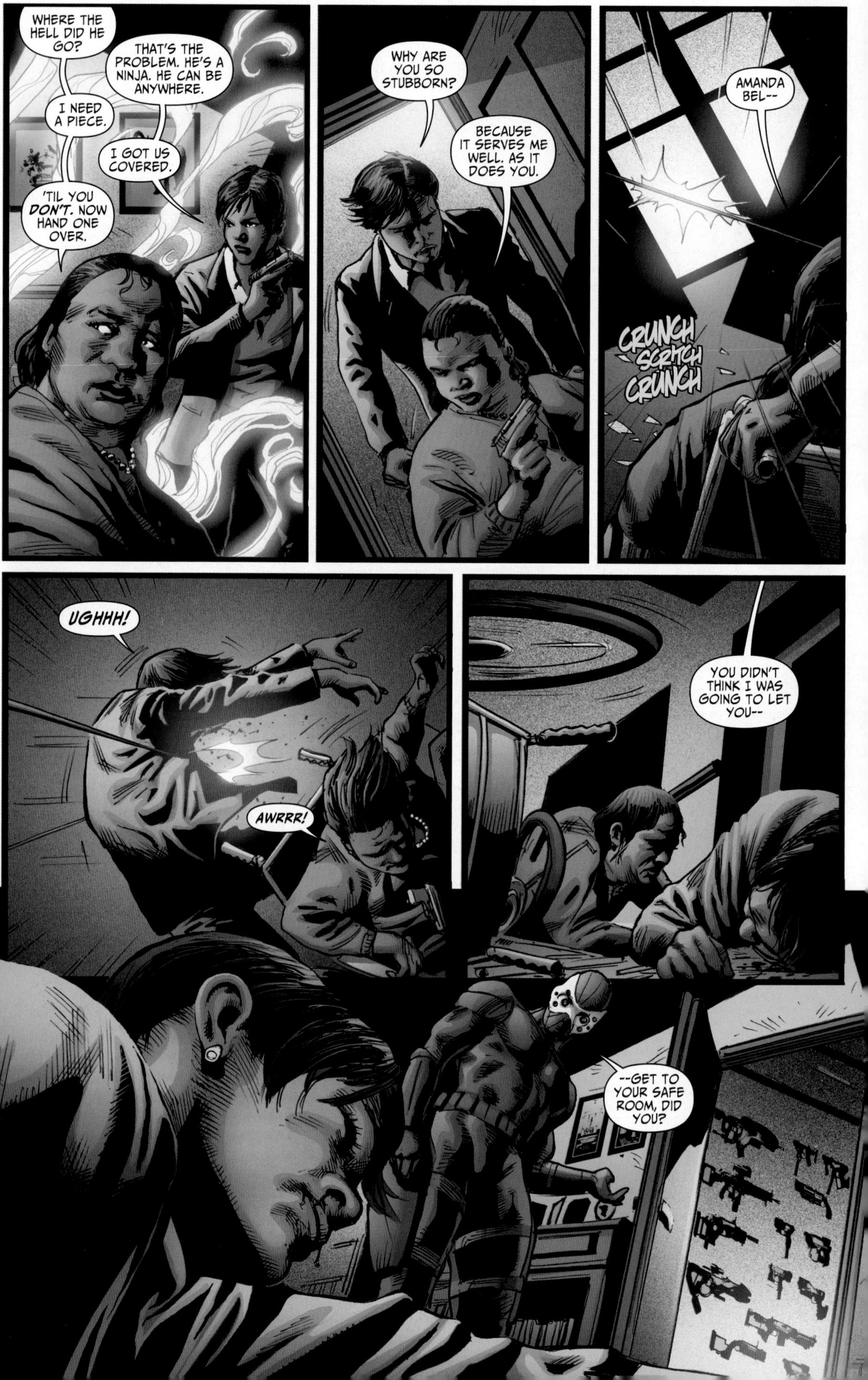
WHERE THE HELL DID HE GO?
THAT'S THE PROBLEM. HE'S A NINJA. HE CAN BE ANYWHERE.
I NEED A PIECE.
I GOT US COVERED.
'TIL YOU DON'T. NOW HAND ONE OVER.
WHY ARE YOU SO STUBBORN?
BECAUSE IT SERVES ME WELL. AS IT DOES YOU.
AMANDA BEL--
CRUNCH SCRITCH CRUNCH
UGHHH!
AWRRR!
YOU DIDN'T THINK I WAS GOING TO LET YOU--
--GET TO YOUR SAFE ROOM, DID YOU?

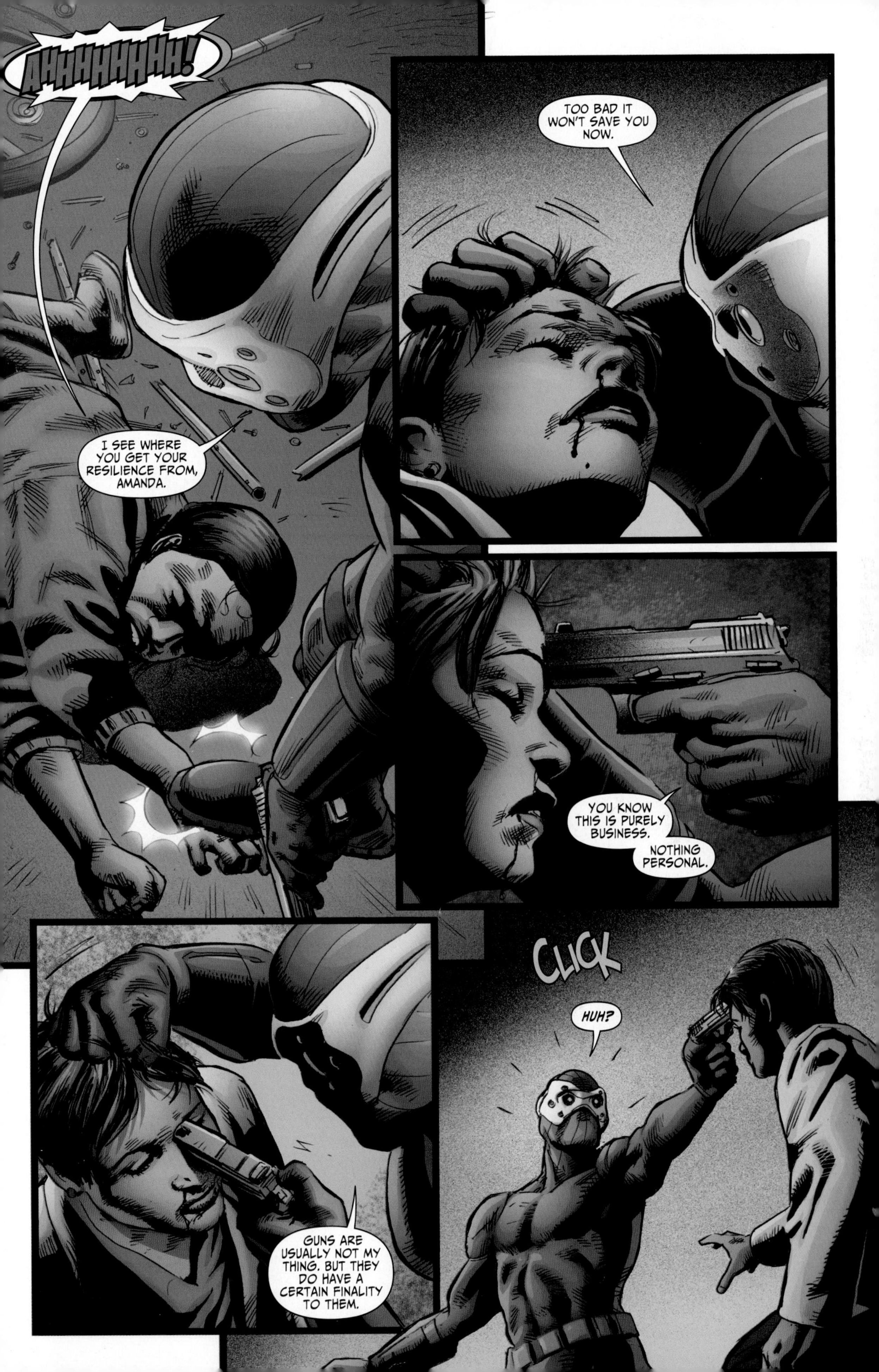
AHHHHHHHH!
I SEE WHERE YOU GET YOUR RESILIENCE FROM, AMANDA.
TOO BAD IT WON'T SAVE YOU NOW.
YOU KNOW THIS IS PURELY BUSINESS.
NOTHING PERSONAL.
GUNS ARE USUALLY NOT MY THING. BUT THEY DO HAVE A CERTAIN FINALITY TO THEM.
CLICK
HUH?

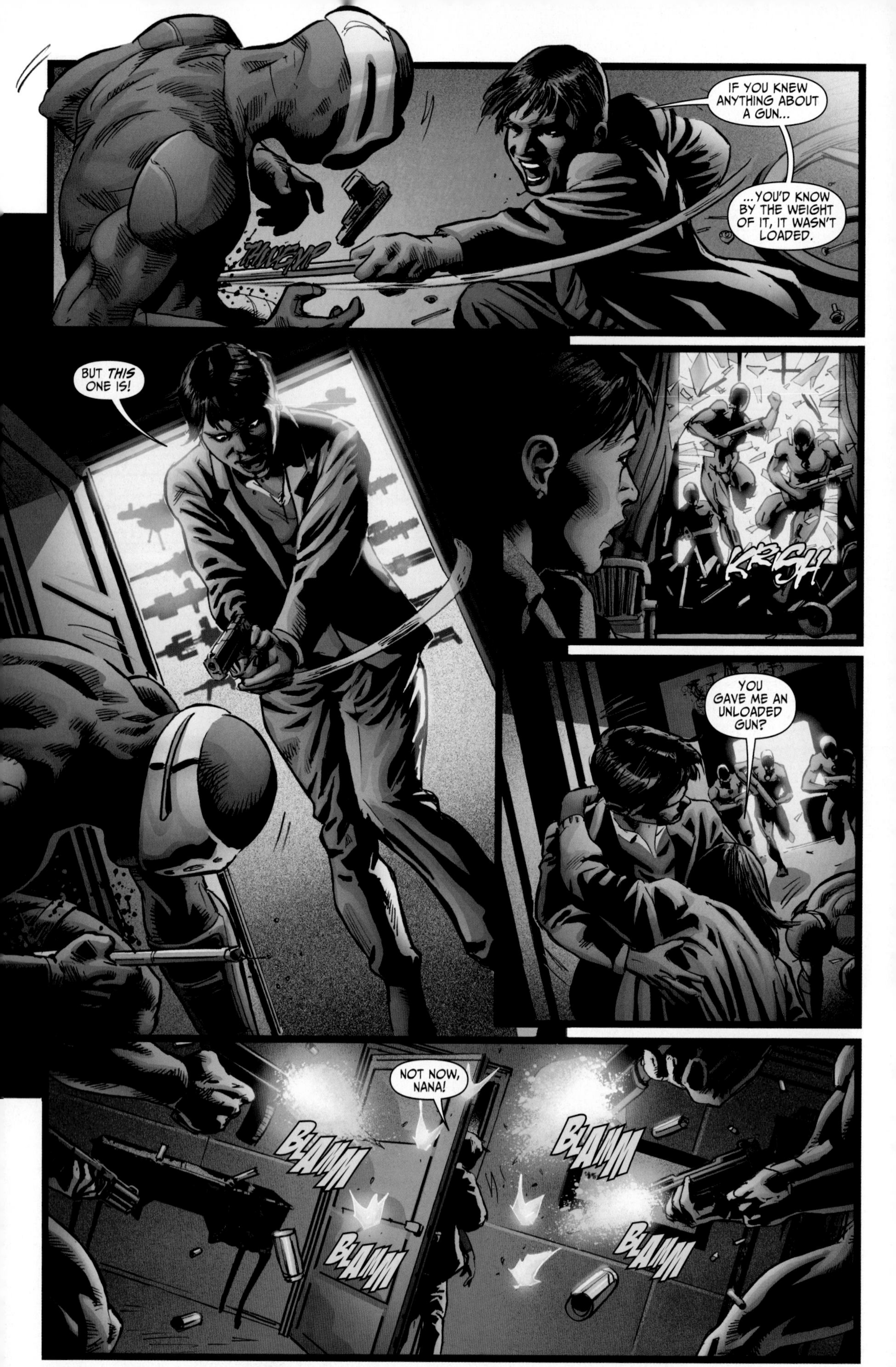
THWEMP
IF YOU KNEW ANYTHING ABOUT A GUN...
...YOU'D KNOW BY THE WEIGHT OF IT, IT WASN'T LOADED.
BUT THIS ONE IS!
KRSH
YOU GAVE ME AN UNLOADED GUN?
NOT NOW, NANA!
BLAMM
BLAMM
BLAMM
BLAMM

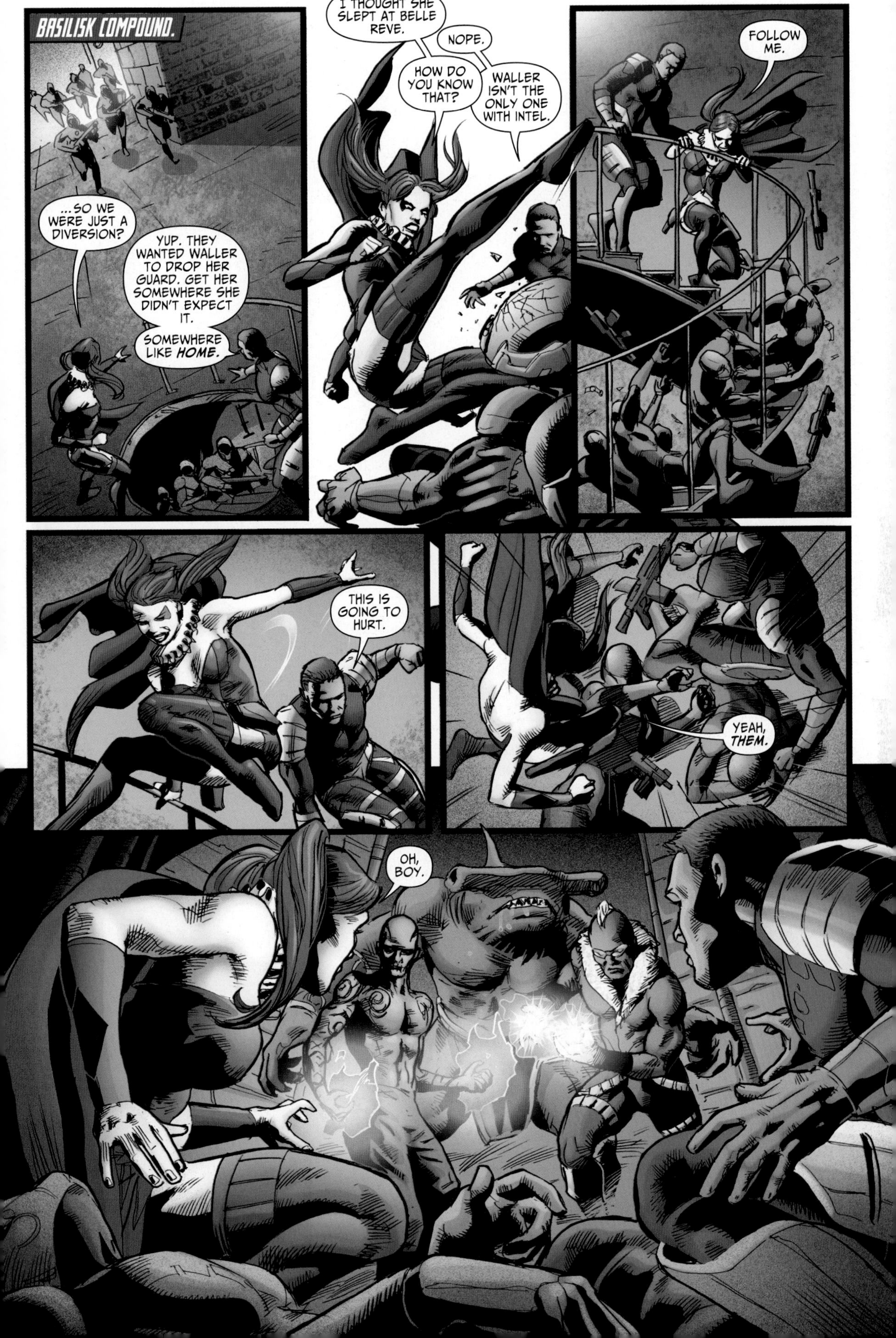
BASILISK COMPOUND.
...SO WE WERE JUST A DIVERSION?
YUP. THEY WANTED WALLER TO DROP HER GUARD. GET HER SOMEWHERE SHE DIDN'T EXPECT IT.
SOMEWHERE LIKE HOME.
I THOUGHT SHE SLEPT AT BELLE REVE.
NOPE.
HOW DO YOU KNOW THAT?
WALLER ISN'T THE ONLY ONE WITH INTEL.
FOLLOW ME.
THIS IS GOING TO HURT.
YEAH, THEM.
OH, BOY.

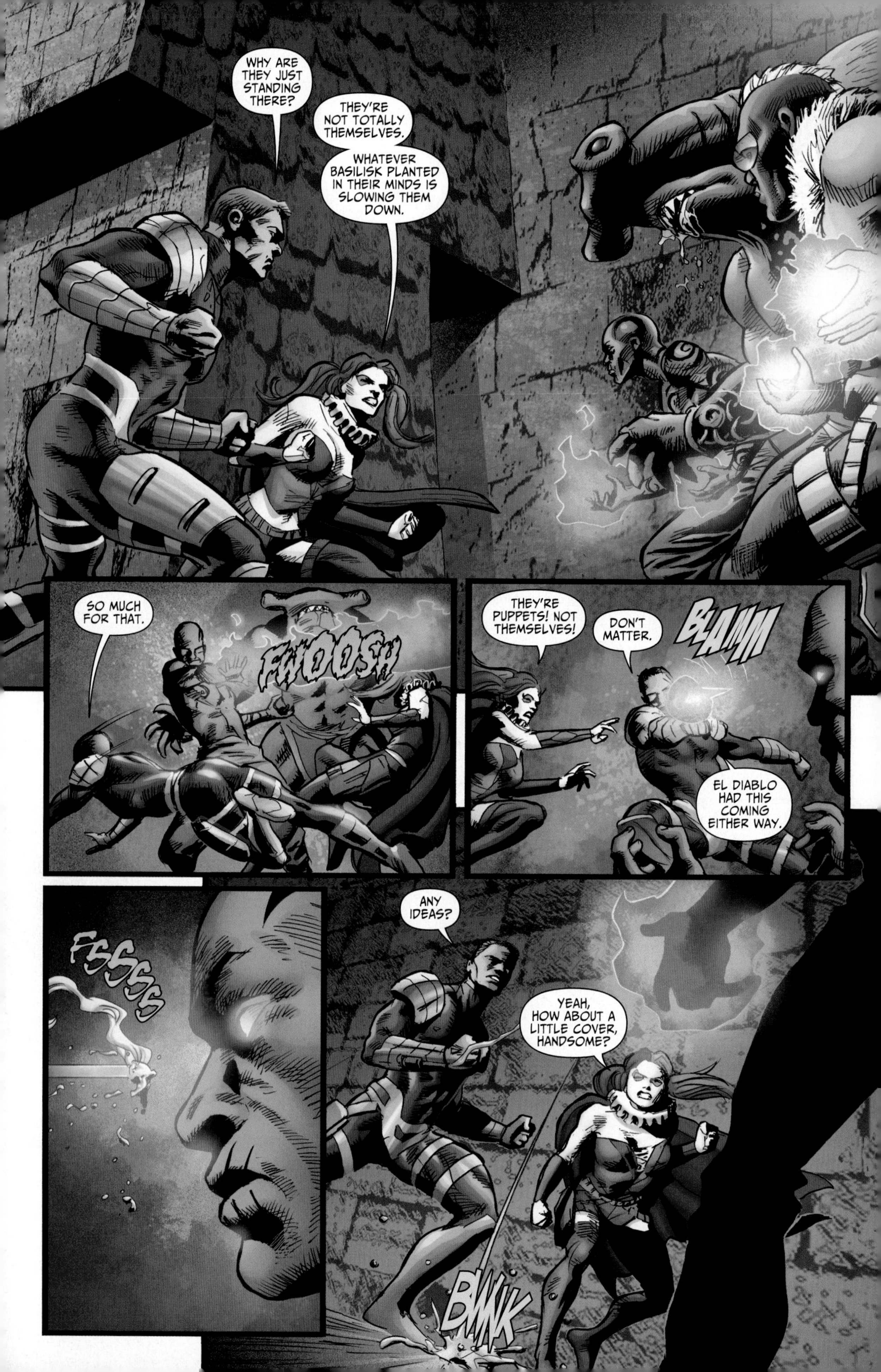

WHY ARE THEY JUST STANDING THERE?
THEY'RE NOT TOTALLY THEMSELVES.
WHATEVER BASILISK PLANTED IN THEIR MINDS IS SLOWING THEM DOWN.
SO MUCH FOR THAT.
FWOOSH
THEY'RE PUPPETS! NOT THEMSELVES!
DON'T MATTER.
BLAMM
EL DIABLO HAD THIS COMING EITHER WAY.
FSSSS
ANY IDEAS?
YEAH, HOW ABOUT A LITTLE COVER, HANDSOME?
BMNK

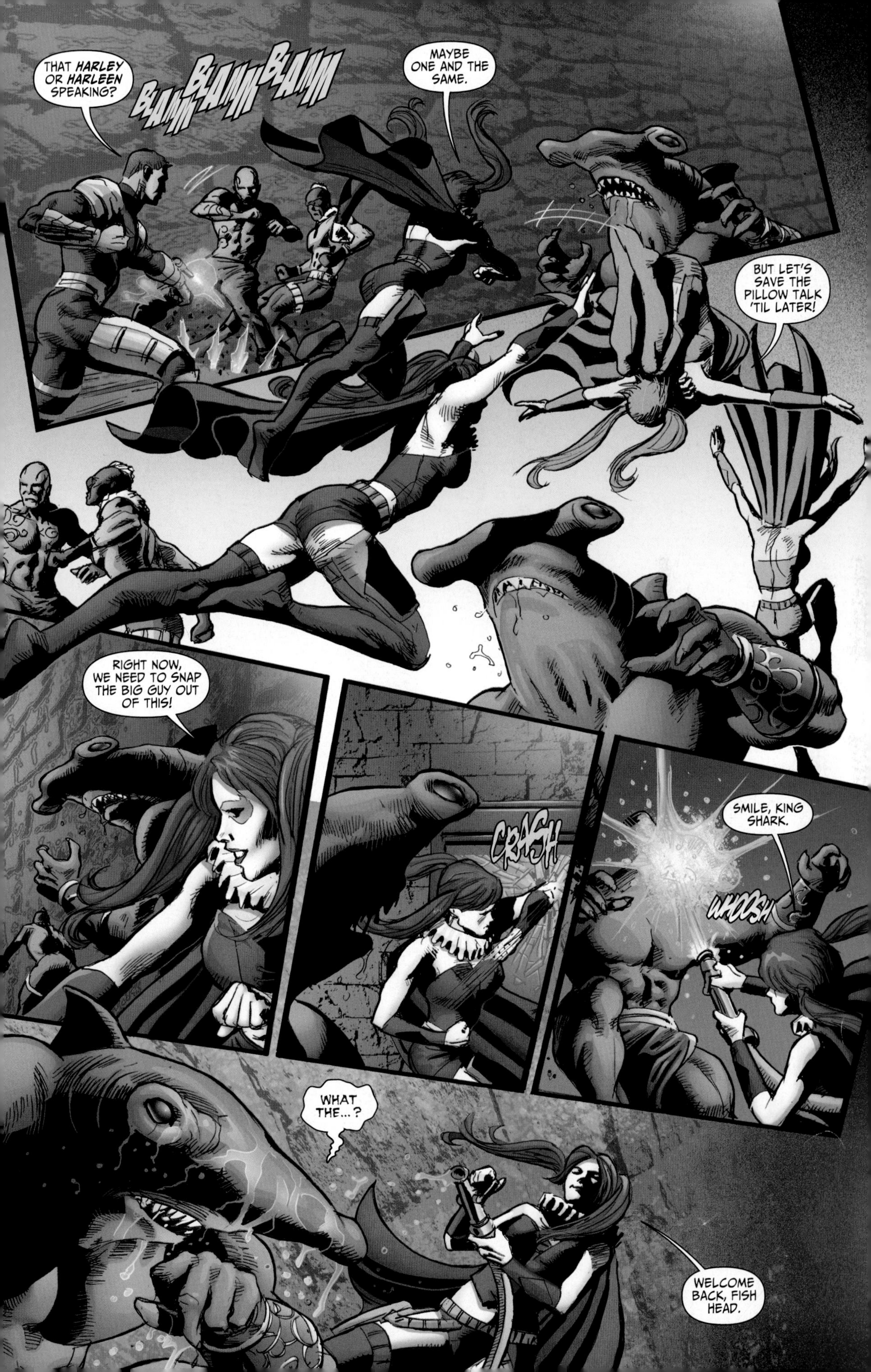
THAT HARLEY OR HARLEEN SPEAKING?
BLAMM BLAMM BLAMM
MAYBE ONE AND THE SAME.
BUT LET'S SAVE THE PILLOW TALK 'TIL LATER!
RIGHT NOW, WE NEED TO SNAP THE BIG GUY OUT OF THIS!
CRASH
SMILE, KING SHARK.
WHOOSH
WHAT THE...?
WELCOME BACK, FISH HEAD.

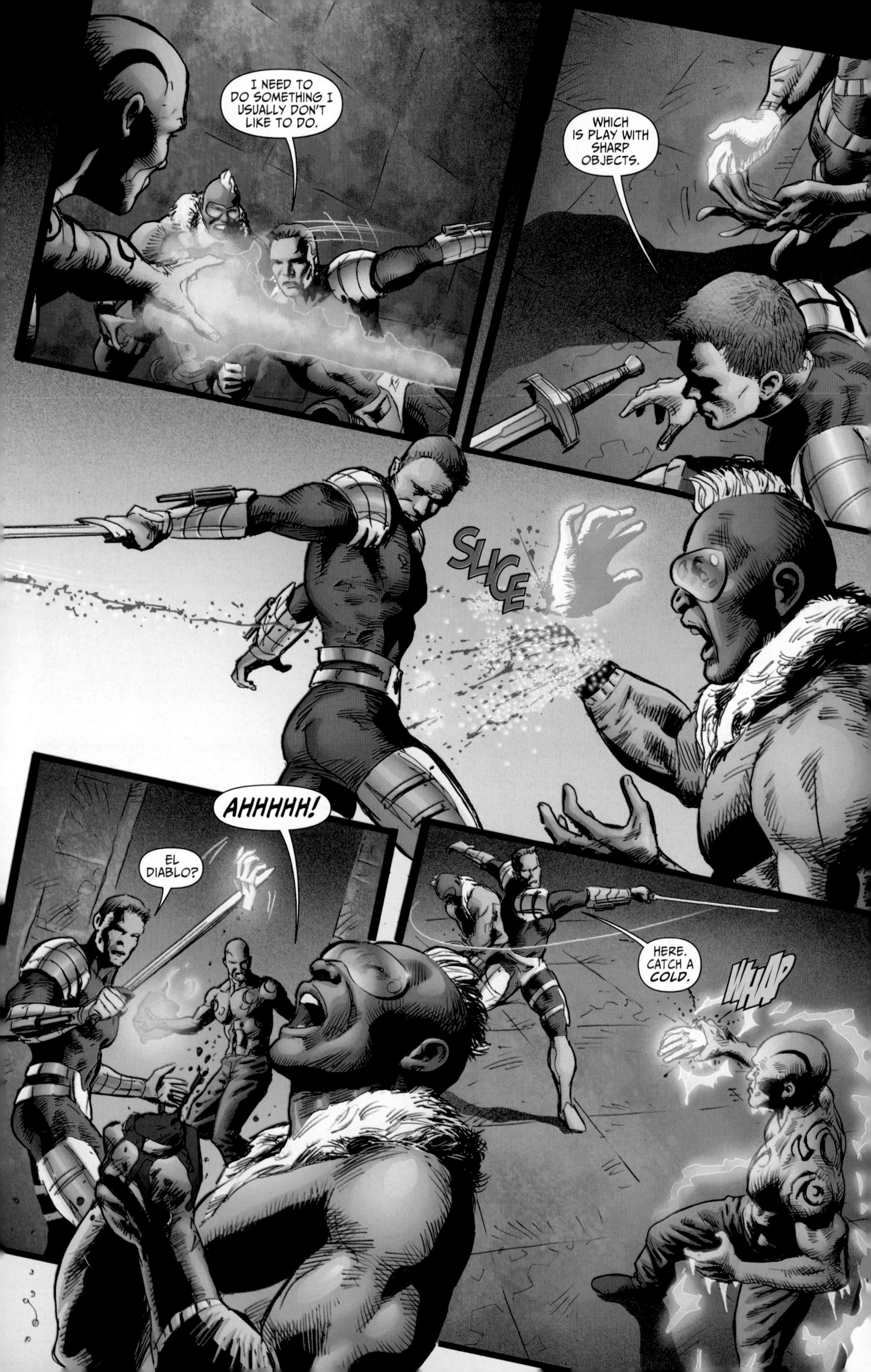
I NEED TO DO SOMETHING I USUALLY DON'T LIKE TO DO.
WHICH IS PLAY WITH SHARP OBJECTS.
SLICE
AHHHHH!
EL DIABLO?
HERE. CATCH A COLD.

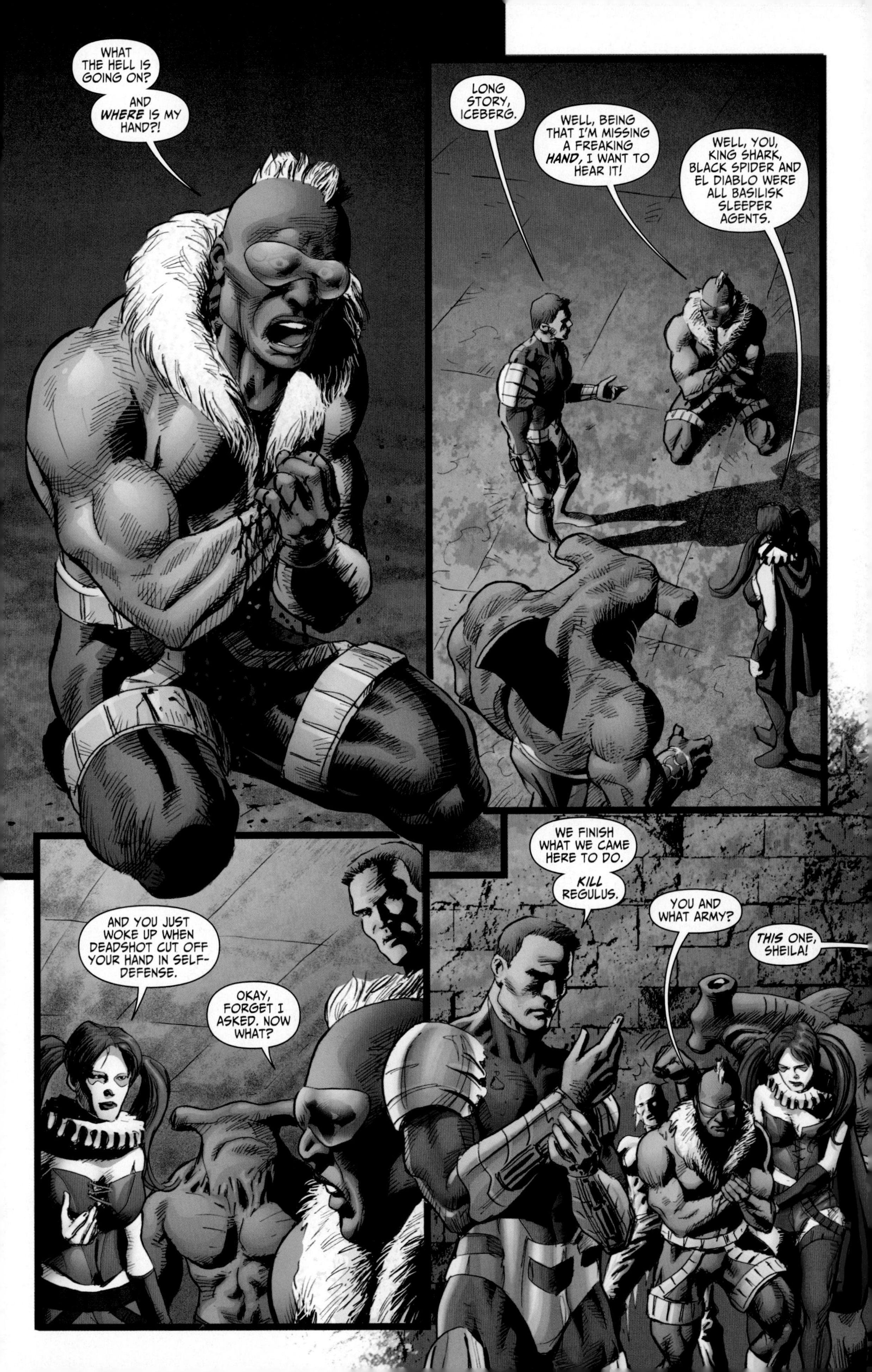
WHAT THE HELL IS GOING ON?
AND *WHERE* IS MY HAND?!
LONG STORY, ICEBERG.
WELL, BEING THAT I'M MISSING A FREAKING *HAND*, I WANT TO HEAR IT!
WELL, YOU, KING SHARK, BLACK SPIDER AND EL DIABLO WERE ALL BASILISK SLEEPER AGENTS.
AND YOU JUST WOKE UP WHEN DEADSHOT CUT OFF YOUR HAND IN SELF-DEFENSE.
OKAY, FORGET I ASKED. NOW WHAT?
WE FINISH WHAT WE CAME HERE TO DO.
KILL REGULUS.
YOU AND WHAT ARMY?
THIS ONE, SHEILA!

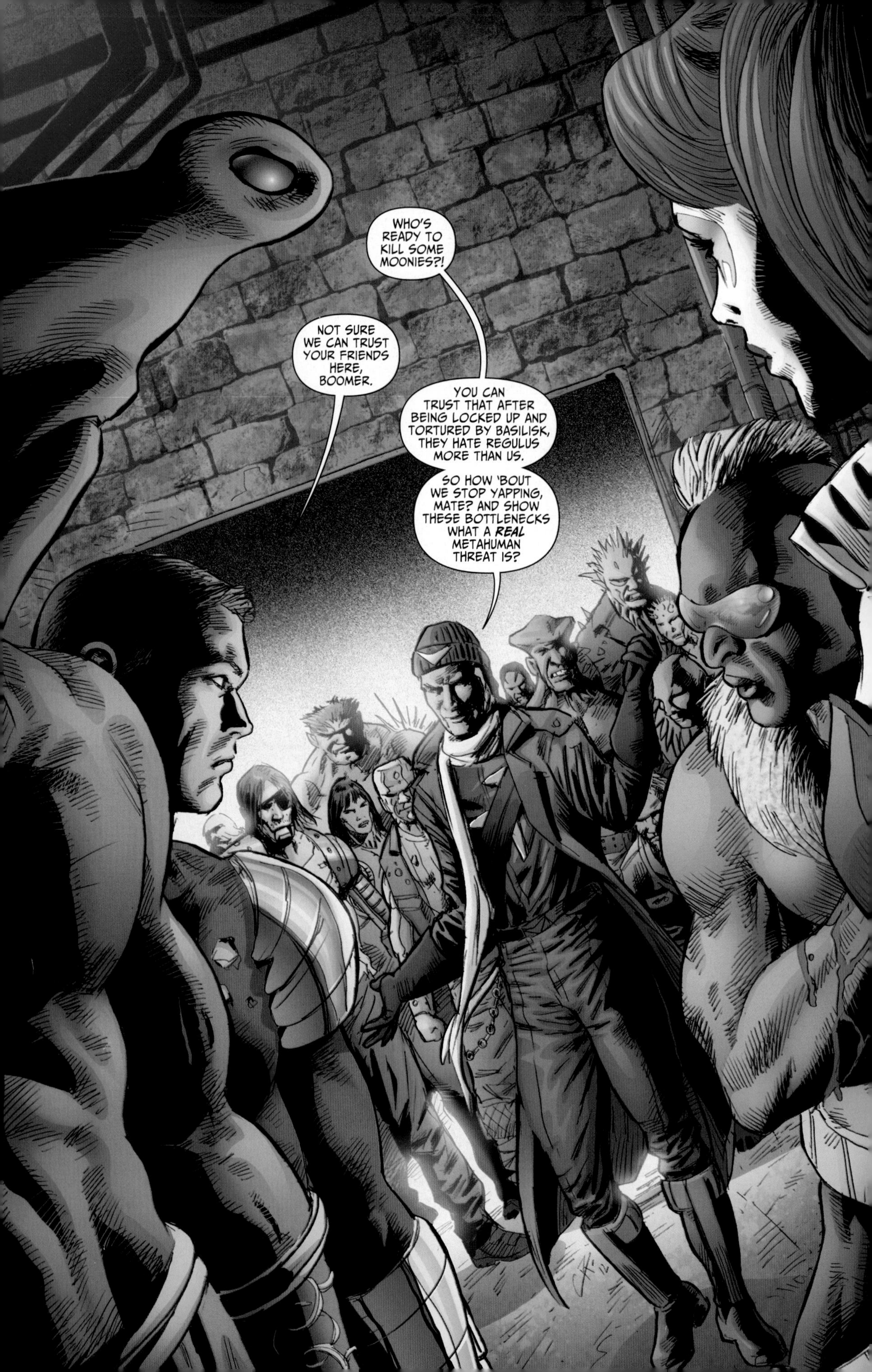
WHO'S READY TO KILL SOME MOONIES?!
NOT SURE WE CAN TRUST YOUR FRIENDS HERE, BOOMER.
YOU CAN TRUST THAT AFTER BEING LOCKED UP AND TORTURED BY BASILISK, THEY HATE REGULUS MORE THAN US.
SO HOW 'BOUT WE STOP YAPPING, MATE? AND SHOW THESE BOTTLENECKS WHAT A *REAL* METAHUMAN THREAT IS?

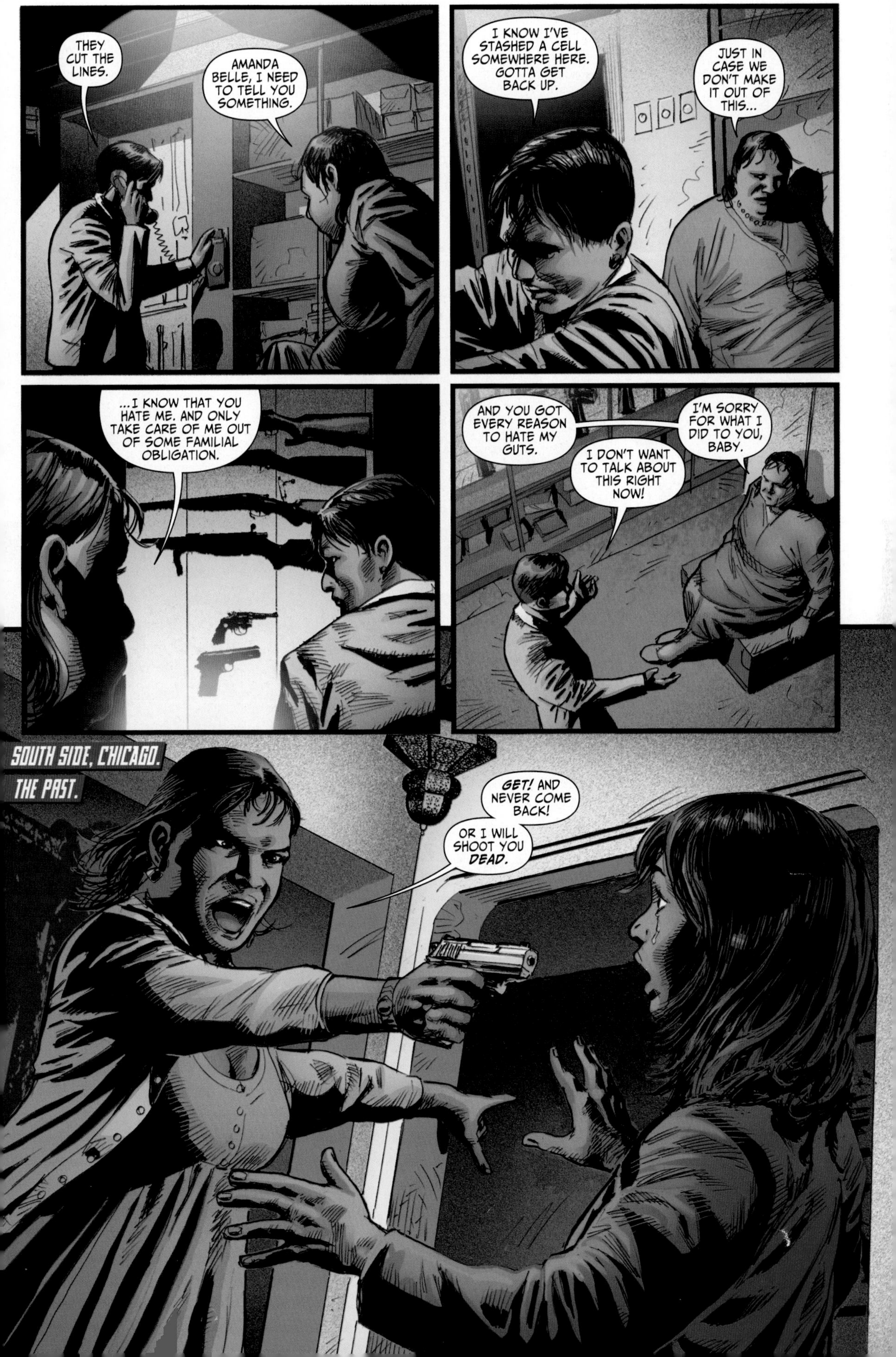
THEY CUT THE LINES.
AMANDA BELLE, I NEED TO TELL YOU SOMETHING.
I KNOW I'VE STASHED A CELL SOMEWHERE HERE. GOTTA GET BACK UP.
JUST IN CASE WE DON'T MAKE IT OUT OF THIS...
...I KNOW THAT YOU HATE ME. AND ONLY TAKE CARE OF ME OUT OF SOME FAMILIAL OBLIGATION.
AND YOU GOT EVERY REASON TO HATE MY GUTS.
I'M SORRY FOR WHAT I DID TO YOU, BABY.
I DON'T WANT TO TALK ABOUT THIS RIGHT NOW!
SOUTH SIDE, CHICAGO.
THE PAST.
GET! AND NEVER COME BACK!
OR I WILL SHOOT YOU DEAD.

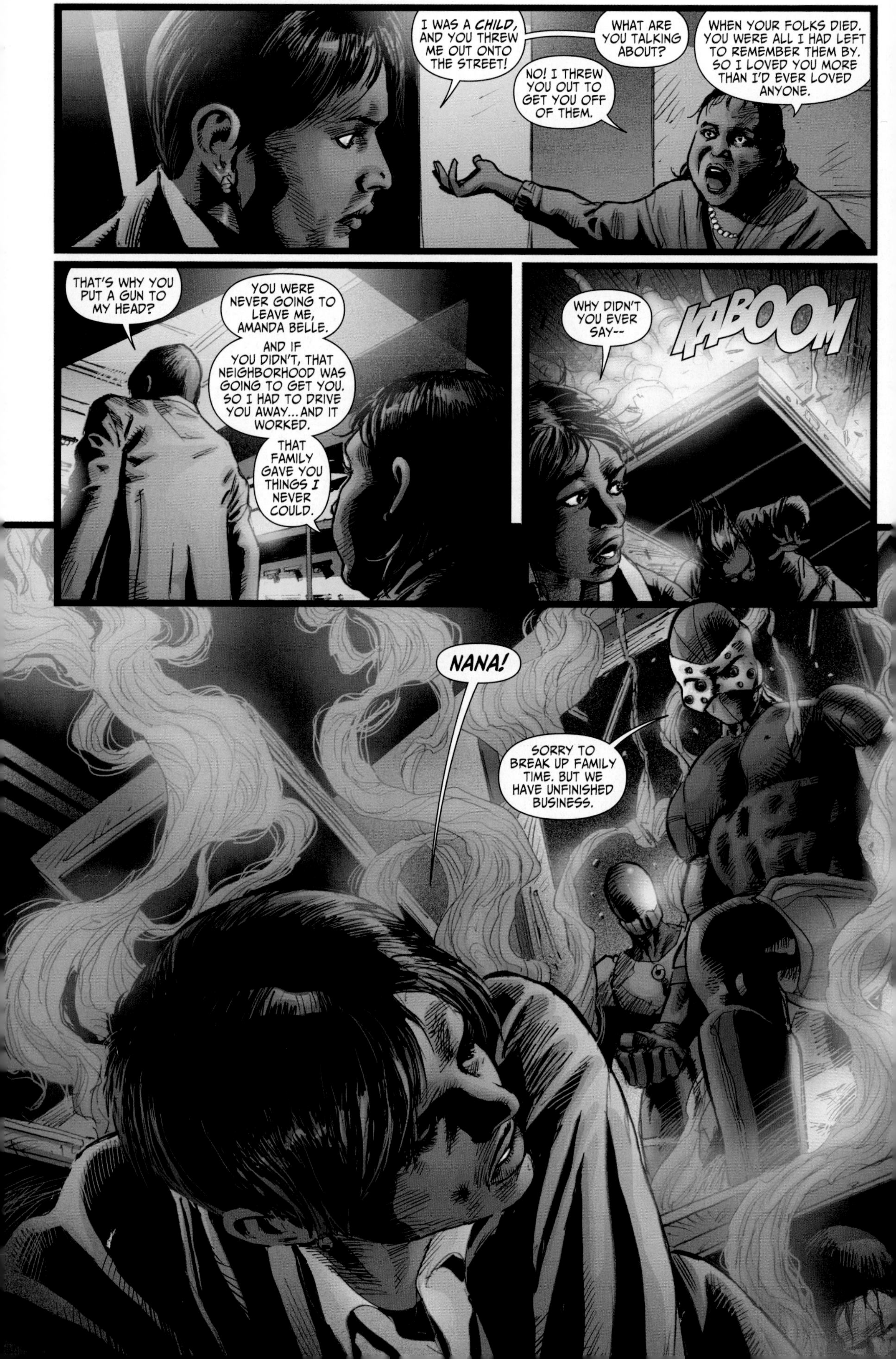
I WAS A *CHILD*, AND YOU THREW ME OUT ONTO THE STREET!
WHAT ARE YOU TALKING ABOUT?
NO! I THREW YOU OUT TO GET YOU OFF OF THEM.
WHEN YOUR FOLKS DIED. YOU WERE ALL I HAD LEFT TO REMEMBER THEM BY. SO I LOVED YOU MORE THAN I'D EVER LOVED ANYONE.
THAT'S WHY YOU PUT A GUN TO MY HEAD?
YOU WERE NEVER GOING TO LEAVE ME, AMANDA BELLE.
AND IF YOU DIDN'T, THAT NEIGHBORHOOD WAS GOING TO GET YOU. SO I HAD TO DRIVE YOU AWAY...AND IT WORKED.
THAT FAMILY GAVE YOU THINGS *I* NEVER COULD.
WHY DIDN'T YOU EVER SAY--
KABOOM
NANA!
SORRY TO BREAK UP FAMILY TIME. BUT WE HAVE UNFINISHED BUSINESS.

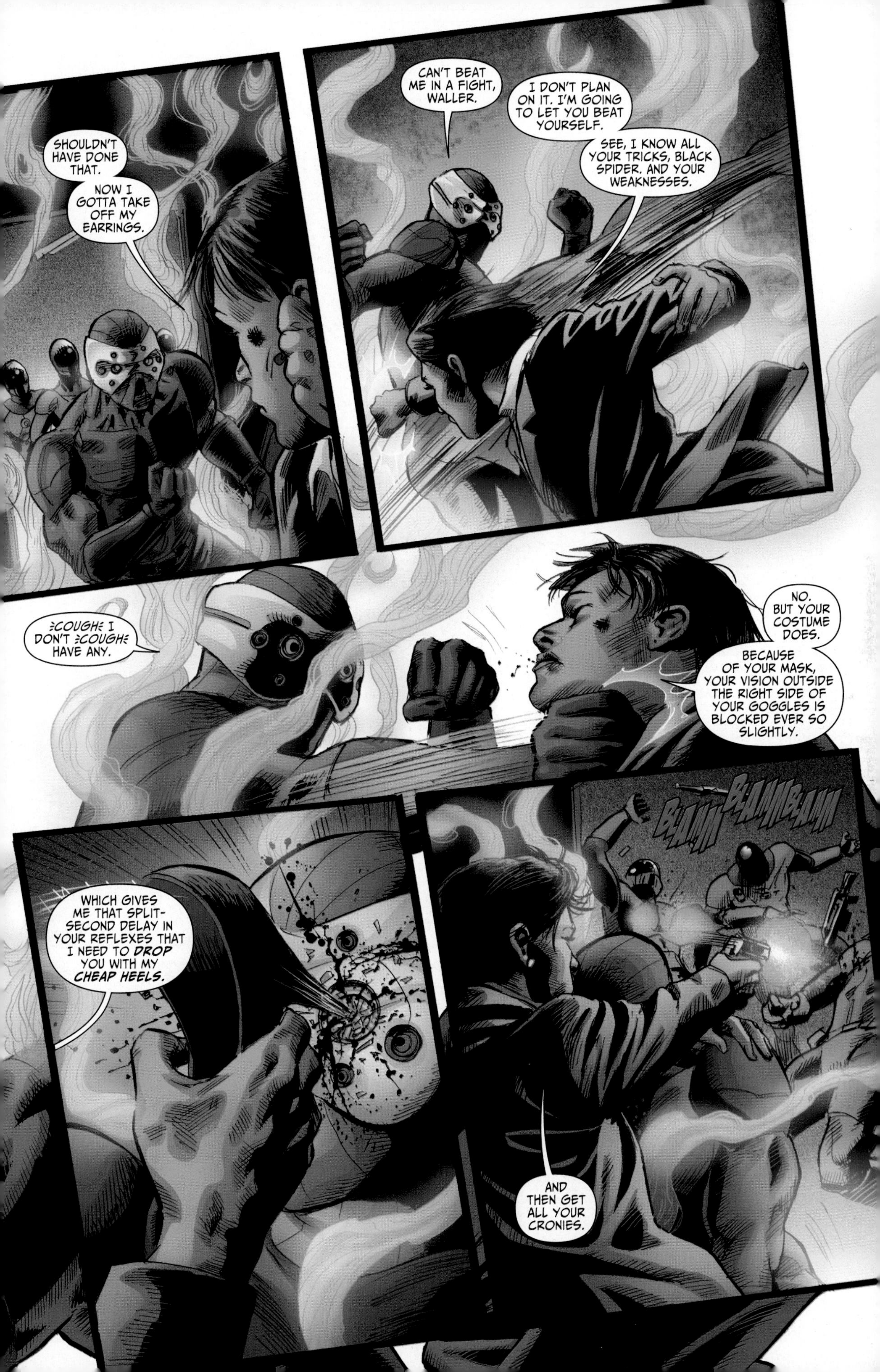
SHOULDN'T HAVE DONE THAT.
NOW I GOTTA TAKE OFF MY EARRINGS.
CAN'T BEAT ME IN A FIGHT, WALLER.
I DON'T PLAN ON IT. I'M GOING TO LET YOU BEAT YOURSELF.
SEE, I KNOW ALL YOUR TRICKS, BLACK SPIDER. AND YOUR WEAKNESSES.
COUGH I DON'T *COUGH* HAVE ANY.
NO. BUT YOUR COSTUME DOES.
BECAUSE OF YOUR MASK, YOUR VISION OUTSIDE THE RIGHT SIDE OF YOUR GOGGLES IS BLOCKED EVER SO SLIGHTLY.
WHICH GIVES ME THAT SPLIT-SECOND DELAY IN YOUR REFLEXES THAT I NEED TO DROP YOU WITH MY CHEAP HEELS.
BLAM BLAM BLAM
AND THEN GET ALL YOUR CRONIES.

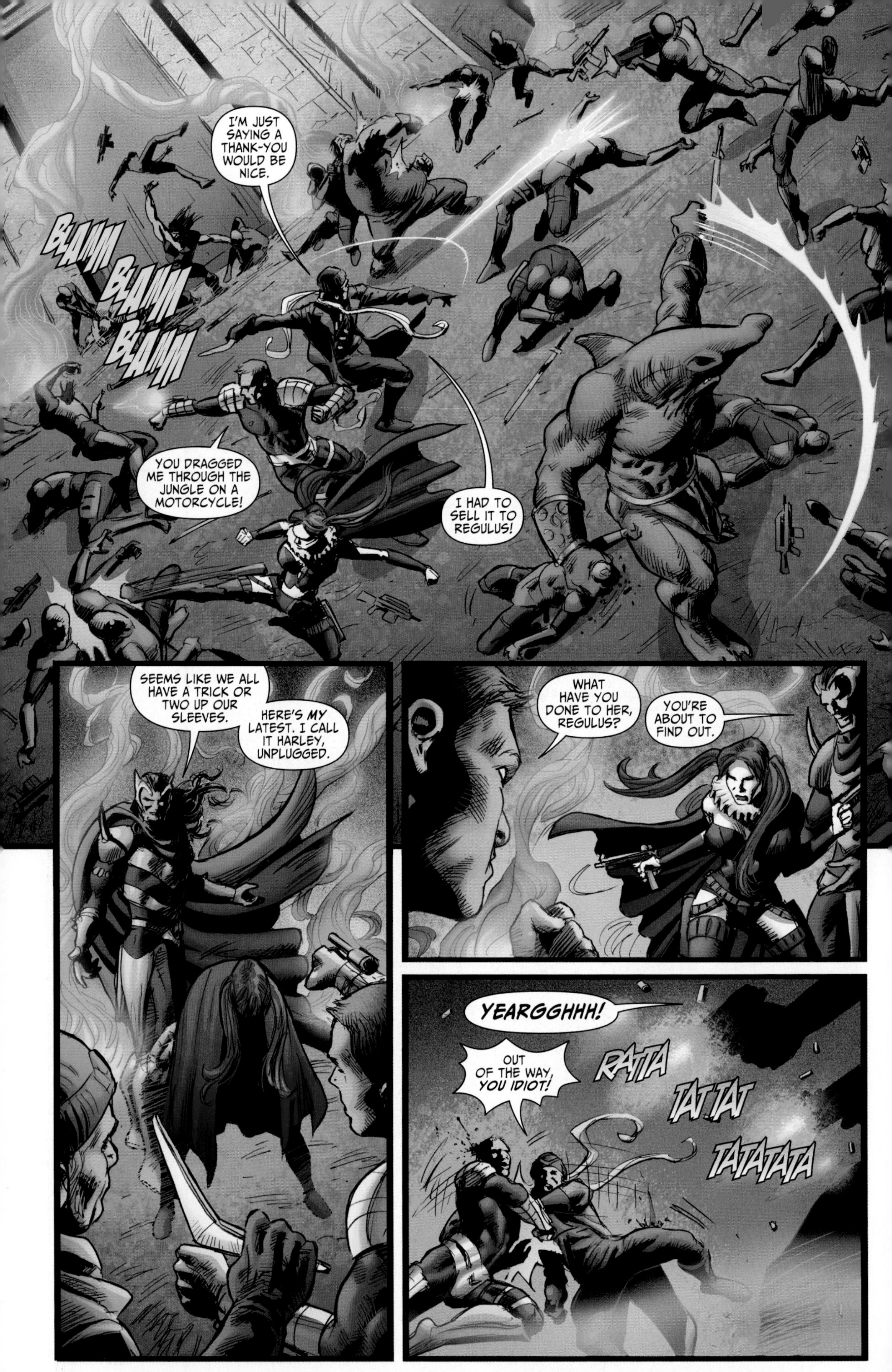
I'M JUST SAYING A THANK-YOU WOULD BE NICE.
BLAMM BLAMM BLAMM
YOU DRAGGED ME THROUGH THE JUNGLE ON A MOTORCYCLE!
I HAD TO SELL IT TO REGULUS!
SEEMS LIKE WE ALL HAVE A TRICK OR TWO UP OUR SLEEVES.
HERE'S MY LATEST. I CALL IT HARLEY, UNPLUGGED.
WHAT HAVE YOU DONE TO HER, REGULUS?
YOU'RE ABOUT TO FIND OUT.
YEARGGHHH!
OUT OF THE WAY, YOU IDIOT!
RATTA TAT TAT TATATATA

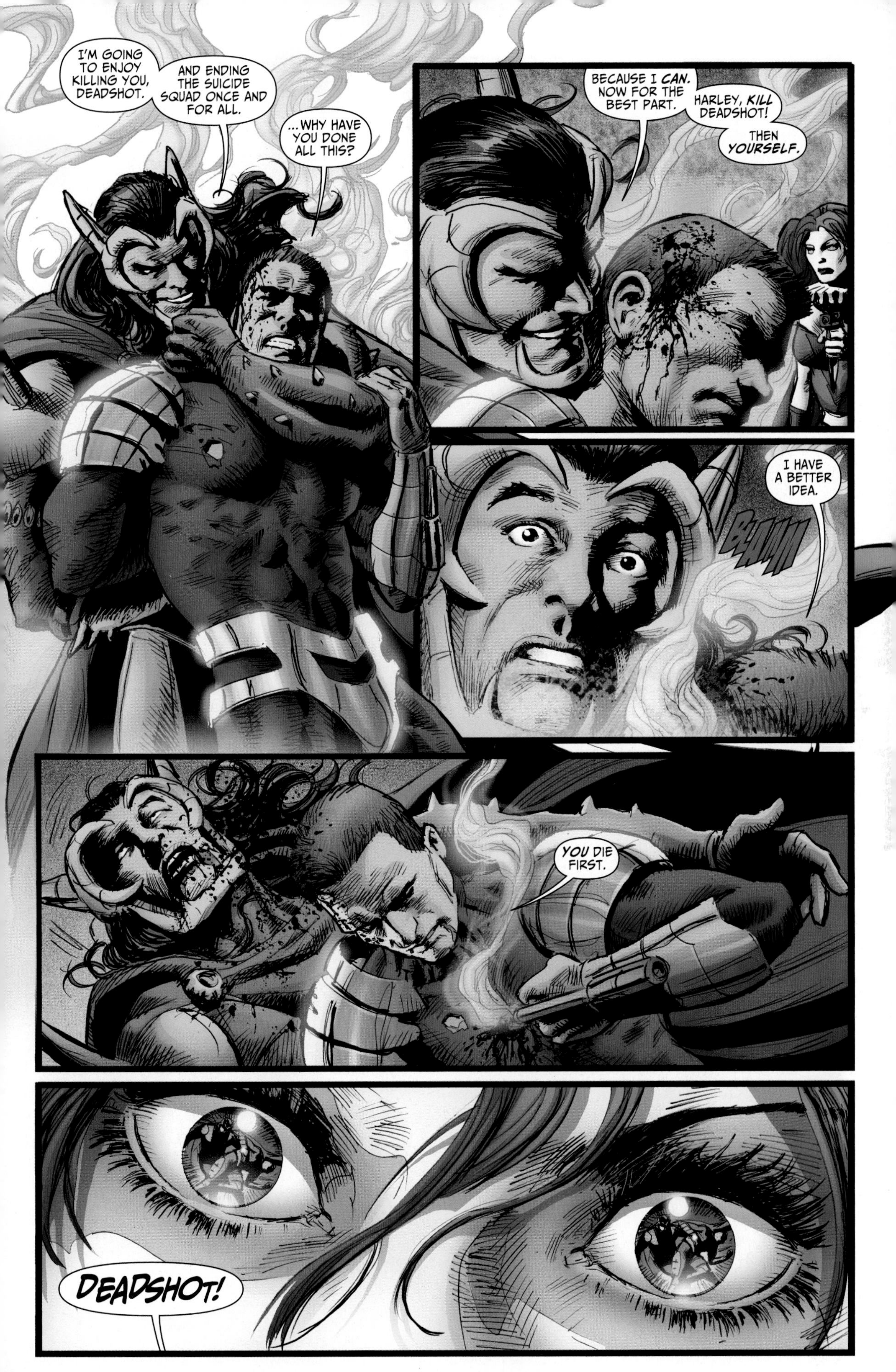
I'M GOING TO ENJOY KILLING YOU, DEADSHOT.
AND ENDING THE SUICIDE SQUAD ONCE AND FOR ALL.
...WHY HAVE YOU DONE ALL THIS?
BECAUSE I CAN. NOW FOR THE BEST PART.
HARLEY, KILL DEADSHOT!
THEN YOURSELF.
I HAVE A BETTER IDEA.
BLAM
YOU DIE FIRST.
DEADSHOT!

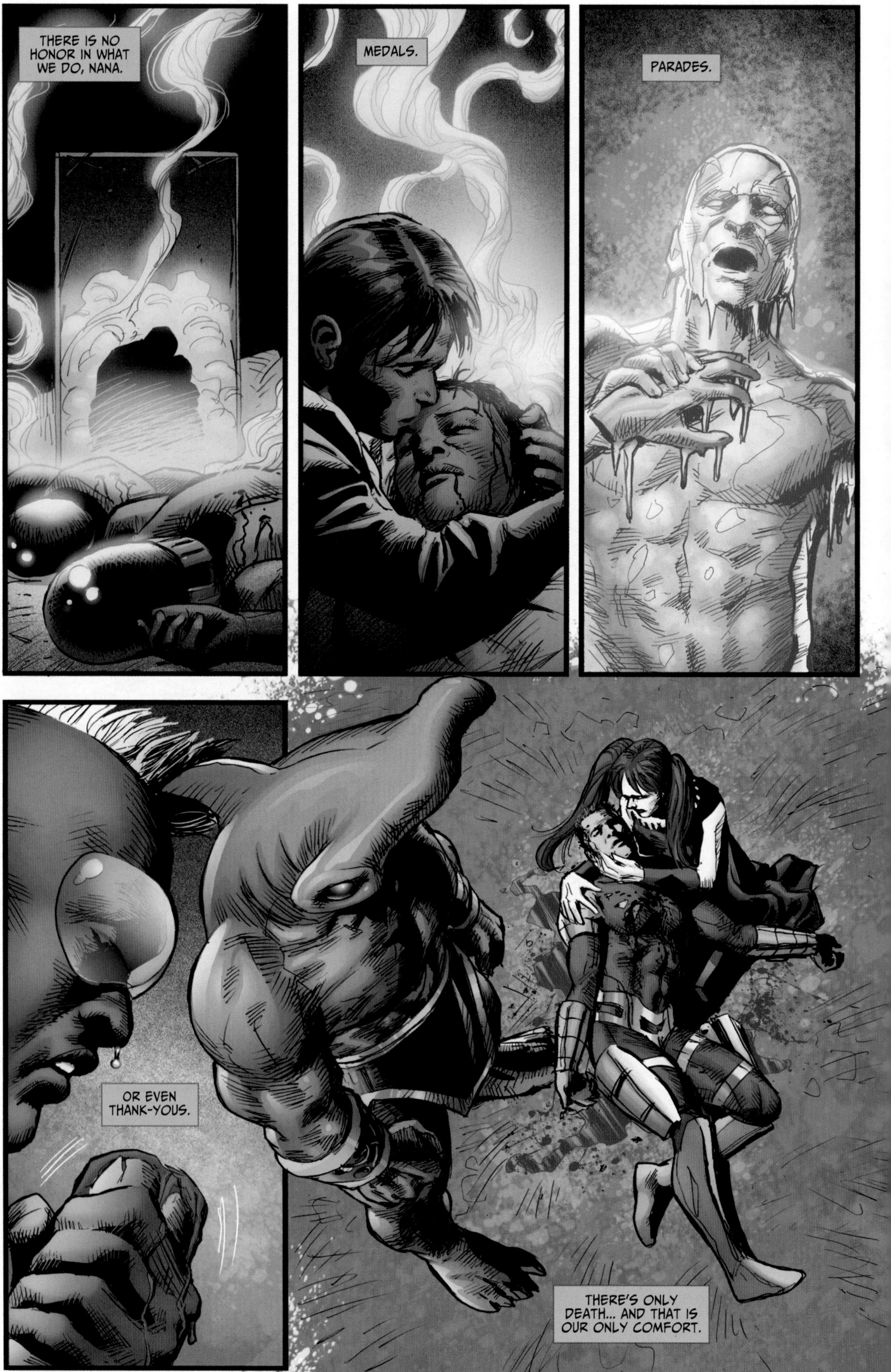
THERE IS NO HONOR IN WHAT WE DO, NANA.
MEDALS.
PARADES.
OR EVEN THANK-YOUS.
THERE'S ONLY DEATH... AND THAT IS OUR ONLY COMFORT.

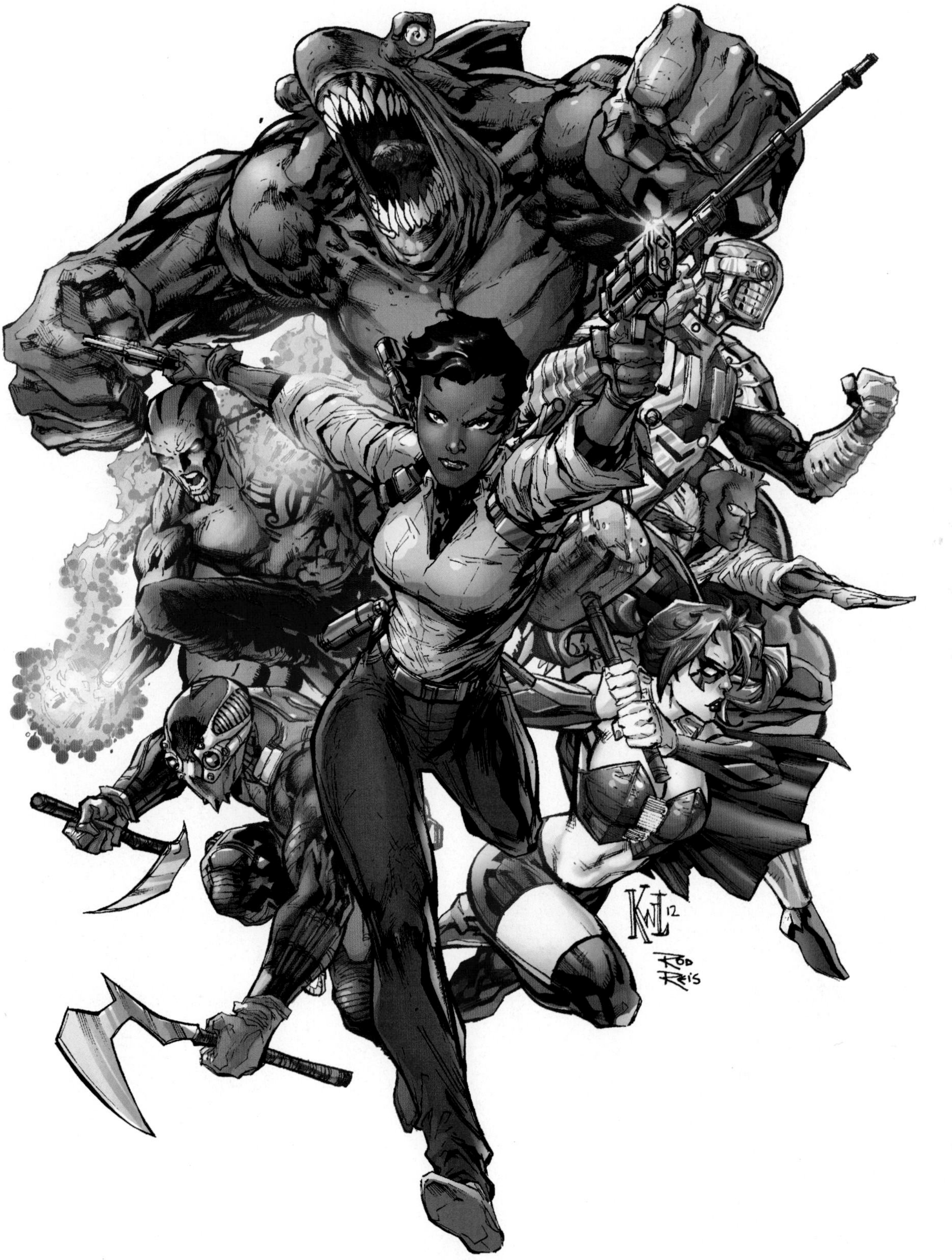
ROD REIS

POINT OF NO RETURN

ADAM GLASS
writer

FERNANDO DAGNINO
artist

cover art by KEN LASHLEY & ROD REIS

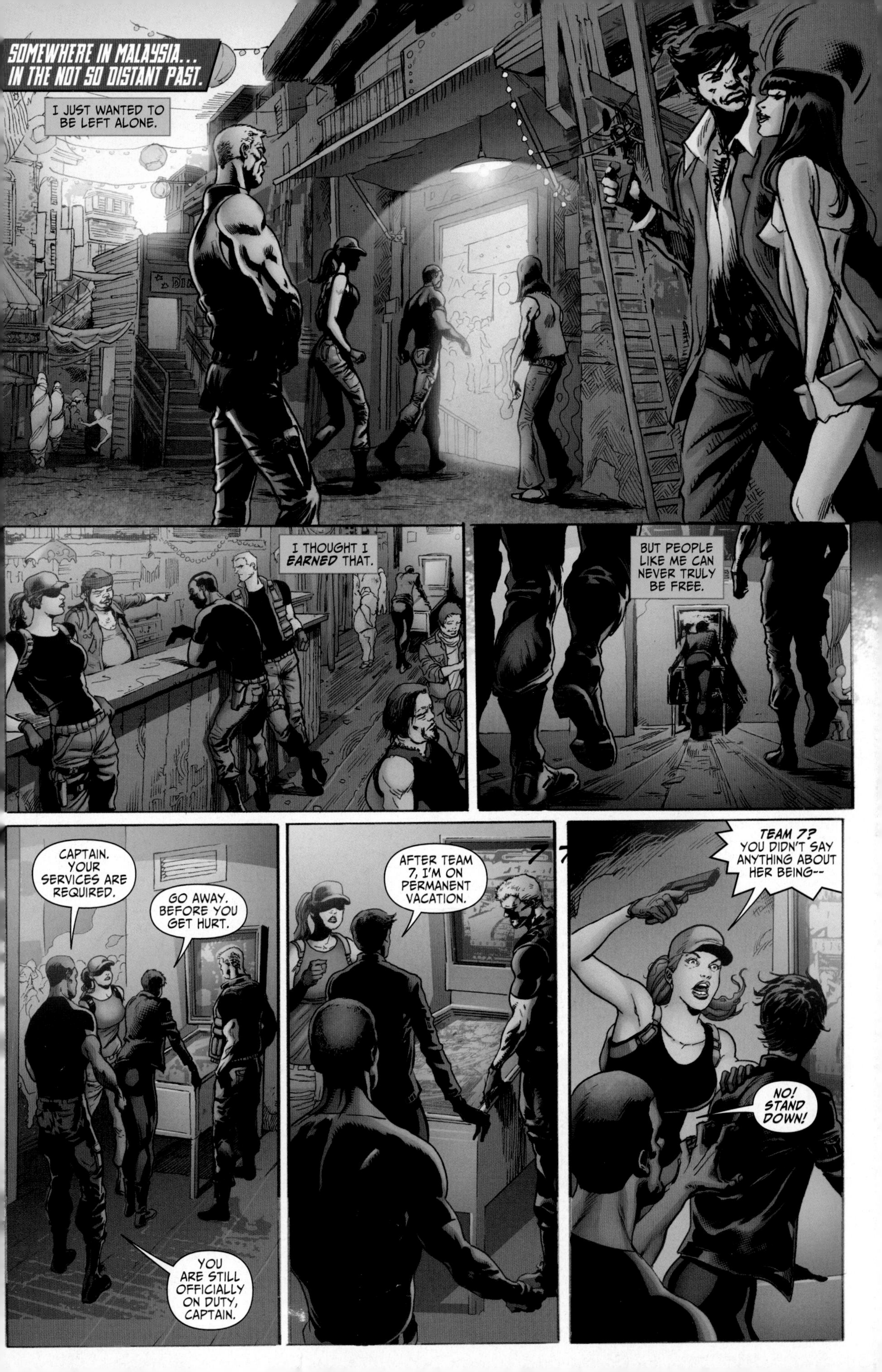
SOMEWHERE IN MALAYSIA... IN THE NOT SO DISTANT PAST.
I JUST WANTED TO BE LEFT ALONE.
I THOUGHT I EARNED THAT.
BUT PEOPLE LIKE ME CAN NEVER TRULY BE FREE.
CAPTAIN. YOUR SERVICES ARE REQUIRED.
GO AWAY. BEFORE YOU GET HURT.
YOU ARE STILL OFFICIALLY ON DUTY, CAPTAIN.
AFTER TEAM 7, I'M ON PERMANENT VACATION.
TEAM 7? YOU DIDN'T SAY ANYTHING ABOUT HER BEING--
NO! STAND DOWN!

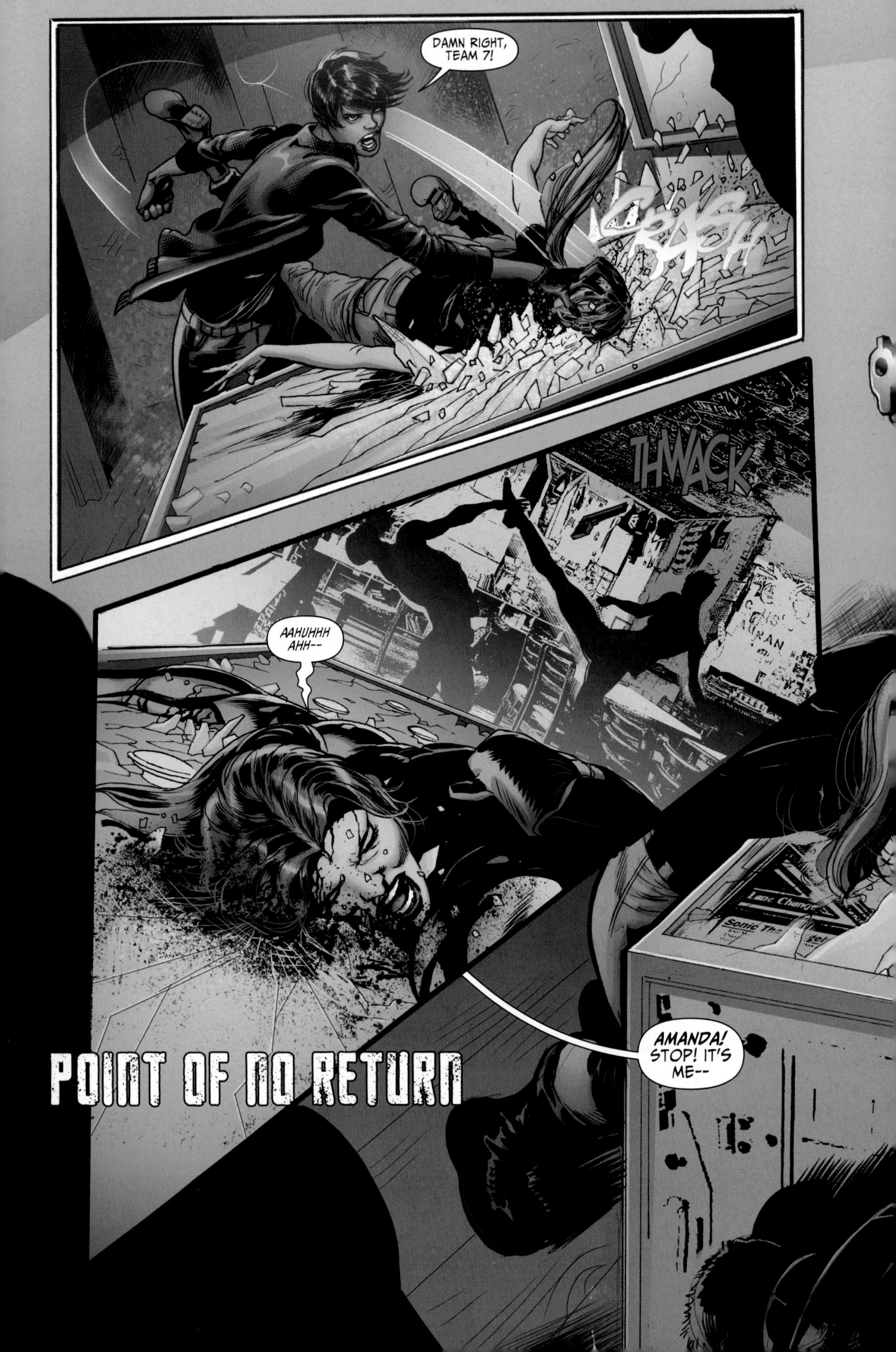
DAMN RIGHT, TEAM 7!
CRASH
THWACK
AAHUHHH AHH--
AMANDA! STOP! IT'S ME--
POINT OF NO RETURN

CLICK

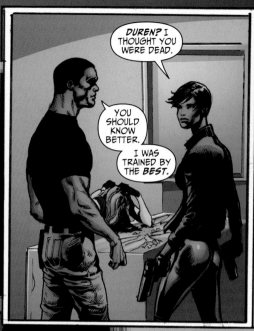

DUREN? I THOUGHT YOU WERE DEAD.

YOU SHOULD KNOW BETTER. I WAS TRAINED BY THE *BEST*.

DAMN YOU, DUREN.

GET OVER HERE.

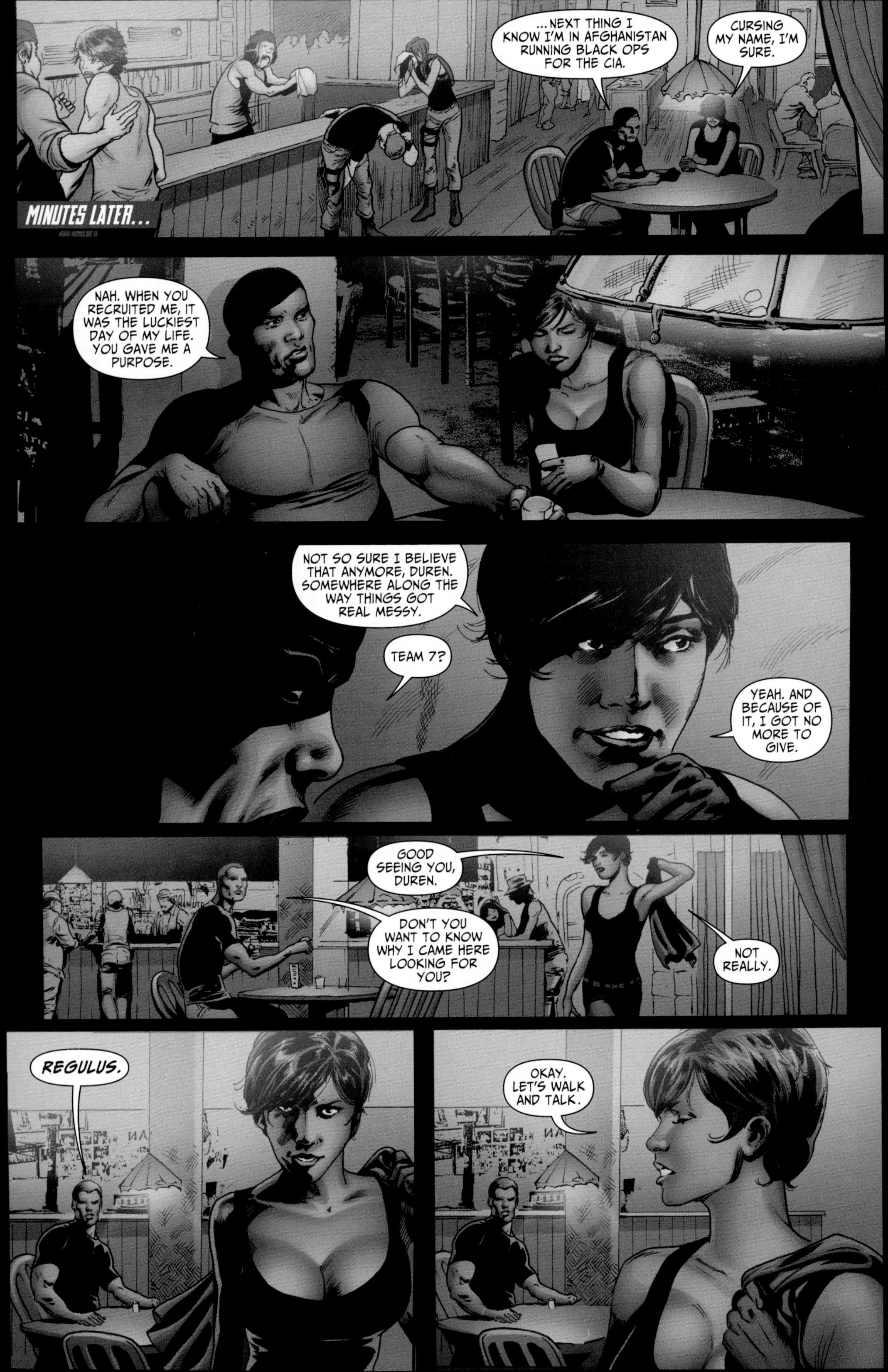
MINUTES LATER...
...NEXT THING I KNOW I'M IN AFGHANISTAN RUNNING BLACK OPS FOR THE CIA.
CURSING MY NAME, I'M SURE.
NAH. WHEN YOU RECRUITED ME, IT WAS THE LUCKIEST DAY OF MY LIFE. YOU GAVE ME A PURPOSE.
NOT SO SURE I BELIEVE THAT ANYMORE, DUREN. SOMEWHERE ALONG THE WAY THINGS GOT REAL MESSY.
TEAM 7?
YEAH. AND BECAUSE OF IT, I GOT NO MORE TO GIVE.
GOOD SEEING YOU, DUREN.
DON'T YOU WANT TO KNOW WHY I CAME HERE LOOKING FOR YOU?
NOT REALLY.
REGULUS.
OKAY. LET'S WALK AND TALK.

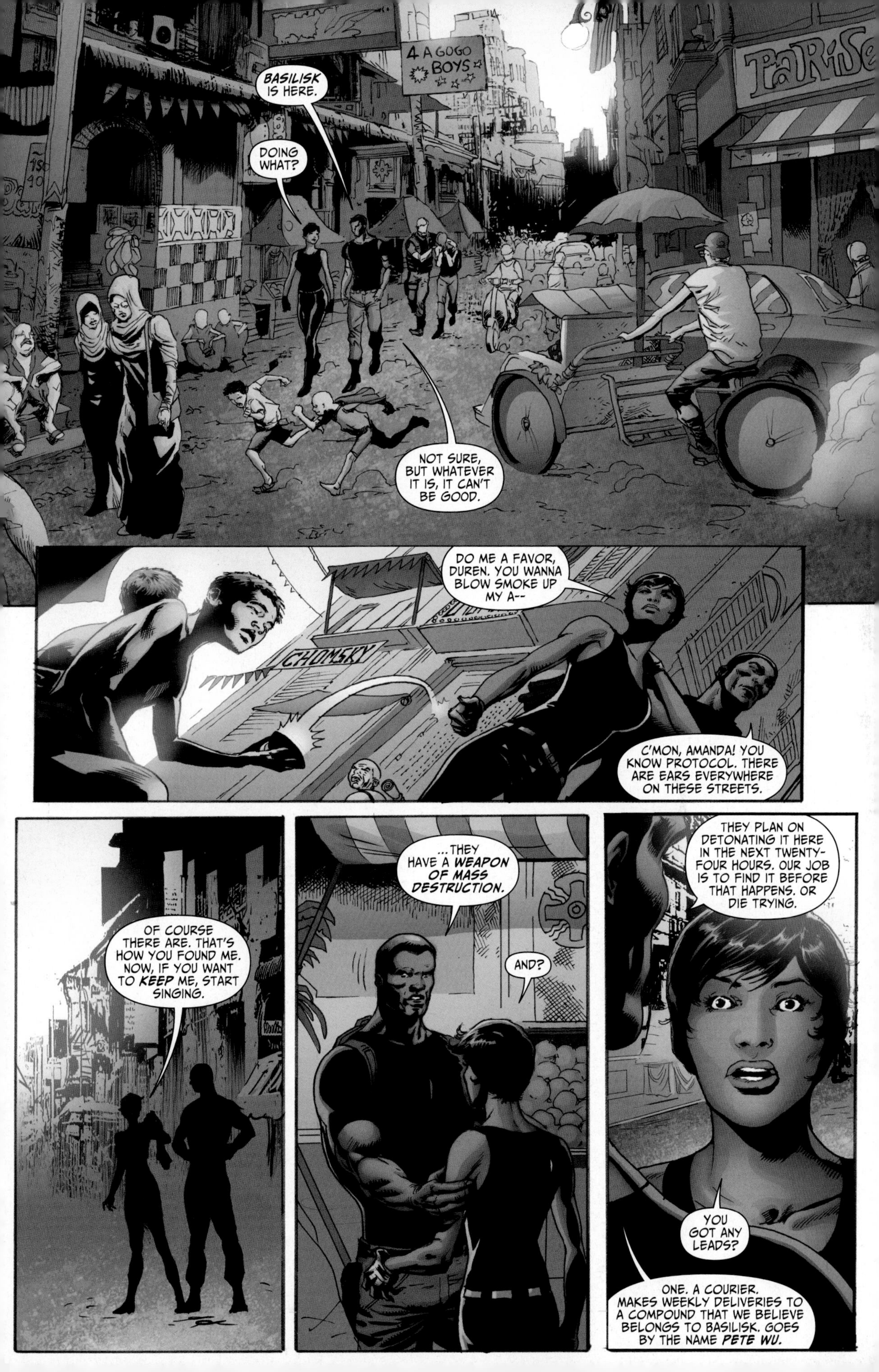
4 A GOGO BOYS
PARISE
BASILISK IS HERE.
DOING WHAT?
NOT SURE, BUT WHATEVER IT IS, IT CAN'T BE GOOD.
CHOMSKY
DO ME A FAVOR, DUREN. YOU WANNA BLOW SMOKE UP MY A--
C'MON, AMANDA! YOU KNOW PROTOCOL. THERE ARE EARS EVERYWHERE ON THESE STREETS.
OF COURSE THERE ARE. THAT'S HOW YOU FOUND ME. NOW, IF YOU WANT TO KEEP ME, START SINGING.
...THEY HAVE A WEAPON OF MASS DESTRUCTION.
AND?
THEY PLAN ON DETONATING IT HERE IN THE NEXT TWENTY-FOUR HOURS. OUR JOB IS TO FIND IT BEFORE THAT HAPPENS. OR DIE TRYING.
YOU GOT ANY LEADS?
ONE. A COURIER. MAKES WEEKLY DELIVERIES TO A COMPOUND THAT WE BELIEVE BELONGS TO BASILISK. GOES BY THE NAME PETE WU.

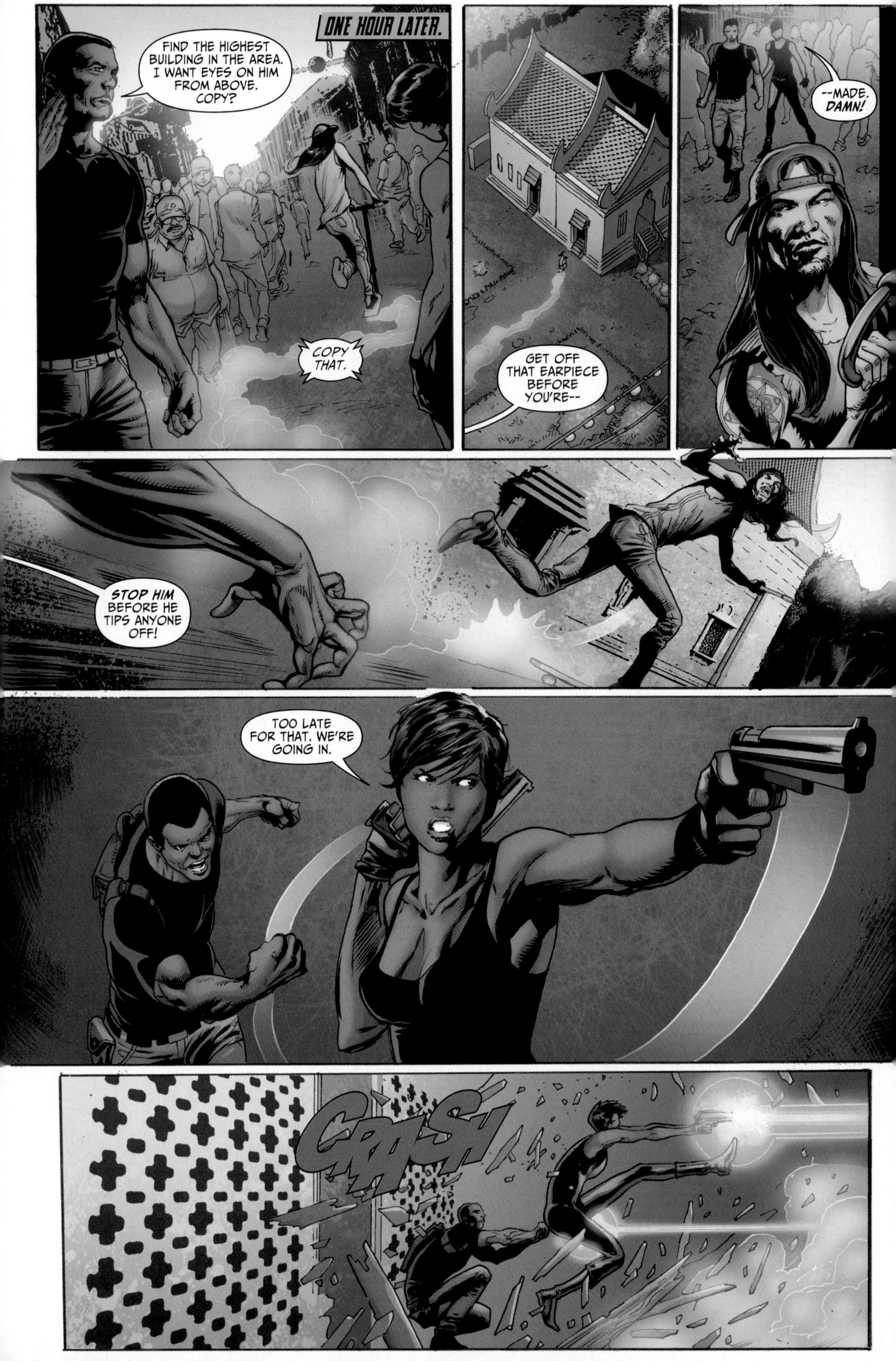
ONE HOUR LATER.
FIND THE HIGHEST BUILDING IN THE AREA. I WANT EYES ON HIM FROM ABOVE. COPY?
COPY THAT.
GET OFF THAT EARPIECE BEFORE YOU'RE--
--MADE. DAMN!
STOP HIM BEFORE HE TIPS ANYONE OFF!
TOO LATE FOR THAT. WE'RE GOING IN.
CRASH

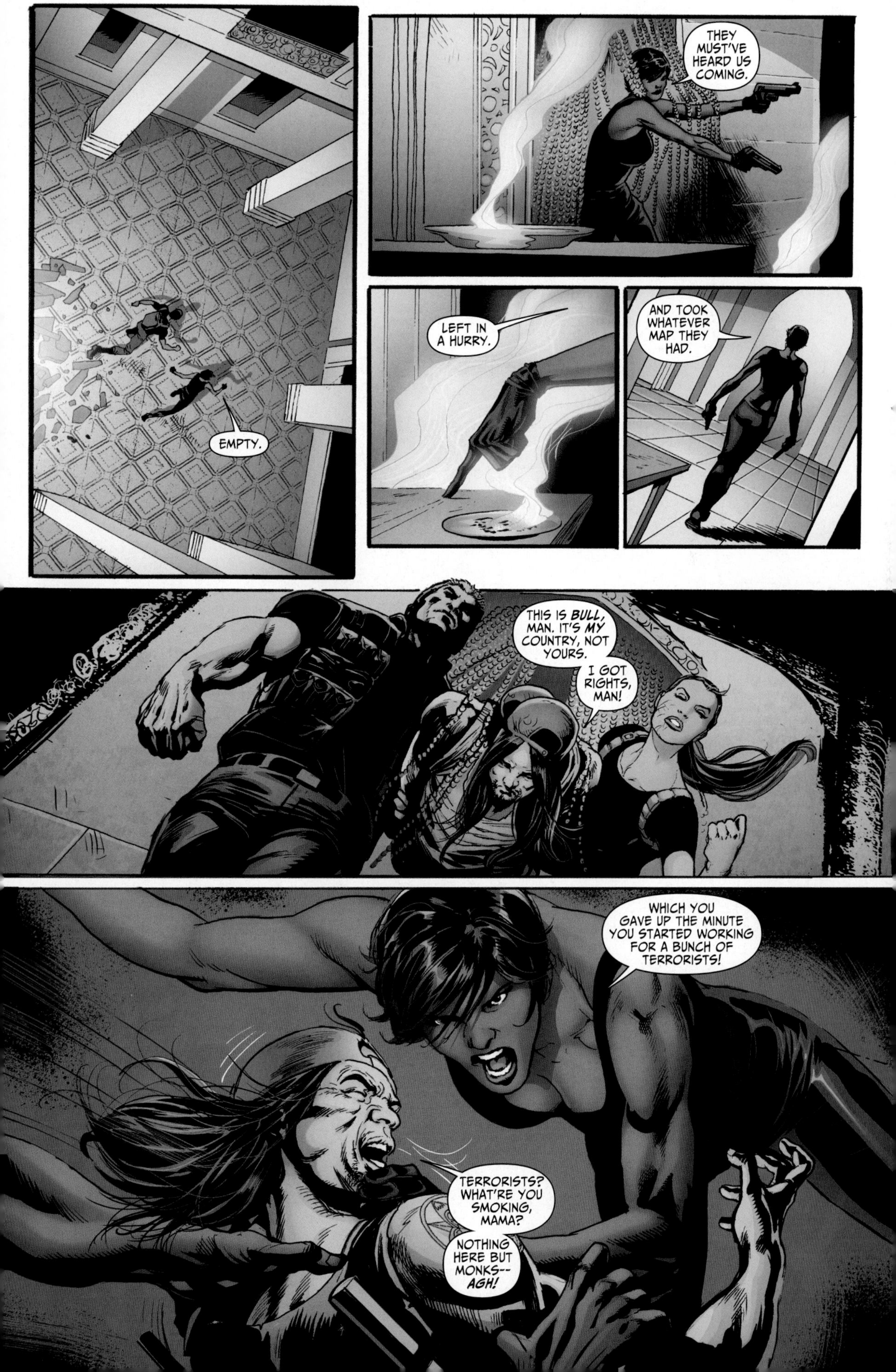
EMPTY.
THEY MUST'VE HEARD US COMING.
LEFT IN A HURRY.
AND TOOK WHATEVER MAP THEY HAD.
THIS IS *BULL*, MAN. IT'S *MY* COUNTRY, NOT YOURS.
I GOT RIGHTS, MAN!
WHICH YOU GAVE UP THE MINUTE YOU STARTED WORKING FOR A BUNCH OF TERRORISTS!
TERRORISTS? WHAT'RE YOU SMOKING, MAMA?
NOTHING HERE BUT MONKS-- *AGH!*

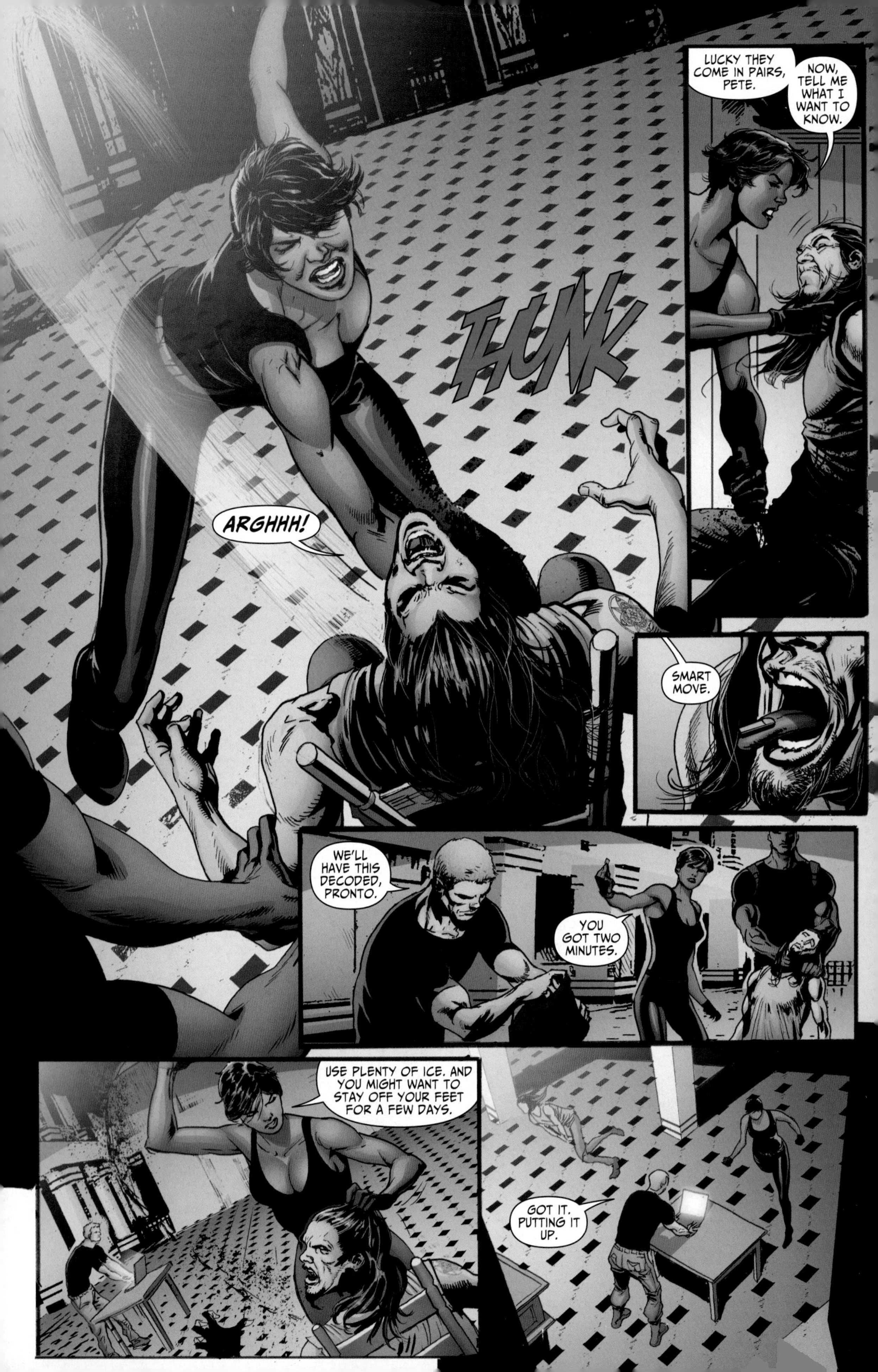
THUNK
ARGHHH!
LUCKY THEY COME IN PAIRS, PETE.
NOW, TELL ME WHAT I WANT TO KNOW.
SMART MOVE.
WE'LL HAVE THIS DECODED, PRONTO.
YOU GOT TWO MINUTES.
USE PLENTY OF ICE. AND YOU MIGHT WANT TO STAY OFF YOUR FEET FOR A FEW DAYS.
GOT IT. PUTTING IT UP.

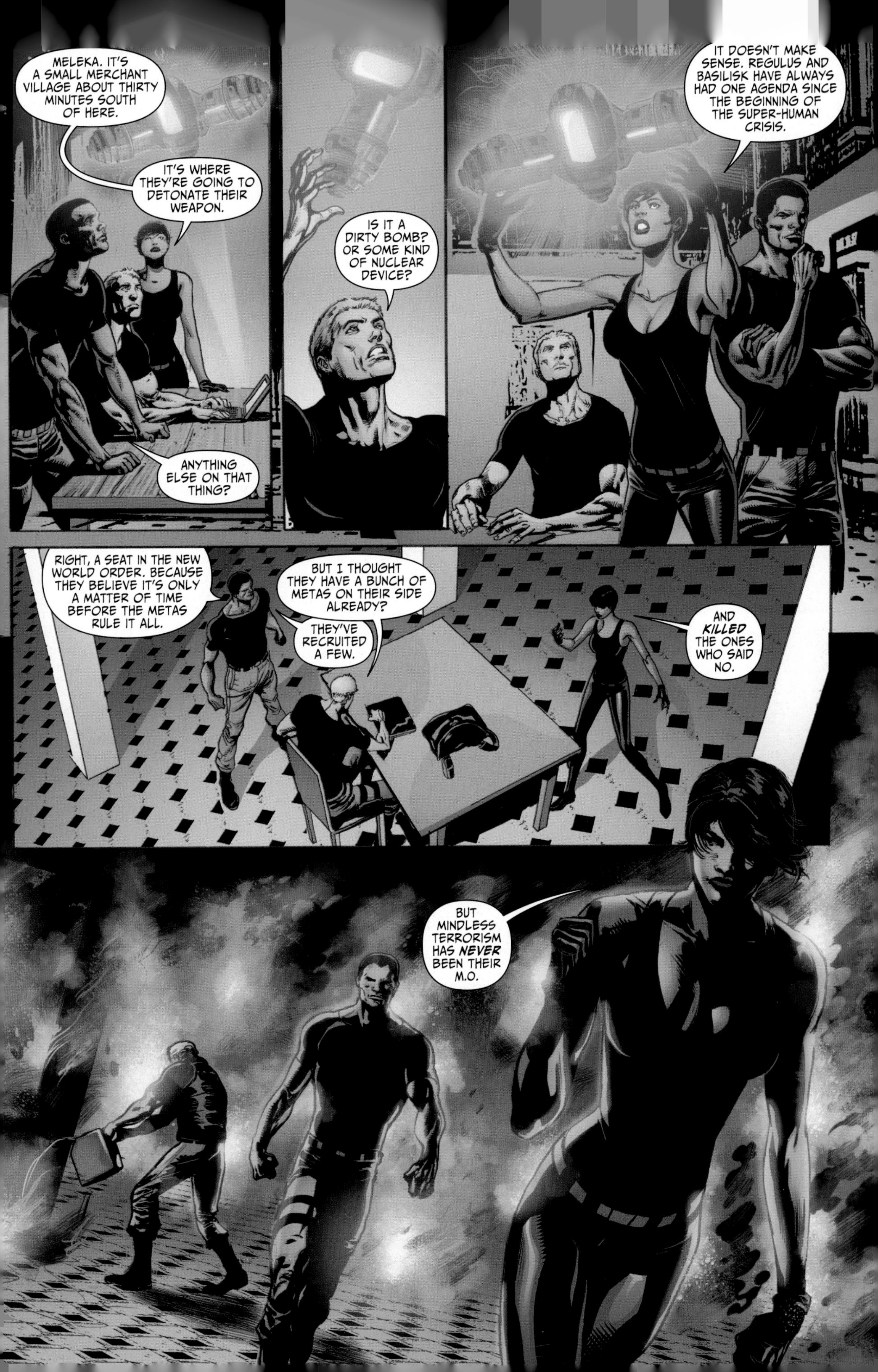
MELEKA. IT'S A SMALL MERCHANT VILLAGE ABOUT THIRTY MINUTES SOUTH OF HERE.
IT'S WHERE THEY'RE GOING TO DETONATE THEIR WEAPON.
ANYTHING ELSE ON THAT THING?
IS IT A DIRTY BOMB? OR SOME KIND OF NUCLEAR DEVICE?
IT DOESN'T MAKE SENSE. REGULUS AND BASILISK HAVE ALWAYS HAD ONE AGENDA SINCE THE BEGINNING OF THE SUPER-HUMAN CRISIS.
RIGHT, A SEAT IN THE NEW WORLD ORDER. BECAUSE THEY BELIEVE IT'S ONLY A MATTER OF TIME BEFORE THE METAS RULE IT ALL.
BUT I THOUGHT THEY HAVE A BUNCH OF METAS ON THEIR SIDE ALREADY?
THEY'VE RECRUITED A FEW.
AND KILLED THE ONES WHO SAID NO.
BUT MINDLESS TERRORISM HAS NEVER BEEN THEIR M.O.

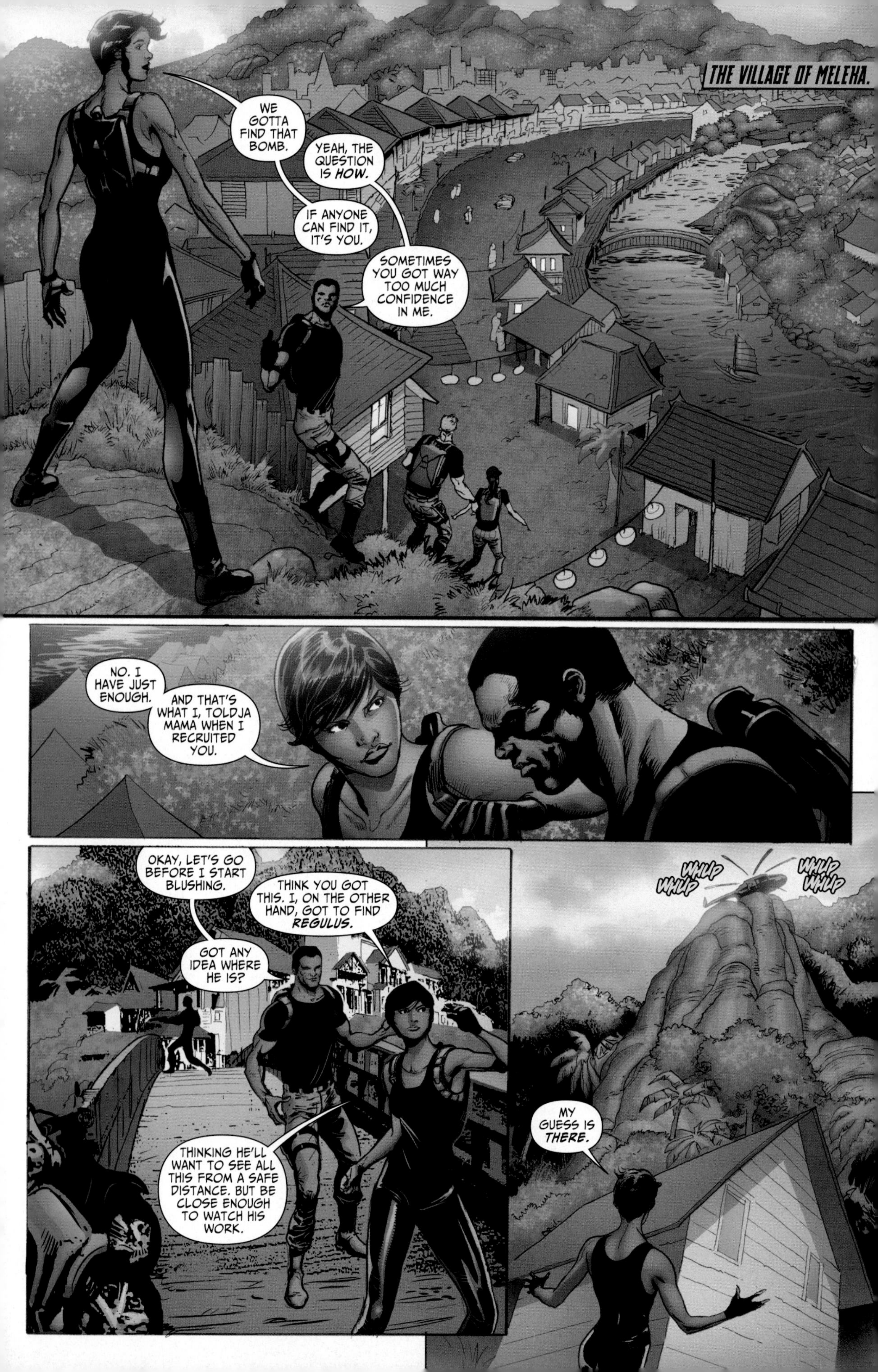
THE VILLAGE OF MELEHA.
WE GOTTA FIND THAT BOMB.
YEAH, THE QUESTION IS HOW.
IF ANYONE CAN FIND IT, IT'S YOU.
SOMETIMES YOU GOT WAY TOO MUCH CONFIDENCE IN ME.
NO. I HAVE JUST ENOUGH.
AND THAT'S WHAT I, TOLDJA MAMA WHEN I RECRUITED YOU.
OKAY, LET'S GO BEFORE I START BLUSHING.
THINK YOU GOT THIS. I, ON THE OTHER HAND, GOT TO FIND REGULUS.
GOT ANY IDEA WHERE HE IS?
THINKING HE'LL WANT TO SEE ALL THIS FROM A SAFE DISTANCE. BUT BE CLOSE ENOUGH TO WATCH HIS WORK.
WHUP WHUP
WHUP WHUP
MY GUESS IS THERE.

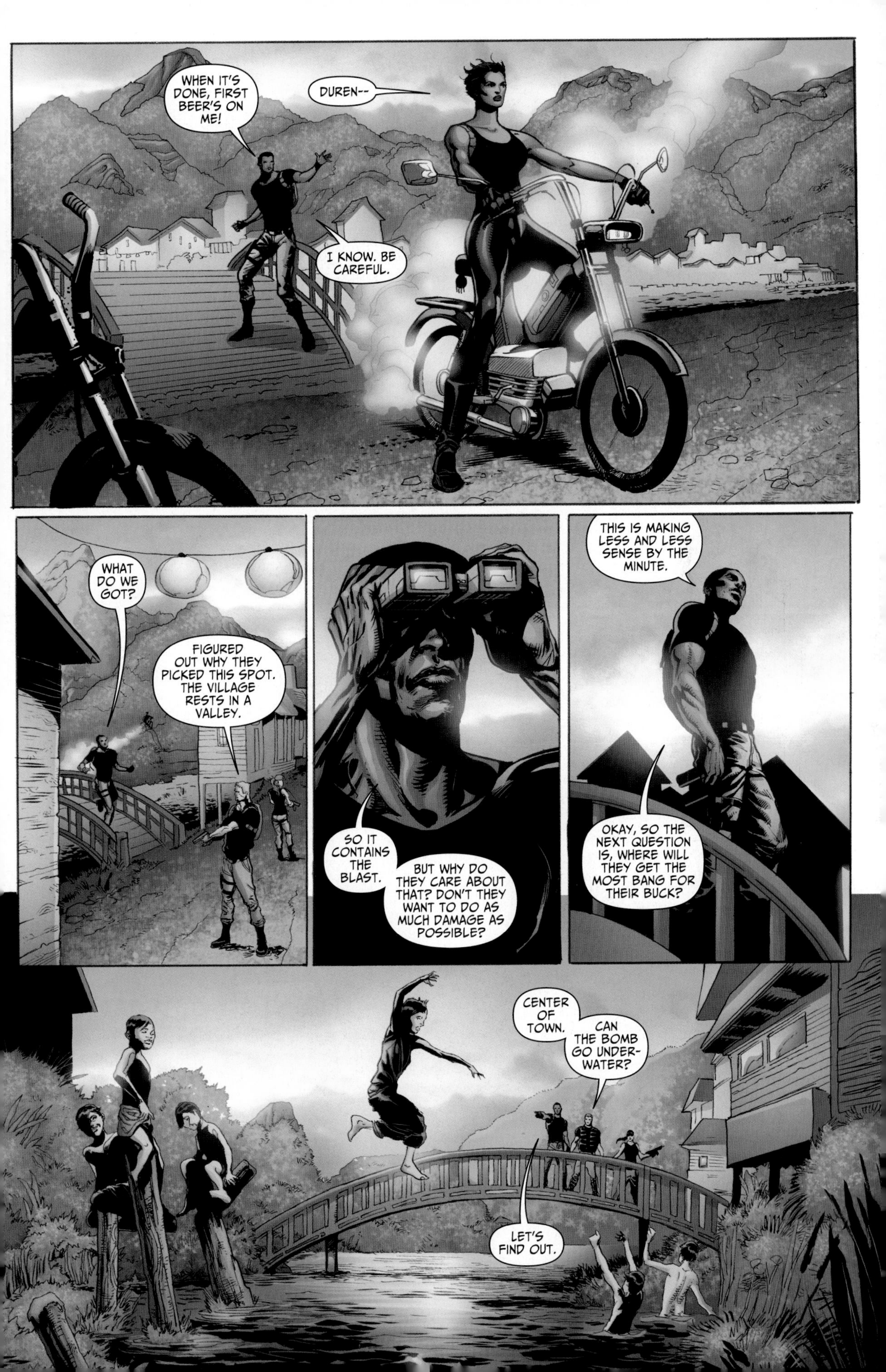
WHEN IT'S DONE, FIRST BEER'S ON ME!
DUREN--
I KNOW. BE CAREFUL.
WHAT DO WE GOT?
FIGURED OUT WHY THEY PICKED THIS SPOT. THE VILLAGE RESTS IN A VALLEY.
SO IT CONTAINS THE BLAST.
BUT WHY DO THEY CARE ABOUT THAT? DON'T THEY WANT TO DO AS MUCH DAMAGE AS POSSIBLE?
THIS IS MAKING LESS AND LESS SENSE BY THE MINUTE.
OKAY, SO THE NEXT QUESTION IS, WHERE WILL THEY GET THE MOST BANG FOR THEIR BUCK?
CENTER OF TOWN.
CAN THE BOMB GO UNDER-WATER?
LET'S FIND OUT.

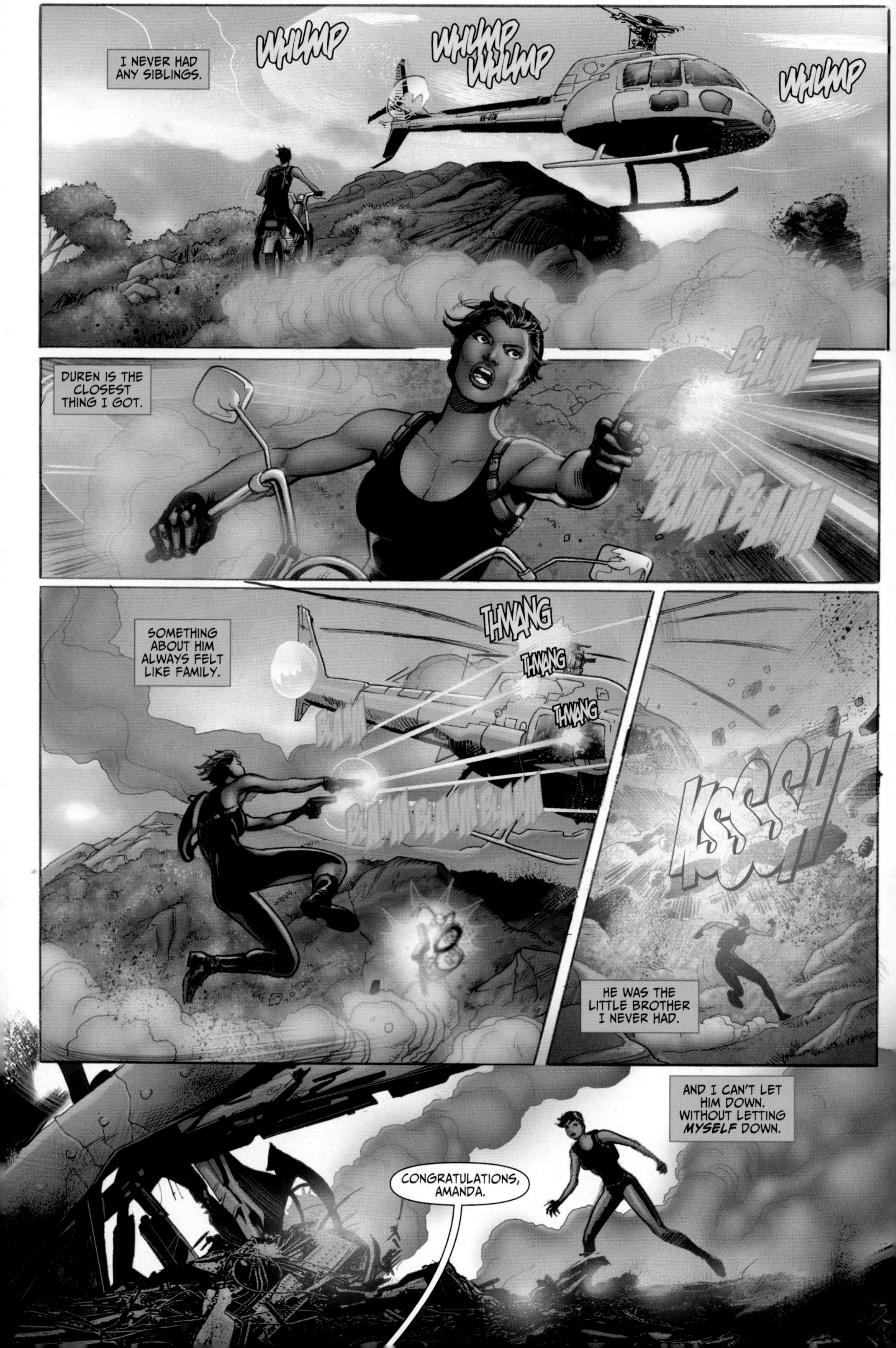
I NEVER HAD ANY SIBLINGS.
WHUMP
WHUMP WHUMP
WHUMP
DUREN IS THE CLOSEST THING I GOT.
BLAM
BLAM BLAM BLAM
SOMETHING ABOUT HIM ALWAYS FELT LIKE FAMILY.
THWANG
THWANG
THWANG
BLAM
BLAM BLAM BLAM
KSSSH
HE WAS THE LITTLE BROTHER I NEVER HAD.
AND I CAN'T LET HIM DOWN. WITHOUT LETTING *MYSELF* DOWN.
CONGRATULATIONS, AMANDA.

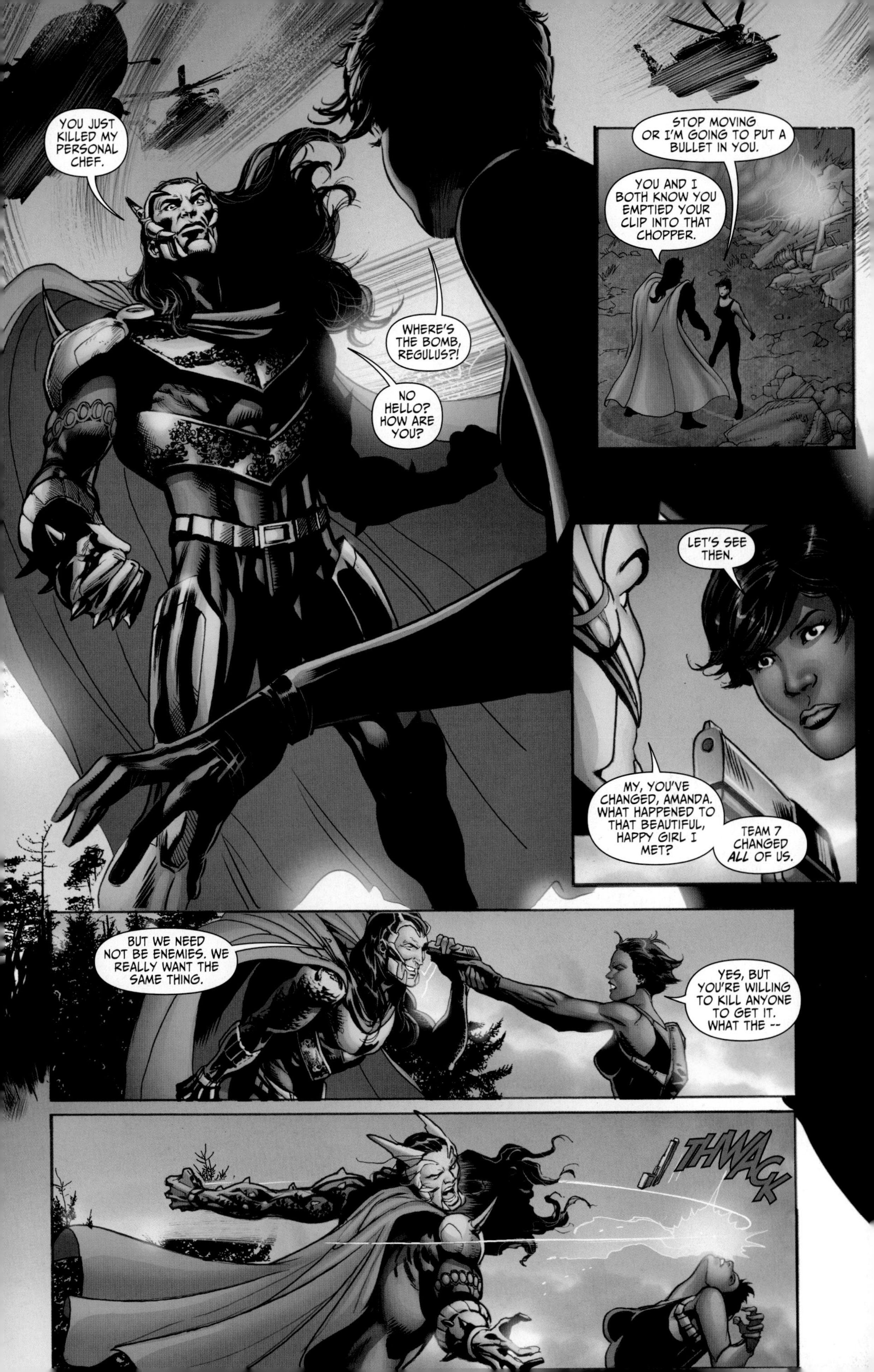
YOU JUST KILLED MY PERSONAL CHEF.
WHERE'S THE BOMB, REGULUS?!
NO HELLO? HOW ARE YOU?
STOP MOVING OR I'M GOING TO PUT A BULLET IN YOU.
YOU AND I BOTH KNOW YOU EMPTIED YOUR CLIP INTO THAT CHOPPER.
LET'S SEE THEN.
MY, YOU'VE CHANGED, AMANDA. WHAT HAPPENED TO THAT BEAUTIFUL, HAPPY GIRL I MET?
TEAM 7 CHANGED ALL OF US.
BUT WE NEED NOT BE ENEMIES. WE REALLY WANT THE SAME THING.
YES, BUT YOU'RE WILLING TO KILL ANYONE TO GET IT. WHAT THE --
THWACK

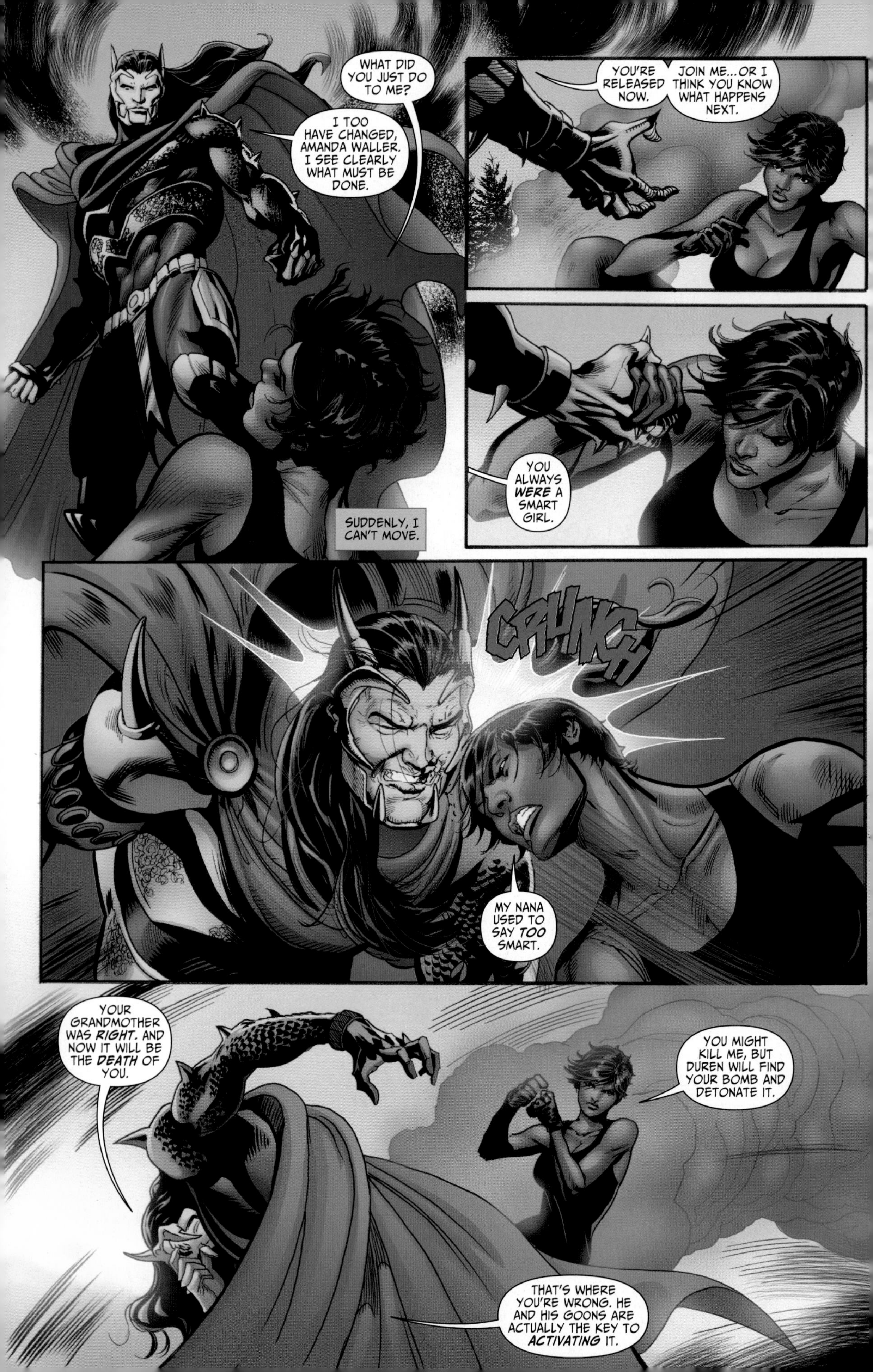
WHAT DID YOU JUST DO TO ME?
I TOO HAVE CHANGED, AMANDA WALLER. I SEE CLEARLY WHAT MUST BE DONE.
SUDDENLY, I CAN'T MOVE.
YOU'RE RELEASED NOW.
JOIN ME...OR I THINK YOU KNOW WHAT HAPPENS NEXT.
YOU ALWAYS WERE A SMART GIRL.
CRUNCH
MY NANA USED TO SAY TOO SMART.
YOUR GRANDMOTHER WAS RIGHT. AND NOW IT WILL BE THE DEATH OF YOU.
YOU MIGHT KILL ME, BUT DUREN WILL FIND YOUR BOMB AND DETONATE IT.
THAT'S WHERE YOU'RE WRONG. HE AND HIS GOONS ARE ACTUALLY THE KEY TO ACTIVATING IT.

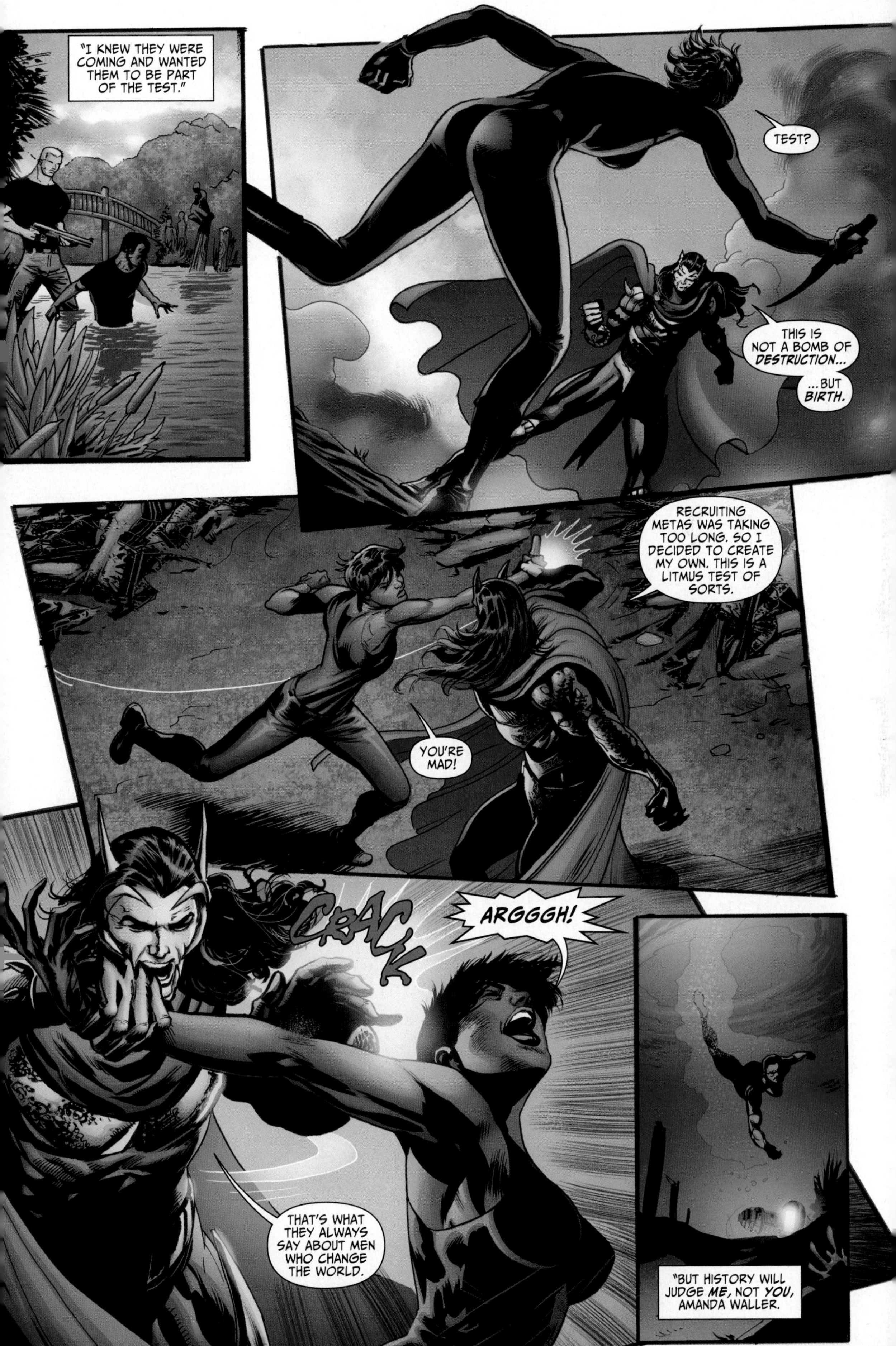
"I KNEW THEY WERE COMING AND WANTED THEM TO BE PART OF THE TEST."
TEST?
THIS IS NOT A BOMB OF *DESTRUCTION...*
...BUT *BIRTH.*
RECRUITING METAS WAS TAKING TOO LONG. SO I DECIDED TO CREATE MY OWN. THIS IS A LITMUS TEST OF SORTS.
YOU'RE MAD!
CRACK
ARGGGH!
THAT'S WHAT THEY ALWAYS SAY ABOUT MEN WHO CHANGE THE WORLD.
"BUT HISTORY WILL JUDGE *ME,* NOT *YOU,* AMANDA WALLER.

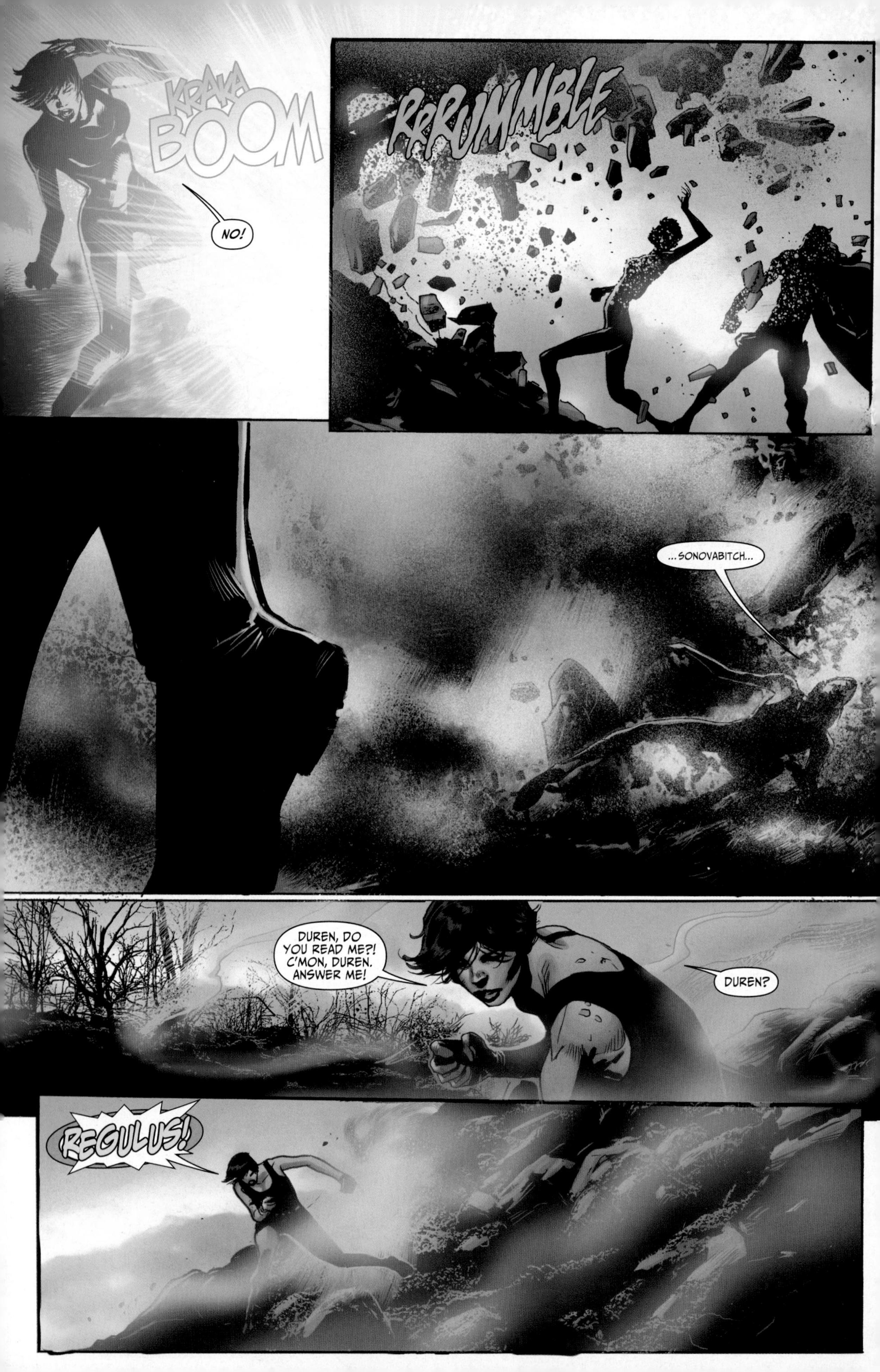
KRAKA BOOM
NO!
RRRUMMBLE
...SONOVABITCH...
DUREN, DO YOU READ ME?! C'MON, DUREN. ANSWER ME!
DUREN?
REGULUS!

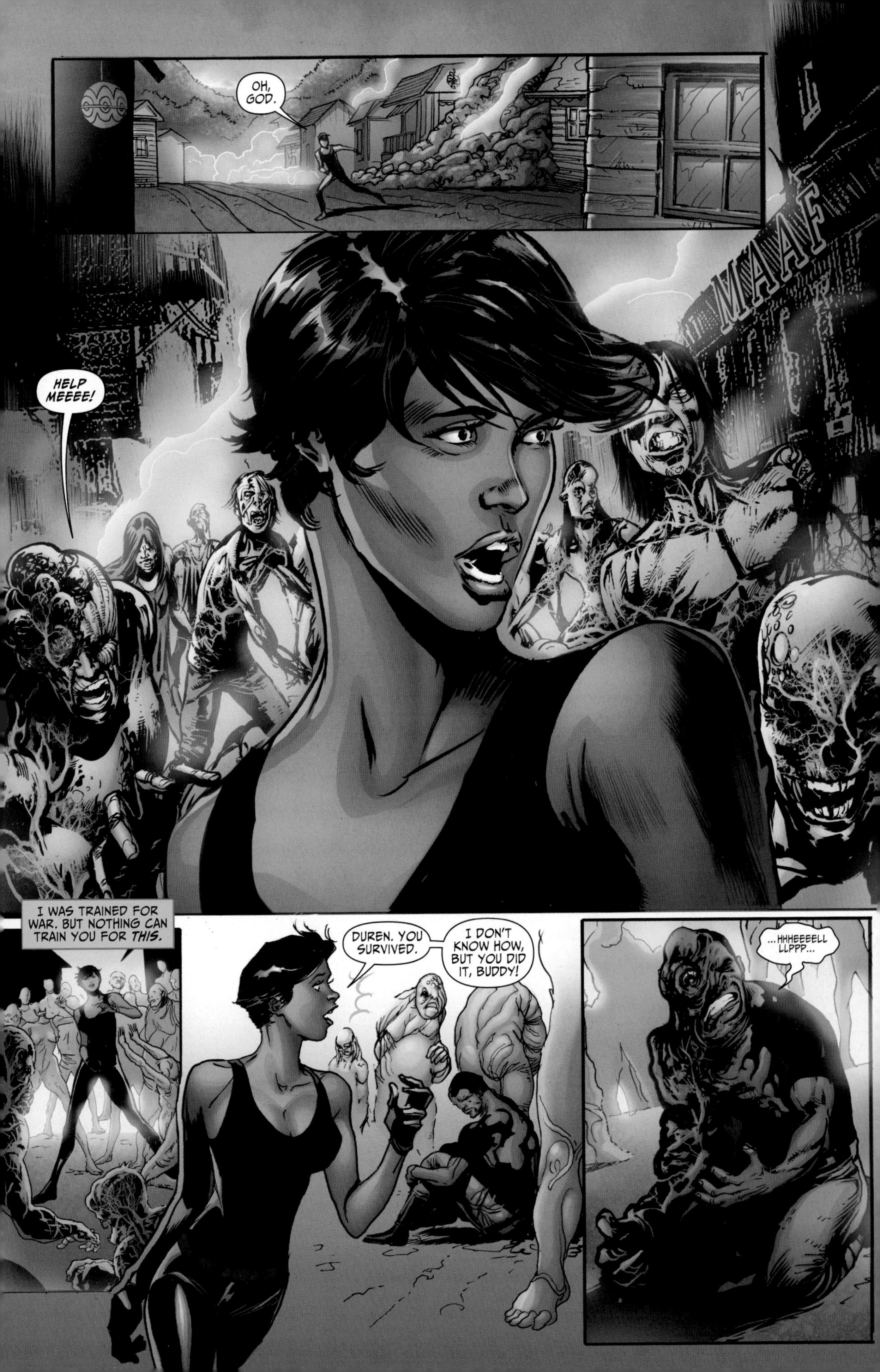
OH, GOD.
HELP MEEEE!
I WAS TRAINED FOR WAR. BUT NOTHING CAN TRAIN YOU FOR *THIS*.
DUREN. YOU SURVIVED.
I DON'T KNOW HOW, BUT YOU DID IT, BUDDY!
...HHHEEEELL LLPPP...

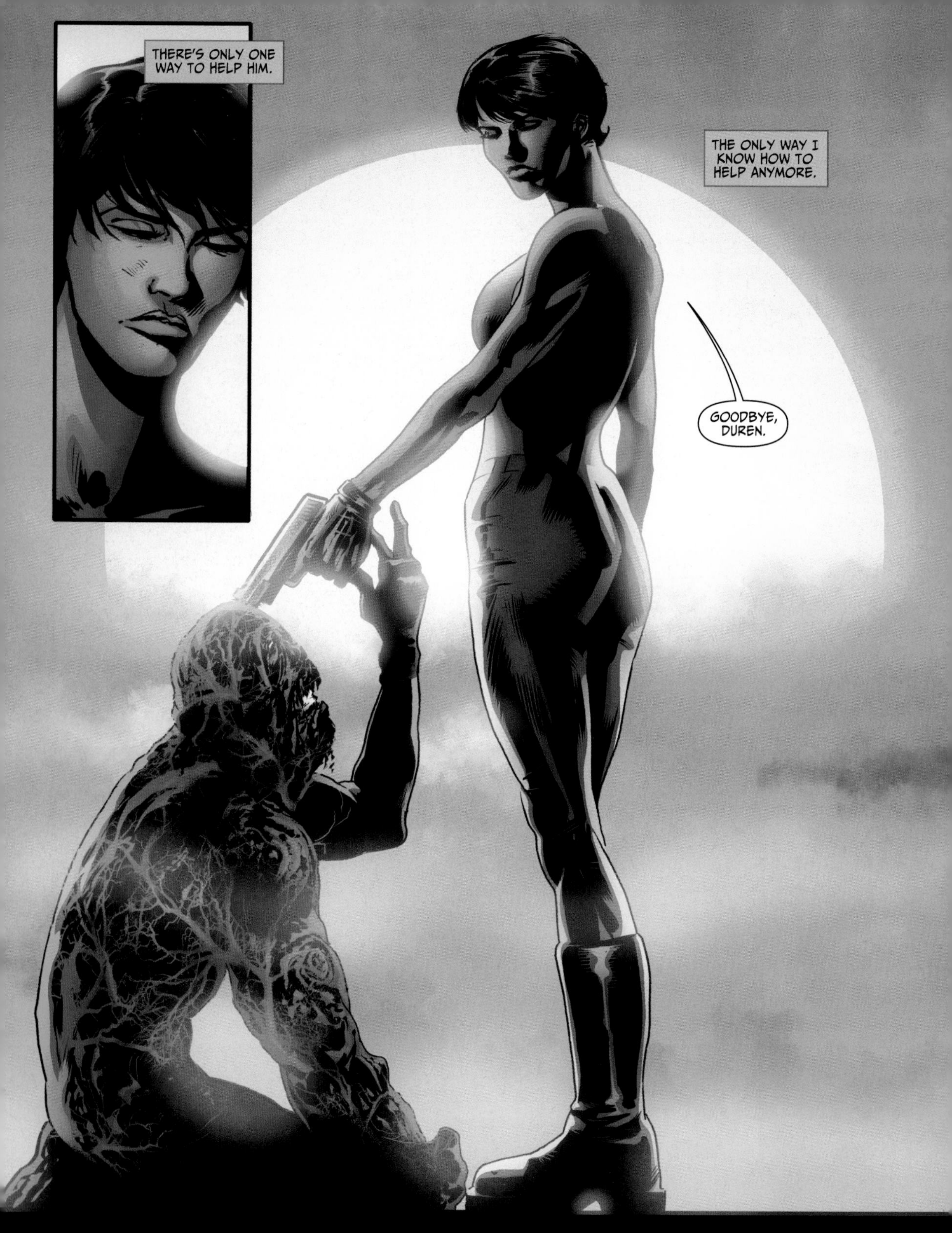
THERE'S ONLY ONE WAY TO HELP HIM.
THE ONLY WAY I KNOW HOW TO HELP ANYMORE.
GOODBYE, DUREN.

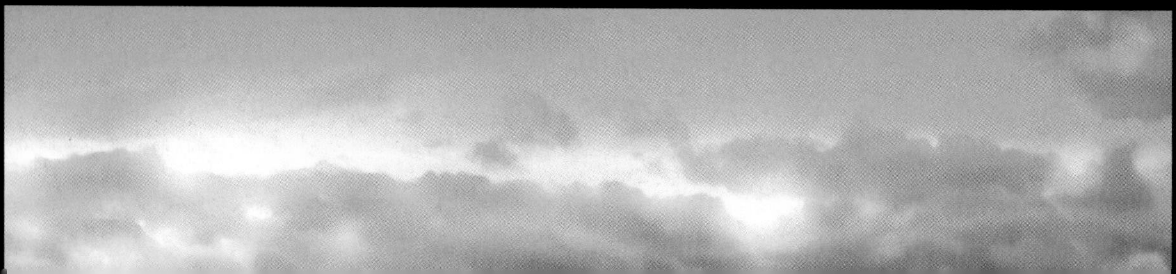

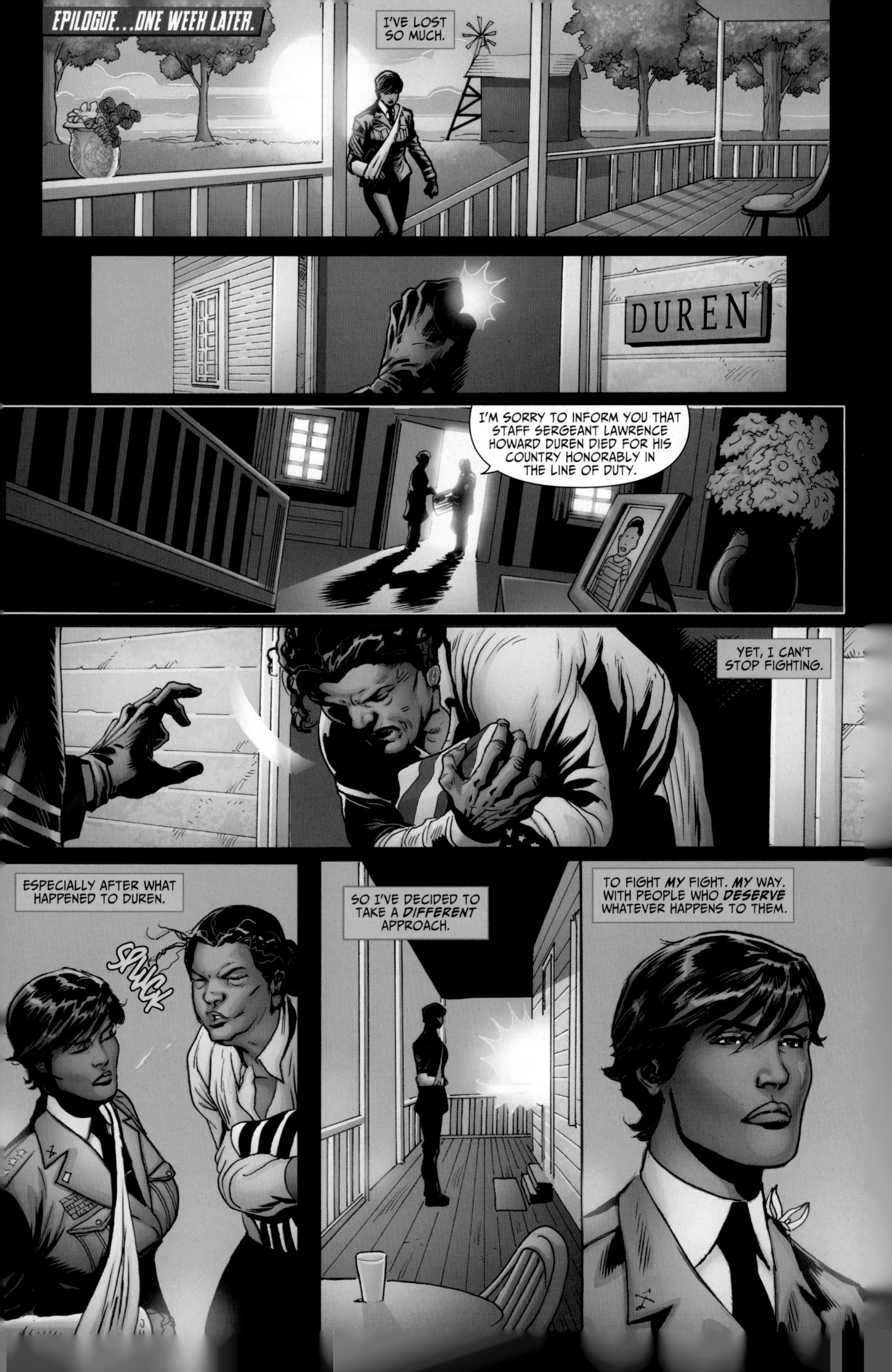
EPILOGUE...ONE WEEK LATER.
I'VE LOST SO MUCH.
DUREN
I'M SORRY TO INFORM YOU THAT STAFF SERGEANT LAWRENCE HOWARD DUREN DIED FOR HIS COUNTRY HONORABLY IN THE LINE OF DUTY.
YET, I CAN'T STOP FIGHTING.
ESPECIALLY AFTER WHAT HAPPENED TO DUREN.
SPLUCK
SO I'VE DECIDED TO TAKE A DIFFERENT APPROACH.
TO FIGHT MY FIGHT. MY WAY. WITH PEOPLE WHO DESERVE WHATEVER HAPPENS TO THEM.

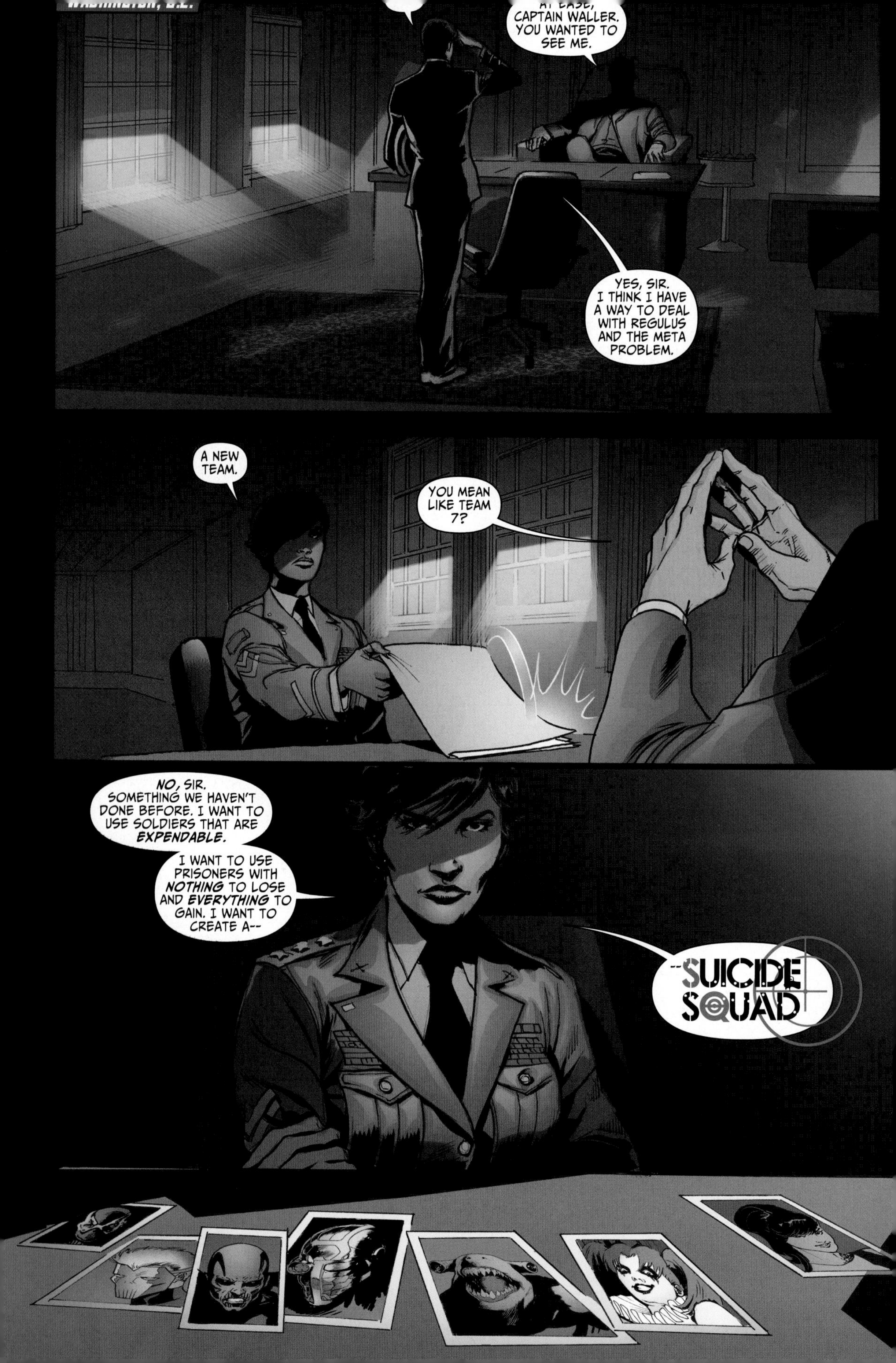
CAPTAIN WALLER. YOU WANTED TO SEE ME.
YES, SIR. I THINK I HAVE A WAY TO DEAL WITH REGULUS AND THE META PROBLEM.
A NEW TEAM.
YOU MEAN LIKE TEAM 7?
NO, SIR. SOMETHING WE HAVEN'T DONE BEFORE. I WANT TO USE SOLDIERS THAT ARE EXPENDABLE.
I WANT TO USE PRISONERS WITH NOTHING TO LOSE AND EVERYTHING TO GAIN. I WANT TO CREATE A--
--SUICIDE SQUAD

REGULUS SKETCHES BY FERNANDO DAGNINO

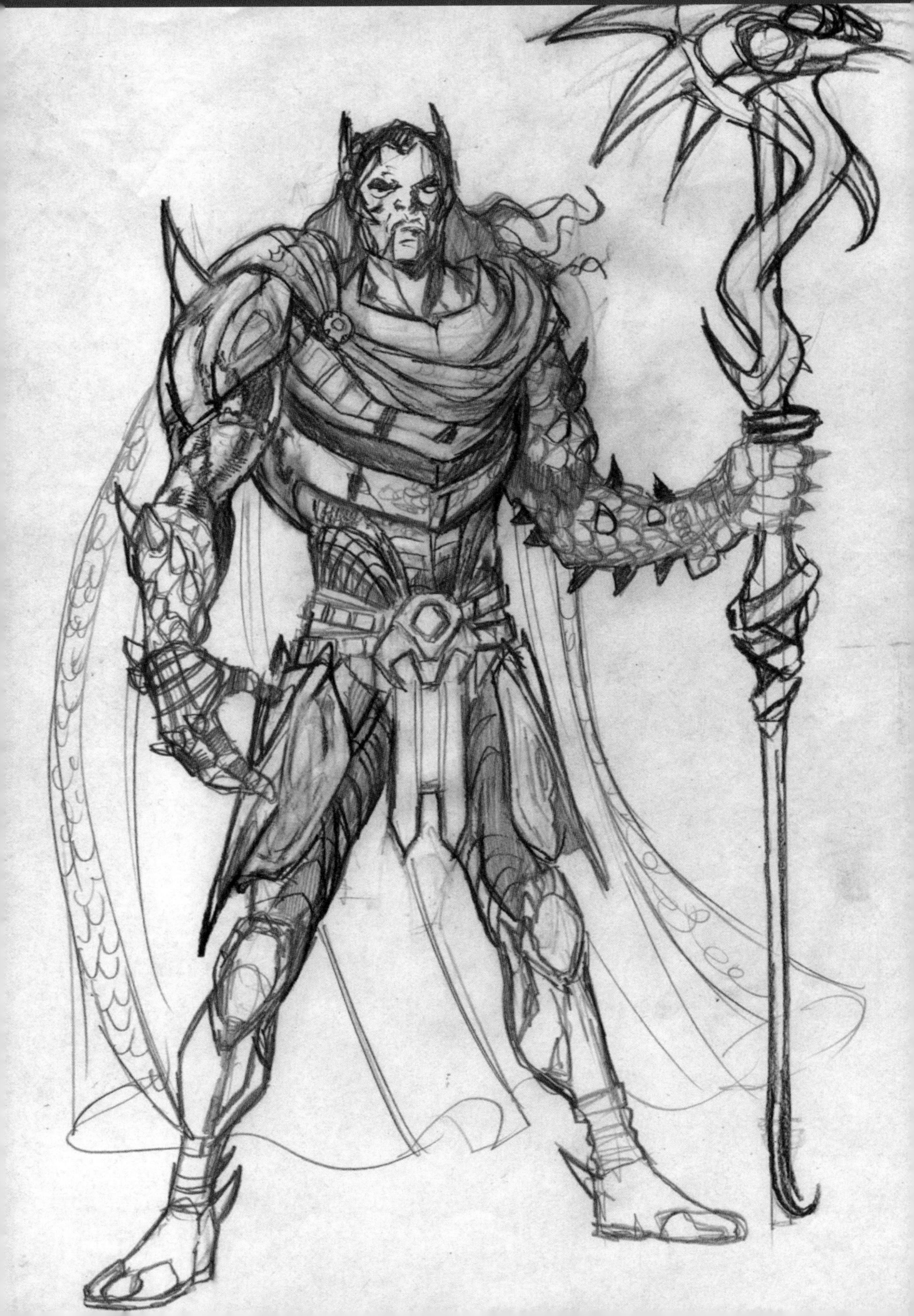

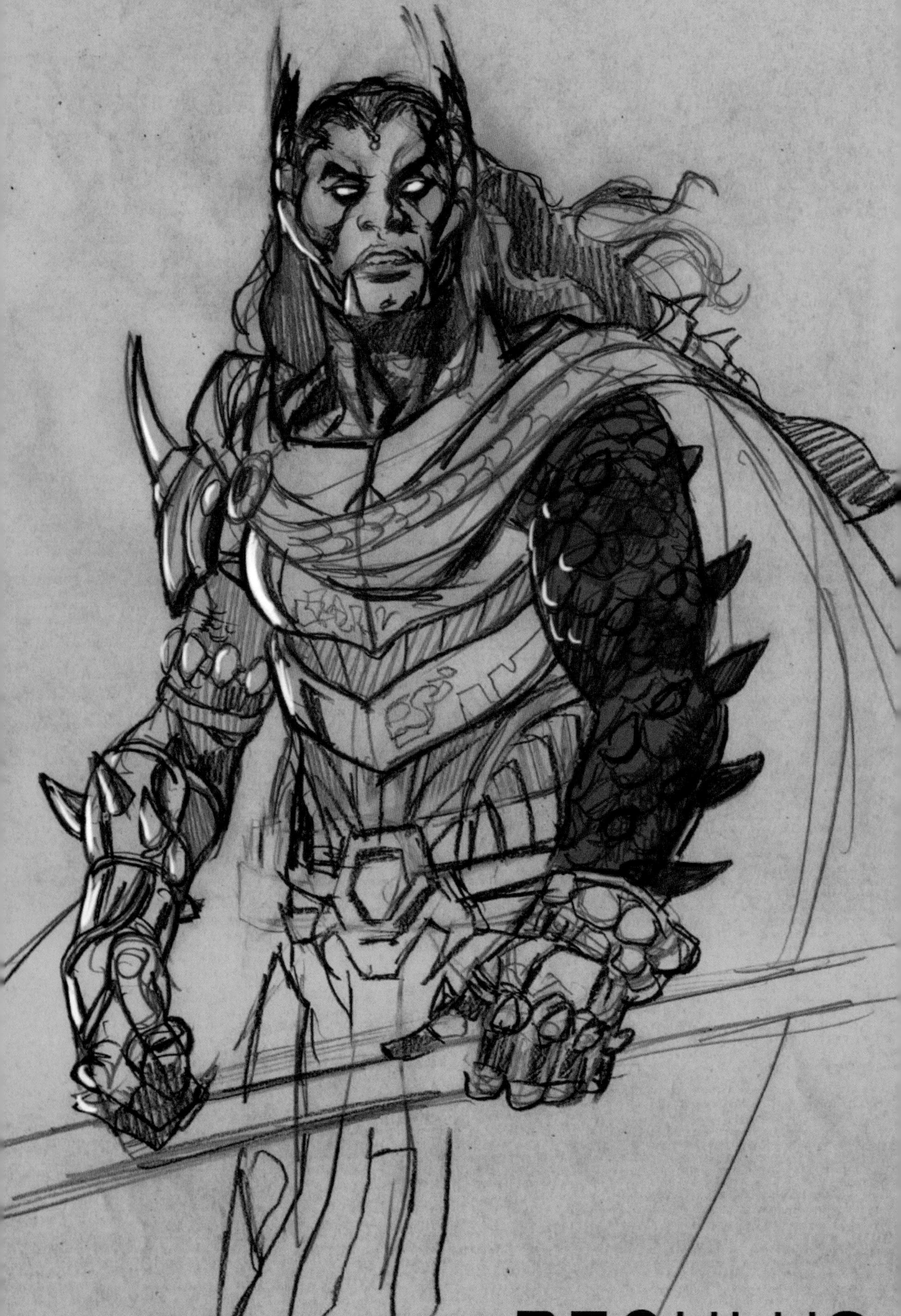

REGULUS

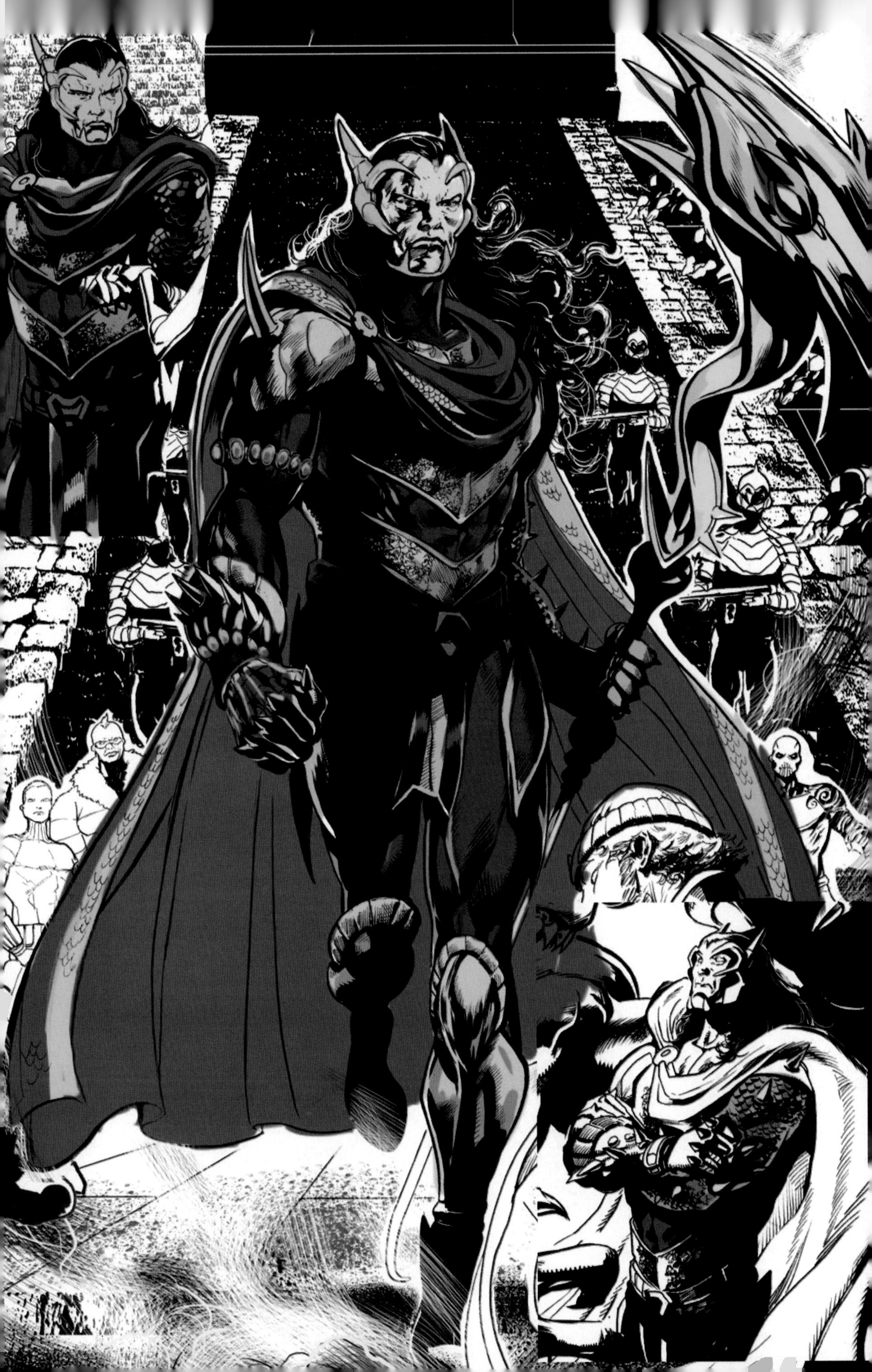

SUICIDE SQUAD
COVER SKETCHES BY KEN LASHLEY

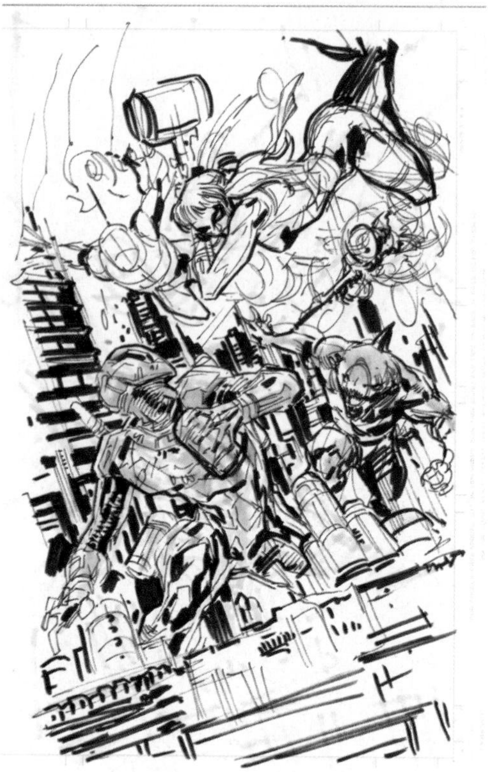

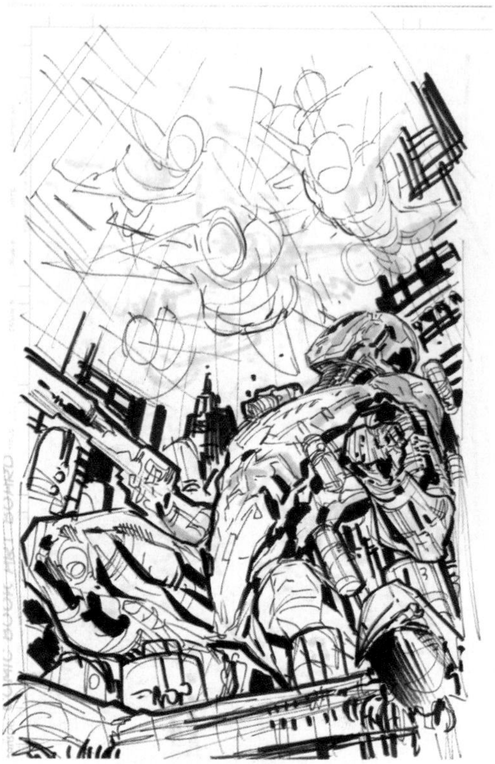

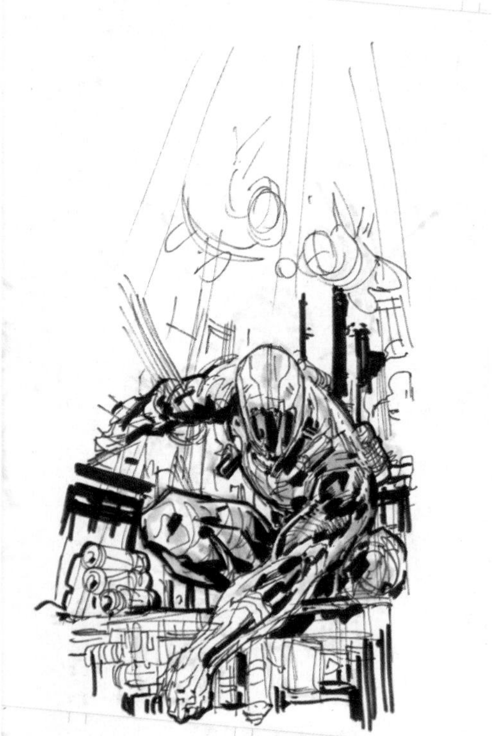

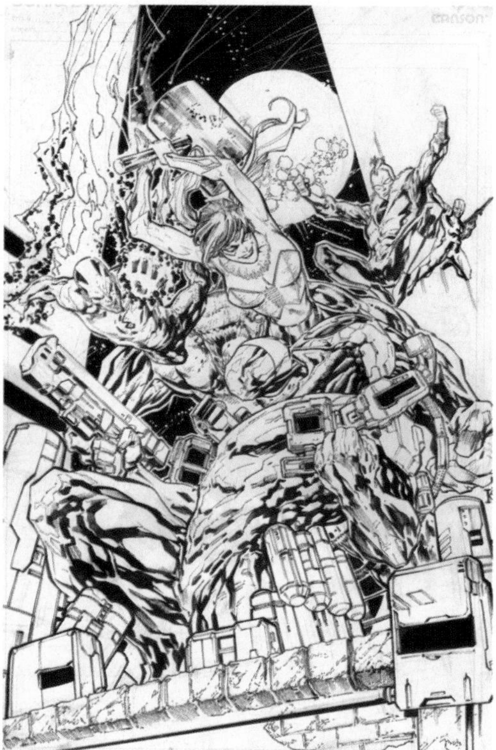

Cover issue #10

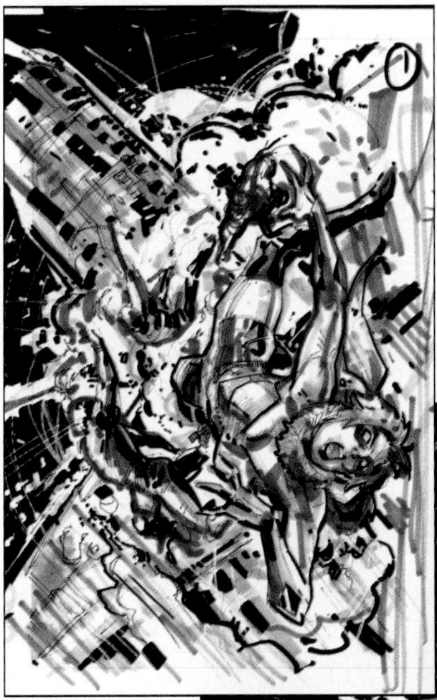

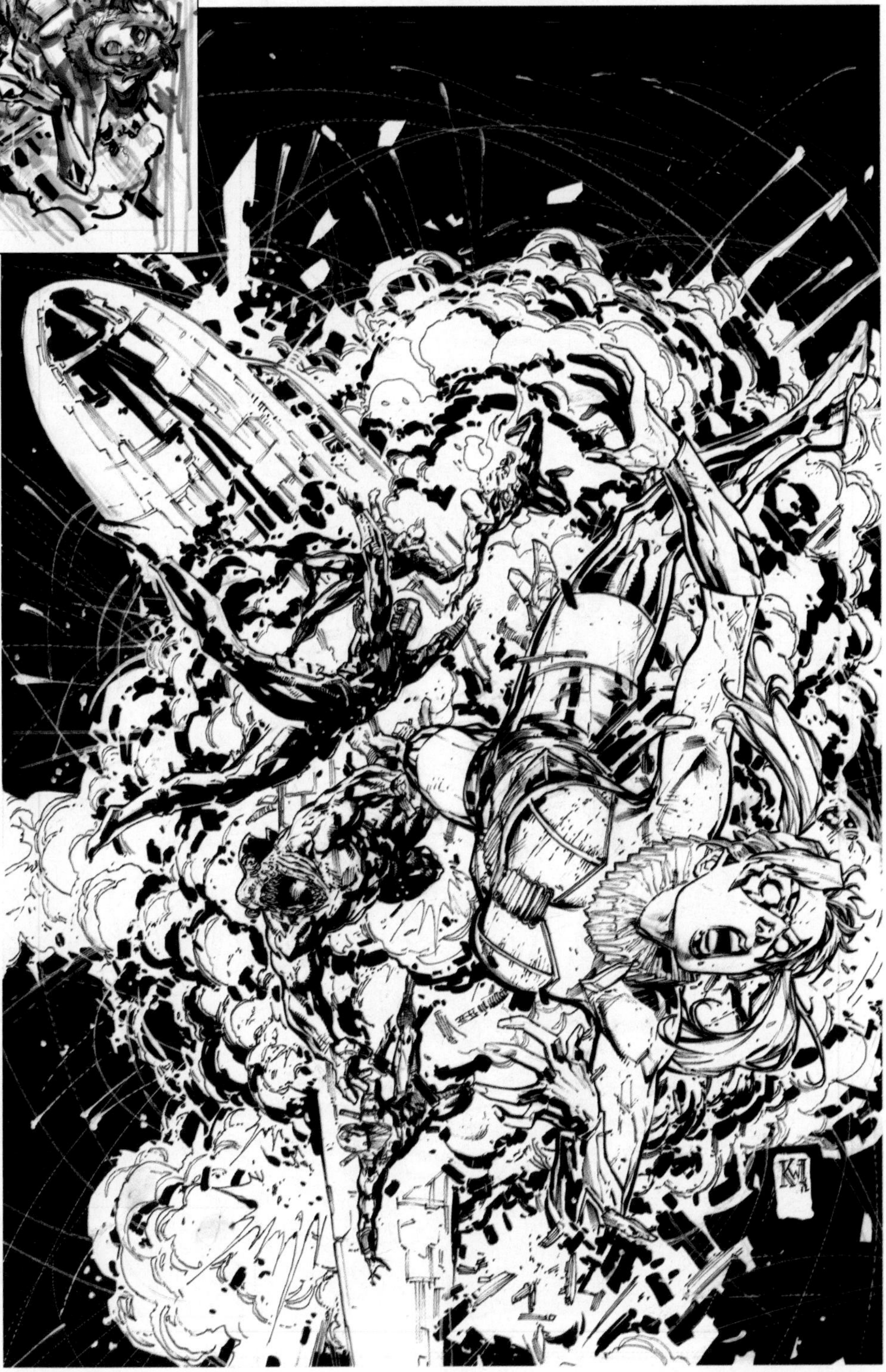

Cover issue #11

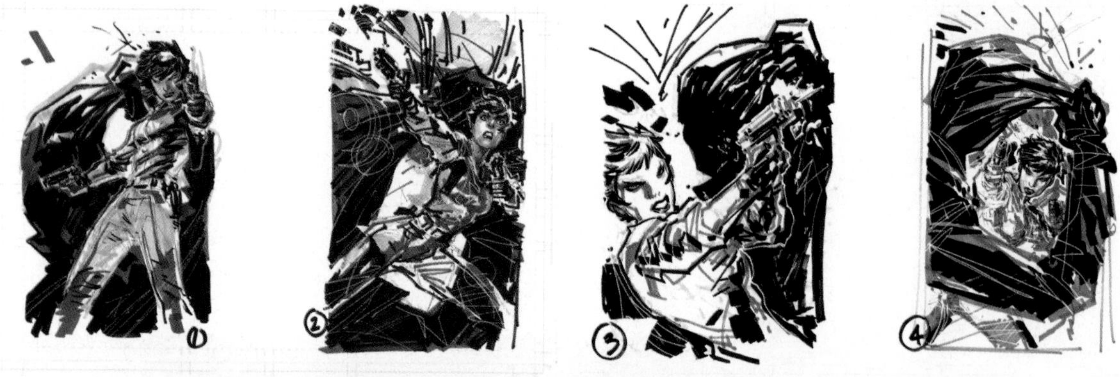

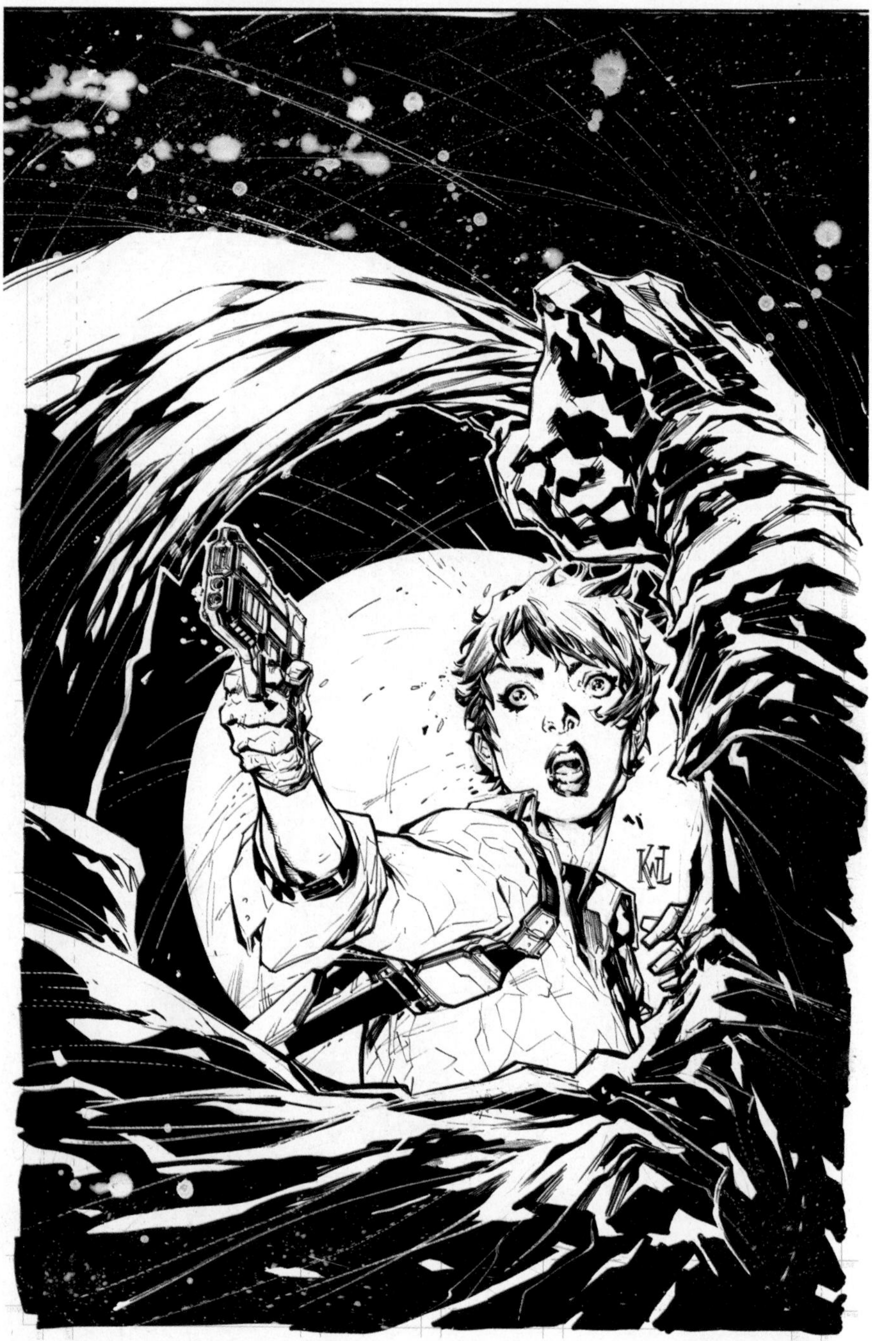

Cover issue #12

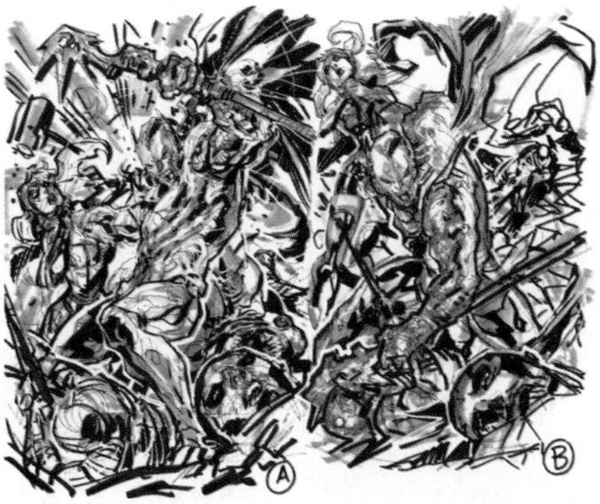
A
B

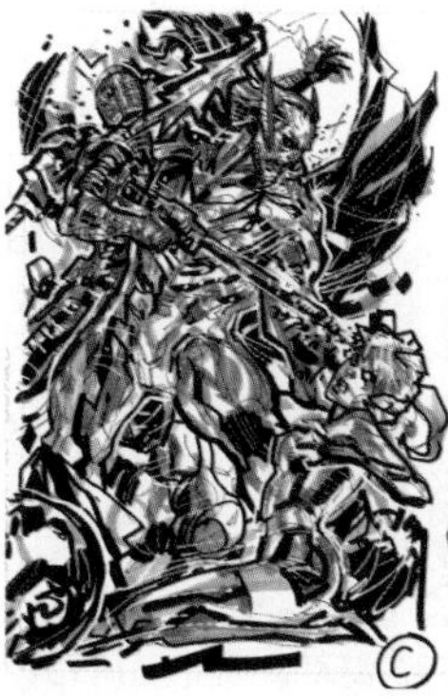
C

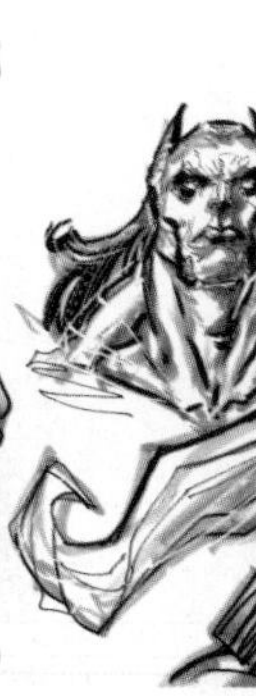

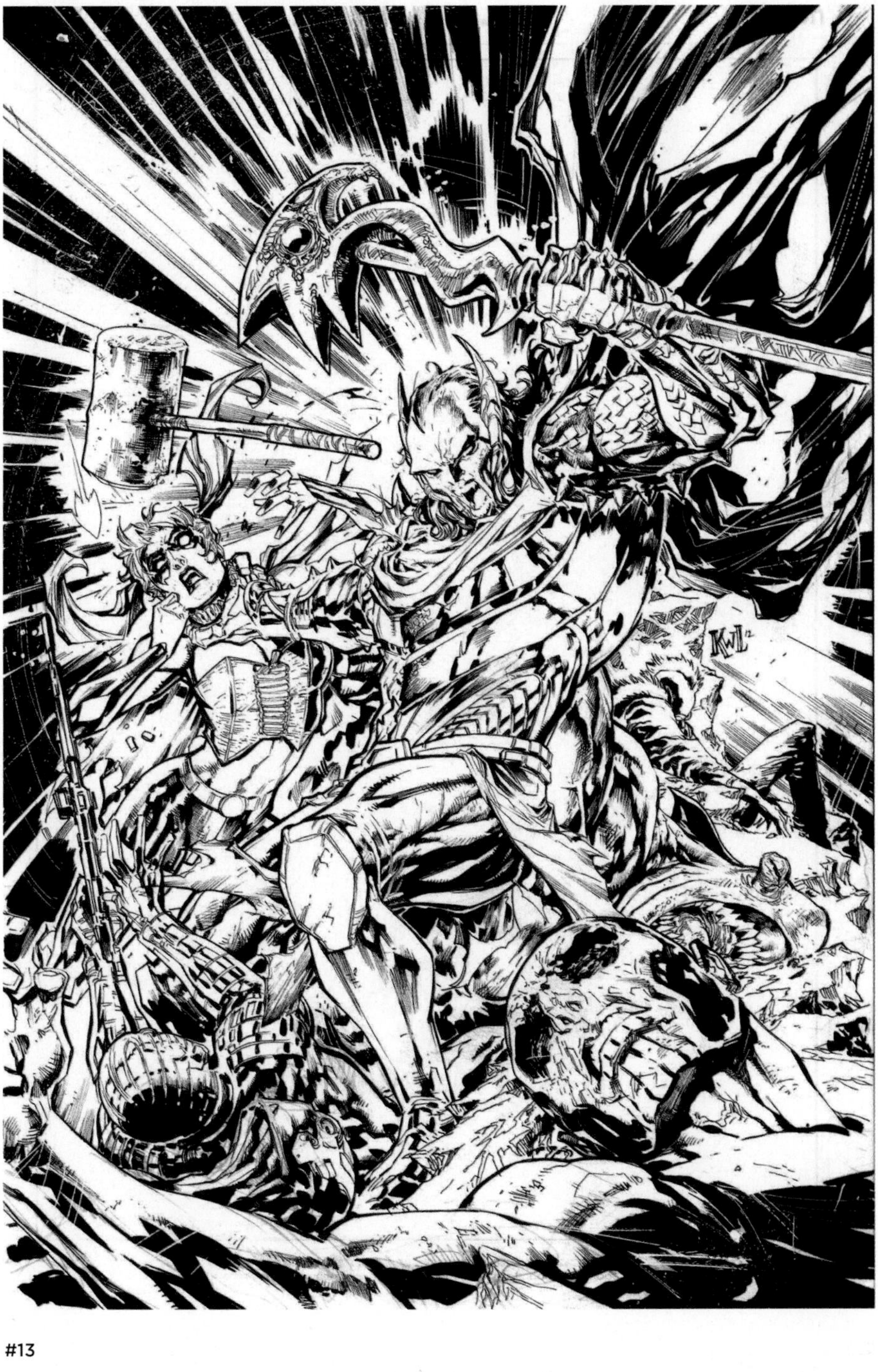

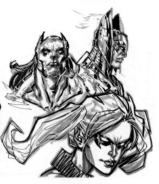

Cover issue #13

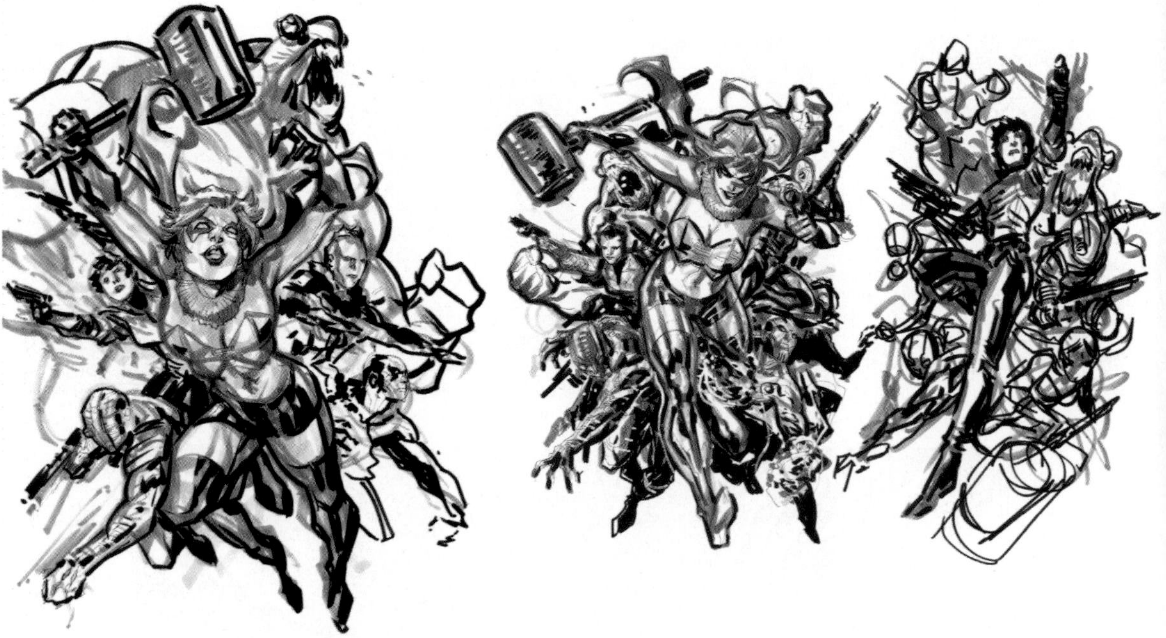

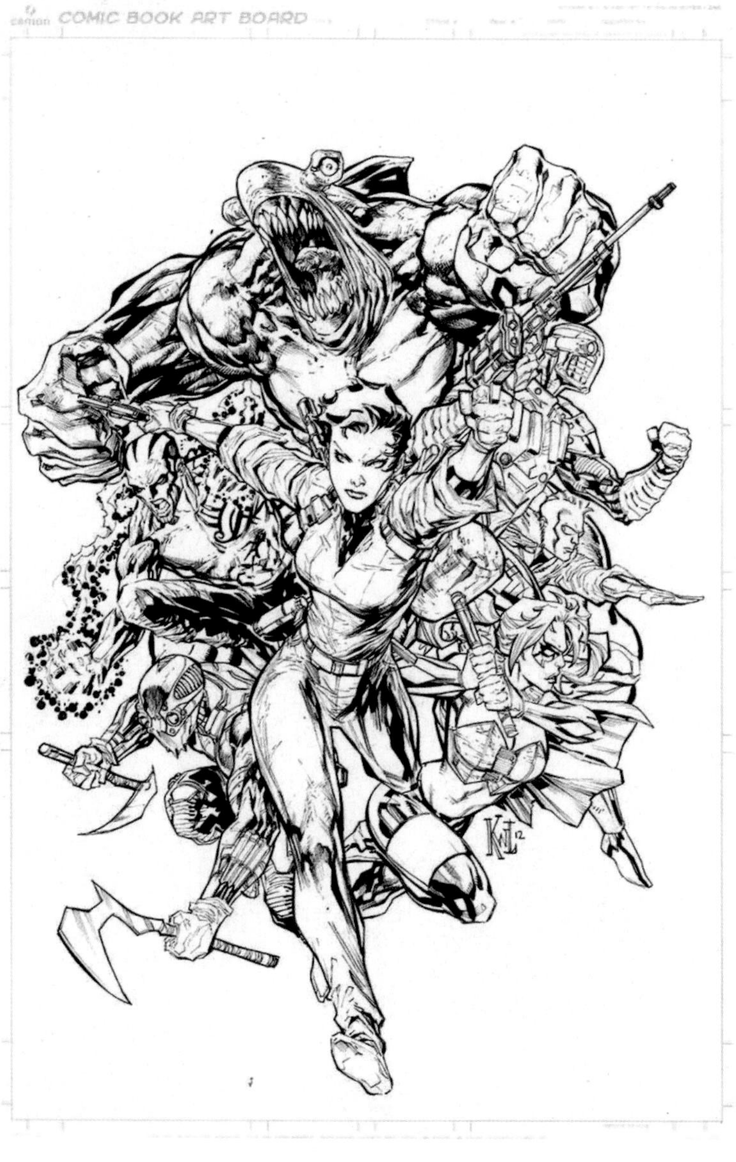
COMIC BOOK ART BOARD

Cover issue #0

DC COMICS™

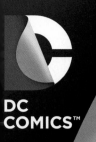

"A pretty irresistible hook. What if the good guys assembled a bunch of bad guys to work as a Dirty Dozen-like superteam and do the dirty work traditional heroes would never touch (or want to know about)?"
—THE ONION/AV CLUB

START AT THE BEGINNING!

SUICIDE SQUAD VOLUME 1: KICKED IN THE TEETH

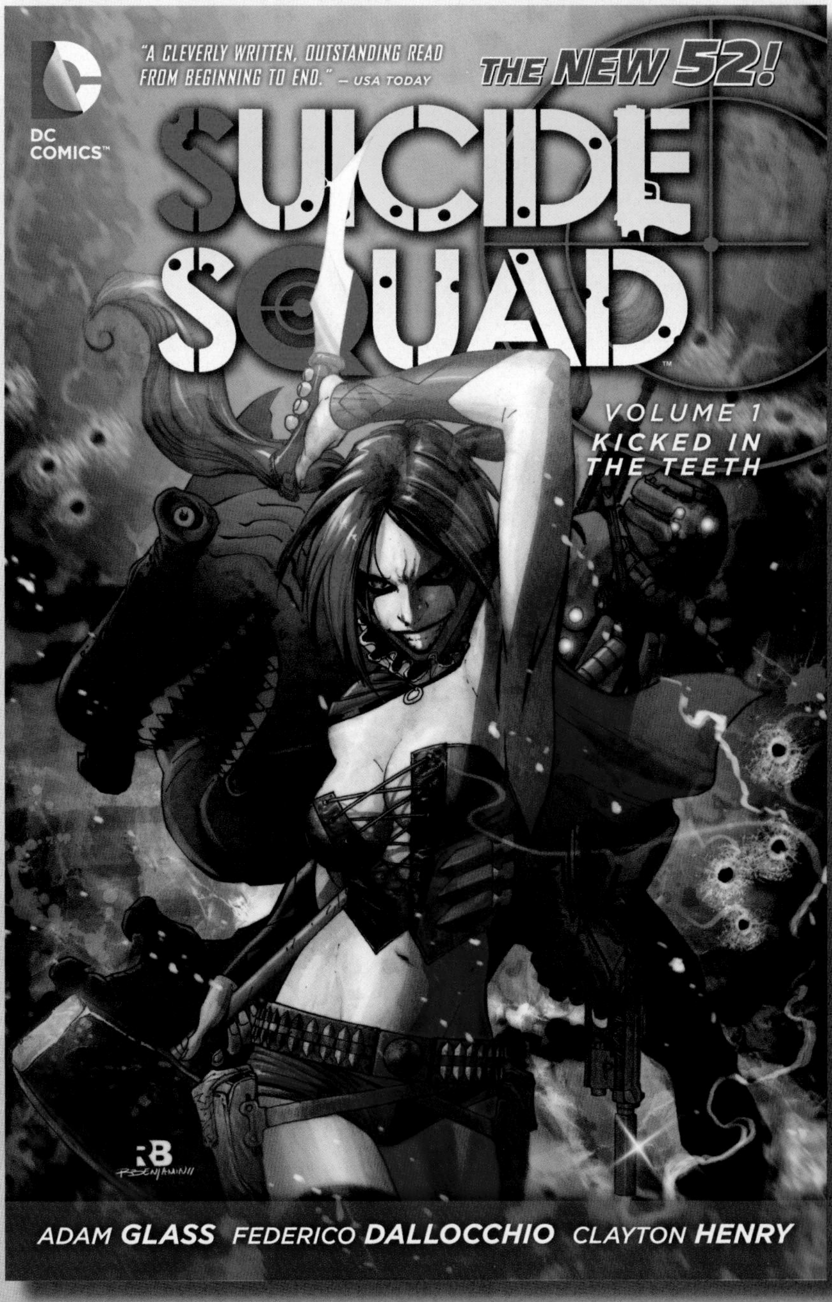
DC COMICS™
"A CLEVERLY WRITTEN, OUTSTANDING READ FROM BEGINNING TO END." – USA TODAY
THE NEW 52!
SUICIDE SQUAD
VOLUME 1
KICKED IN THE TEETH
ADAM GLASS FEDERICO DALLOCCHIO CLAYTON HENRY

DEATHSTROKE VOLUME 1: LEGACY

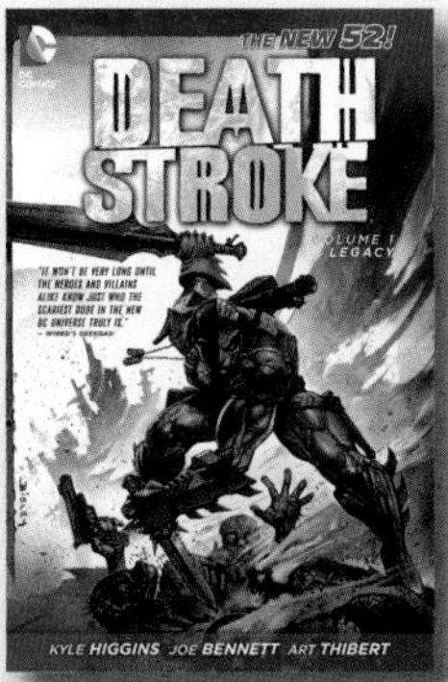
THE NEW 52!
DEATH STROKE
VOLUME 1 LEGACY
KYLE HIGGINS JOE BENNETT ART THIBERT

MEN OF WAR VOLUME 1: UNEASY COMPANY

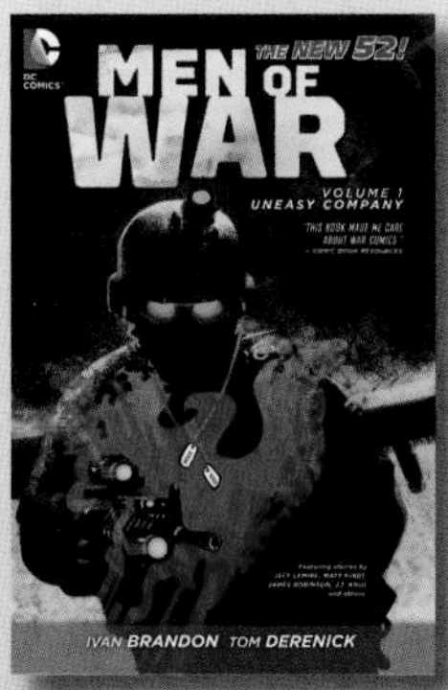
THE NEW 52!
MEN OF WAR
VOLUME 1 UNEASY COMPANY
IVAN BRANDON TOM DERENICK

HAWK & DOVE VOLUME 1: FIRST STRIKES

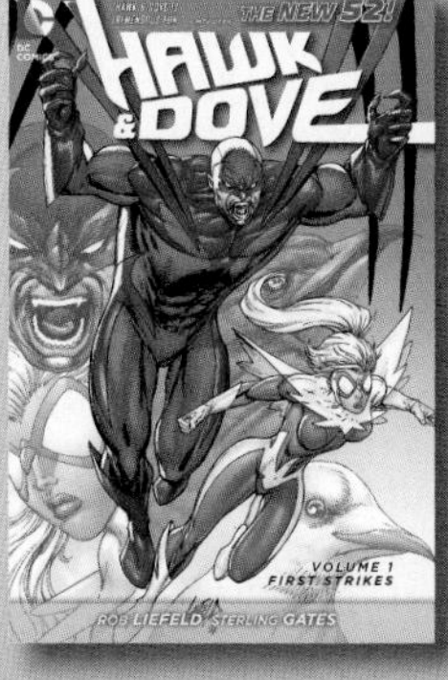
THE NEW 52!
HAWK & DOVE
VOLUME 1 FIRST STRIKES
ROB LIEFELD STERLING GATES

DC COMICS™

"A stunning debut. This is definitely in the top rank of the revamp."
—THE ONION / AV CLUB

"Snyder and Capullo reach new heights of collaboration here, with Capullo making inspired storytelling choices that add additional layers to Snyder's narration and dialog."
—VANITY FAIR

START AT THE BEGINNING!

BATMAN VOLUME 1: THE COURT OF OWLS

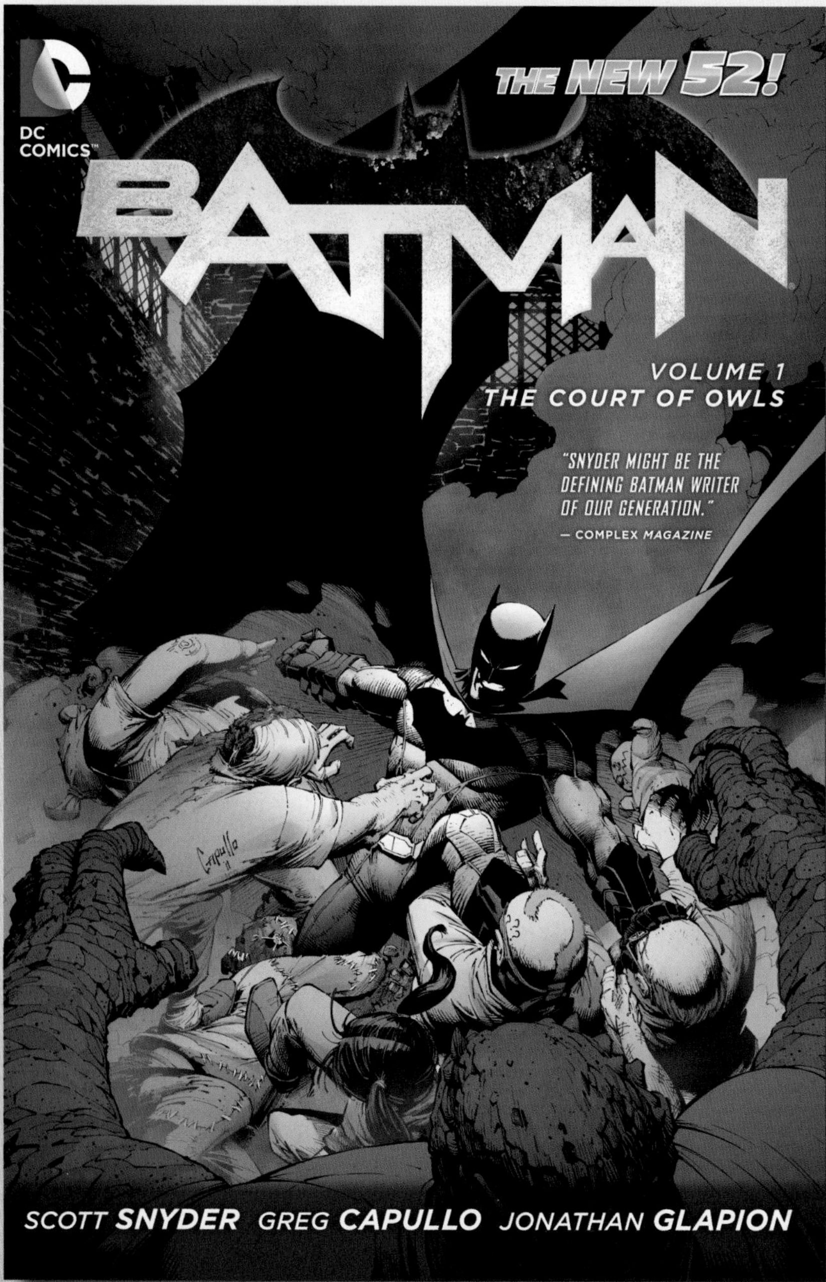

DC COMICS™
THE NEW 52!
BATMAN
VOLUME 1
THE COURT OF OWLS
"SNYDER MIGHT BE THE DEFINING BATMAN WRITER OF OUR GENERATION."
— COMPLEX MAGAZINE
SCOTT SNYDER GREG CAPULLO JONATHAN GLAPION

BATMAN & ROBIN VOLUME 1: BORN TO KILL

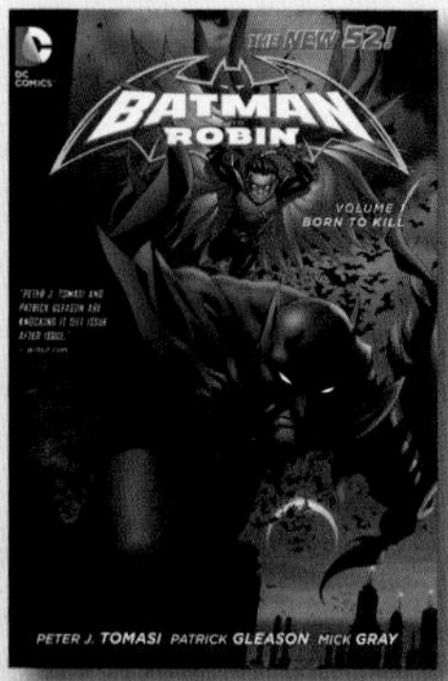

THE NEW 52!
BATMAN ROBIN
VOLUME 1
BORN TO KILL
PETER J. TOMASI PATRICK GLEASON MICK GRAY

BATMAN: DETECTIVE COMICS VOLUME 1: FACES OF DEATH

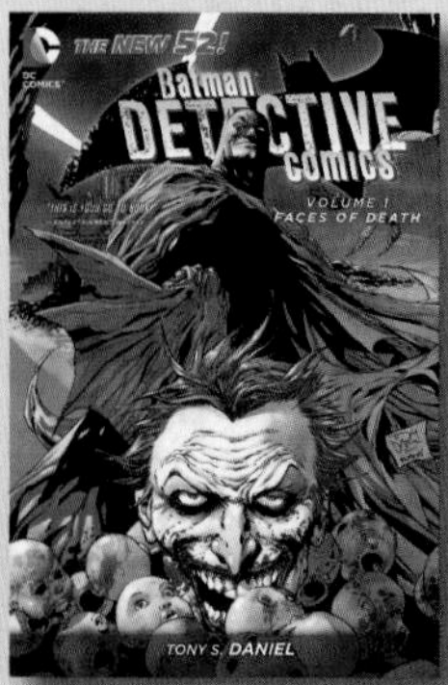

THE NEW 52!
Batman
DETECTIVE
COMICS
VOLUME 1
FACES OF DEATH
TONY S. DANIEL

BATMAN: THE DARK KNIGHT VOLUME 1: KNIGHT TERRORS

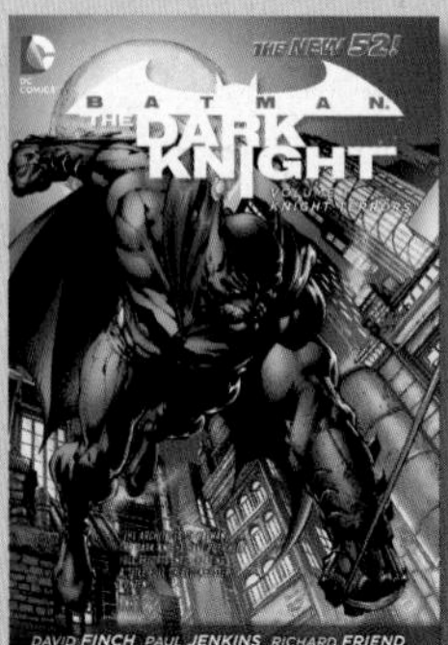

THE NEW 52!
BATMAN
THE DARK KNIGHT
DAVID FINCH PAUL JENKINS RICHARD FRIEND

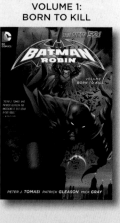

"If you don't love it from the very first page, you're not human."
—MTV GEEK

"ANIMAL MAN has the sensational Jeff Lemire at the helm."
—ENTERTAINMENT WEEKLY

START AT THE BEGINNING!

ANIMAL MAN
VOLUME 1: THE HUNT

JUSTICE LEAGUE DARK
VOLUME 1:
IN THE DARK

RESURRECTION MAN
VOLUME 1:
DEAD AGAIN

FRANKENSTEIN
AGENT OF S.H.A.D.E.
VOLUME 1: WAR OF
THE MONSTERS

VOLUME 1
THE HUNT

"TRAVEL FOREMAN'S ART IS INNOVATIVE AND EXCELLENTLY CREEPY... AS LEMIRE'S EVERYMAN HERO MAKES HIS MARK IN THE NEW DC UNIVERSE."
— USA TODAY

JEFF LEMIRE TRAVEL FOREMAN

DC COMICS™

"Simone and artist Ardian Syaf not only do justice to Babs' legacy, but build in a new complexity that is the starting point for a future full of new storytelling possibilities. A hell of a ride."
—IGN

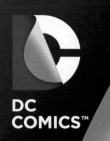

START AT THE BEGINNING!

BATGIRL VOLUME 1: THE DARKEST REFLECTION

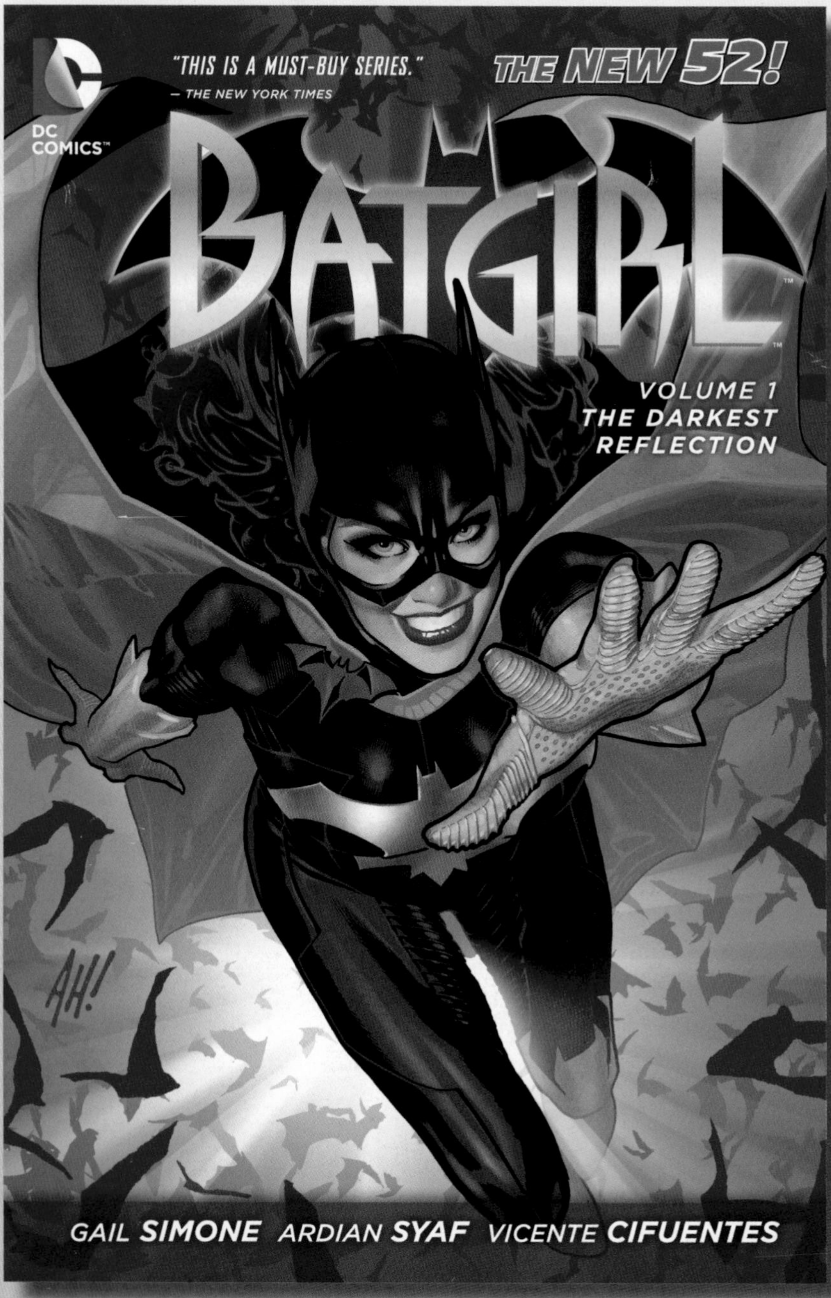
DC COMICS™
"THIS IS A MUST-BUY SERIES."
— THE NEW YORK TIMES
THE NEW 52!
BATGIRL
VOLUME 1
THE DARKEST REFLECTION
GAIL SIMONE ARDIAN SYAF VICENTE CIFUENTES

BATWOMAN VOLUME 1: HYDROLOGY

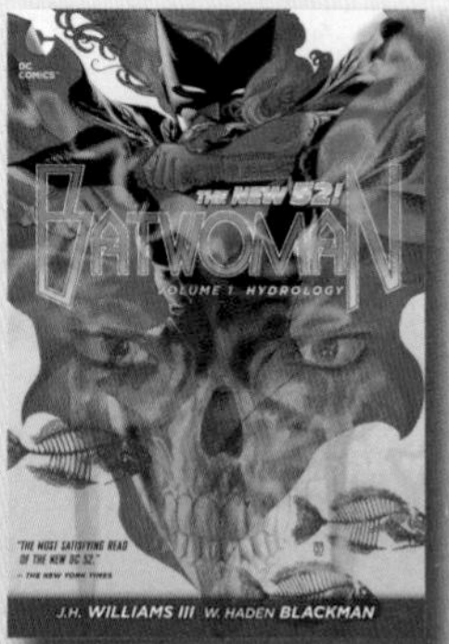
THE NEW 52!
BATWOMAN
VOLUME 1: HYDROLOGY
J.H. WILLIAMS III W. HADEN BLACKMAN

RED HOOD AND THE OUTLAWS VOLUME 1: REDEMPTION

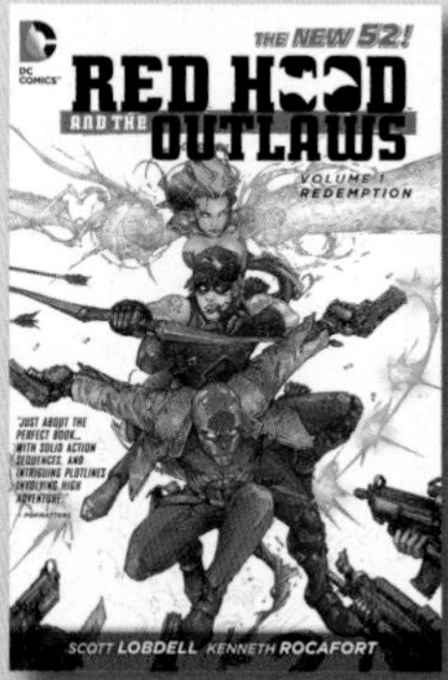
THE NEW 52!
RED HOOD AND THE OUTLAWS
VOLUME 1 REDEMPTION
SCOTT LOBDELL KENNETH ROCAFORT

BATWING VOLUME 1: THE LOST KINGDOM

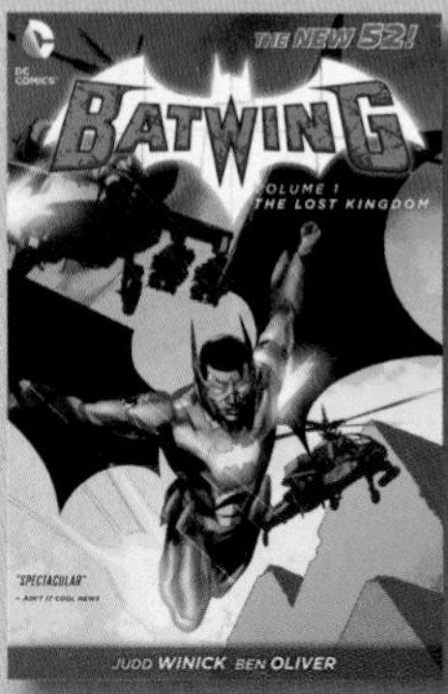
THE NEW 52!
BATWING
VOLUME 1 THE LOST KINGDOM
"SPECTACULAR"
JUDD WINICK BEN OLIVER